KENJI TSURUBUCHI

4

Touge Oni

PRIMAL GODS IN ANCIENT TIMES

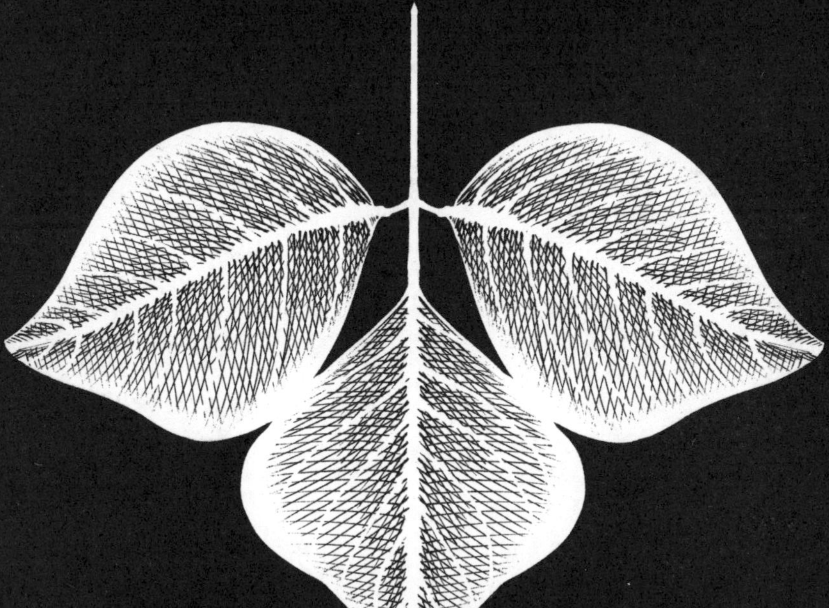

"The history of the province of Izumo.
...ghly begins in the east and
...west. [...] It is named Izumo
... Mizuomitsuno-no-Mikoto
...*mo tatsu'*—clouds aplenty.
... yakumo-tatsu Izumo."
...etteer of Izumo Province—

Contents

CHAPTER XII

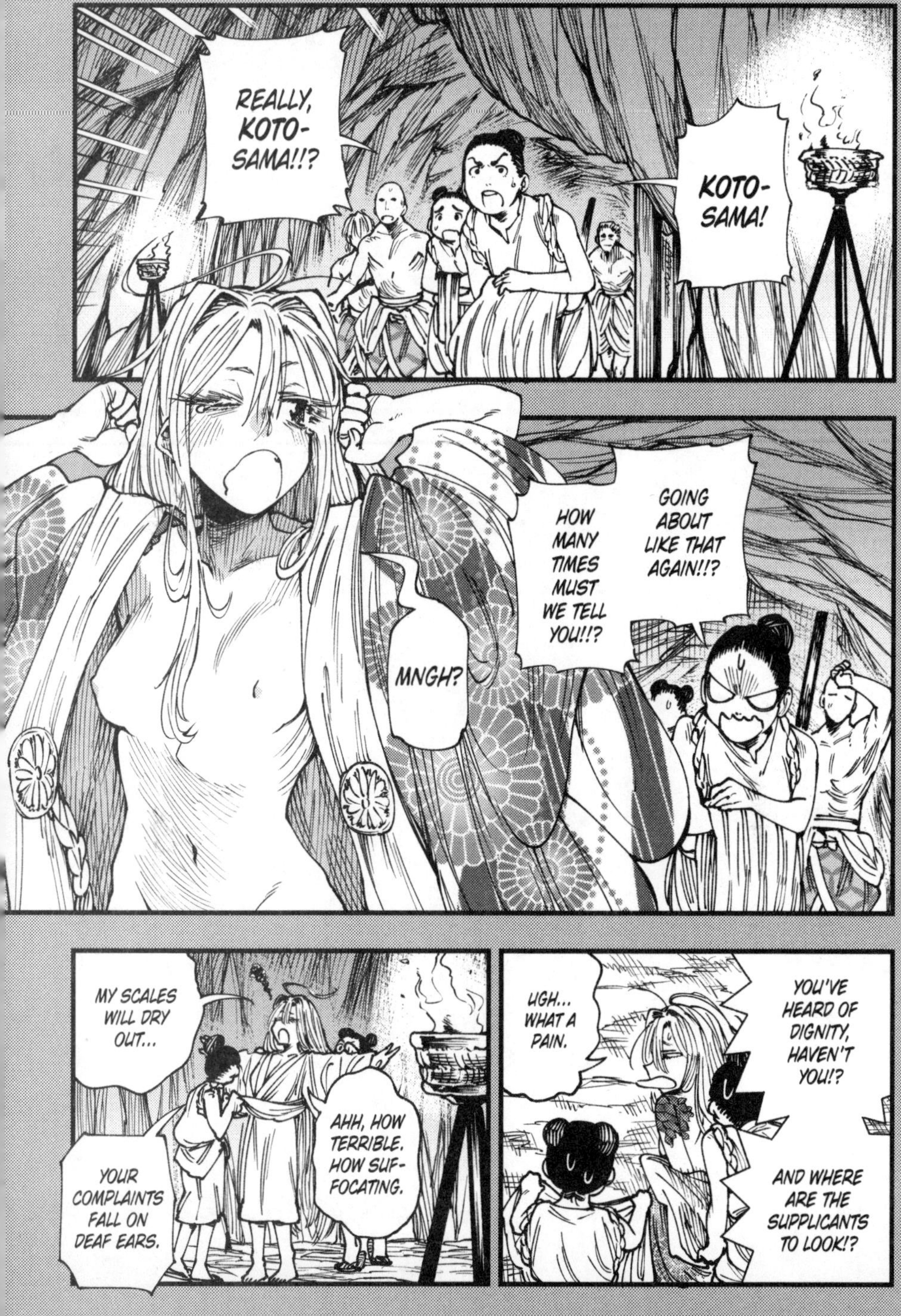
KOTO-SAMA!
REALLY, KOTO-SAMA!!?
GOING ABOUT LIKE THAT AGAIN!!?
HOW MANY TIMES MUST WE TELL YOU!!?
MNGH?
YOU'VE HEARD OF DIGNITY, HAVEN'T YOU!?
UGH... WHAT A PAIN.
AND WHERE ARE THE SUPPLICANTS TO LOOK!?
MY SCALES WILL DRY OUT...
AHH, HOW TERRIBLE. HOW SUF-FOCATING.
YOUR COMPLAINTS FALL ON DEAF EARS.

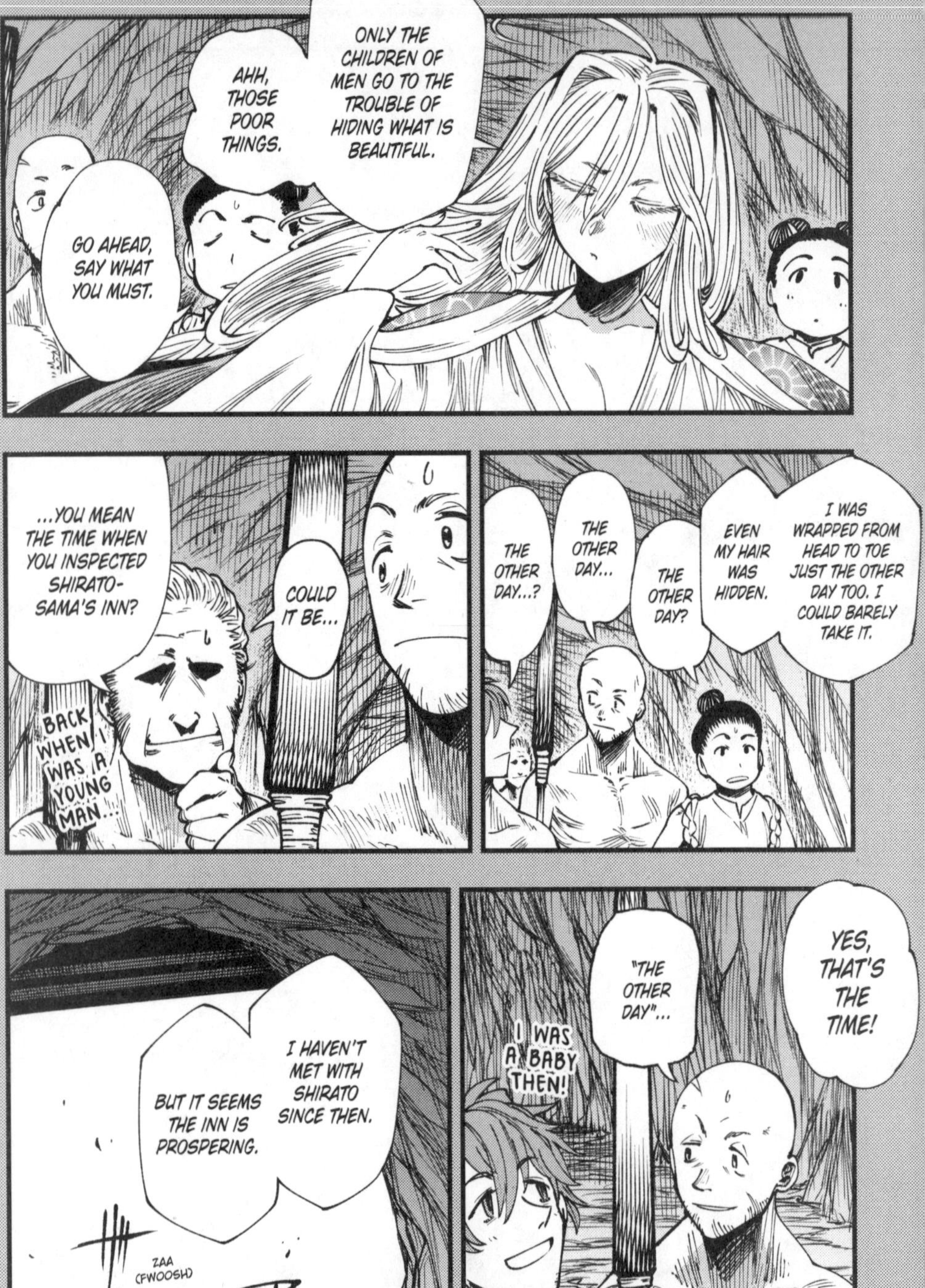
ONLY THE CHILDREN OF MEN GO TO THE TROUBLE OF HIDING WHAT IS BEAUTIFUL.
AHH, THOSE POOR THINGS.
GO AHEAD, SAY WHAT YOU MUST.
I WAS WRAPPED FROM HEAD TO TOE JUST THE OTHER DAY TOO. I COULD BARELY TAKE IT.
EVEN MY HAIR WAS HIDDEN.
THE OTHER DAY?
THE OTHER DAY...
THE OTHER DAY...?
COULD IT BE...
...YOU MEAN THE TIME WHEN YOU INSPECTED SHIRATO-SAMA'S INN?
BACK WHEN I WAS A YOUNG MAN...
YES, THAT'S THE TIME!
"THE OTHER DAY"...
I WAS A BABY THEN!
I HAVEN'T MET WITH SHIRATO SINCE THEN.
BUT IT SEEMS THE INN IS PROSPERING.
ZAA (FWOOSH)

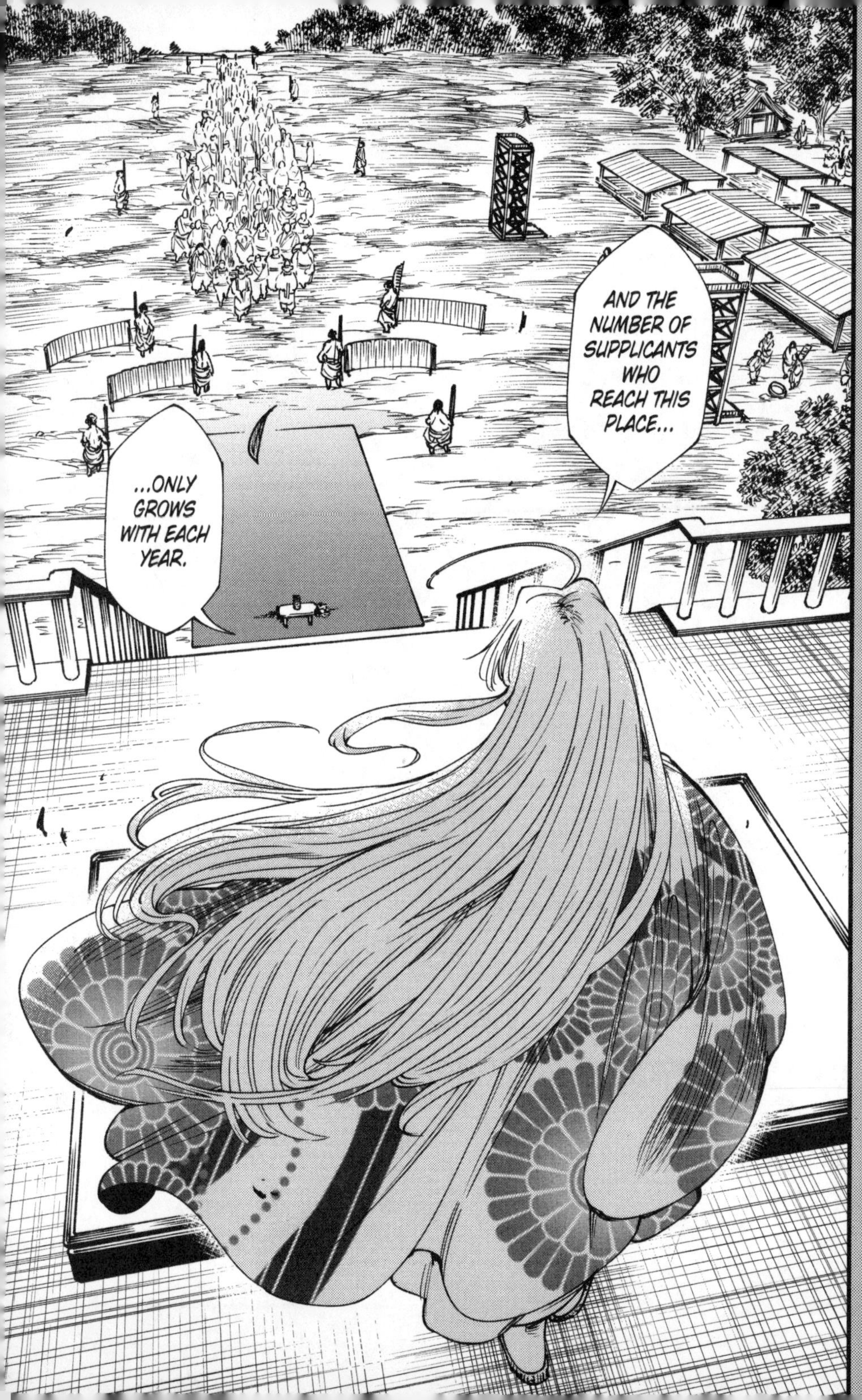
AND THE NUMBER OF SUPPLICANTS WHO REACH THIS PLACE...
...ONLY GROWS WITH EACH YEAR.

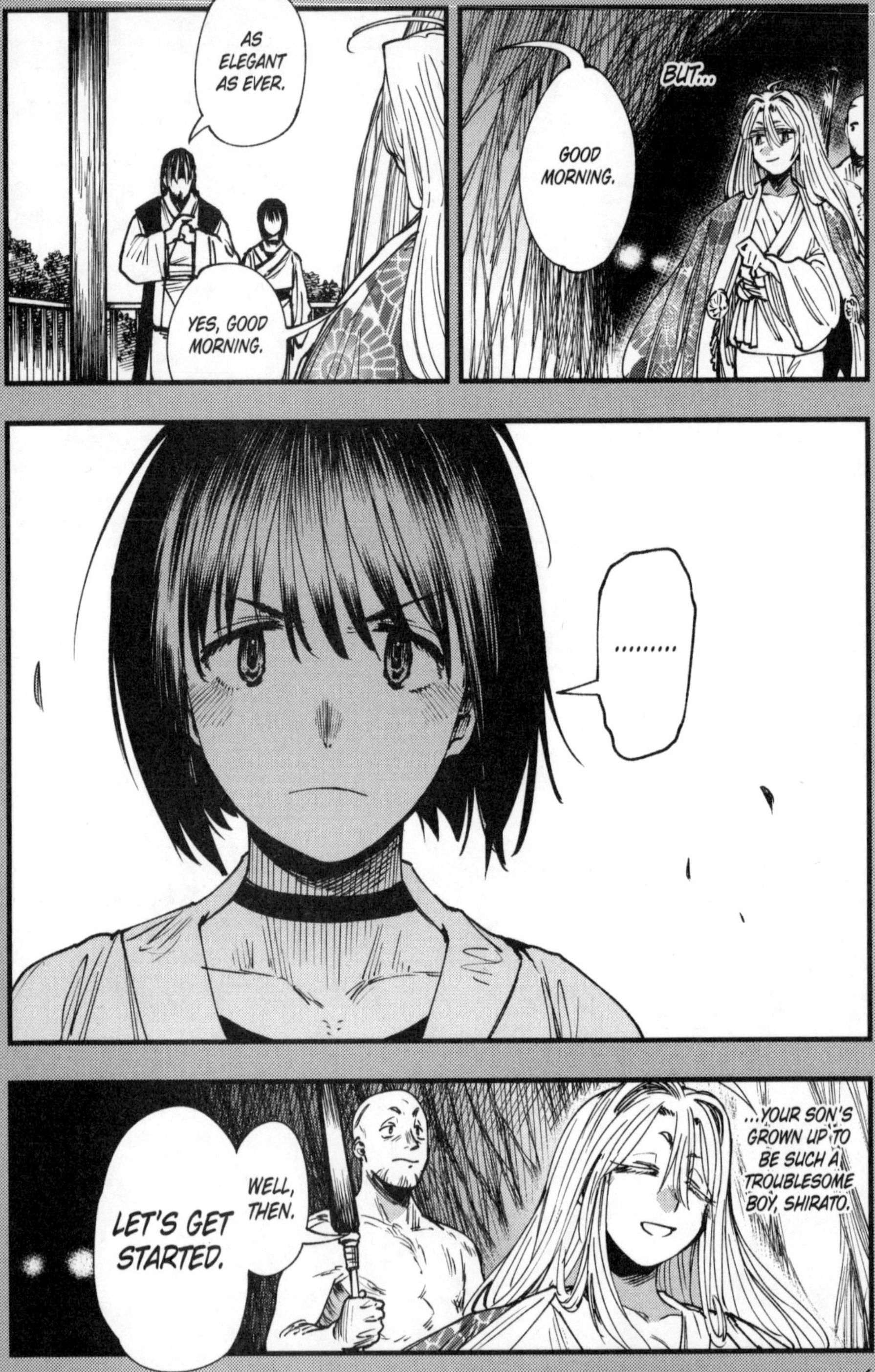
BUT...
GOOD MORNING.
AS ELEGANT AS EVER.
YES, GOOD MORNING.
....
...YOUR SON'S GROWN UP TO BE SUCH A TROUBLESOME BOY, SHIRATO.
WELL, THEN.
LET'S GET STARTED.

CHAPTER XII THE TALE OF MOUNT KATSURAGI: THE SUPPLICANTS

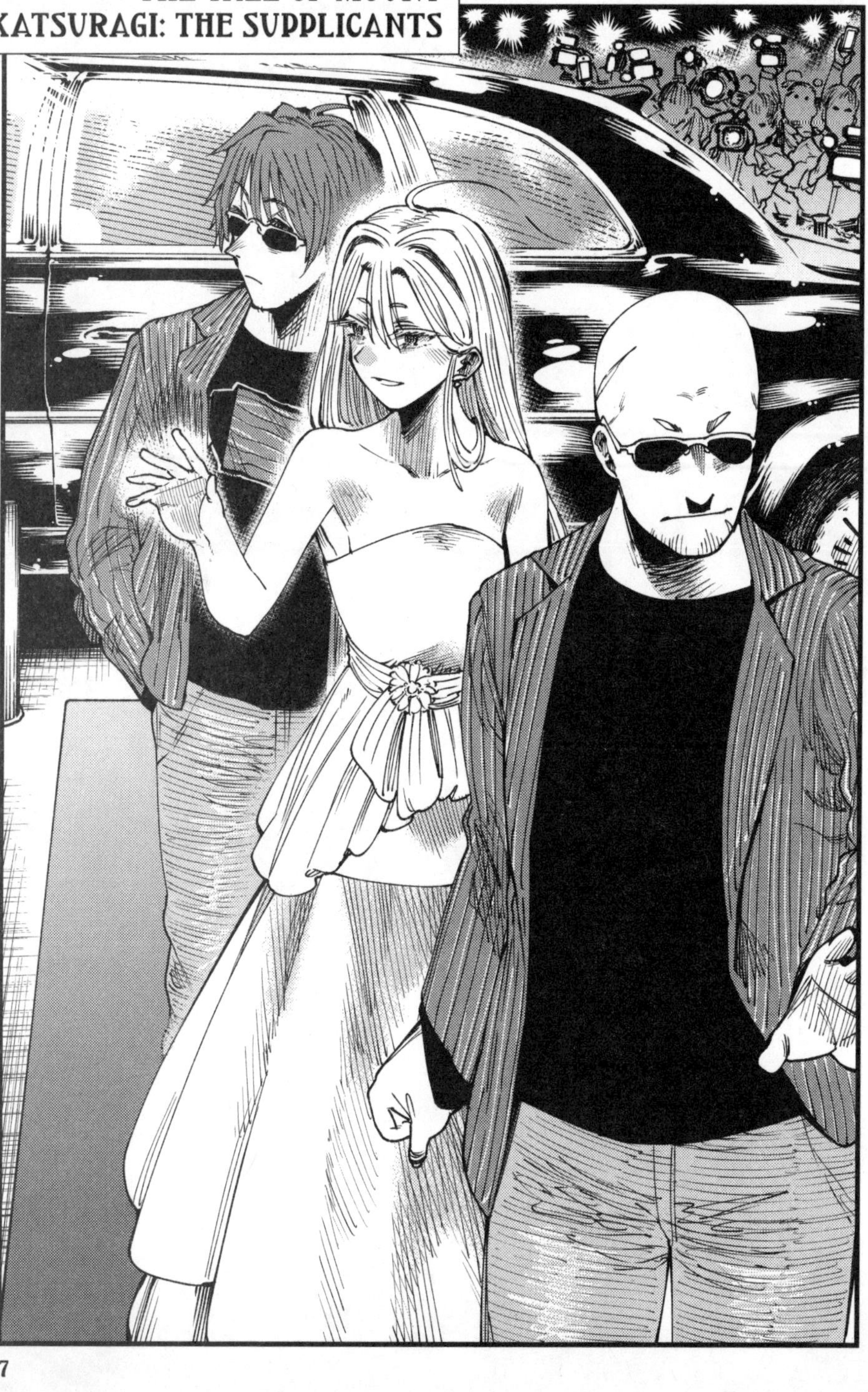

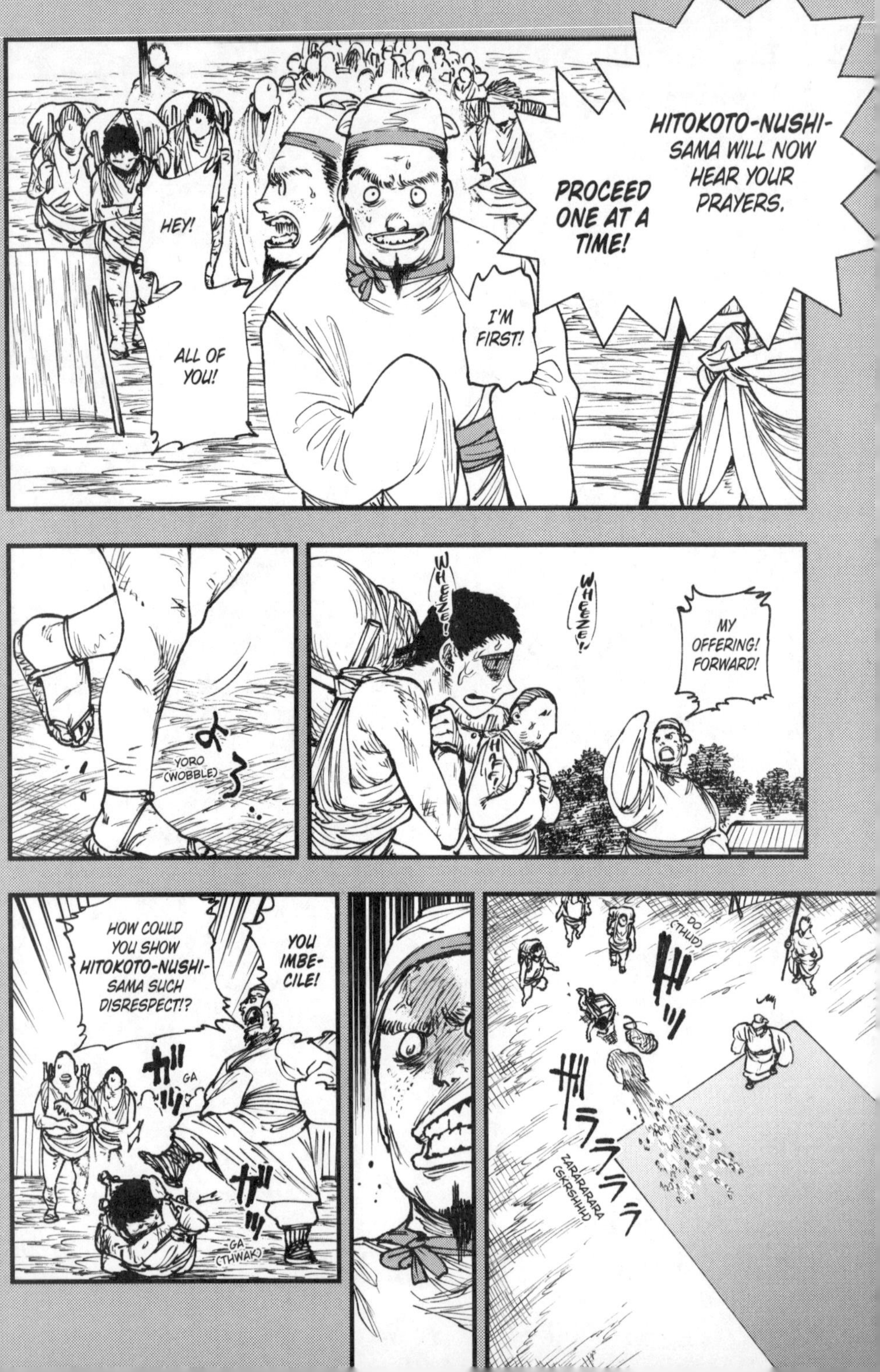
HITOKOTO-NUSHI-SAMA WILL NOW HEAR YOUR PRAYERS.
PROCEED ONE AT A TIME!
I'M FIRST!
HEY!
ALL OF YOU!
MY OFFERING! FORWARD!
WHEEZE!
WHEEZE!
HAF!
YORO (WOBBLE)
DO (THUD)
ZARARARARA (SKRSHHH)
YOU IMBE-CILE!
HOW COULD YOU SHOW HITOKOTO-NUSHI-SAMA SUCH DISRESPECT!?
GA
GA (THWAK)

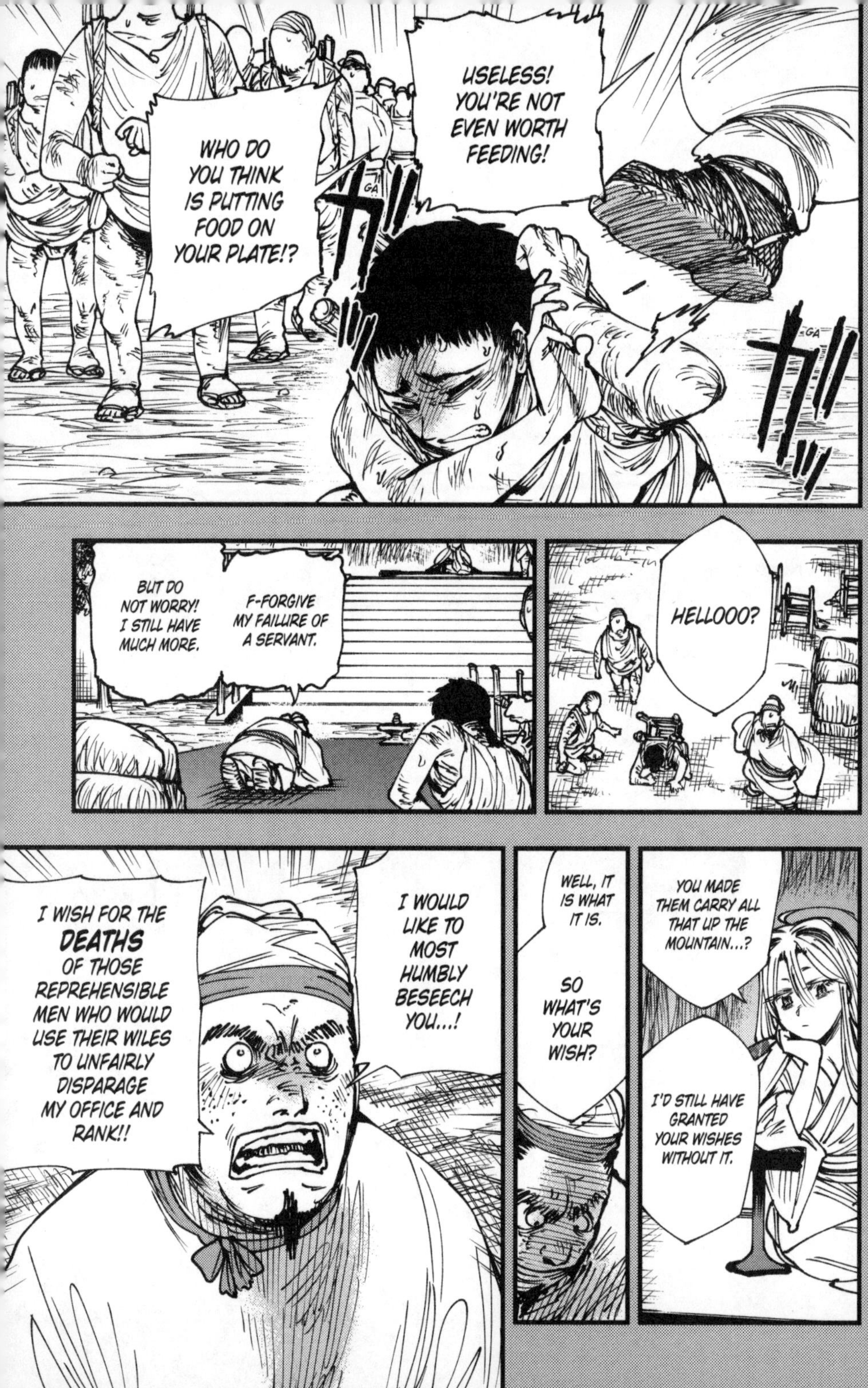
USELESS! YOU'RE NOT EVEN WORTH FEEDING!
GA
WHO DO YOU THINK IS PUTTING FOOD ON YOUR PLATE!?
GA
HELLOOO?
F-FORGIVE MY FAILURE OF A SERVANT.
BUT DO NOT WORRY! I STILL HAVE MUCH MORE.
YOU MADE THEM CARRY ALL THAT UP THE MOUNTAIN...?
I'D STILL HAVE GRANTED YOUR WISHES WITHOUT IT.
WELL, IT IS WHAT IT IS.
SO WHAT'S YOUR WISH?
I WOULD LIKE TO MOST HUMBLY BESEECH YOU...!
I WISH FOR THE DEATHS OF THOSE REPREHENSIBLE MEN WHO WOULD USE THEIR WILES TO UNFAIRLY DISPARAGE MY OFFICE AND RANK!!

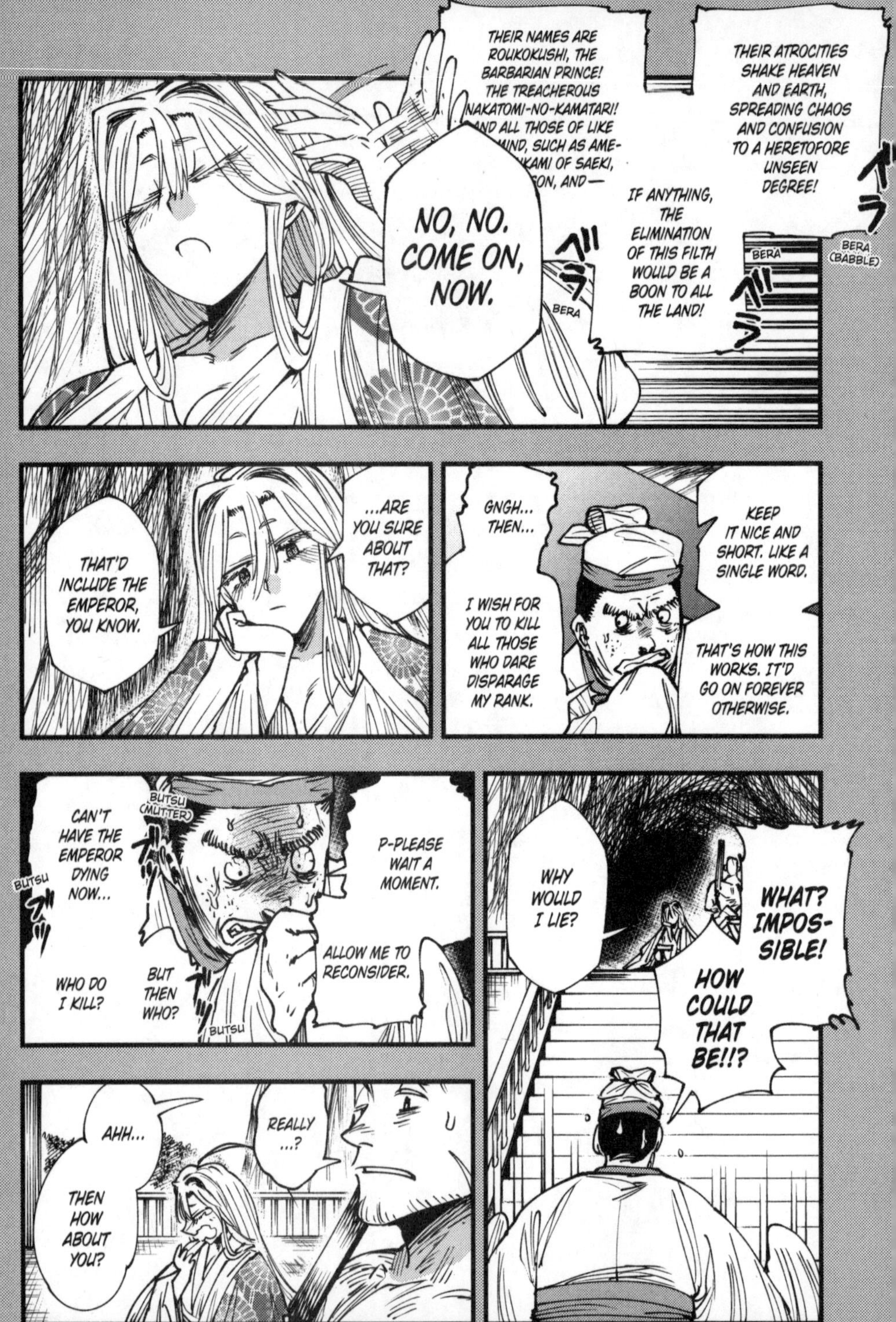
THEIR NAMES ARE ROUKOKUSHI, THE BARBARIAN PRINCE! THE TREACHEROUS NAKATOMI-NO-KAMATARI! AND ALL THOSE OF LIKE MIND, SUCH AS AME- KAMI OF SAEKI, SON, AND—
THEIR ATROCITIES SHAKE HEAVEN AND EARTH, SPREADING CHAOS AND CONFUSION TO A HERETOFORE UNSEEN DEGREE!
BERA (BABBLE)
BERA
IF ANYTHING, THE ELIMINATION OF THIS FILTH WOULD BE A BOON TO ALL THE LAND!
BERA
NO, NO. COME ON, NOW.
KEEP IT NICE AND SHORT. LIKE A SINGLE WORD.
THAT'S HOW THIS WORKS. IT'D GO ON FOREVER OTHERWISE.
GNGH... THEN...
I WISH FOR YOU TO KILL ALL THOSE WHO DARE DISPARAGE MY RANK.
...ARE YOU SURE ABOUT THAT?
THAT'D INCLUDE THE EMPEROR, YOU KNOW.
WHAT? IMPOSSIBLE!
HOW COULD THAT BE!!?
WHY WOULD I LIE?
P-PLEASE WAIT A MOMENT.
ALLOW ME TO RECONSIDER.
BUTSU (MUTTER)
CAN'T HAVE THE EMPEROR DYING NOW...
BUTSU
BUT THEN WHO?
WHO DO I KILL?
BUTSU
REALLY ...?
AHH...
THEN HOW ABOUT YOU?

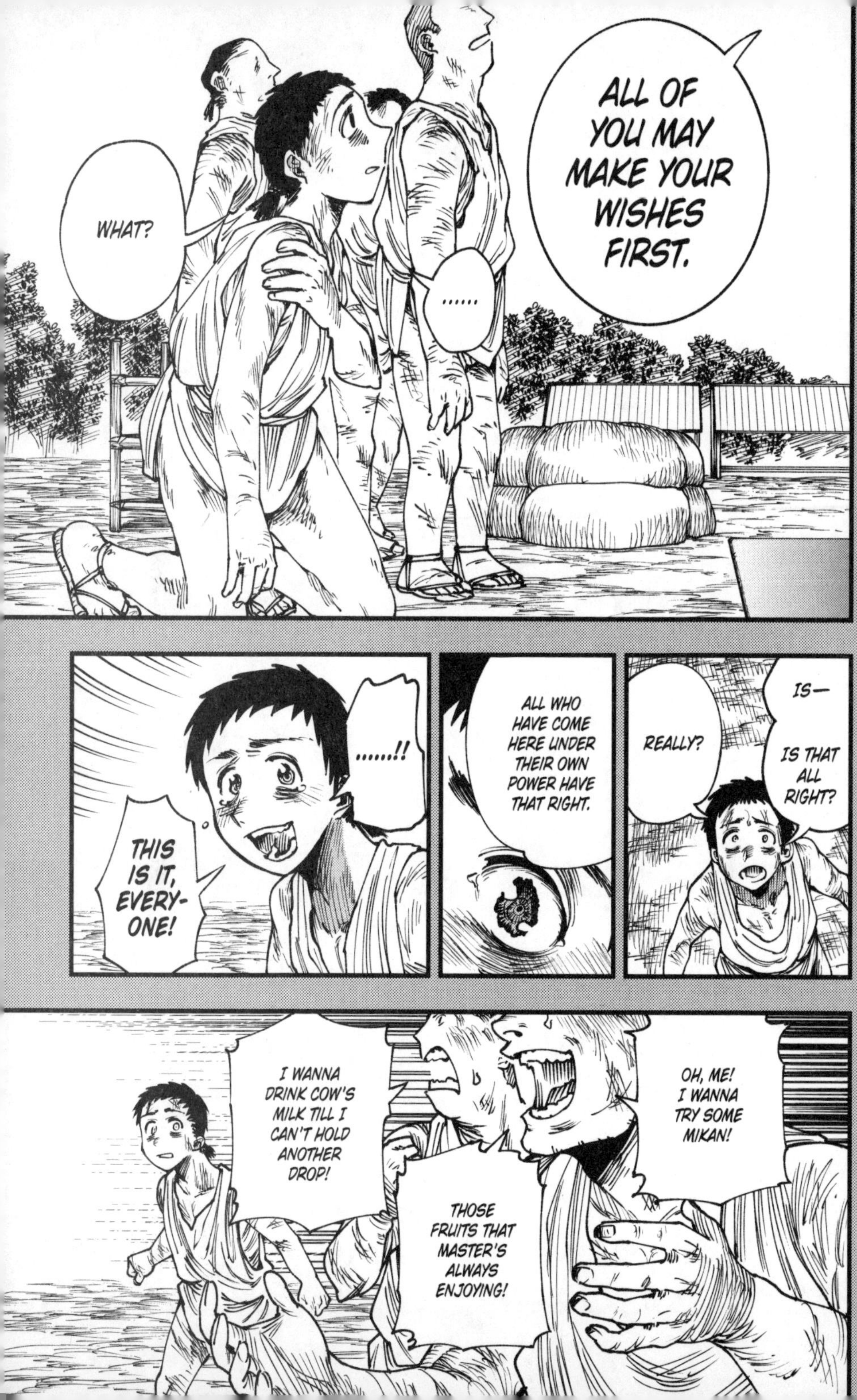
ALL OF YOU MAY MAKE YOUR WISHES FIRST.
......
WHAT?
IS— IS THAT ALL RIGHT?
REALLY?
ALL WHO HAVE COME HERE UNDER THEIR OWN POWER HAVE THAT RIGHT.
......!!
THIS IS IT, EVERY-ONE!
OH, ME! I WANNA TRY SOME MIKAN!
THOSE FRUITS THAT MASTER'S ALWAYS ENJOYING!
I WANNA DRINK COW'S MILK TILL I CAN'T HOLD ANOTHER DROP!

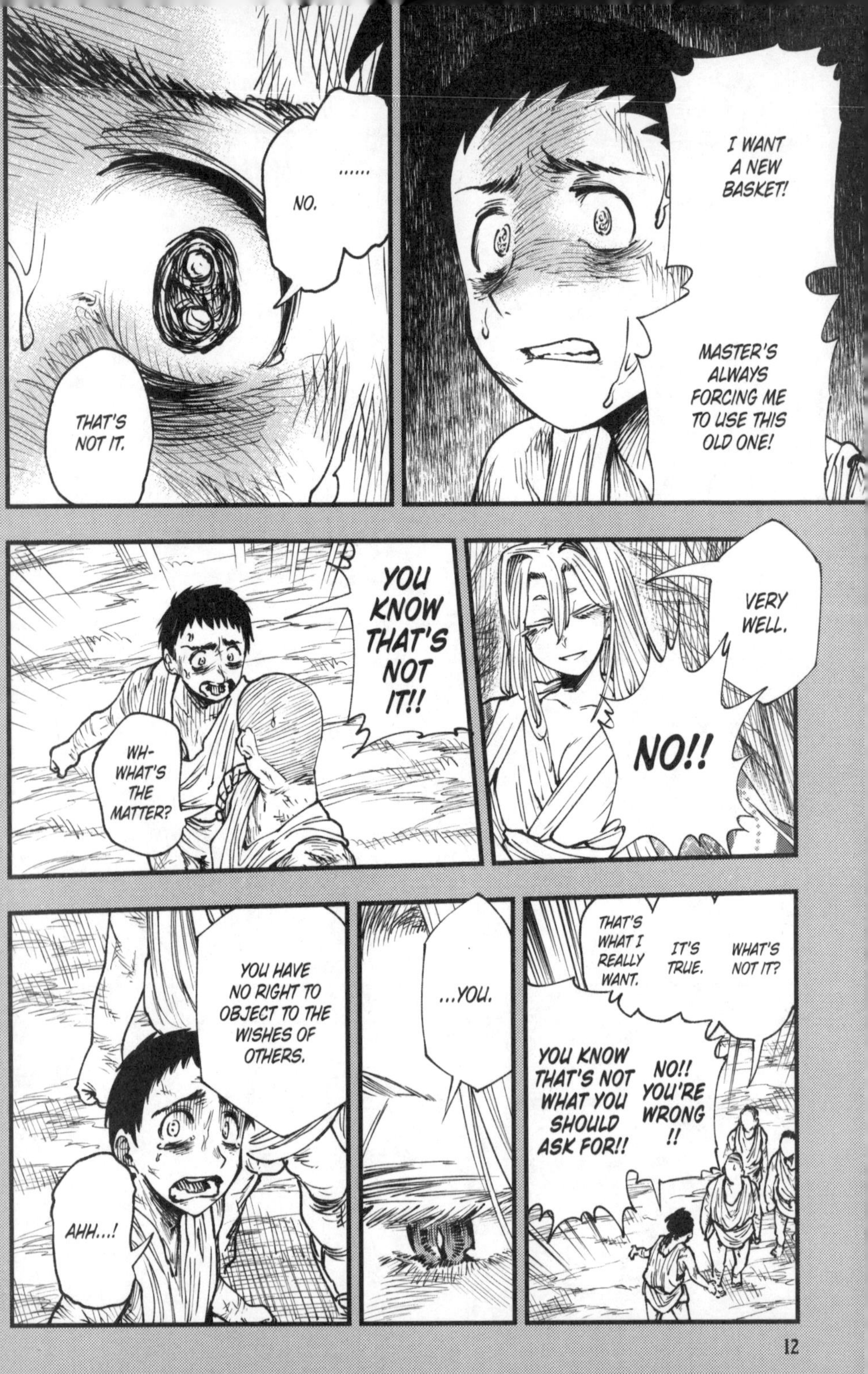
I WANT A NEW BASKET!
MASTER'S ALWAYS FORCING ME TO USE THIS OLD ONE!
......
NO.
THAT'S NOT IT.
VERY WELL.
NO!!
YOU KNOW THAT'S NOT IT!!
WH-WHAT'S THE MATTER?
WHAT'S NOT IT?
IT'S TRUE.
THAT'S WHAT I REALLY WANT.
NO!! YOU'RE WRONG!!
YOU KNOW THAT'S NOT WHAT YOU SHOULD ASK FOR!!
...YOU.
YOU HAVE NO RIGHT TO OBJECT TO THE WISHES OF OTHERS.
AHH...!

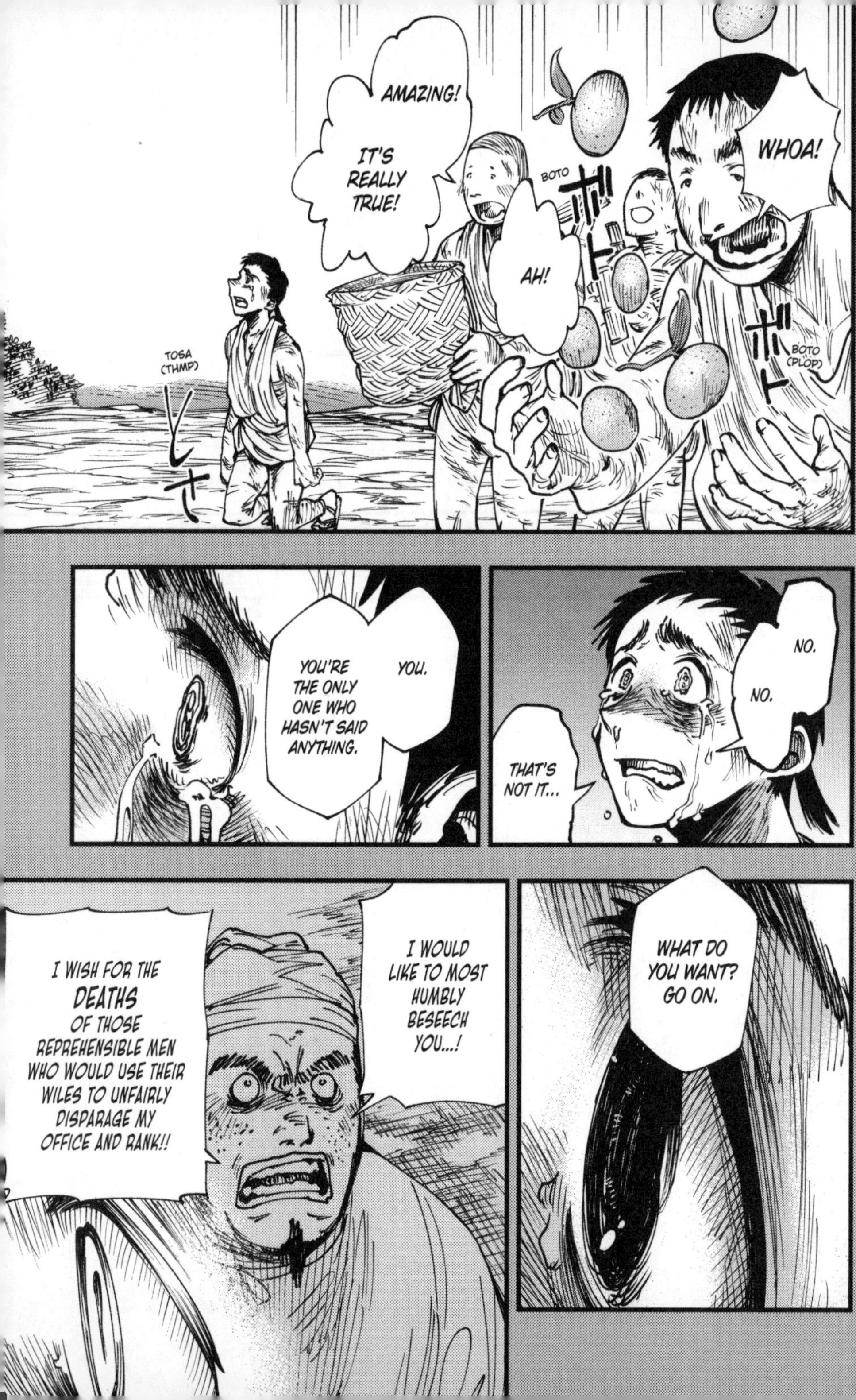
WHOA!
BOTO (PLOP)
BOTO
AH!
AMAZING!
IT'S REALLY TRUE!
TOSA (THMP)
NO.
NO.
THAT'S NOT IT...
YOU.
YOU'RE THE ONLY ONE WHO HASN'T SAID ANYTHING.
WHAT DO YOU WANT? GO ON.
I WOULD LIKE TO MOST HUMBLY BESEECH YOU...!
I WISH FOR THE DEATHS OF THOSE REPREHENSIBLE MEN WHO WOULD USE THEIR WILES TO UNFAIRLY DISPARAGE MY OFFICE AND RANK!!

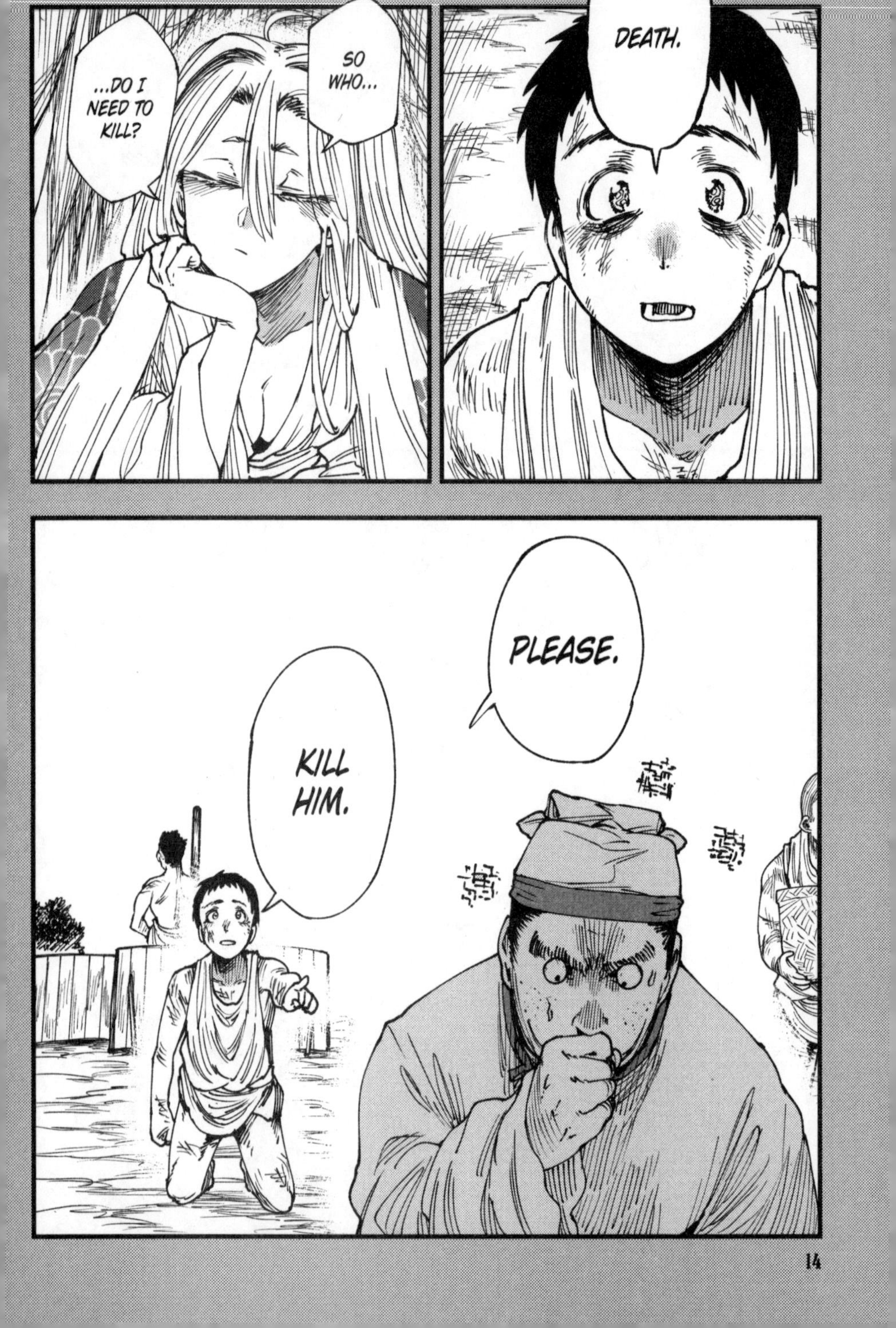
DEATH.
SO WHO...
...DO I NEED TO KILL?
PLEASE.
KILL HIM.

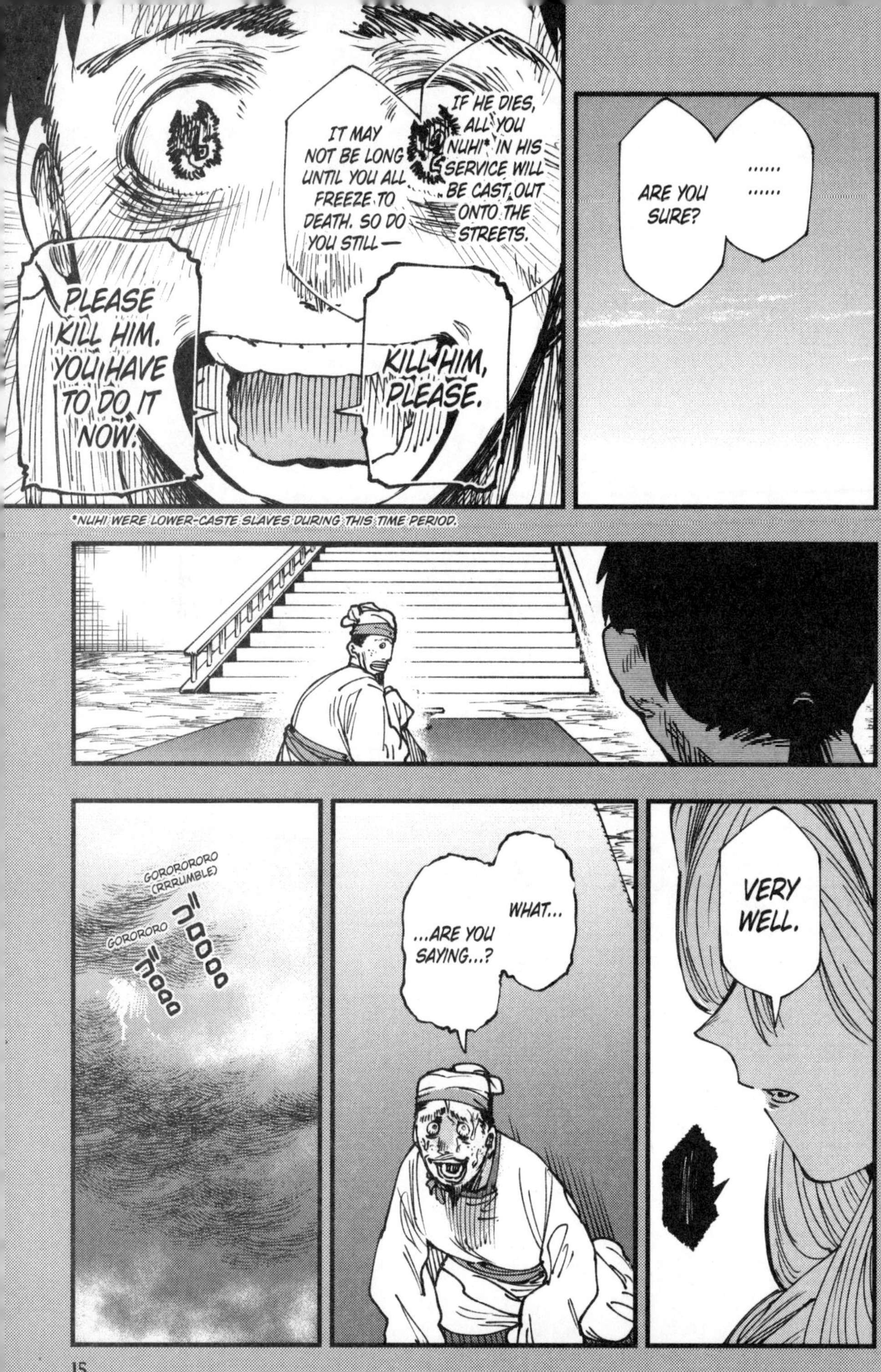

......
......
ARE YOU SURE?
IF HE DIES, ALL YOU NUHI* IN HIS SERVICE WILL BE CAST OUT ONTO THE STREETS.
IT MAY NOT BE LONG UNTIL YOU ALL FREEZE TO DEATH. SO DO YOU STILL—
KILL HIM, PLEASE.
PLEASE KILL HIM. YOU HAVE TO DO IT NOW.
VERY WELL.
WHAT...
...ARE YOU SAYING...?
GORORORORO (RRRUMBLE)
ゴロロロロ
GORORORO
ゴロロロ

*NUHI WERE LOWER-CASTE SLAVES DURING THIS TIME PERIOD.

KHHI!

DOSAFU
(THWUMP)

OHH
....!

AHH!
MAS-
TER!

MAS-
TER!?

MAS-
TER?

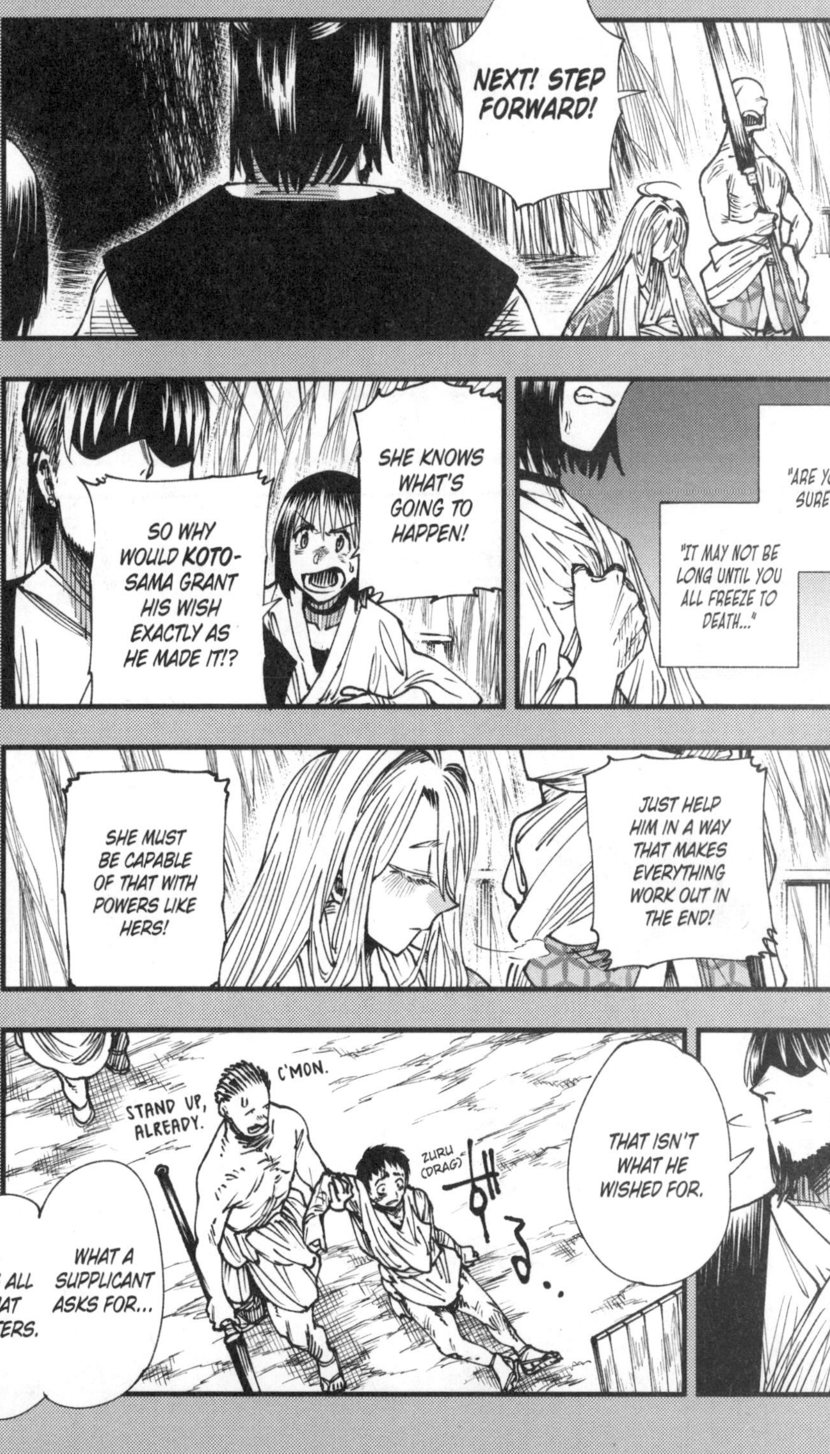
NEXT! STEP FORWARD!
"ARE YOU SURE?
"IT MAY NOT BE LONG UNTIL YOU ALL FREEZE TO DEATH..."
SHE KNOWS WHAT'S GOING TO HAPPEN!
SO WHY WOULD KOTO-SAMA GRANT HIS WISH EXACTLY AS HE MADE IT!?
JUST HELP HIM IN A WAY THAT MAKES EVERYTHING WORK OUT IN THE END!
SHE MUST BE CAPABLE OF THAT WITH POWERS LIKE HERS!
THAT ISN'T WHAT HE WISHED FOR.
C'MON.
STAND UP, ALREADY.
ZURU (DRAG)
WHAT A SUPPLICANT ASKS FOR...
...IS ALL THAT MATTERS.

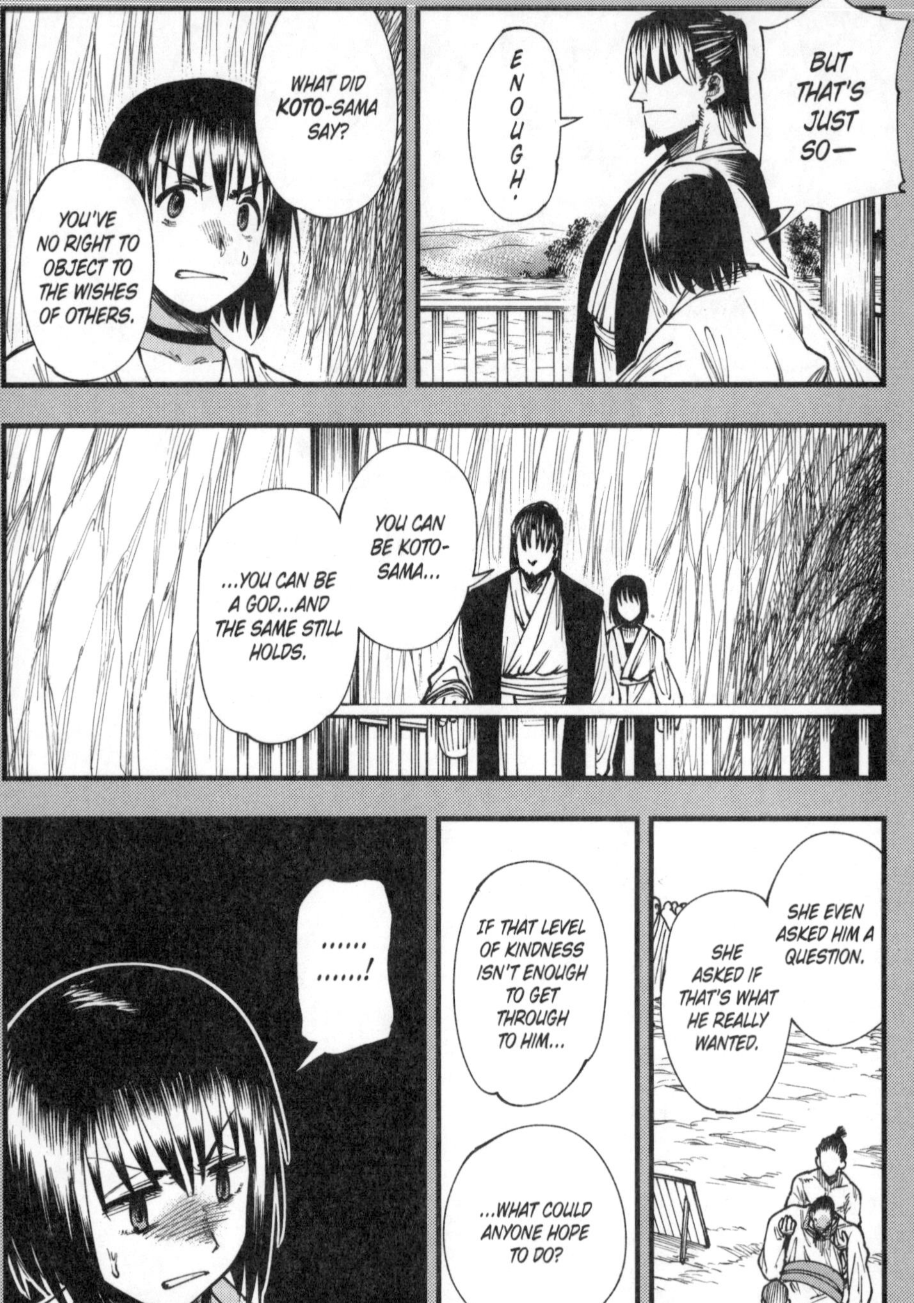
BUT THAT'S JUST SO—
ENOUGH.
WHAT DID KOTO-SAMA SAY?
YOU'VE NO RIGHT TO OBJECT TO THE WISHES OF OTHERS.
YOU CAN BE KOTO-SAMA...
...YOU CAN BE A GOD...AND THE SAME STILL HOLDS.
SHE EVEN ASKED HIM A QUESTION.
SHE ASKED IF THAT'S WHAT HE REALLY WANTED.
IF THAT LEVEL OF KINDNESS ISN'T ENOUGH TO GET THROUGH TO HIM...
...WHAT COULD ANYONE HOPE TO DO?
......
......!

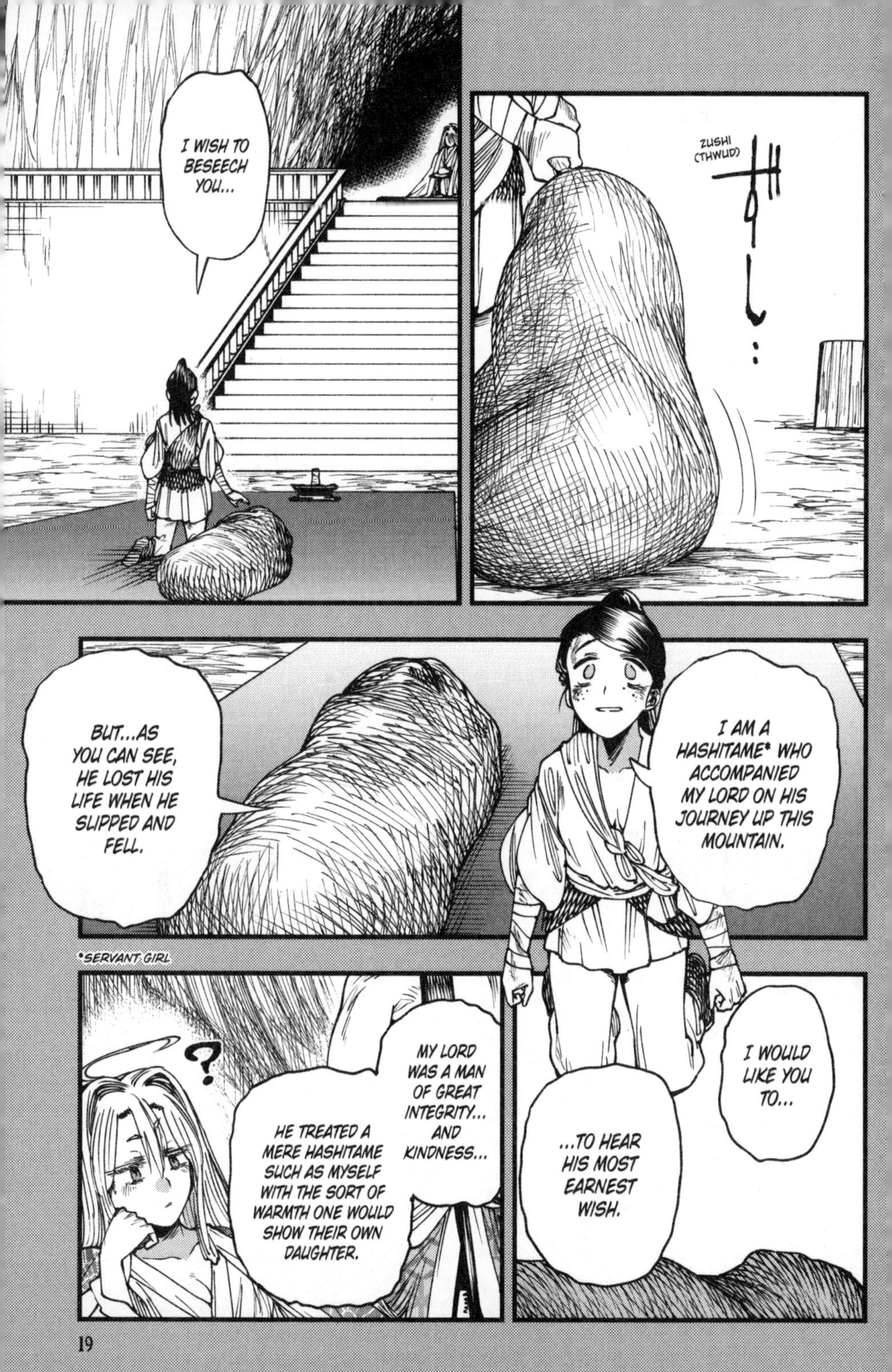
ZUSHI (THWUD)
ずし…
I WISH TO BESEECH YOU…
I AM A HASHITAME* WHO ACCOMPANIED MY LORD ON HIS JOURNEY UP THIS MOUNTAIN.
BUT…AS YOU CAN SEE, HE LOST HIS LIFE WHEN HE SLIPPED AND FELL.
*SERVANT GIRL
I WOULD LIKE YOU TO…
…TO HEAR HIS MOST EARNEST WISH.
MY LORD WAS A MAN OF GREAT INTEGRITY… AND KINDNESS…
HE TREATED A MERE HASHITAME SUCH AS MYSELF WITH THE SORT OF WARMTH ONE WOULD SHOW THEIR OWN DAUGHTER.
?

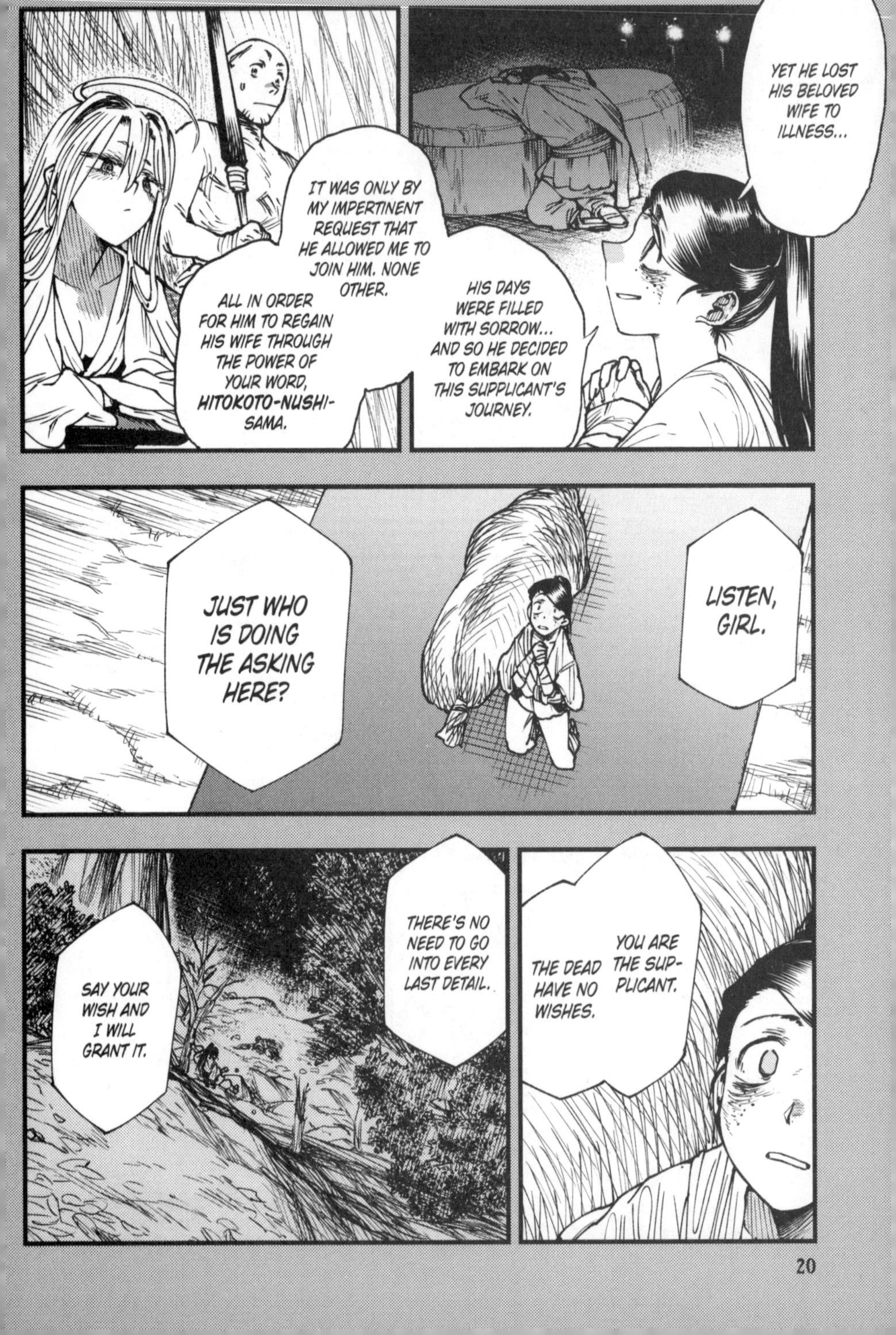
YET HE LOST HIS BELOVED WIFE TO ILLNESS...
HIS DAYS WERE FILLED WITH SORROW... AND SO HE DECIDED TO EMBARK ON THIS SUPPLICANT'S JOURNEY.
IT WAS ONLY BY MY IMPERTINENT REQUEST THAT HE ALLOWED ME TO JOIN HIM. NONE OTHER.
ALL IN ORDER FOR HIM TO REGAIN HIS WIFE THROUGH THE POWER OF YOUR WORD, **HITOKOTO-NUSHI-SAMA.**
LISTEN, GIRL.
JUST WHO IS DOING THE ASKING HERE?
YOU ARE THE SUPPLICANT.
THE DEAD HAVE NO WISHES.
THERE'S NO NEED TO GO INTO EVERY LAST DETAIL.
SAY YOUR WISH AND I WILL GRANT IT.

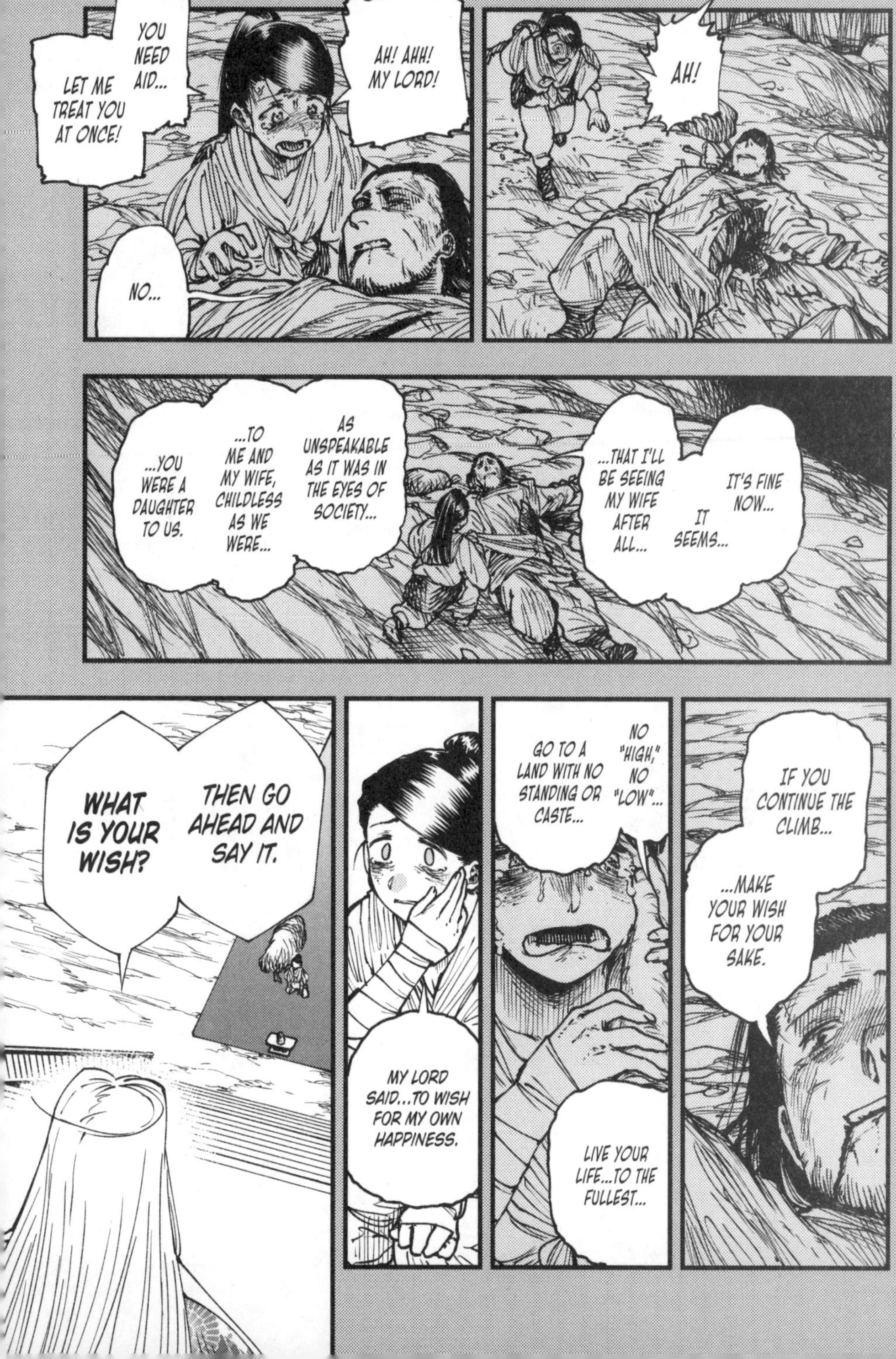
AH!
AH! AHH! MY LORD!
YOU NEED AID...
LET ME TREAT YOU AT ONCE!
NO...
IT'S FINE NOW...
IT SEEMS...
...THAT I'LL BE SEEING MY WIFE AFTER ALL...
AS UNSPEAKABLE AS IT WAS IN THE EYES OF SOCIETY...
...TO ME AND MY WIFE, CHILDLESS AS WE WERE...
...YOU WERE A DAUGHTER TO US.
IF YOU CONTINUE THE CLIMB...
...MAKE YOUR WISH FOR YOUR SAKE.
NO "HIGH," NO "LOW"...
GO TO A LAND WITH NO STANDING OR CASTE...
LIVE YOUR LIFE...TO THE FULLEST...
MY LORD SAID...TO WISH FOR MY OWN HAPPINESS.
THEN GO AHEAD AND SAY IT.
WHAT IS YOUR WISH?

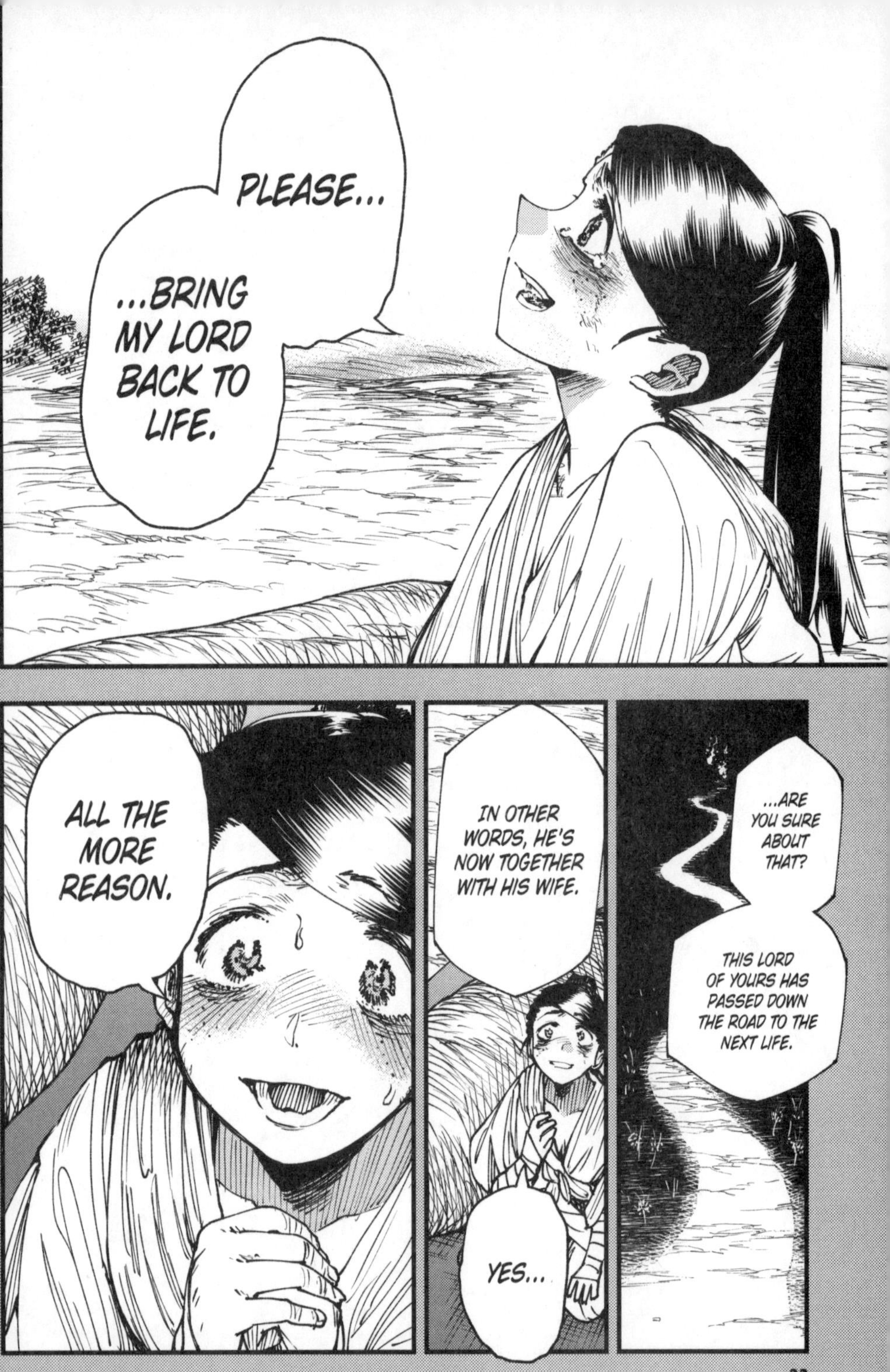
PLEASE...
...BRING MY LORD BACK TO LIFE.
...ARE YOU SURE ABOUT THAT?
THIS LORD OF YOURS HAS PASSED DOWN THE ROAD TO THE NEXT LIFE.
IN OTHER WORDS, HE'S NOW TOGETHER WITH HIS WIFE.
YES...
ALL THE MORE REASON.

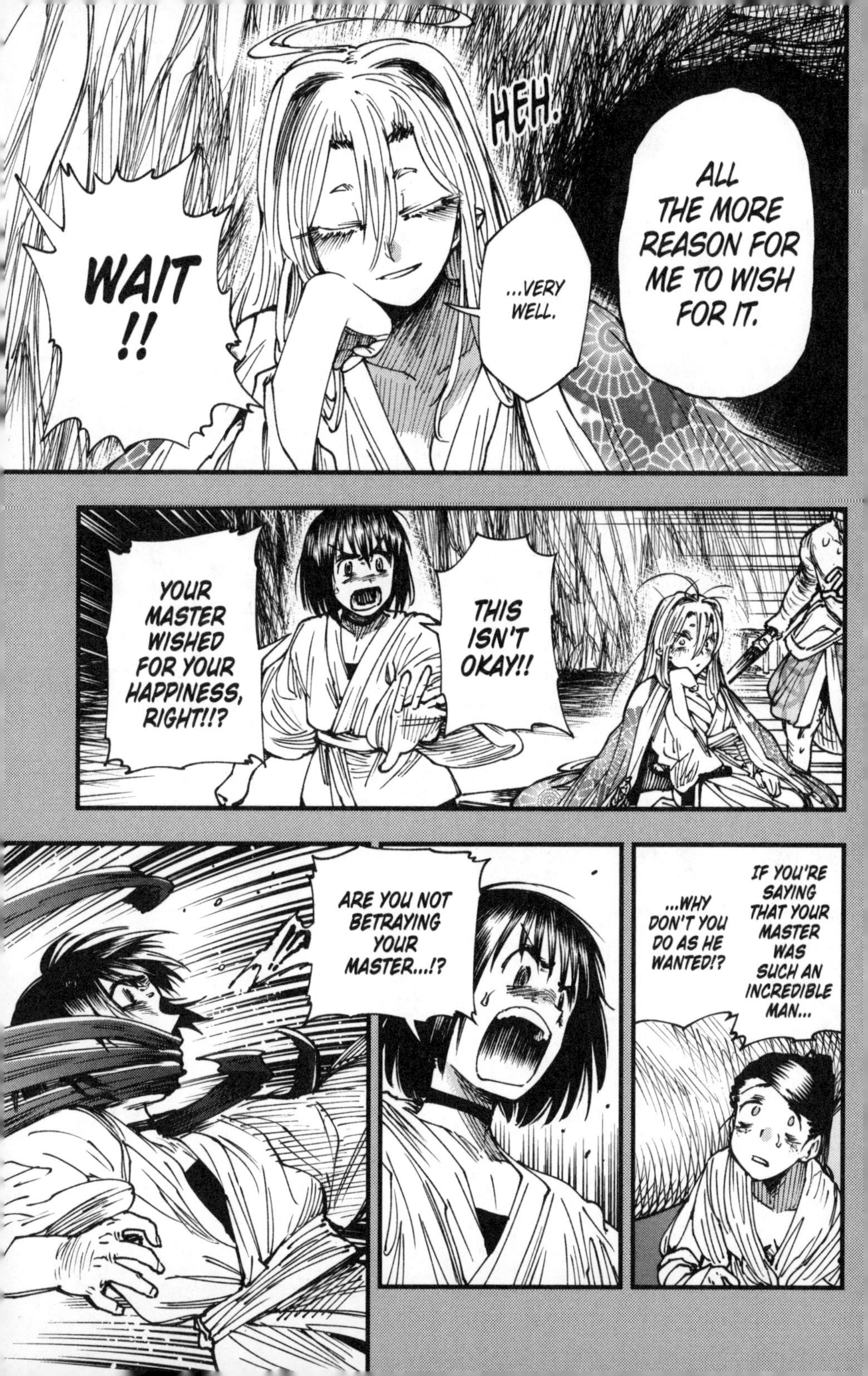
HEH.
ALL THE MORE REASON FOR ME TO WISH FOR IT.
...VERY WELL.
WAIT!!
THIS ISN'T OKAY!!
YOUR MASTER WISHED FOR YOUR HAPPINESS, RIGHT!!?
IF YOU'RE SAYING THAT YOUR MASTER WAS SUCH AN INCREDIBLE MAN...
...WHY DON'T YOU DO AS HE WANTED!?
ARE YOU NOT BETRAYING YOUR MASTER...!?
!!

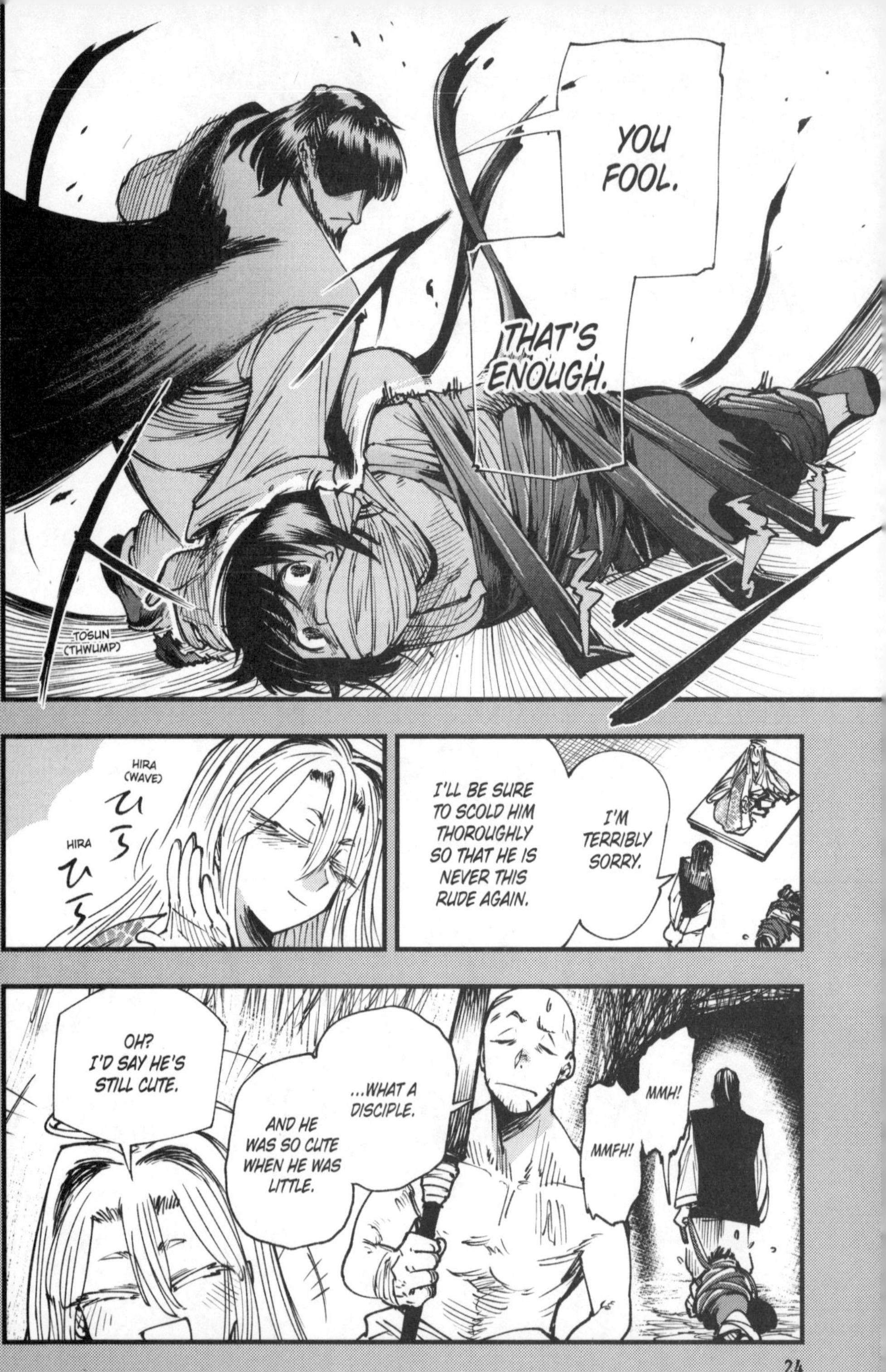
YOU FOOL.
THAT'S ENOUGH.
TOSUN (THWUMP)
I'M TERRIBLY SORRY.
I'LL BE SURE TO SCOLD HIM THOROUGHLY SO THAT HE IS NEVER THIS RUDE AGAIN.
HIRA (WAVE)
ひら
HIRA
ひら
MMH!
MMFH!
...WHAT A DISCIPLE.
AND HE WAS SO CUTE WHEN HE WAS LITTLE.
OH? I'D SAY HE'S STILL CUTE.

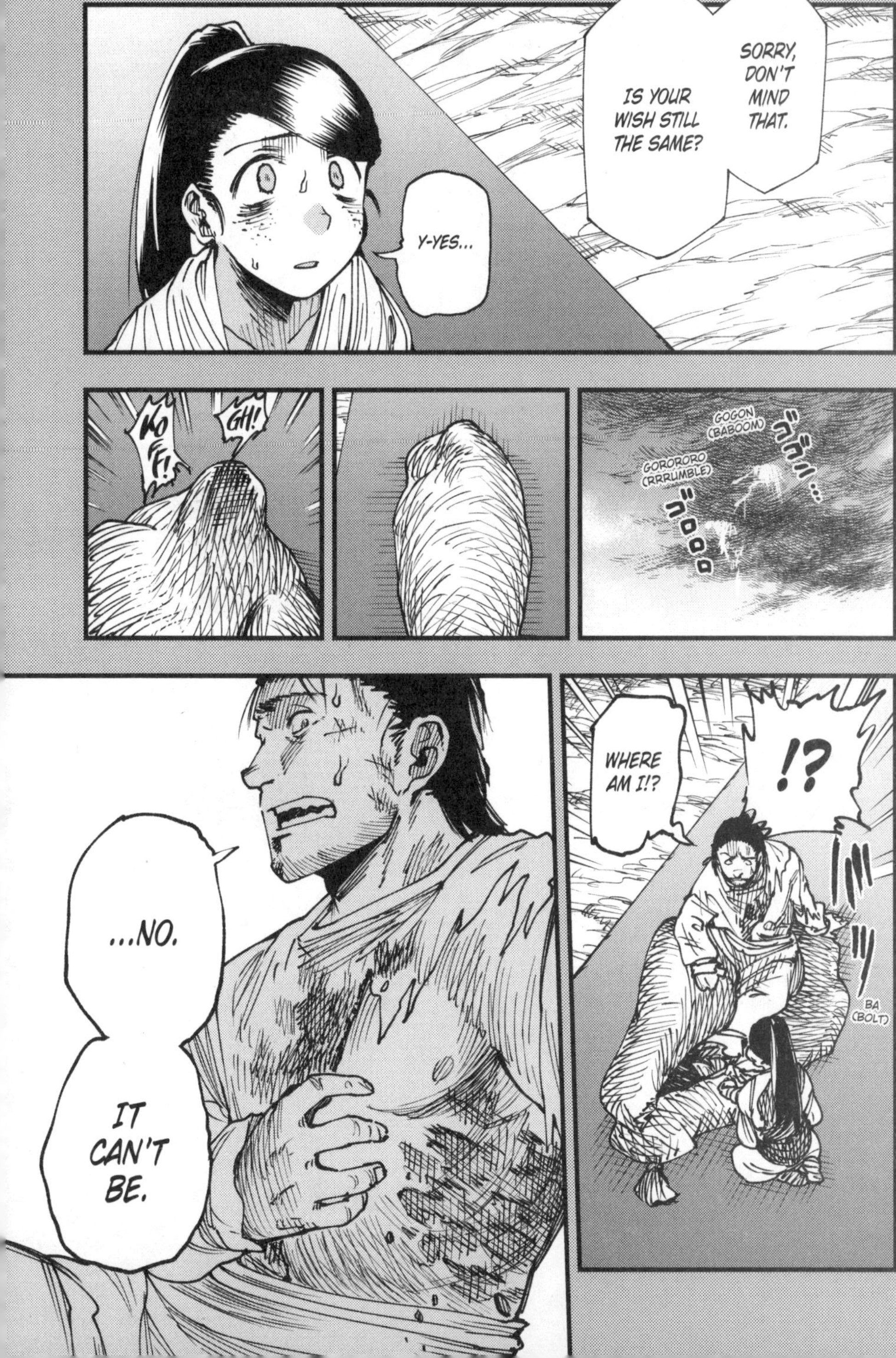
SORRY, DON'T MIND THAT.
IS YOUR WISH STILL THE SAME?
Y-YES...
GOGON (BABOOM)
GORORORO (RRRUMBLE)
GH!
KOFF!
!?
WHERE AM I!?
BA (BOLT)
...NO.
IT CAN'T BE.

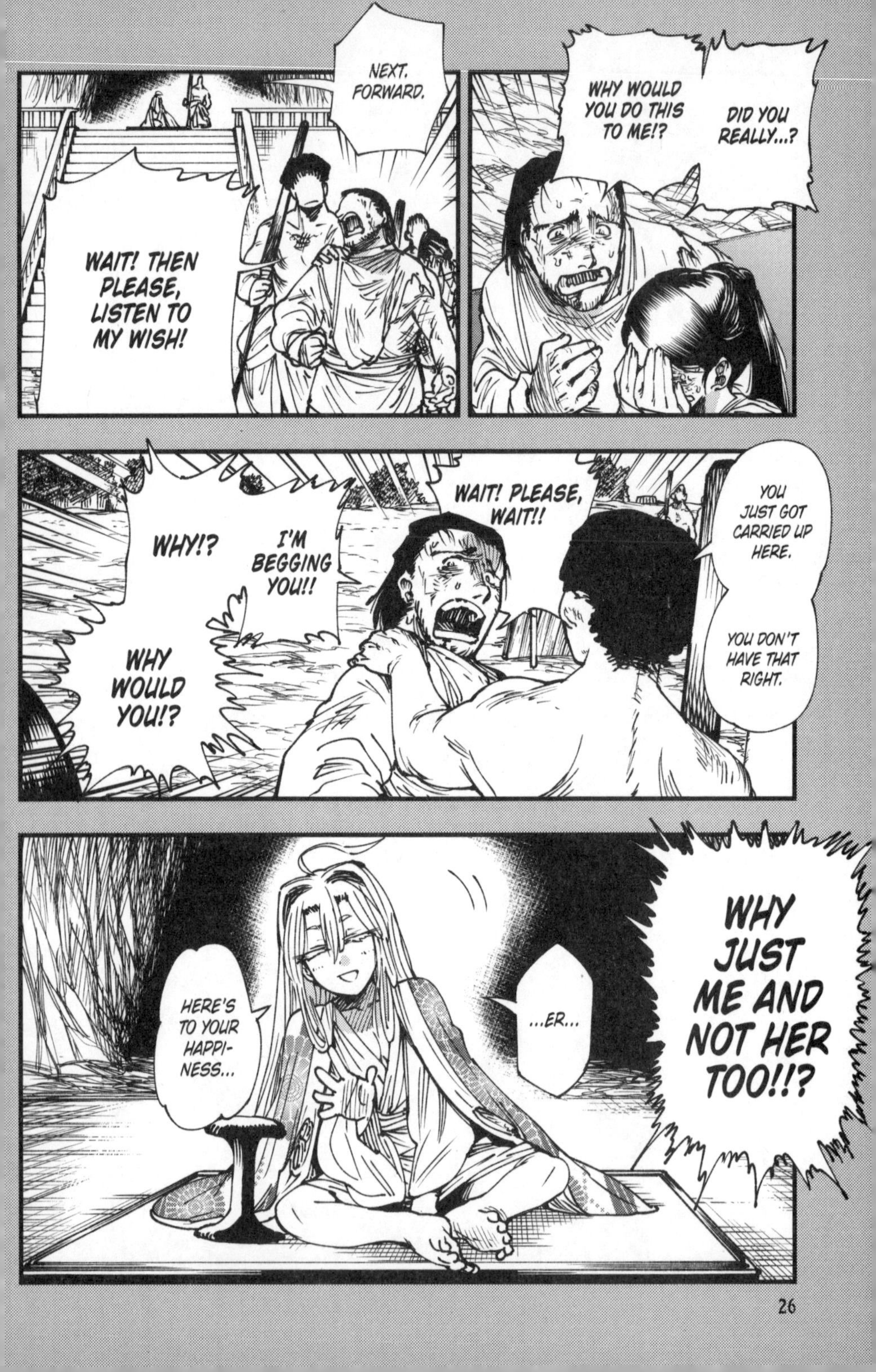
WHY WOULD YOU DO THIS TO ME!?
DID YOU REALLY...?
NEXT. FORWARD.
WAIT! THEN PLEASE, LISTEN TO MY WISH!
YOU JUST GOT CARRIED UP HERE.
YOU DON'T HAVE THAT RIGHT.
WAIT! PLEASE, WAIT!!
I'M BEGGING YOU!!
WHY!?
WHY WOULD YOU!?
WHY JUST ME AND NOT HER TOO!!?
...ER...
HERE'S TO YOUR HAPPINESS...

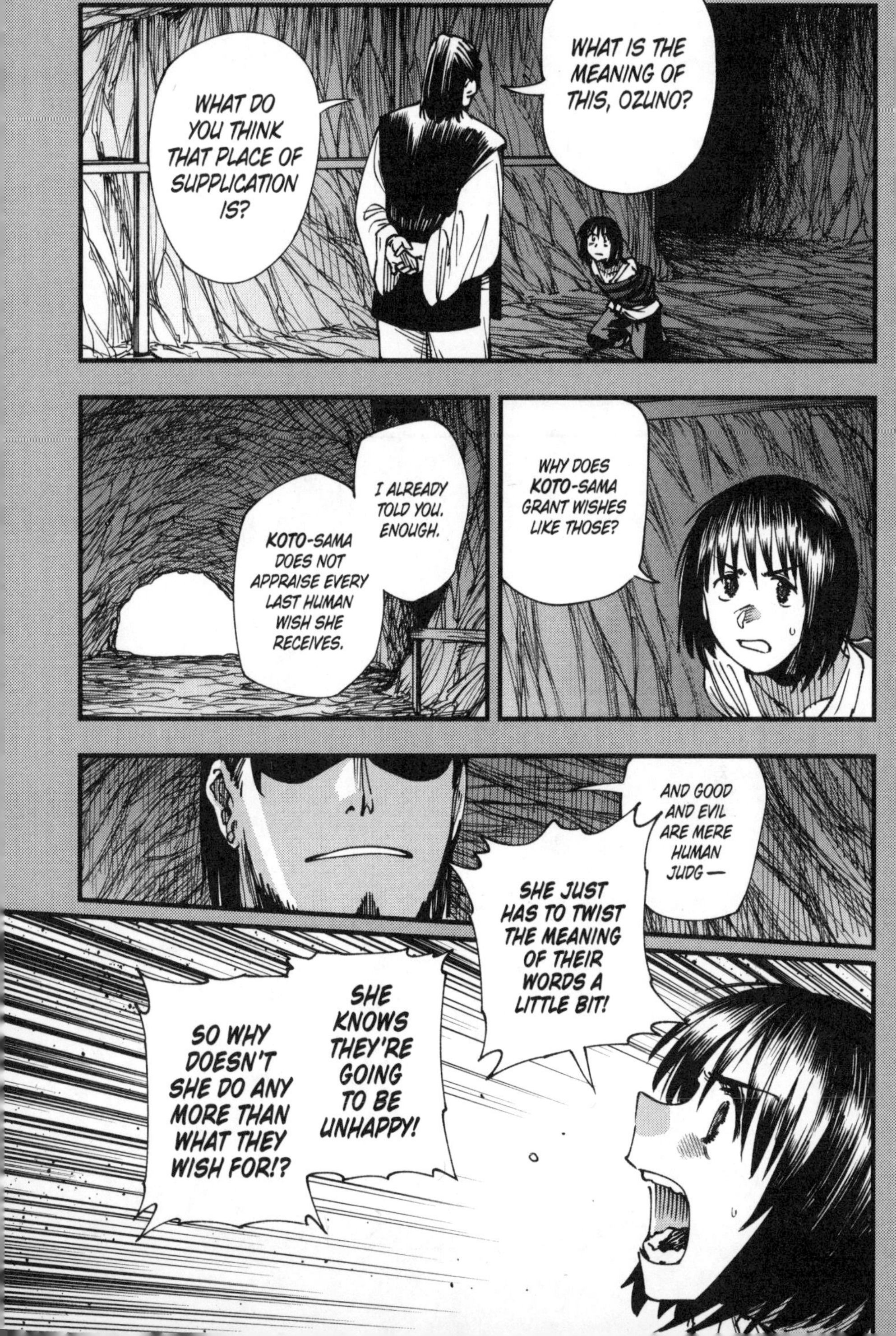
WHAT IS THE MEANING OF THIS, OZUNO?
WHAT DO YOU THINK THAT PLACE OF SUPPLICATION IS?
WHY DOES KOTO-SAMA GRANT WISHES LIKE THOSE?
I ALREADY TOLD YOU. ENOUGH.
KOTO-SAMA DOES NOT APPRAISE EVERY LAST HUMAN WISH SHE RECEIVES.
AND GOOD AND EVIL ARE MERE HUMAN JUDG—
SHE JUST HAS TO TWIST THE MEANING OF THEIR WORDS A LITTLE BIT!
SHE KNOWS THEY'RE GOING TO BE UNHAPPY!
SO WHY DOESN'T SHE DO ANY MORE THAN WHAT THEY WISH FOR!?

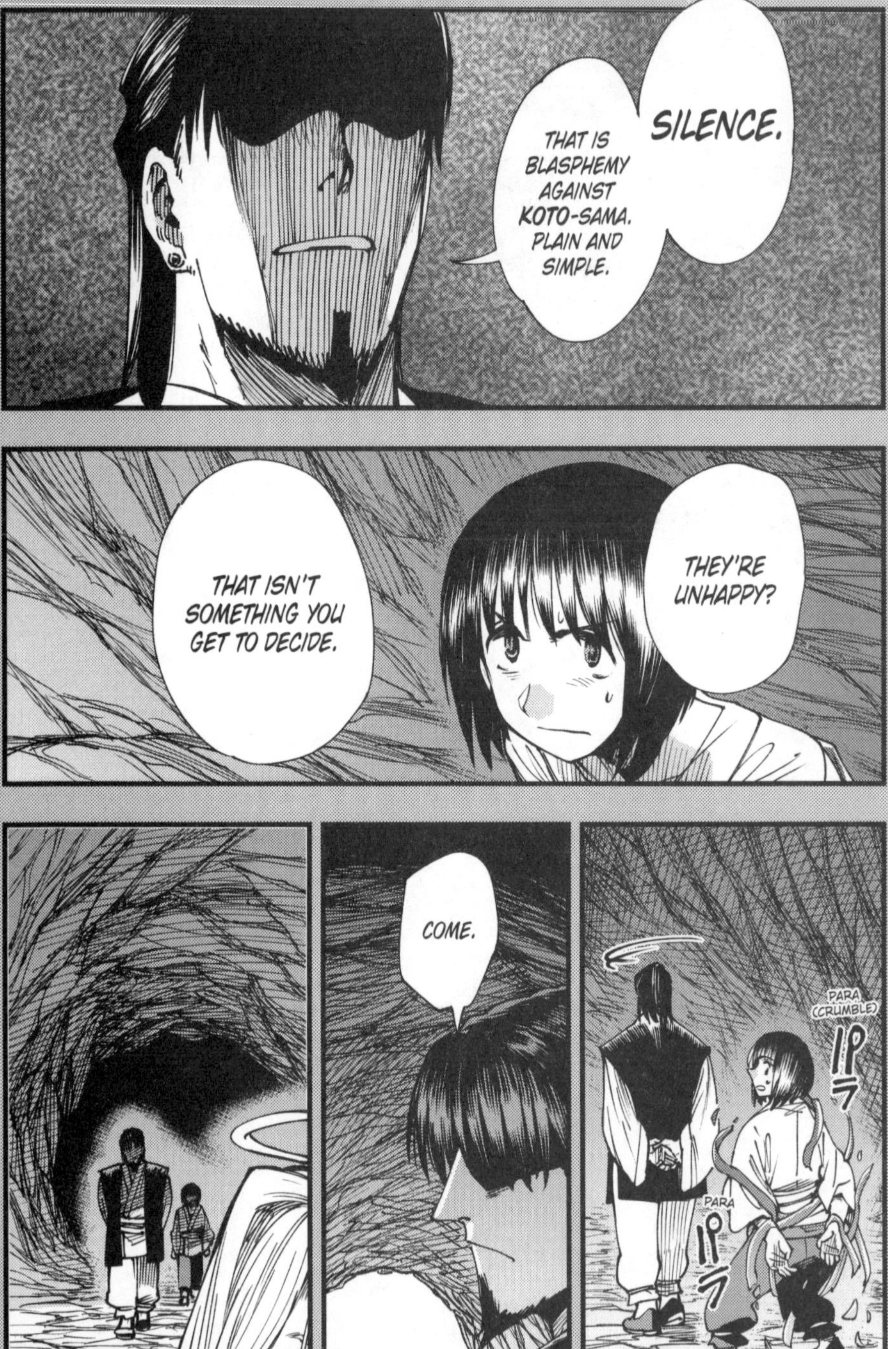
SILENCE.
THAT IS BLASPHEMY AGAINST KOTO-SAMA. PLAIN AND SIMPLE.
THEY'RE UNHAPPY?
THAT ISN'T SOMETHING YOU GET TO DECIDE.
PARA (CRUMBLE)
パラ
PARA
パラ
COME.

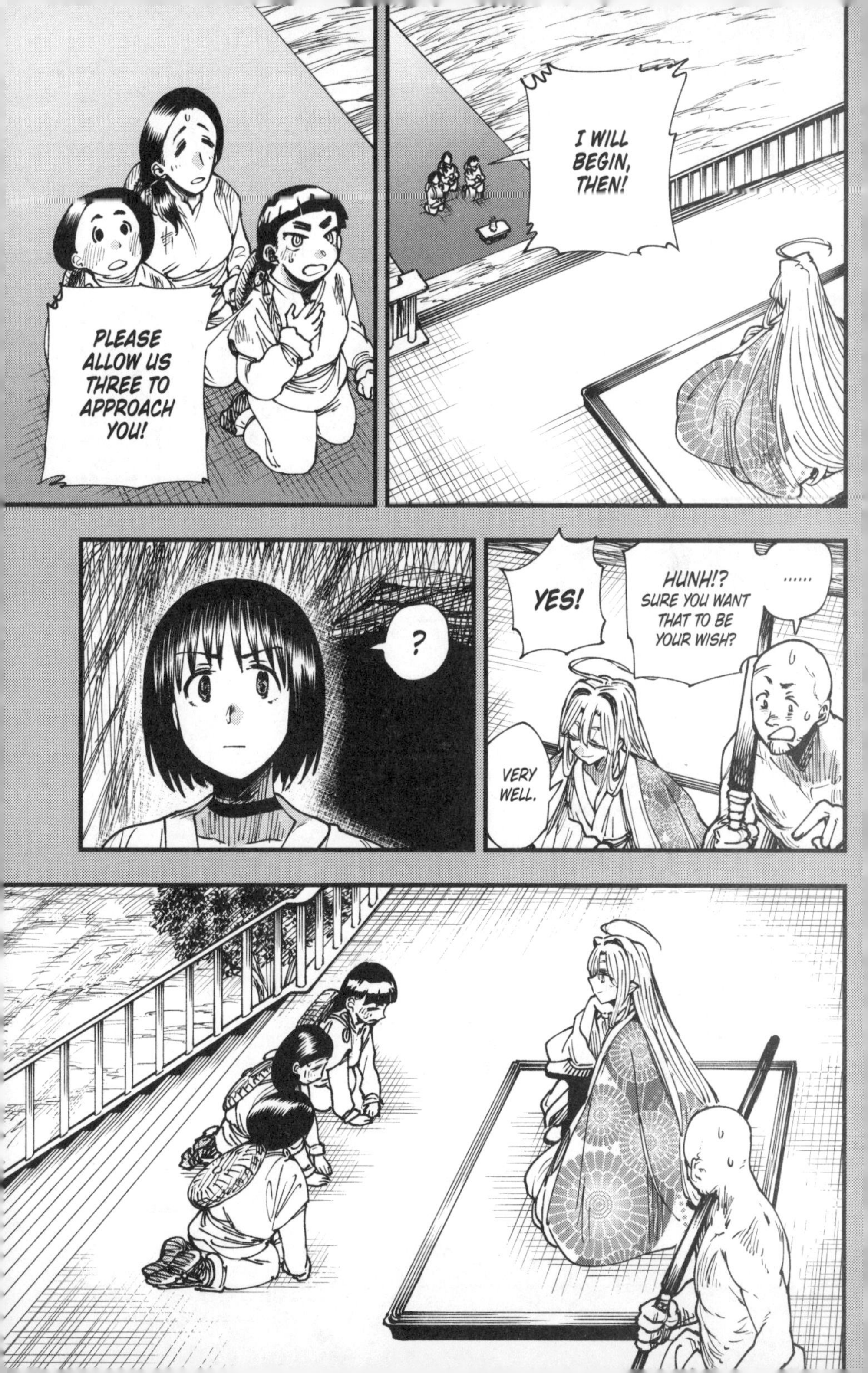
I WILL BEGIN, THEN!
PLEASE ALLOW US THREE TO APPROACH YOU!
......
HUNH!? SURE YOU WANT THAT TO BE YOUR WISH?
YES!
VERY WELL.
?

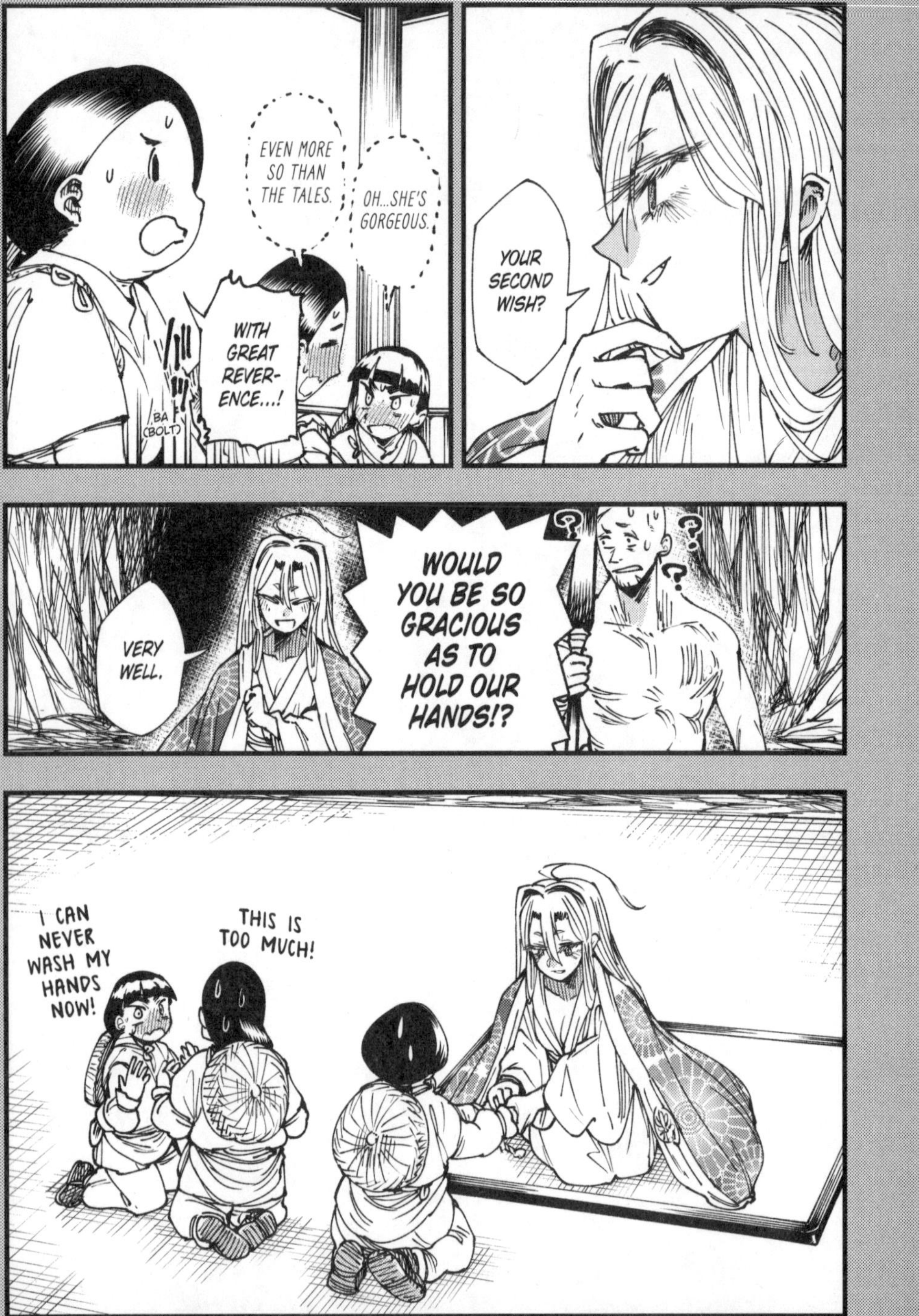
YOUR SECOND WISH?
OH...SHE'S GORGEOUS.
EVEN MORE SO THAN THE TALES.
WITH GREAT REVERENCE...!
BA (BOLT)
WOULD YOU BE SO GRACIOUS AS TO HOLD OUR HANDS!?
VERY WELL.
THIS IS TOO MUCH!
I CAN NEVER WASH MY HANDS NOW!

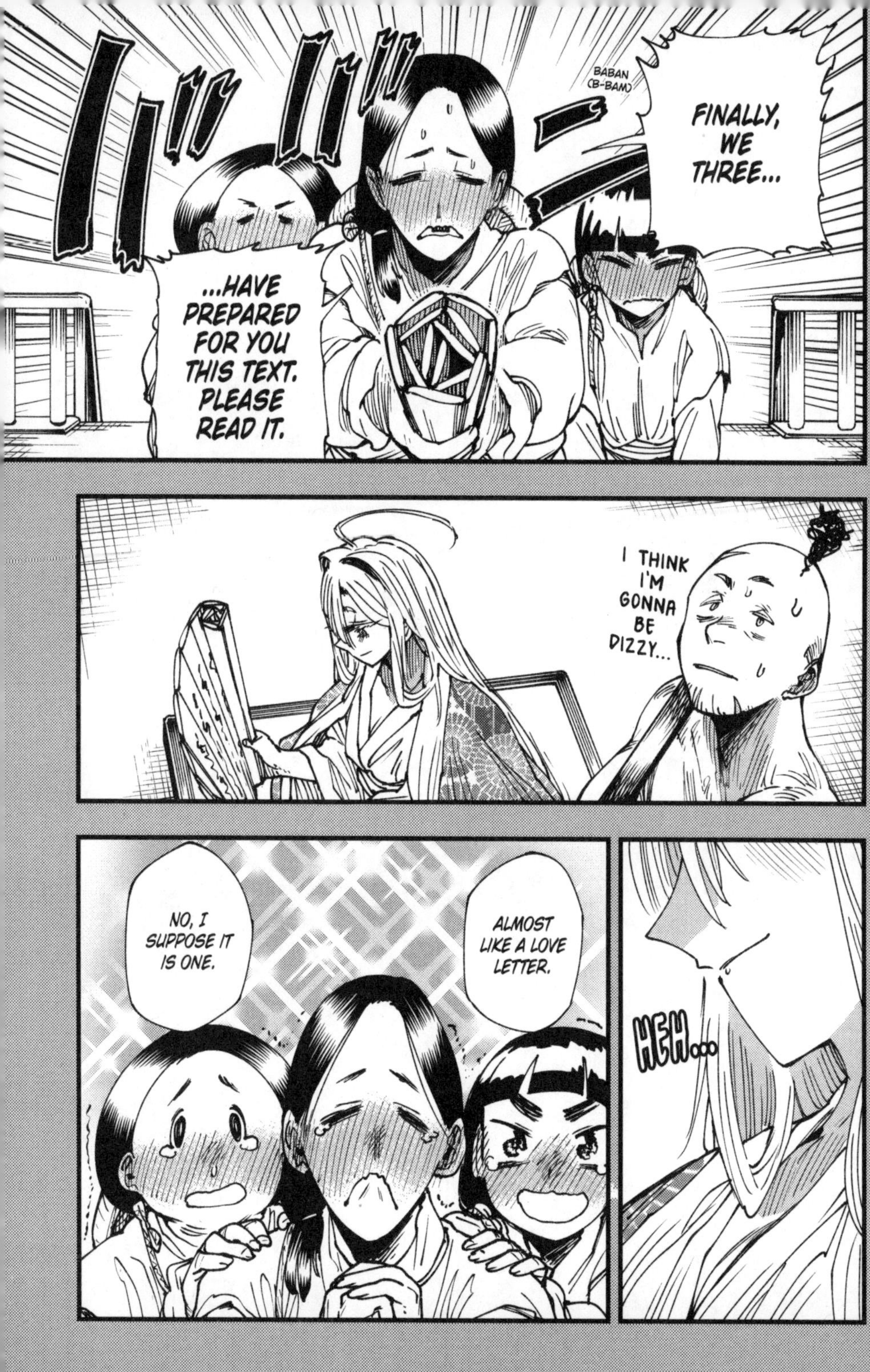
BABAN (B-BAM)
FINALLY, WE THREE...
...HAVE PREPARED FOR YOU THIS TEXT. PLEASE READ IT.
I THINK I'M GONNA BE DIZZY...
HEH...
ALMOST LIKE A LOVE LETTER.
NO, I SUPPOSE IT IS ONE.

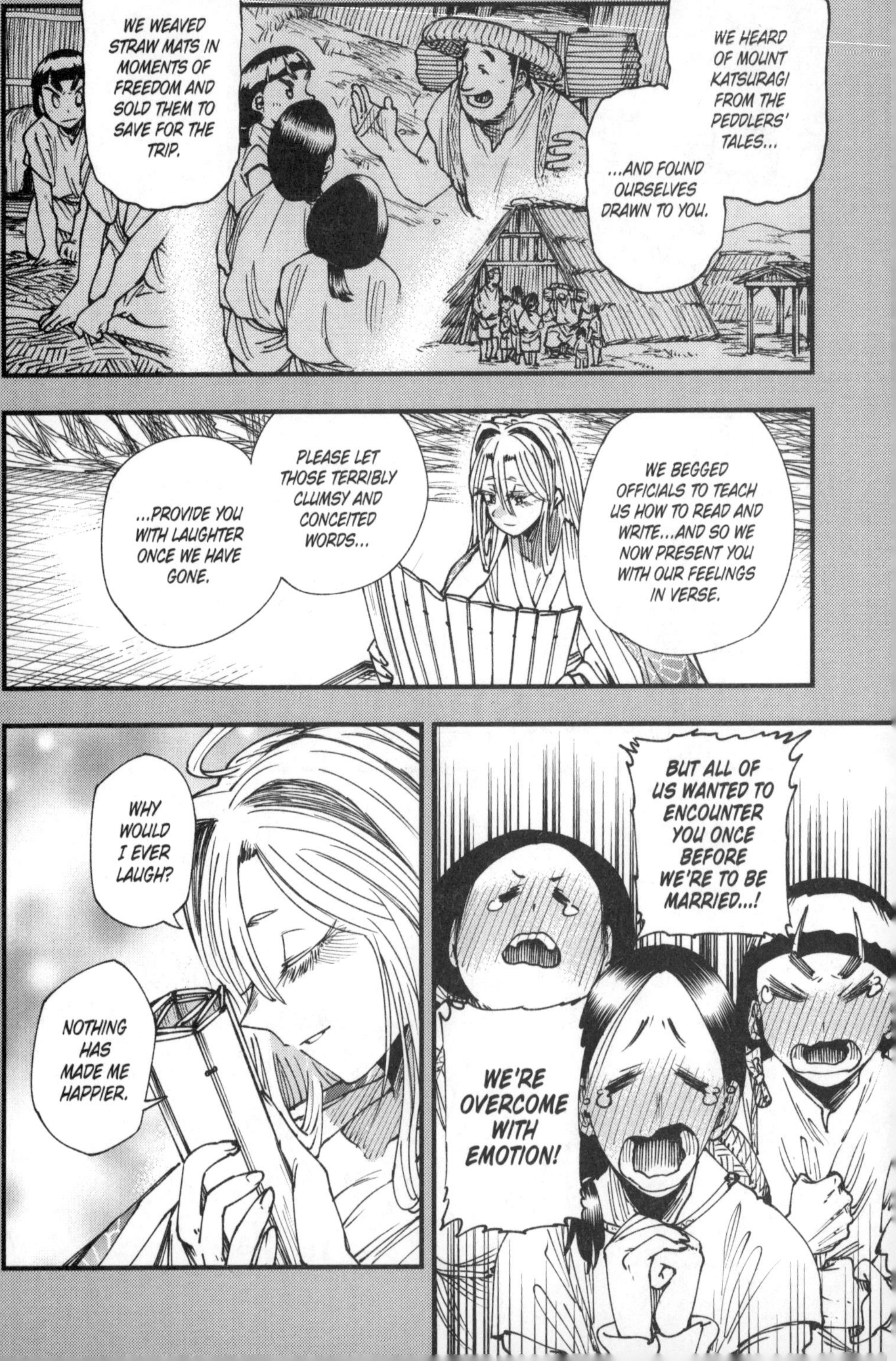
WE HEARD OF MOUNT KATSURAGI FROM THE PEDDLERS' TALES...
...AND FOUND OURSELVES DRAWN TO YOU.
WE WEAVED STRAW MATS IN MOMENTS OF FREEDOM AND SOLD THEM TO SAVE FOR THE TRIP.
WE BEGGED OFFICIALS TO TEACH US HOW TO READ AND WRITE...AND SO WE NOW PRESENT YOU WITH OUR FEELINGS IN VERSE.
PLEASE LET THOSE TERRIBLY CLUMSY AND CONCEITED WORDS...
...PROVIDE YOU WITH LAUGHTER ONCE WE HAVE GONE.
BUT ALL OF US WANTED TO ENCOUNTER YOU ONCE BEFORE WE'RE TO BE MARRIED...!
WE'RE OVERCOME WITH EMOTION!
WHY WOULD I EVER LAUGH?
NOTHING HAS MADE ME HAPPIER.

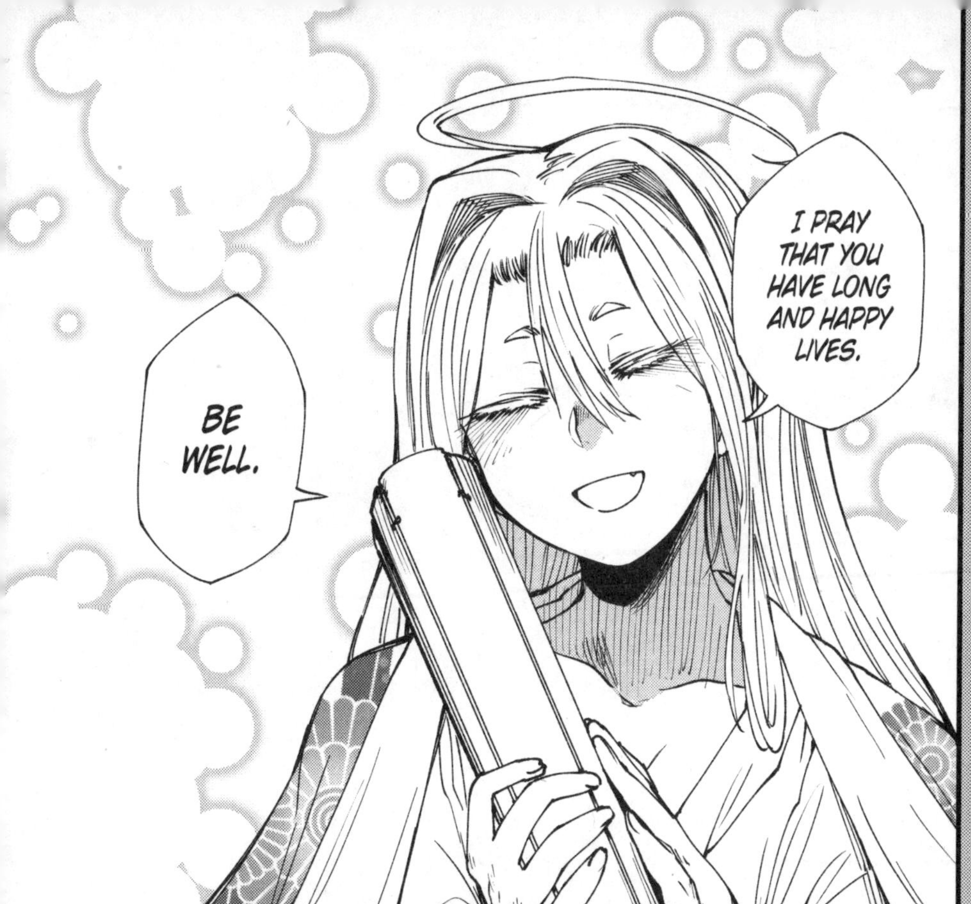
I PRAY THAT YOU HAVE LONG AND HAPPY LIVES.
BE WELL.

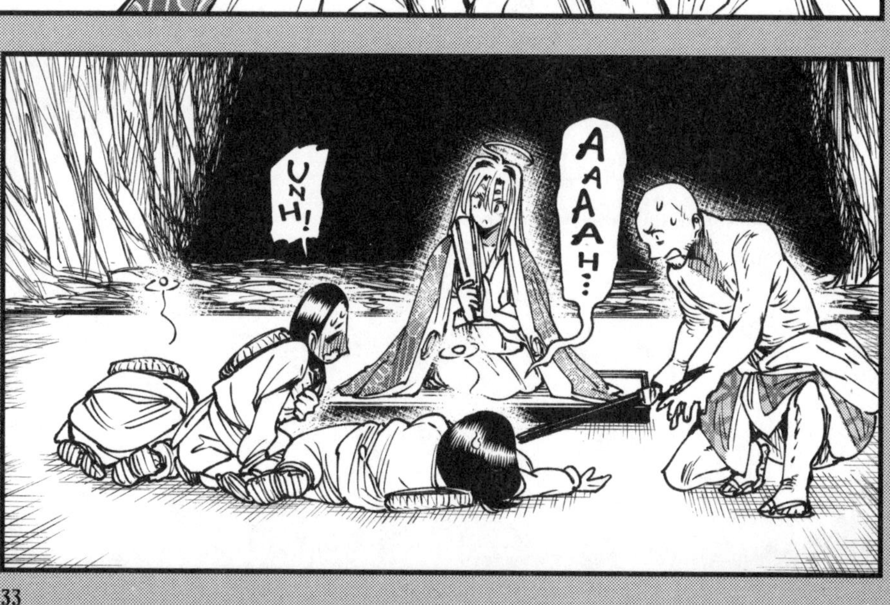
AAAAH...
UNH!

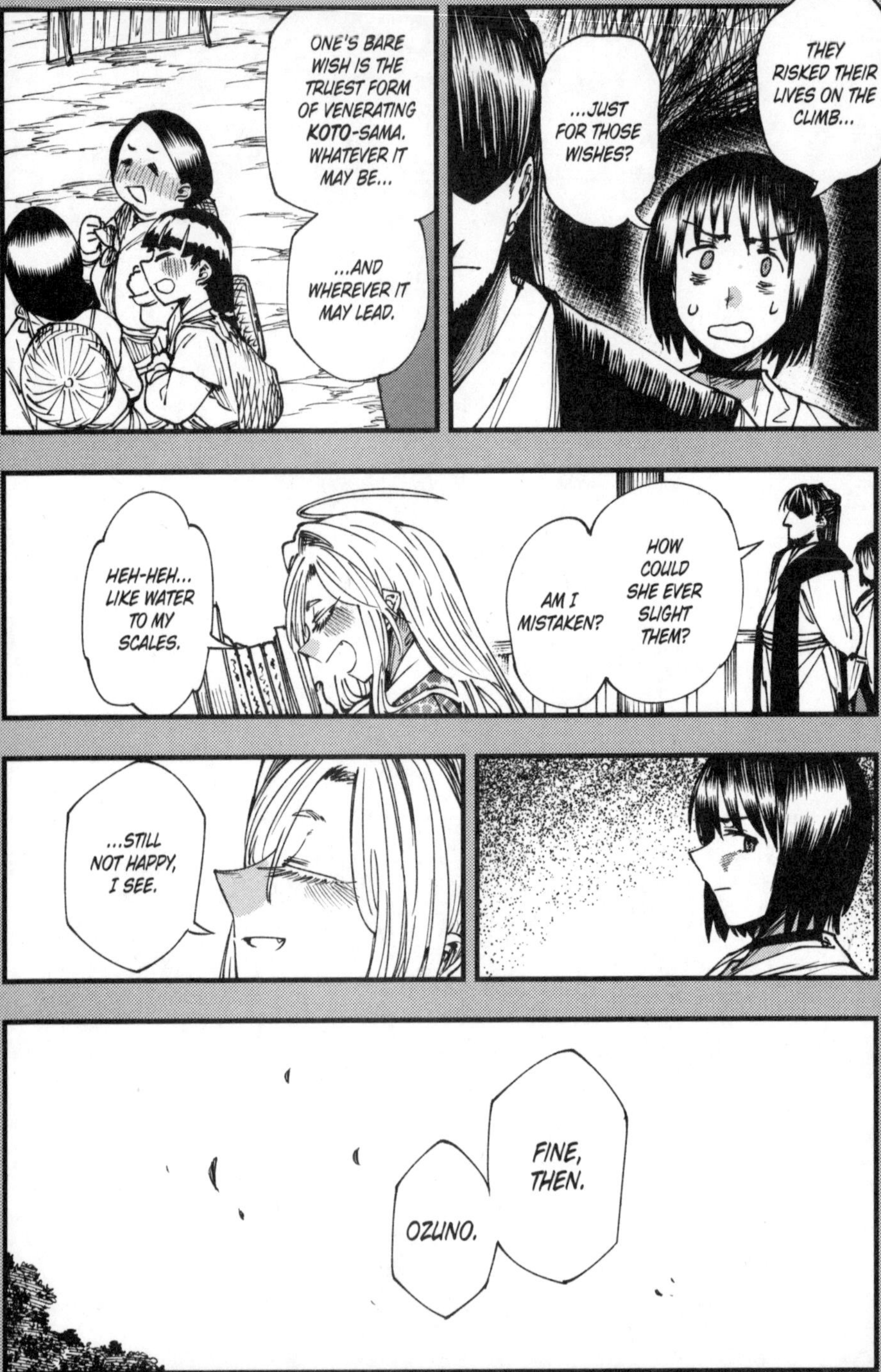
THEY RISKED THEIR LIVES ON THE CLIMB...
...JUST FOR THOSE WISHES?
ONE'S BARE WISH IS THE TRUEST FORM OF VENERATING KOTO-SAMA. WHATEVER IT MAY BE...
...AND WHEREVER IT MAY LEAD.
HOW COULD SHE EVER SLIGHT THEM?
AM I MISTAKEN?
HEH-HEH... LIKE WATER TO MY SCALES.
...STILL NOT HAPPY, I SEE.
FINE, THEN.
OZUNO.

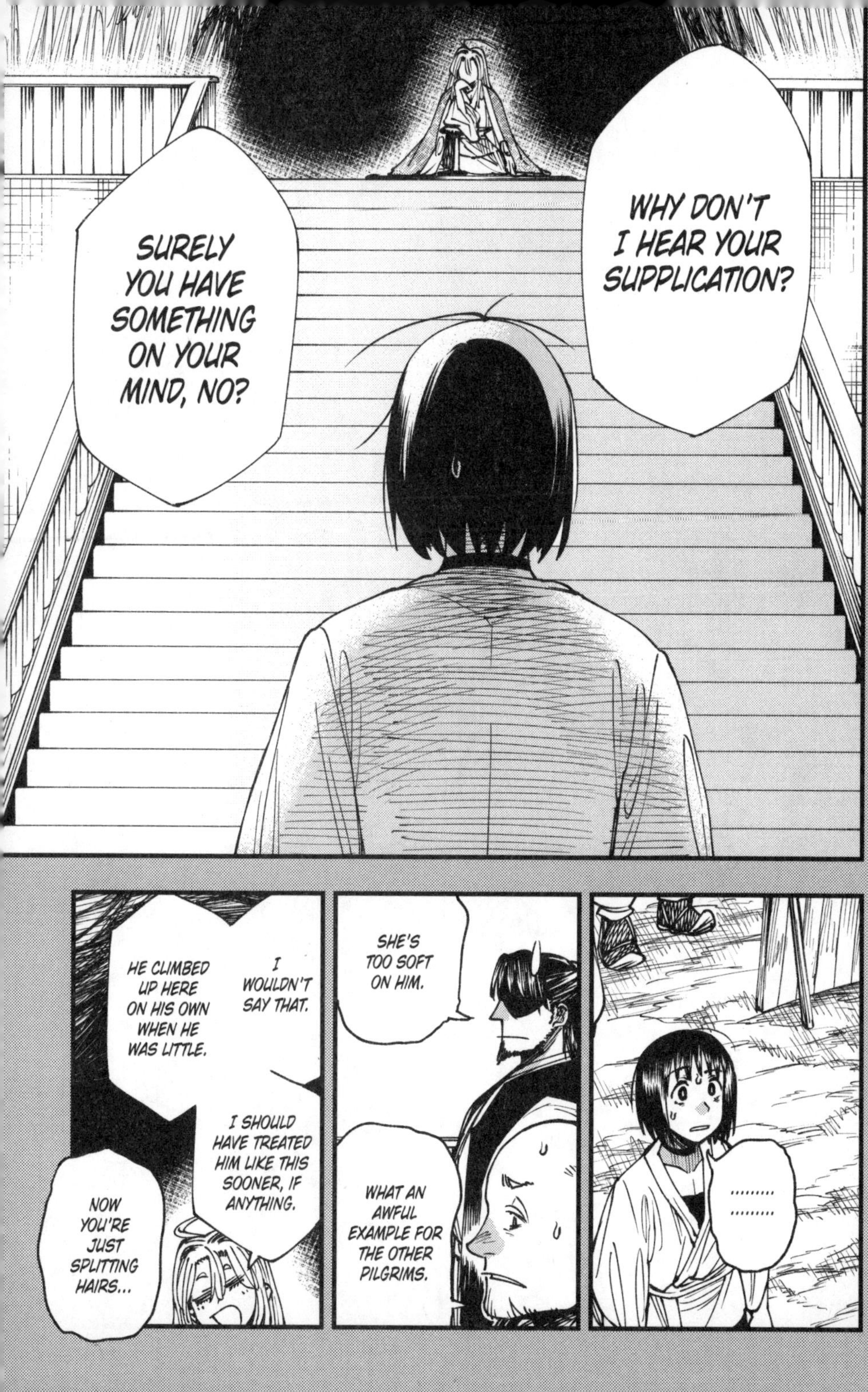
WHY DON'T I HEAR YOUR SUPPLICATION?
SURELY YOU HAVE SOMETHING ON YOUR MIND, NO?
....
SHE'S TOO SOFT ON HIM.
WHAT AN AWFUL EXAMPLE FOR THE OTHER PILGRIMS.
I WOULDN'T SAY THAT.
HE CLIMBED UP HERE ON HIS OWN WHEN HE WAS LITTLE.
I SHOULD HAVE TREATED HIM LIKE THIS SOONER, IF ANYTHING.
NOW YOU'RE JUST SPLITTING HAIRS...

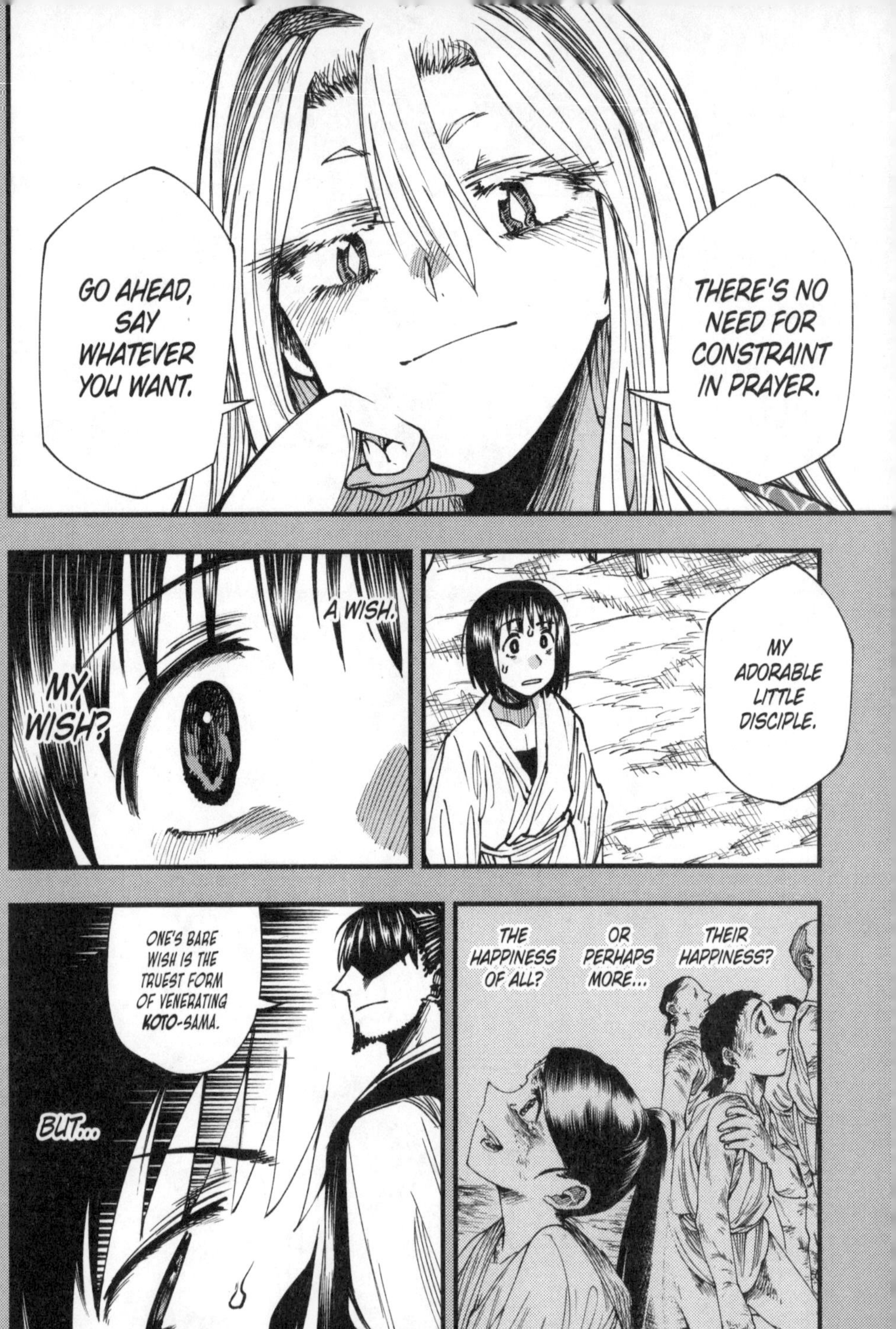
THERE'S NO NEED FOR CONSTRAINT IN PRAYER.
GO AHEAD, SAY WHATEVER YOU WANT.
MY ADORABLE LITTLE DISCIPLE.
A WISH.
MY WISH?
THE HAPPINESS OF ALL?
OR PERHAPS MORE...
THEIR HAPPINESS?
ONE'S BARE WISH IS THE TRUEST FORM OF VENERATING KOTO-SAMA.
BUT...

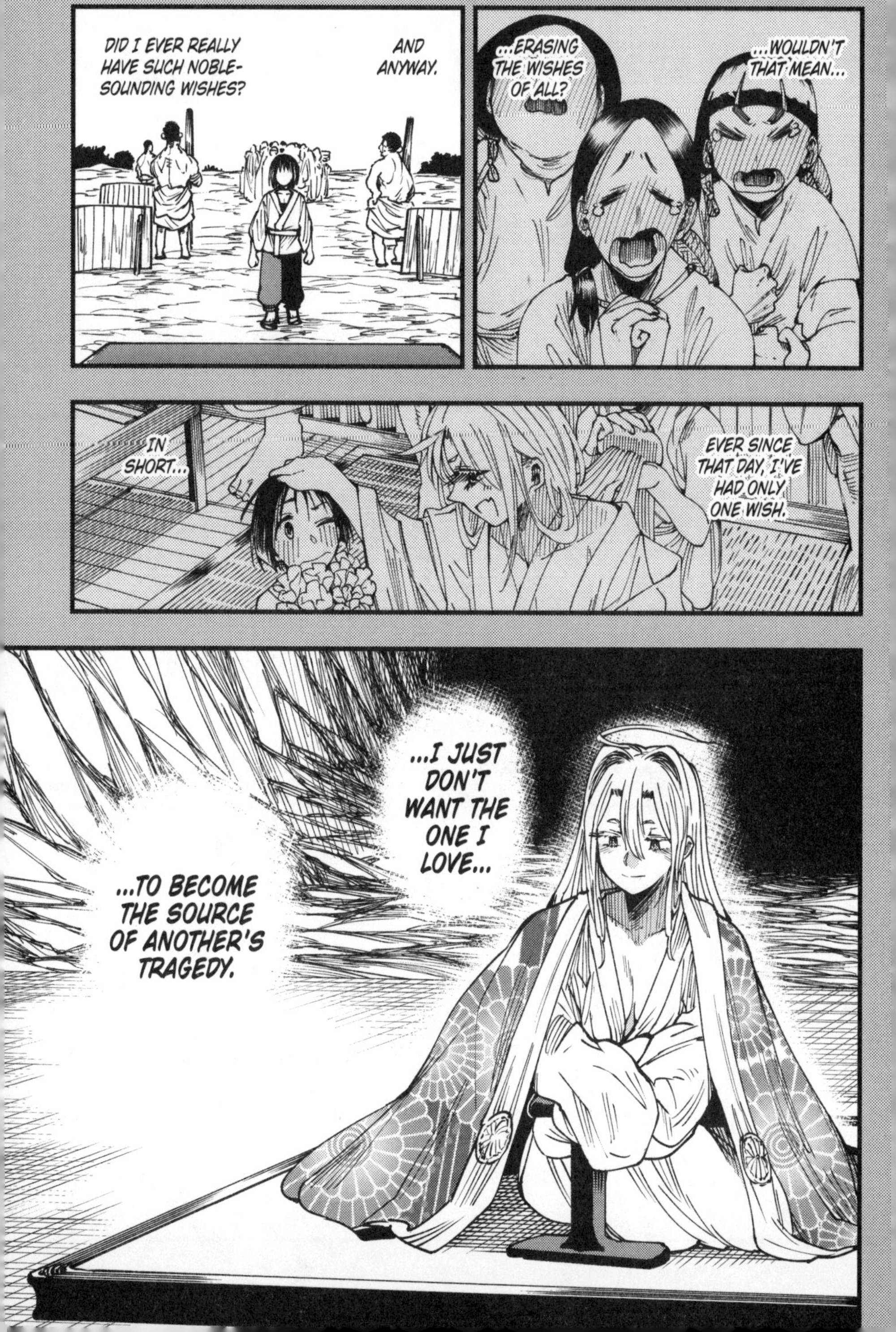
...WOULDN'T THAT MEAN...
...ERASING THE WISHES OF ALL?
AND ANYWAY.
DID I EVER REALLY HAVE SUCH NOBLE-SOUNDING WISHES?
EVER SINCE THAT DAY, I'VE HAD ONLY ONE WISH.
IN SHORT...
...I JUST DON'T WANT THE ONE I LOVE...
...TO BECOME THE SOURCE OF ANOTHER'S TRAGEDY.

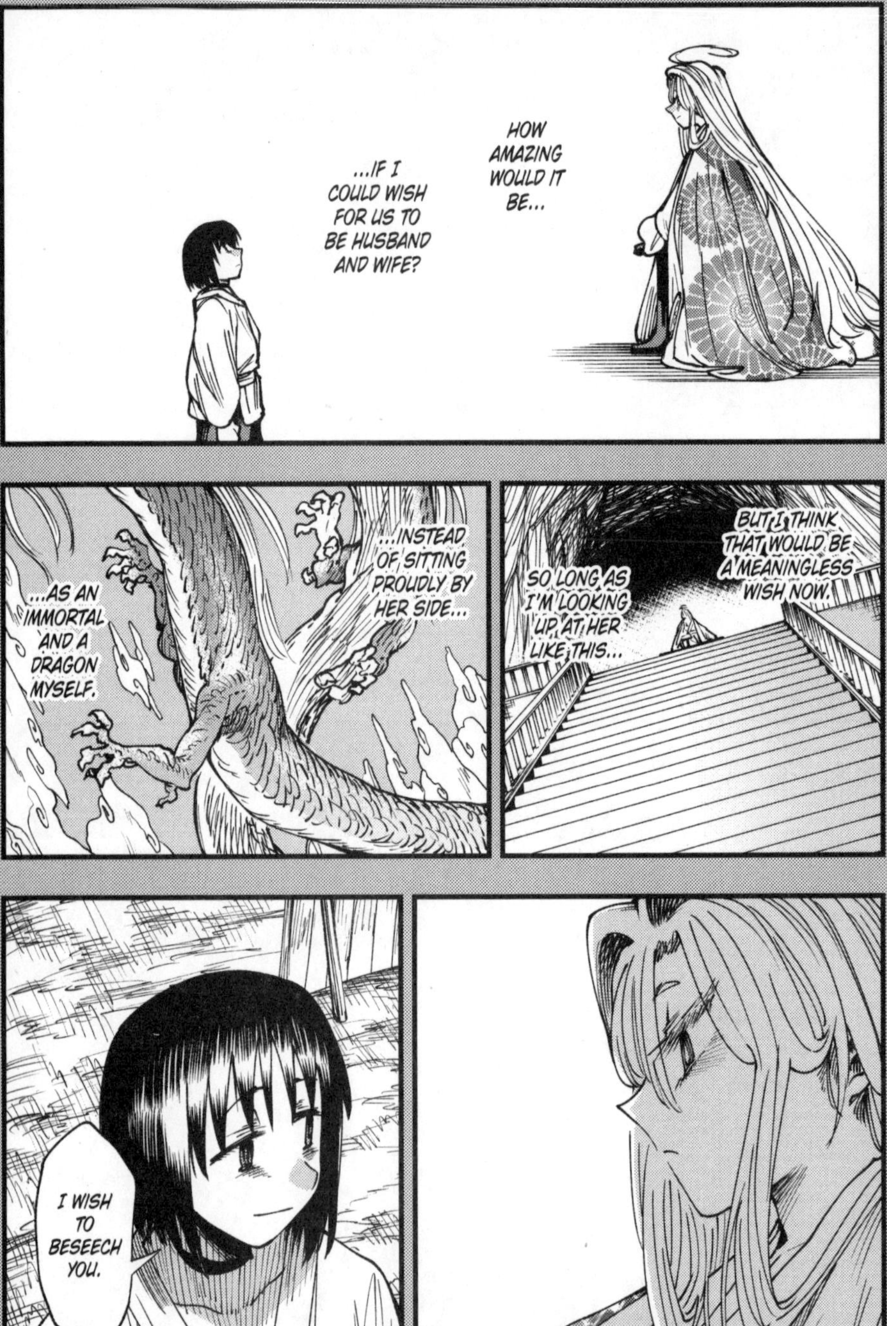
HOW AMAZING WOULD IT BE...
...IF I COULD WISH FOR US TO BE HUSBAND AND WIFE?
BUT I THINK THAT WOULD BE A MEANINGLESS WISH NOW.
SO LONG AS I'M LOOKING UP AT HER LIKE THIS...
...INSTEAD OF SITTING PROUDLY BY HER SIDE...
...AS AN IMMORTAL AND A DRAGON MYSELF.
I WISH TO BESEECH YOU.

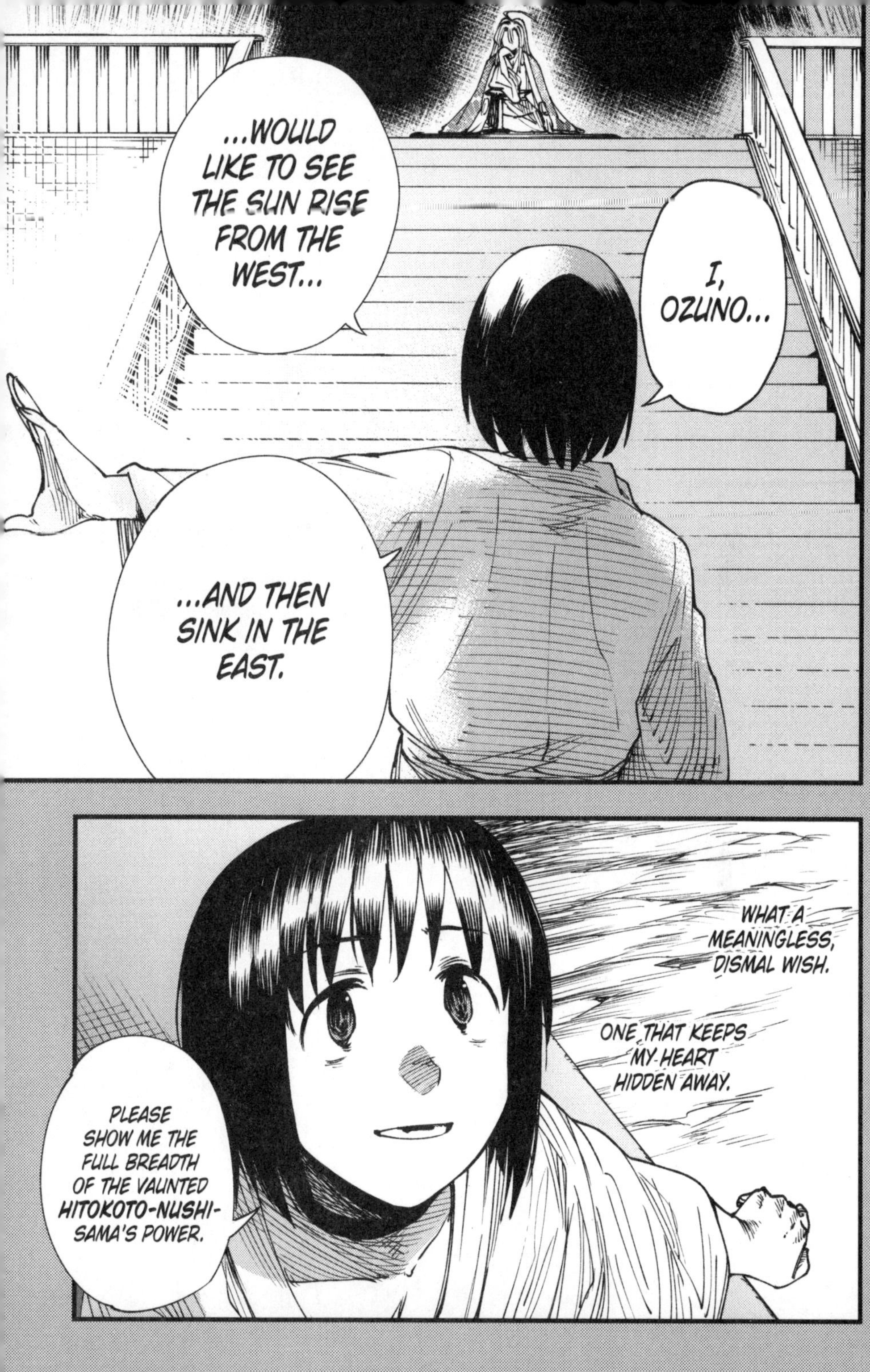
I, OZUNO...
...WOULD LIKE TO SEE THE SUN RISE FROM THE WEST...
...AND THEN SINK IN THE EAST.
WHAT A MEANINGLESS, DISMAL WISH.
ONE THAT KEEPS MY HEART HIDDEN AWAY.
PLEASE SHOW ME THE FULL BREADTH OF THE VAUNTED HITOKOTO-NUSHI-SAMA'S POWER.

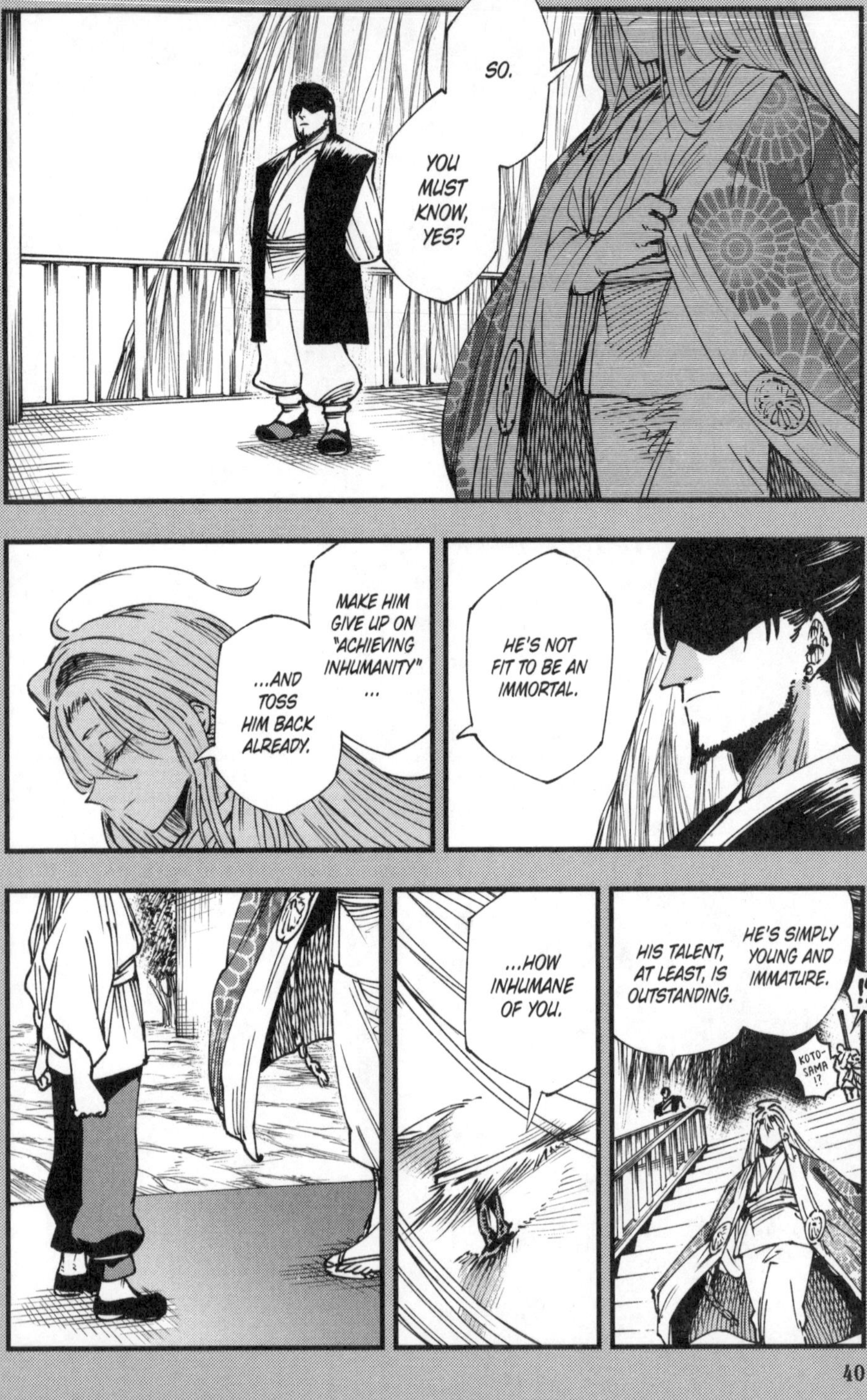
SO.
YOU MUST KNOW, YES?
HE'S NOT FIT TO BE AN IMMORTAL.
MAKE HIM GIVE UP ON "ACHIEVING INHUMANITY" ...
...AND TOSS HIM BACK ALREADY.
HE'S SIMPLY YOUNG AND IMMATURE.
HIS TALENT, AT LEAST, IS OUTSTANDING.
!?
KOTO-SAMA!?
...HOW INHUMANE OF YOU.

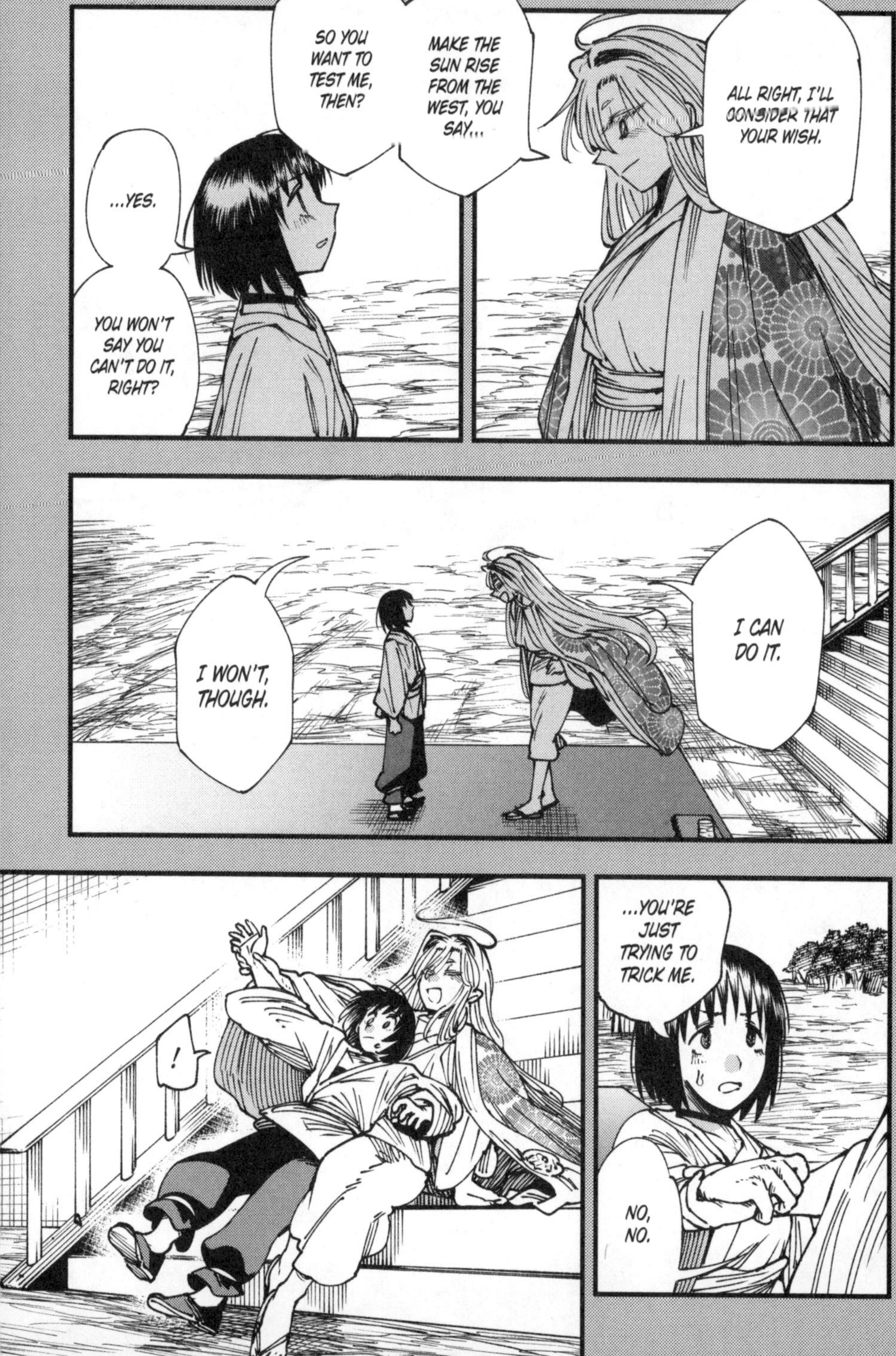
ALL RIGHT, I'LL CONSIDER THAT YOUR WISH.
MAKE THE SUN RISE FROM THE WEST, YOU SAY...
SO YOU WANT TO TEST ME, THEN?
...YES.
YOU WON'T SAY YOU CAN'T DO IT, RIGHT?
I CAN DO IT.
I WON'T, THOUGH.
...YOU'RE JUST TRYING TO TRICK ME.
NO, NO.
!

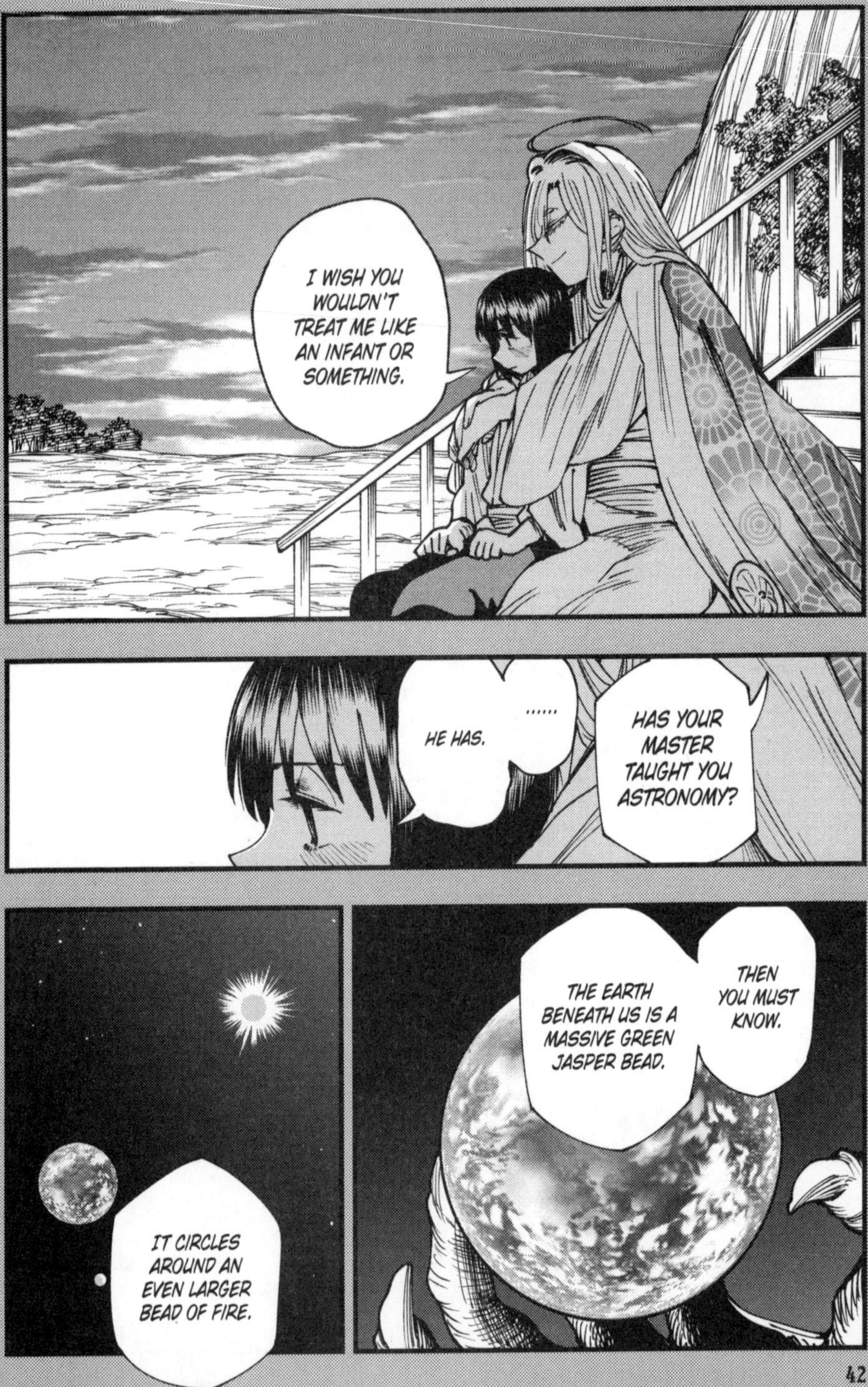
I WISH YOU WOULDN'T TREAT ME LIKE AN INFANT OR SOMETHING.
HAS YOUR MASTER TAUGHT YOU ASTRONOMY?
......
HE HAS.
THEN YOU MUST KNOW.
THE EARTH BENEATH US IS A MASSIVE GREEN JASPER BEAD.
IT CIRCLES AROUND AN EVEN LARGER BEAD OF FIRE.

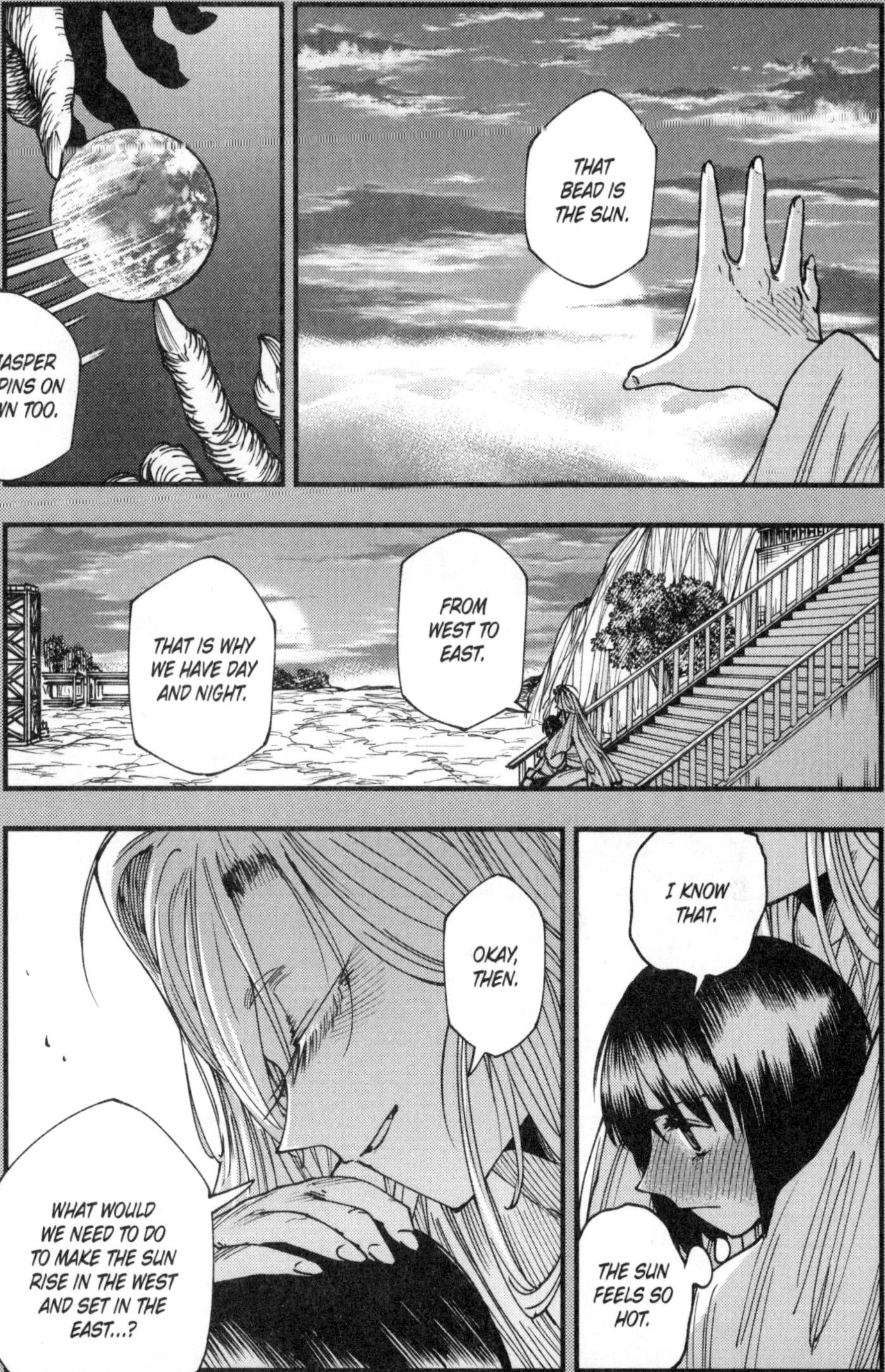
THAT BEAD IS THE SUN.
THE JASPER ONE SPINS ON ITS OWN TOO.
FROM WEST TO EAST.
THAT IS WHY WE HAVE DAY AND NIGHT.
I KNOW THAT.
THE SUN FEELS SO HOT.
OKAY, THEN.
WHAT WOULD WE NEED TO DO TO MAKE THE SUN RISE IN THE WEST AND SET IN THE EAST...?

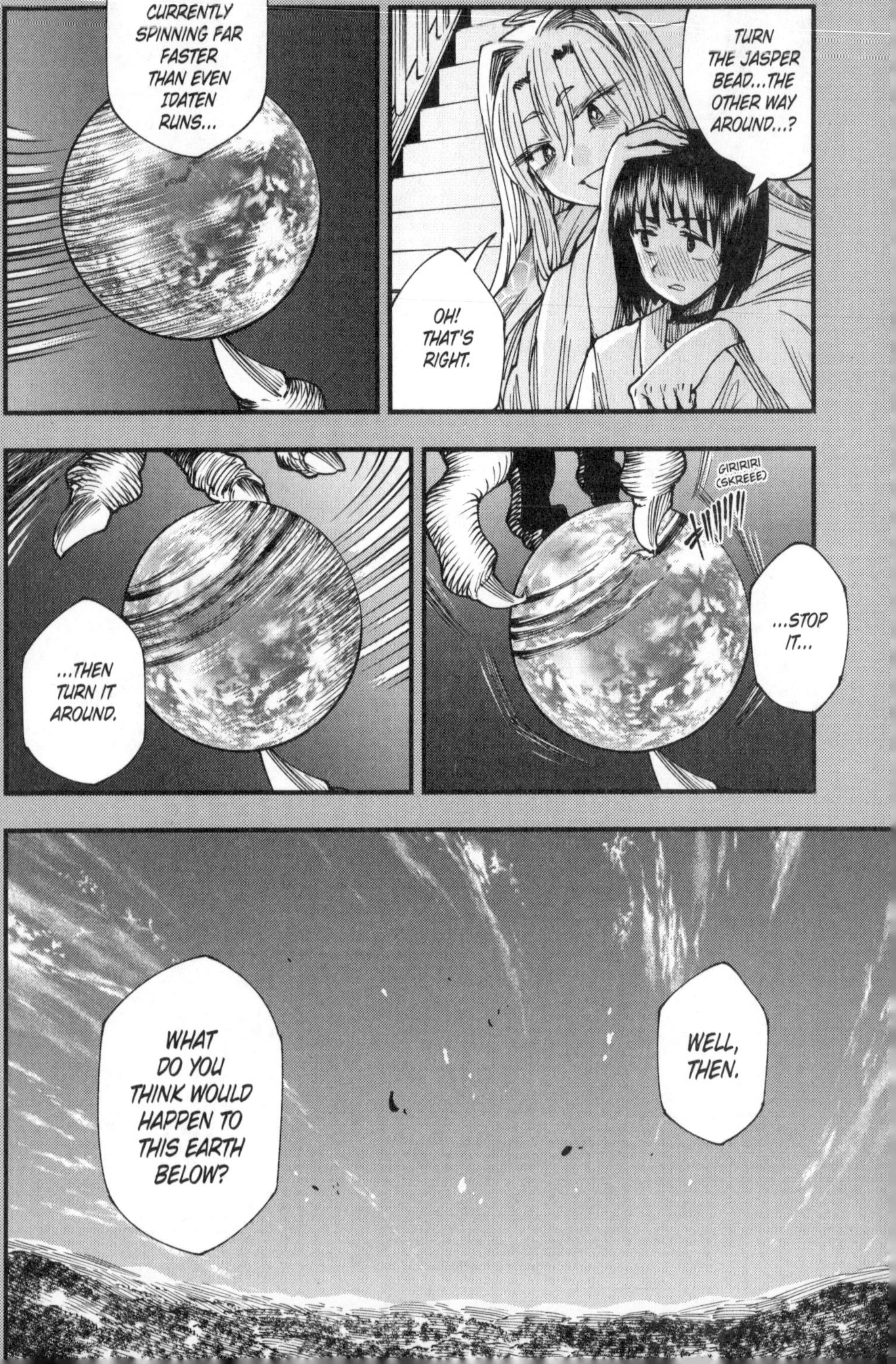
TURN THE JASPER BEAD...THE OTHER WAY AROUND...?
OH! THAT'S RIGHT.
TAKE THE BEAD CURRENTLY SPINNING FAR FASTER THAN EVEN IDATEN RUNS...
GIRIRIRI (SKREEE)
...STOP IT...
...THEN TURN IT AROUND.
WELL, THEN.
WHAT DO YOU THINK WOULD HAPPEN TO THIS EARTH BELOW?

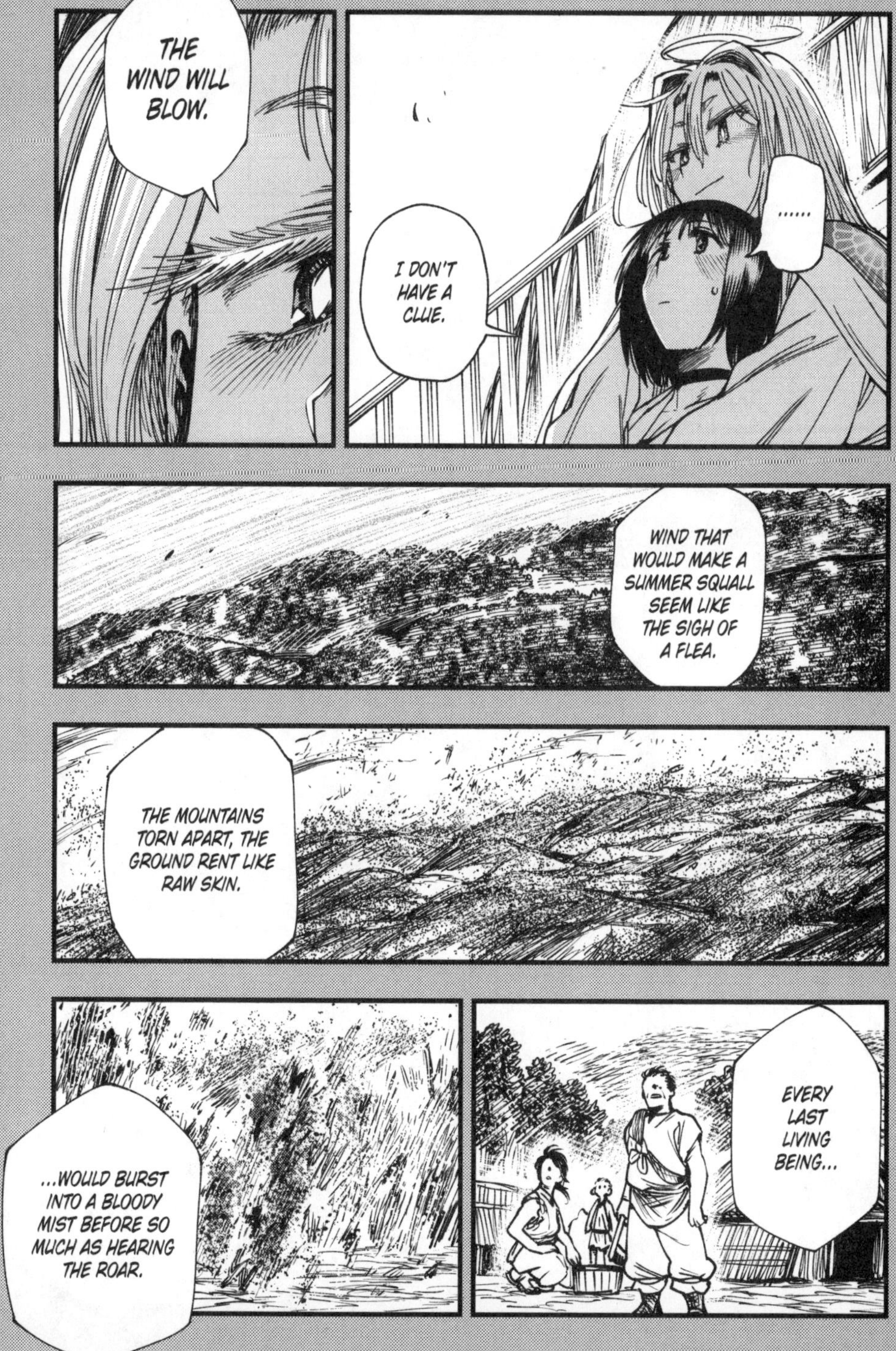
......
I DON'T HAVE A CLUE.
THE WIND WILL BLOW.
WIND THAT WOULD MAKE A SUMMER SQUALL SEEM LIKE THE SIGH OF A FLEA.
THE MOUNTAINS TORN APART, THE GROUND RENT LIKE RAW SKIN.
EVERY LAST LIVING BEING...
...WOULD BURST INTO A BLOODY MIST BEFORE SO MUCH AS HEARING THE ROAR.

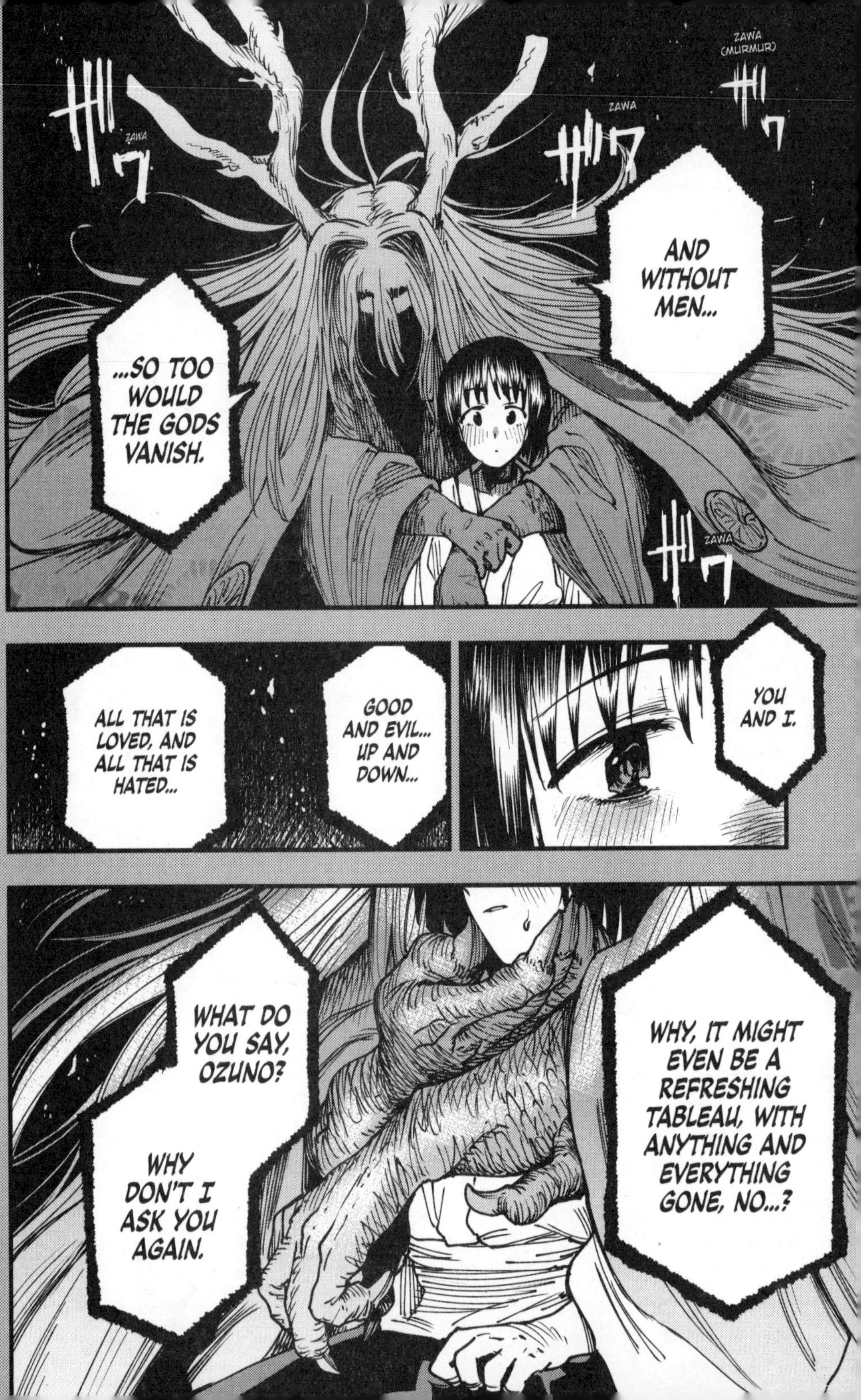
ZAWA (MURMUR)
ZAWA
AND WITHOUT MEN...
ZAWA
...SO TOO WOULD THE GODS VANISH.
ZAWA
YOU AND I.
GOOD AND EVIL... UP AND DOWN...
ALL THAT IS LOVED, AND ALL THAT IS HATED...
WHY, IT MIGHT EVEN BE A REFRESHING TABLEAU, WITH ANYTHING AND EVERYTHING GONE, NO...?
WHAT DO YOU SAY, OZUNO?
WHY DON'T I ASK YOU AGAIN.

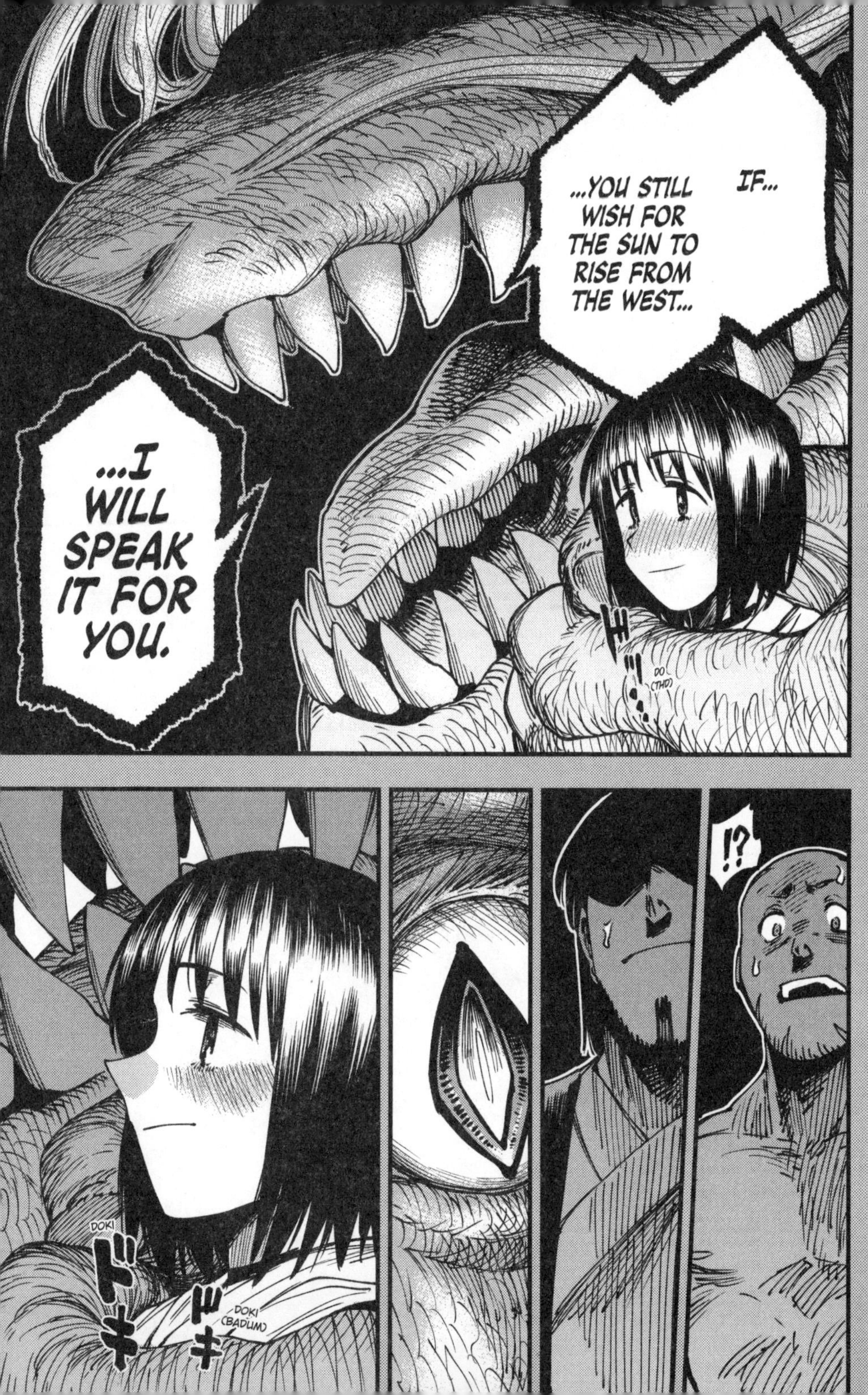
IF...
...YOU STILL WISH FOR THE SUN TO RISE FROM THE WEST...
...I WILL SPEAK IT FOR YOU.
DO (THD)
!?
DOKI
DOKI (BADUM)

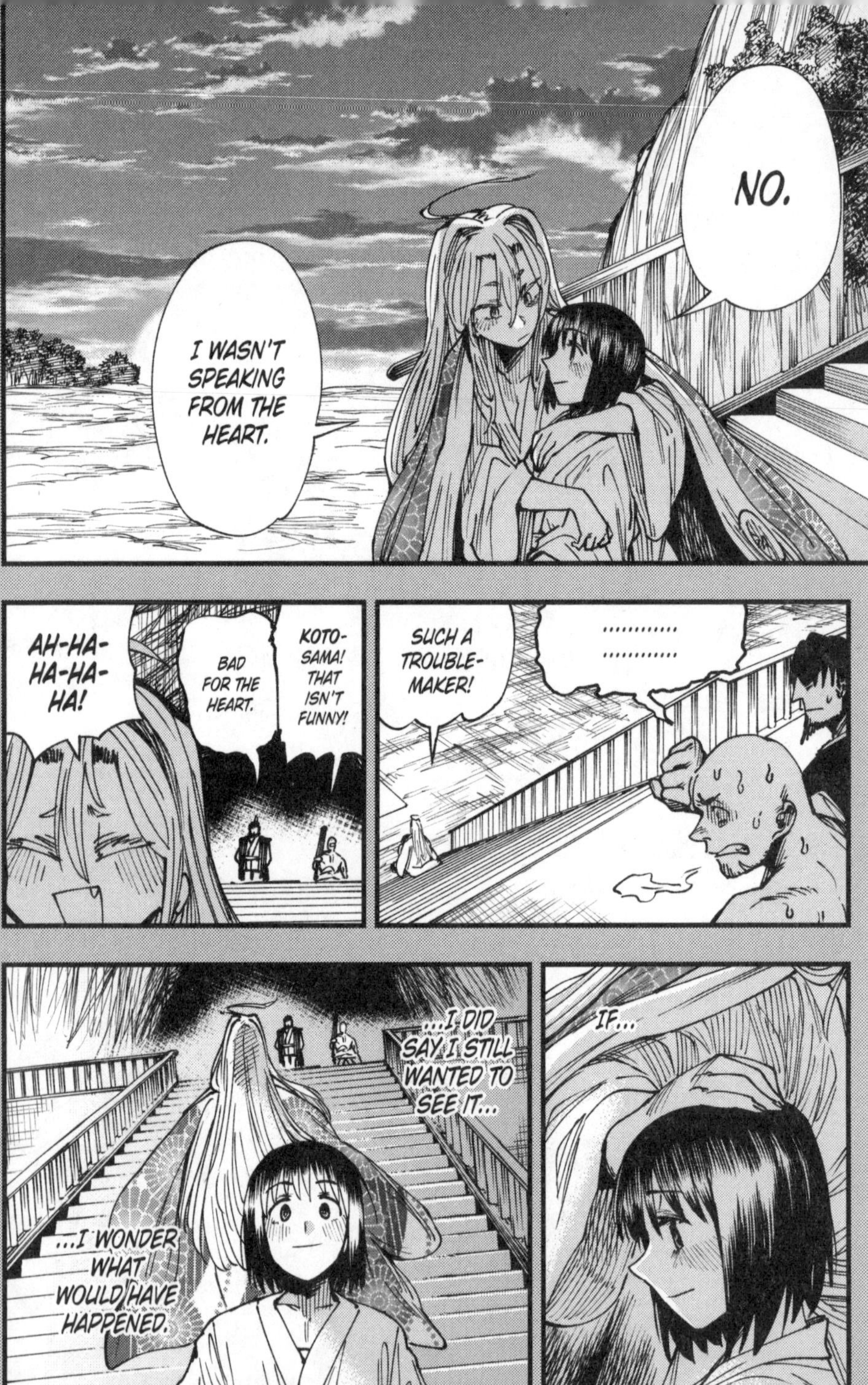
NO.
I WASN'T SPEAKING FROM THE HEART.
....
....
SUCH A TROUBLE-MAKER!
KOTO-SAMA! THAT ISN'T FUNNY!
BAD FOR THE HEART.
AH-HA-HA-HA-HA!
IF...
...I DID SAY I STILL WANTED TO SEE IT...
...I WONDER WHAT WOULD HAVE HAPPENED.

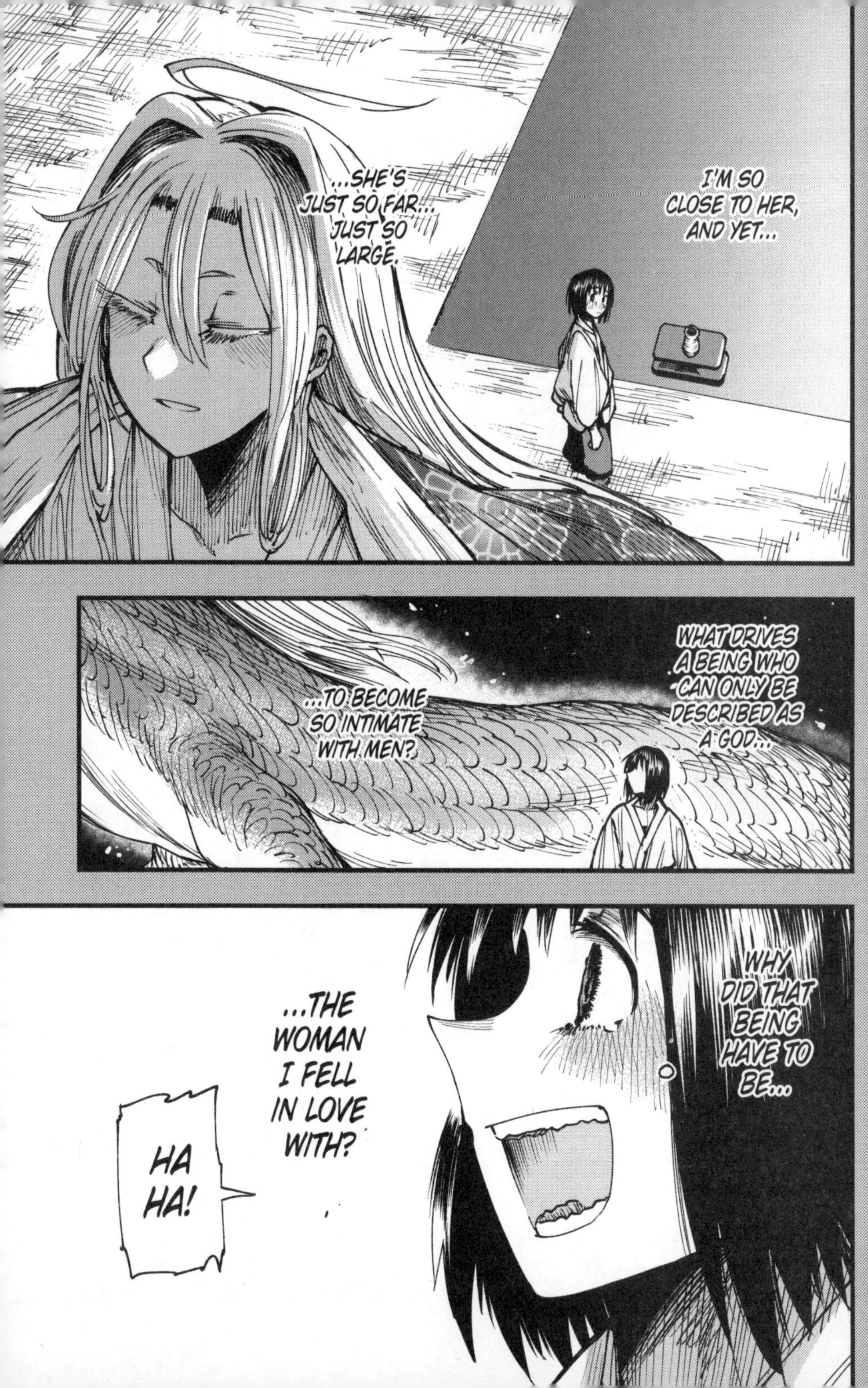
I'M SO CLOSE TO HER, AND YET...
...SHE'S JUST SO FAR... JUST SO LARGE.
WHAT DRIVES A BEING WHO CAN ONLY BE DESCRIBED AS A GOD...
...TO BECOME SO INTIMATE WITH MEN?
WHY DID THAT BEING HAVE TO BE...
...THE WOMAN I FELL IN LOVE WITH?
HA HA!

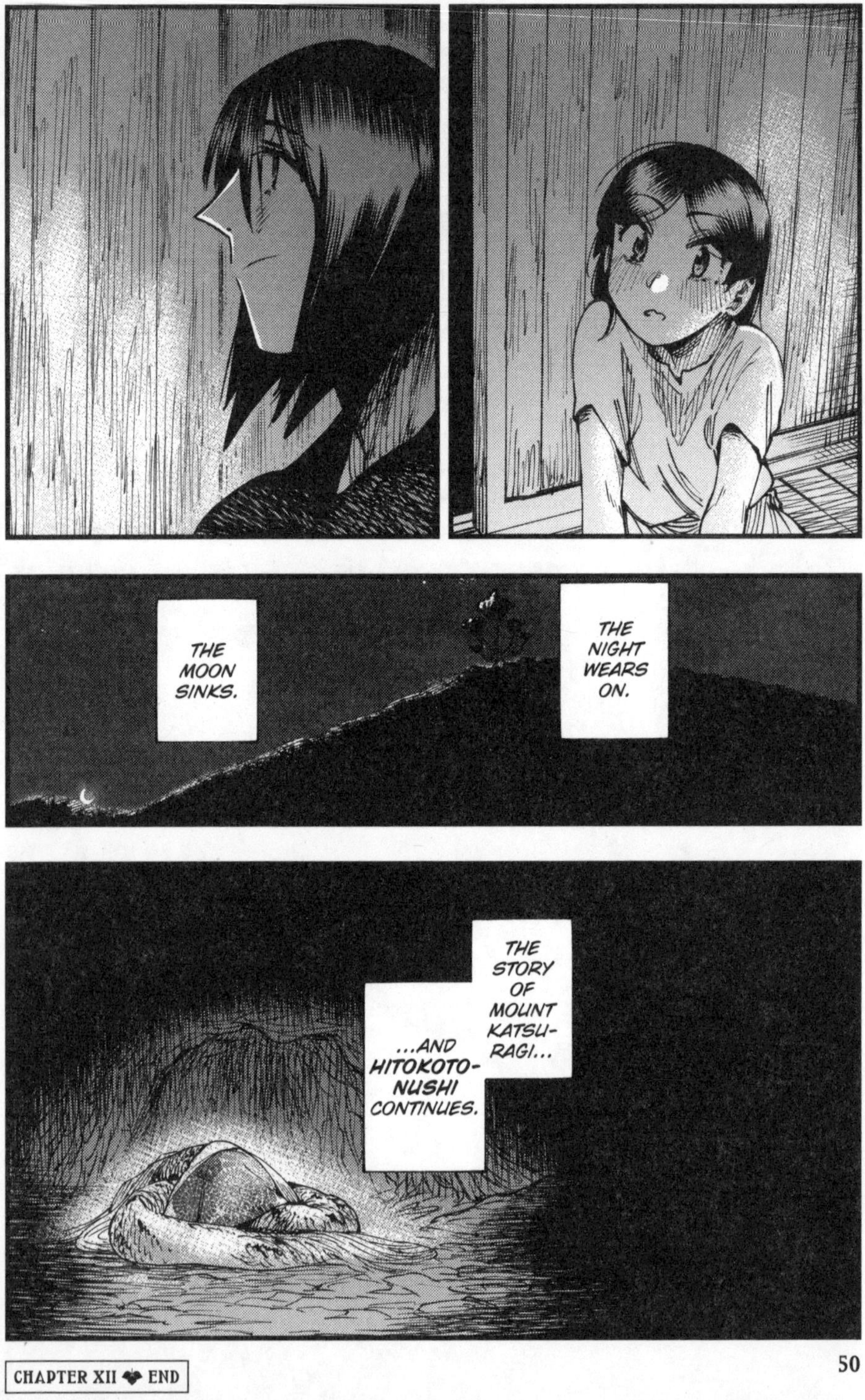
THE NIGHT WEARS ON.
THE MOON SINKS.
THE STORY OF MOUNT KATSU-RAGI...
...AND HITOKOTO-NUSHI CONTINUES.

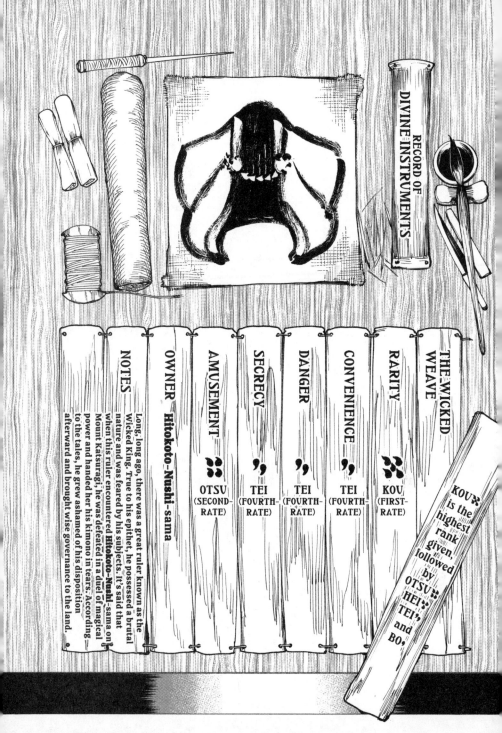

RECORD OF DIVINE INSTRUMENTS

THE WICKED WEAVE

RARITY	❀❀❀ KOU (FIRST-RATE)
CONVENIENCE	" TEI (FOURTH-RATE)
DANGER	" TEI (FOURTH-RATE)
SECRECY	" TEI (FOURTH-RATE)
AMUSEMENT	❀❀ OTSU (SECOND-RATE)

OWNER Hitokoto-Nushi-sama

NOTES
Long, long ago, there was a great ruler known as the Wicked King. True to his epithet, he possessed a brutal nature and was feared by his subjects. It's said that when this ruler encountered **Hitokoto-Nushi**-sama on Mount Katsuragi, he was defeated in a duel of magical power and handed her his kimono in tears. According to the tales, he grew ashamed of his disposition afterward and brought wise governance to the land.

KOU❀ is the highest rank given, followed by OTSU❀ HEI" TEI" and BO'

Touge Oni

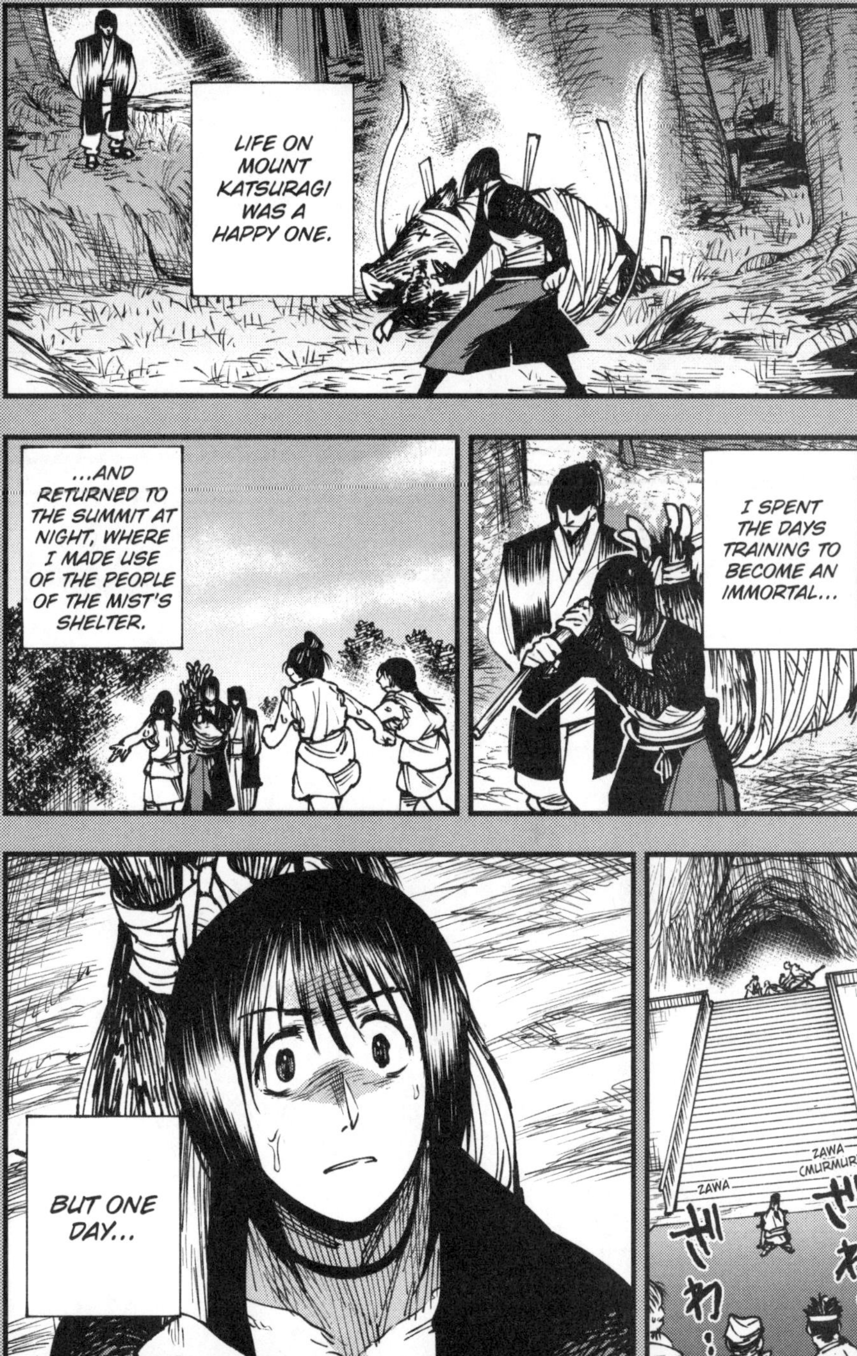
LIFE ON MOUNT KATSURAGI WAS A HAPPY ONE.
I SPENT THE DAYS TRAINING TO BECOME AN IMMORTAL...
...AND RETURNED TO THE SUMMIT AT NIGHT, WHERE I MADE USE OF THE PEOPLE OF THE MIST'S SHELTER.
ZAWA (MURMUR)
ざわ…
ZAWA
ざわ…
BUT ONE DAY...

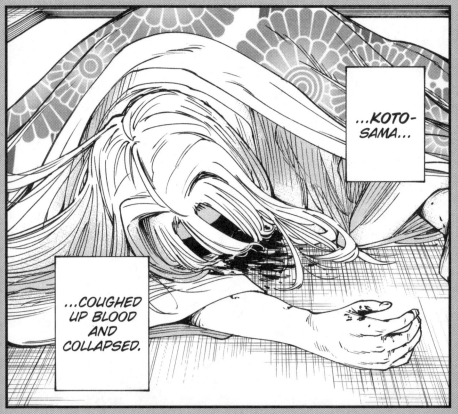

...KOTO-
SAMA...

...COUGHED
UP BLOOD
AND
COLLAPSED.

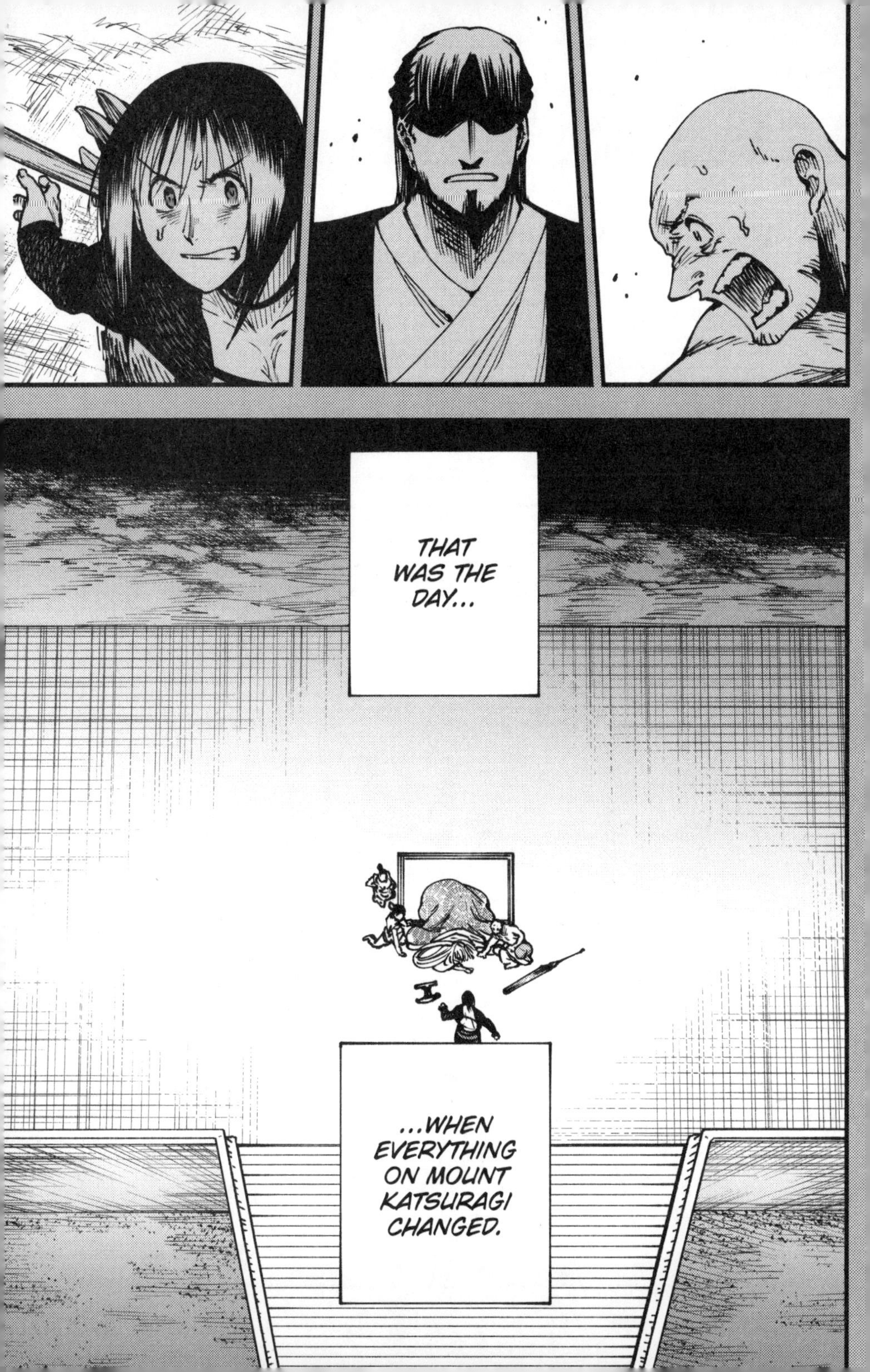
THAT WAS THE DAY...
...WHEN EVERYTHING ON MOUNT KATSURAGI CHANGED.

Chapter XIII The Tale of Mount Katsuragi: The Mist Vanishes

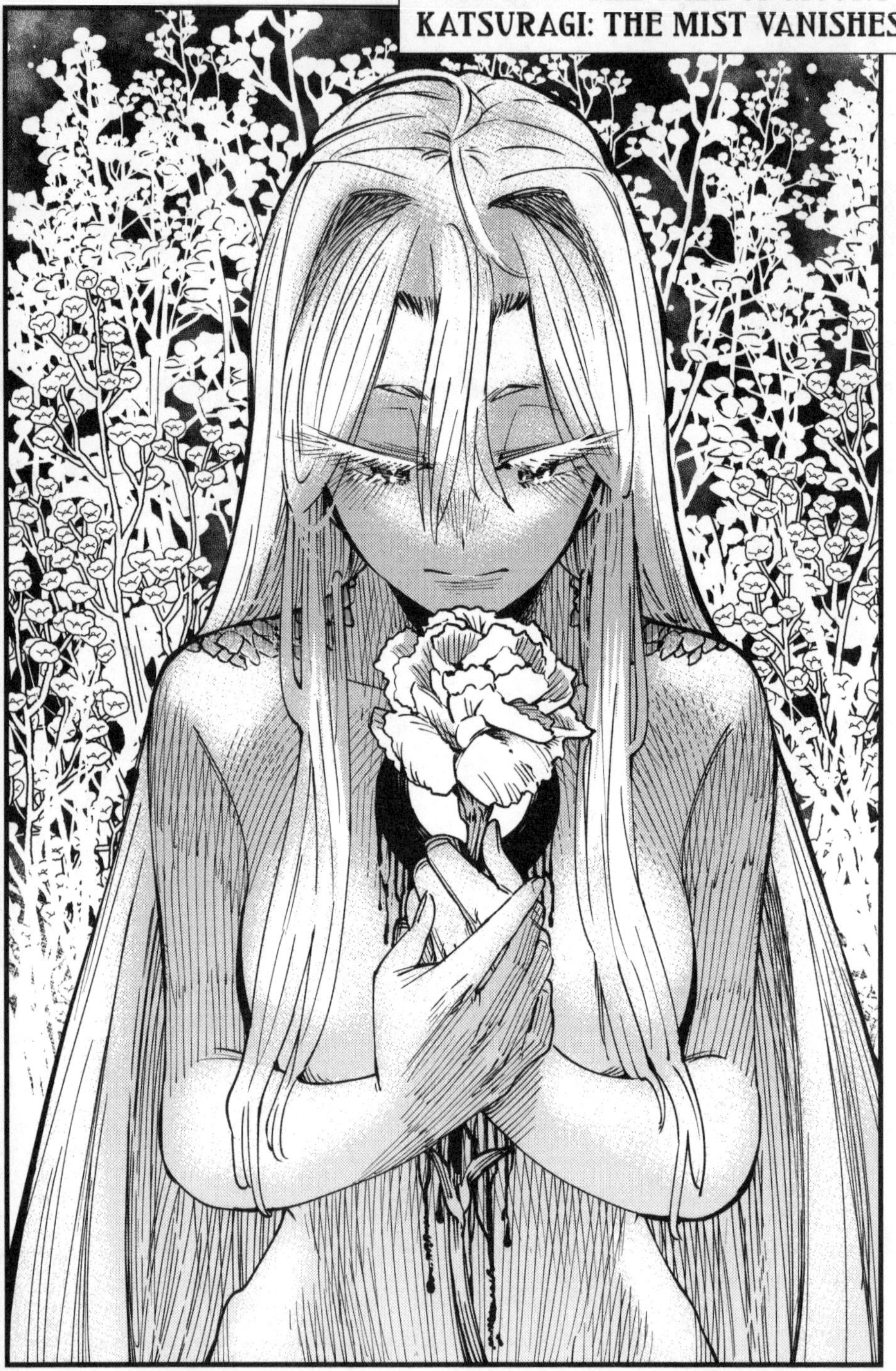

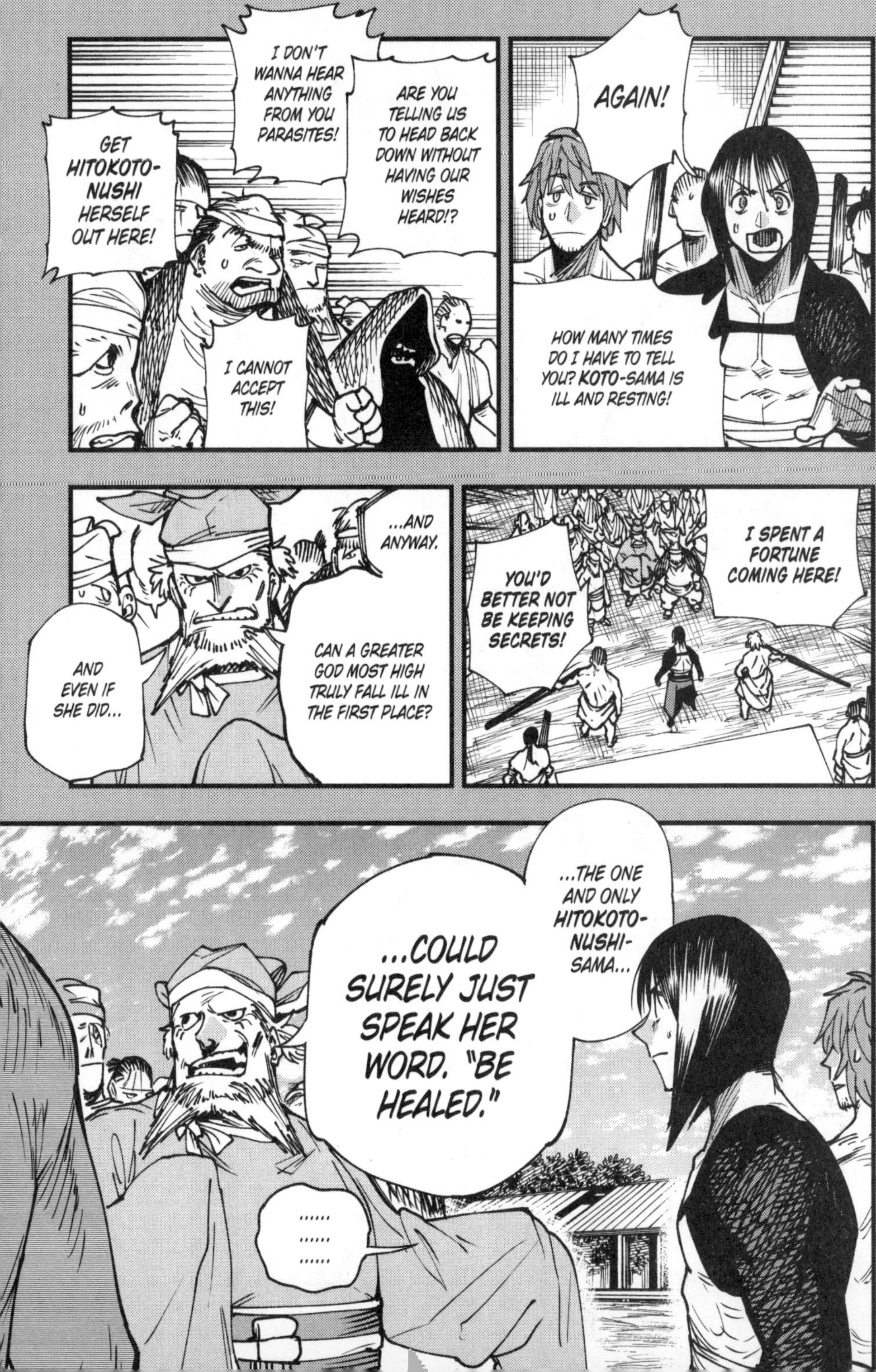
AGAIN!
HOW MANY TIMES DO I HAVE TO TELL YOU? KOTO-SAMA IS ILL AND RESTING!
ARE YOU TELLING US TO HEAD BACK DOWN WITHOUT HAVING OUR WISHES HEARD!?
I DON'T WANNA HEAR ANYTHING FROM YOU PARASITES!
GET HITOKOTO-NUSHI HERSELF OUT HERE!
I CANNOT ACCEPT THIS!
I SPENT A FORTUNE COMING HERE!
YOU'D BETTER NOT BE KEEPING SECRETS!
...AND ANYWAY.
CAN A GREATER GOD MOST HIGH TRULY FALL ILL IN THE FIRST PLACE?
AND EVEN IF SHE DID...
...THE ONE AND ONLY HITOKOTO-NUSHI-SAMA...
...COULD SURELY JUST SPEAK HER WORD. "BE HEALED."
....

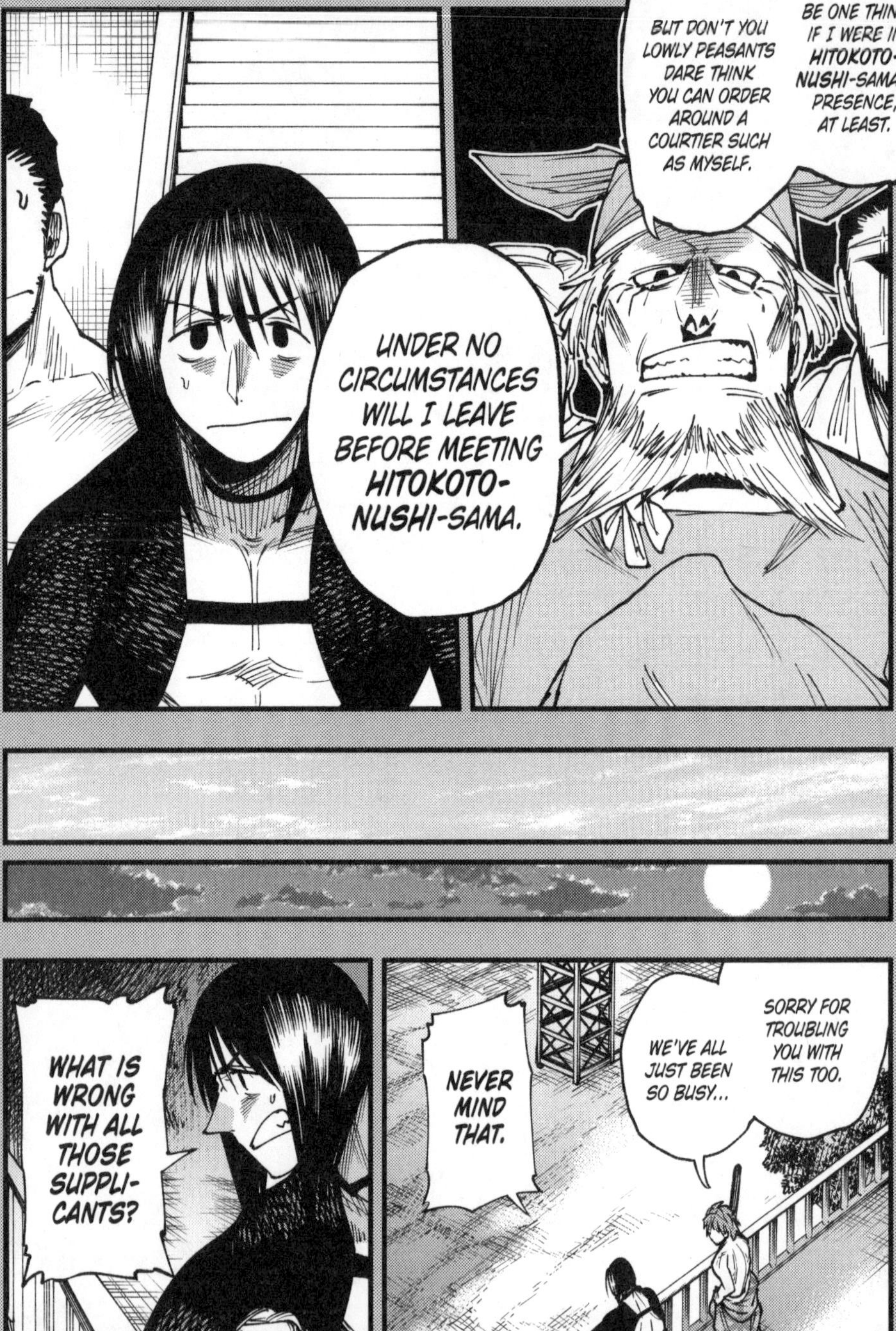
IT WOULD BE ONE THING IF I WERE IN HITOKOTO-NUSHI-SAMA'S PRESENCE, AT LEAST.
BUT DON'T YOU LOWLY PEASANTS DARE THINK YOU CAN ORDER AROUND A COURTIER SUCH AS MYSELF.
UNDER NO CIRCUMSTANCES WILL I LEAVE BEFORE MEETING HITOKOTO-NUSHI-SAMA.
SORRY FOR TROUBLING YOU WITH THIS TOO.
WE'VE ALL JUST BEEN SO BUSY...
NEVER MIND THAT.
WHAT IS WRONG WITH ALL THOSE SUPPLI-CANTS?

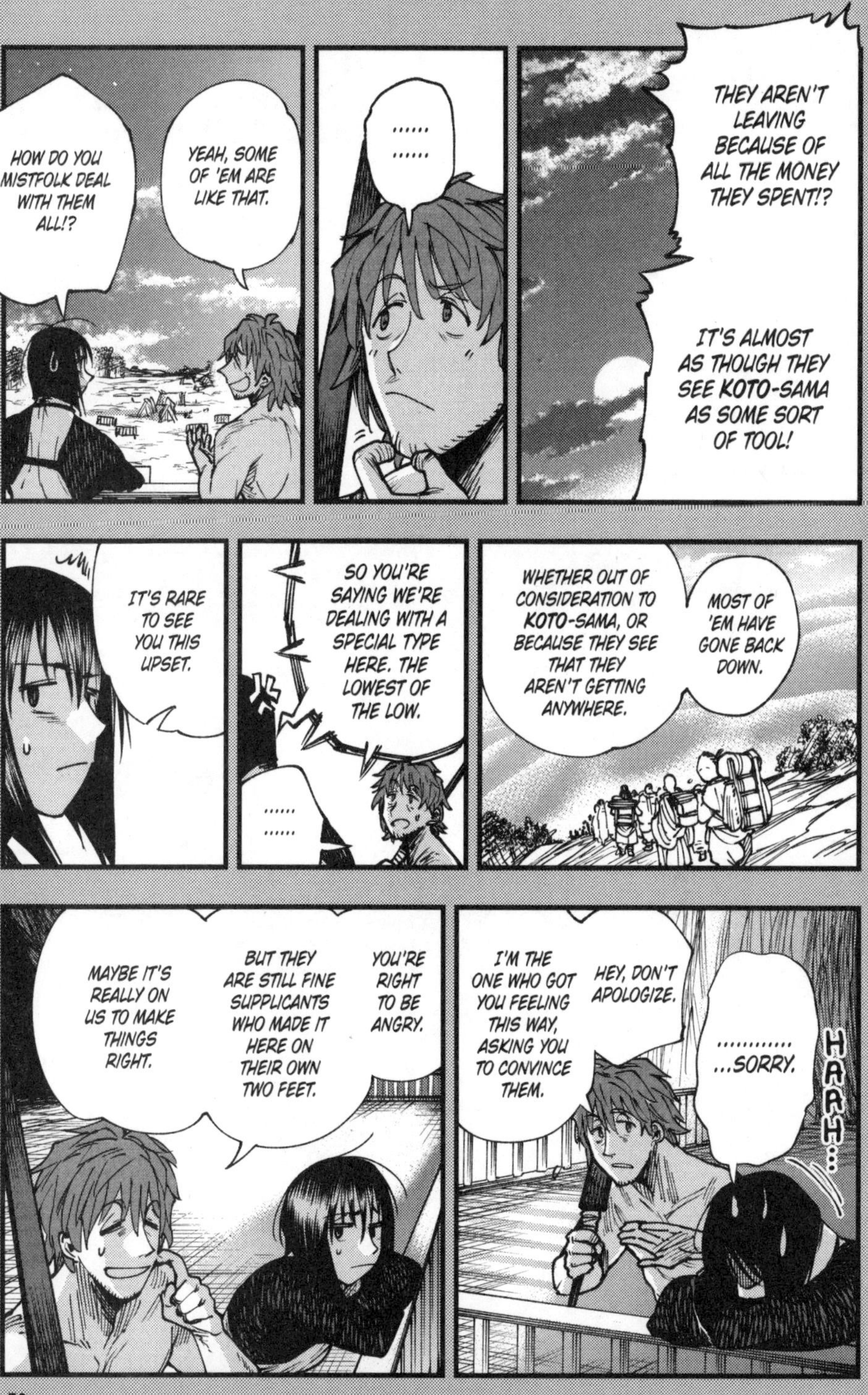
THEY AREN'T LEAVING BECAUSE OF ALL THE MONEY THEY SPENT!?
IT'S ALMOST AS THOUGH THEY SEE KOTO-SAMA AS SOME SORT OF TOOL!
....
YEAH, SOME OF 'EM ARE LIKE THAT.
HOW DO YOU MISTFOLK DEAL WITH THEM ALL!?
MOST OF 'EM HAVE GONE BACK DOWN.
WHETHER OUT OF CONSIDERATION TO KOTO-SAMA, OR BECAUSE THEY SEE THAT THEY AREN'T GETTING ANYWHERE.
SO YOU'RE SAYING WE'RE DEALING WITH A SPECIAL TYPE HERE. THE LOWEST OF THE LOW.
....
IT'S RARE TO SEE YOU THIS UPSET.
HAAAH...
....SORRY.
HEY, DON'T APOLOGIZE.
I'M THE ONE WHO GOT YOU FEELING THIS WAY, ASKING YOU TO CONVINCE THEM.
YOU'RE RIGHT TO BE ANGRY.
BUT THEY ARE STILL FINE SUPPLICANTS WHO MADE IT HERE ON THEIR OWN TWO FEET.
MAYBE IT'S REALLY ON US TO MAKE THINGS RIGHT.

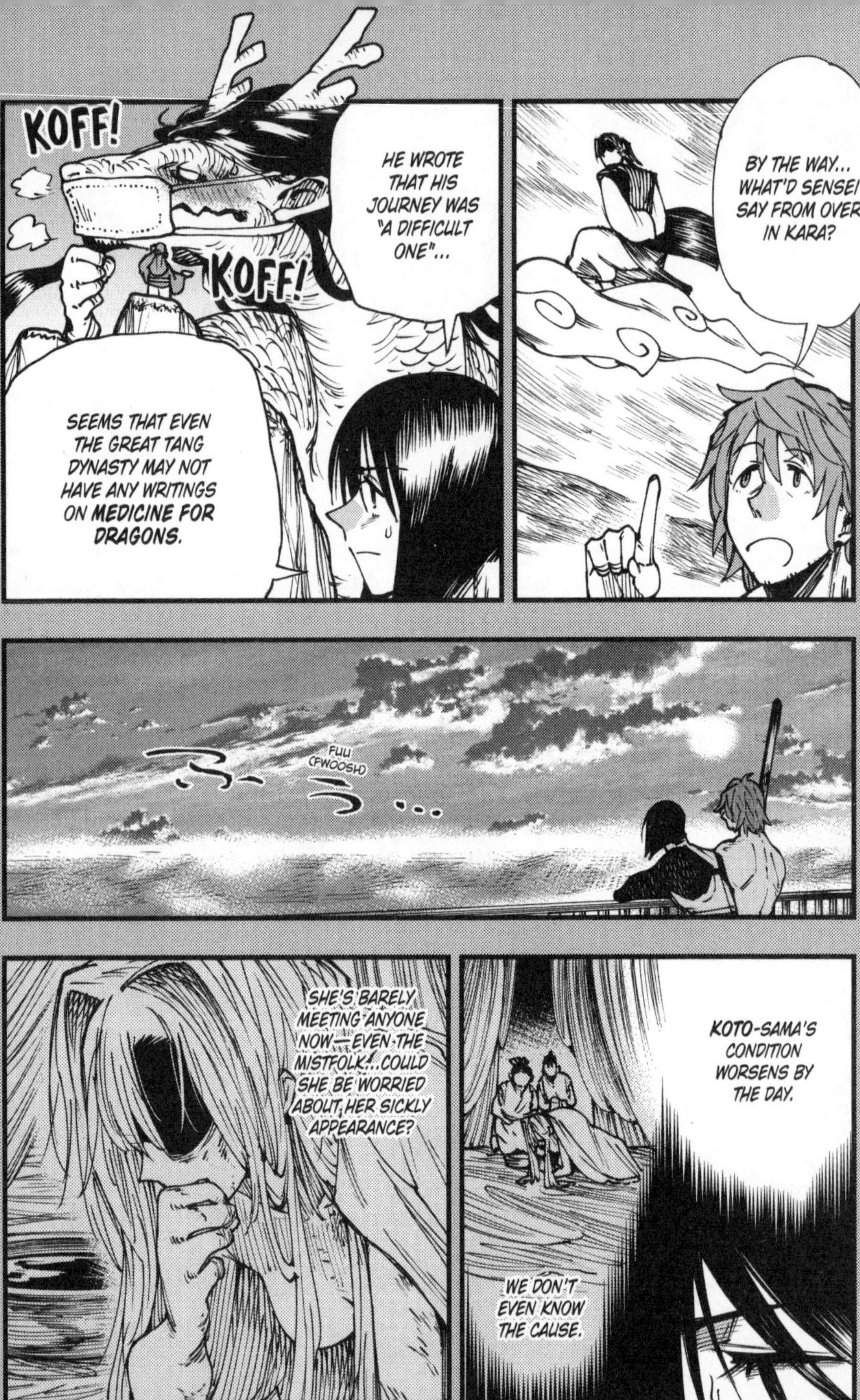
BY THE WAY... WHAT'D SENSEI SAY FROM OVER IN KARA?
KOFF!
HE WROTE THAT HIS JOURNEY WAS "A DIFFICULT ONE"...
KOFF!
SEEMS THAT EVEN THE GREAT TANG DYNASTY MAY NOT HAVE ANY WRITINGS ON MEDICINE FOR DRAGONS.
FUU (FWOOSH)
KOTO-SAMA'S CONDITION WORSENS BY THE DAY.
WE DON'T EVEN KNOW THE CAUSE.
SHE'S BARELY MEETING ANYONE NOW—EVEN THE MISTFOLK...COULD SHE BE WORRIED ABOUT HER SICKLY APPEARANCE?

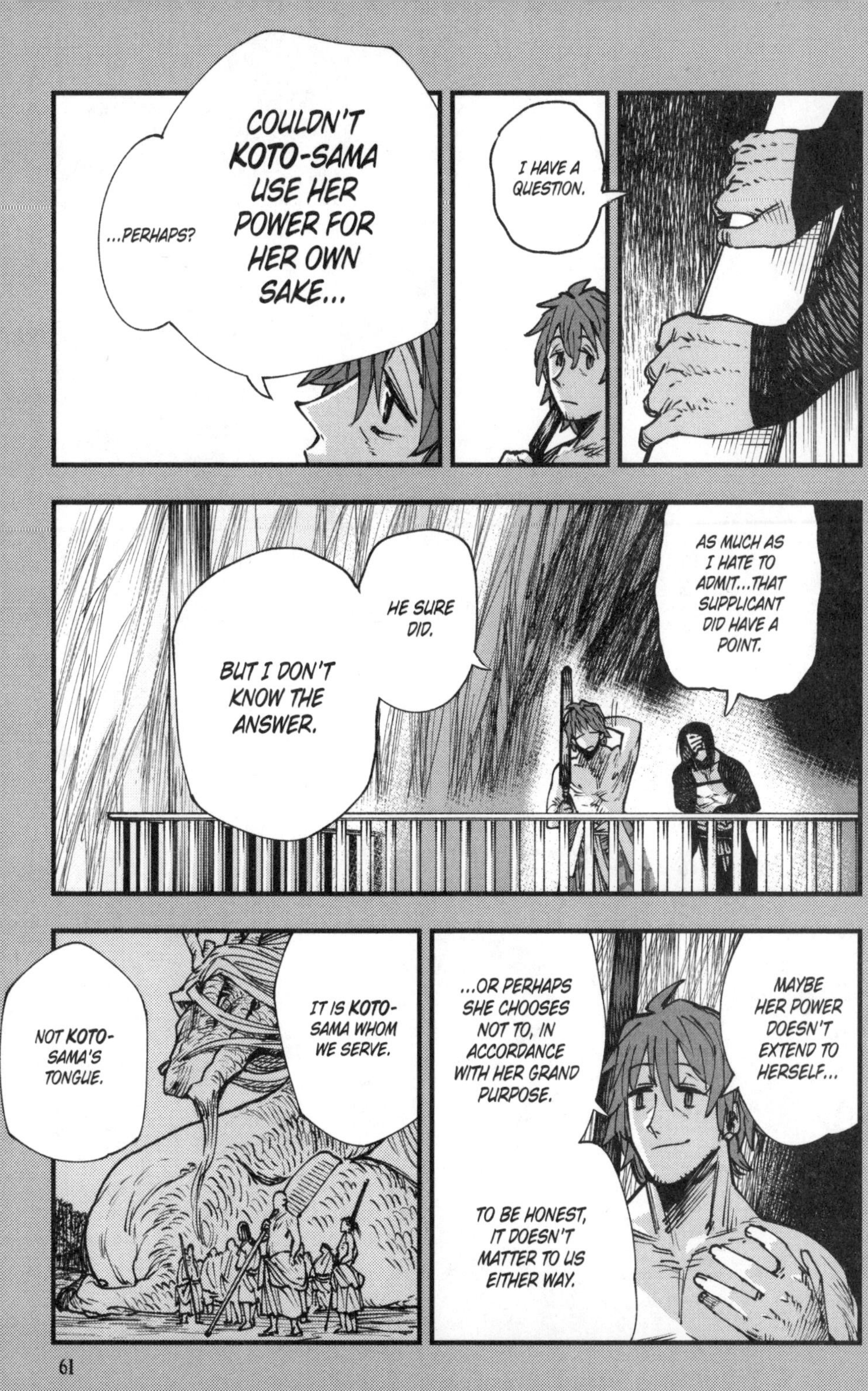
I HAVE A QUESTION.
COULDN'T KOTO-SAMA USE HER POWER FOR HER OWN SAKE...
...PERHAPS?
AS MUCH AS I HATE TO ADMIT...THAT SUPPLICANT DID HAVE A POINT.
HE SURE DID.
BUT I DON'T KNOW THE ANSWER.
MAYBE HER POWER DOESN'T EXTEND TO HERSELF...
...OR PERHAPS SHE CHOOSES NOT TO, IN ACCORDANCE WITH HER GRAND PURPOSE.
TO BE HONEST, IT DOESN'T MATTER TO US EITHER WAY.
IT IS KOTO-SAMA WHOM WE SERVE.
NOT KOTO-SAMA'S TONGUE.

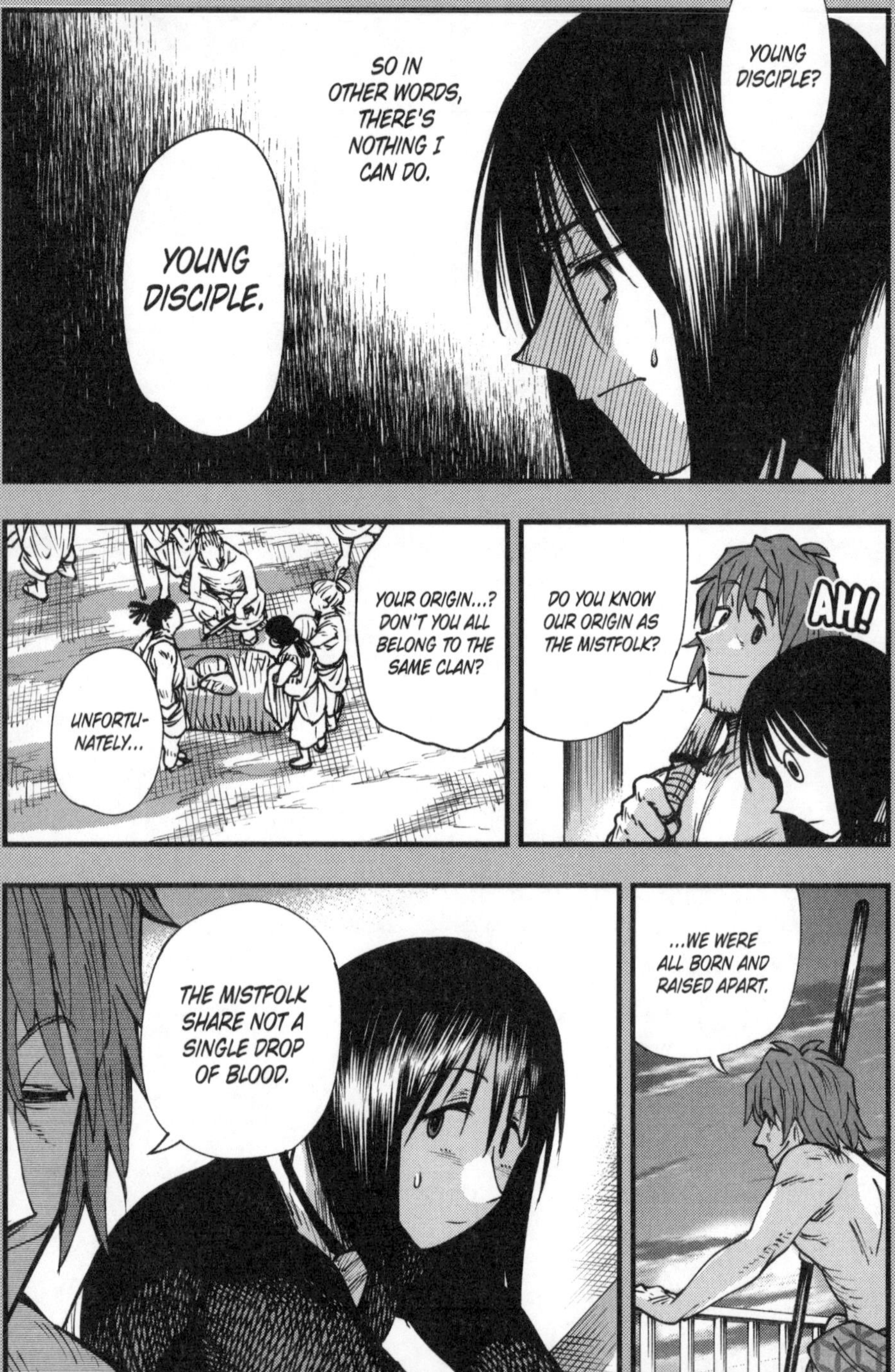
YOUNG DISCIPLE?
SO IN OTHER WORDS, THERE'S NOTHING I CAN DO.
YOUNG DISCIPLE.
AH!
DO YOU KNOW OUR ORIGIN AS THE MISTFOLK?
YOUR ORIGIN...? DON'T YOU ALL BELONG TO THE SAME CLAN?
UNFORTU-NATELY...
...WE WERE ALL BORN AND RAISED APART.
THE MISTFOLK SHARE NOT A SINGLE DROP OF BLOOD.

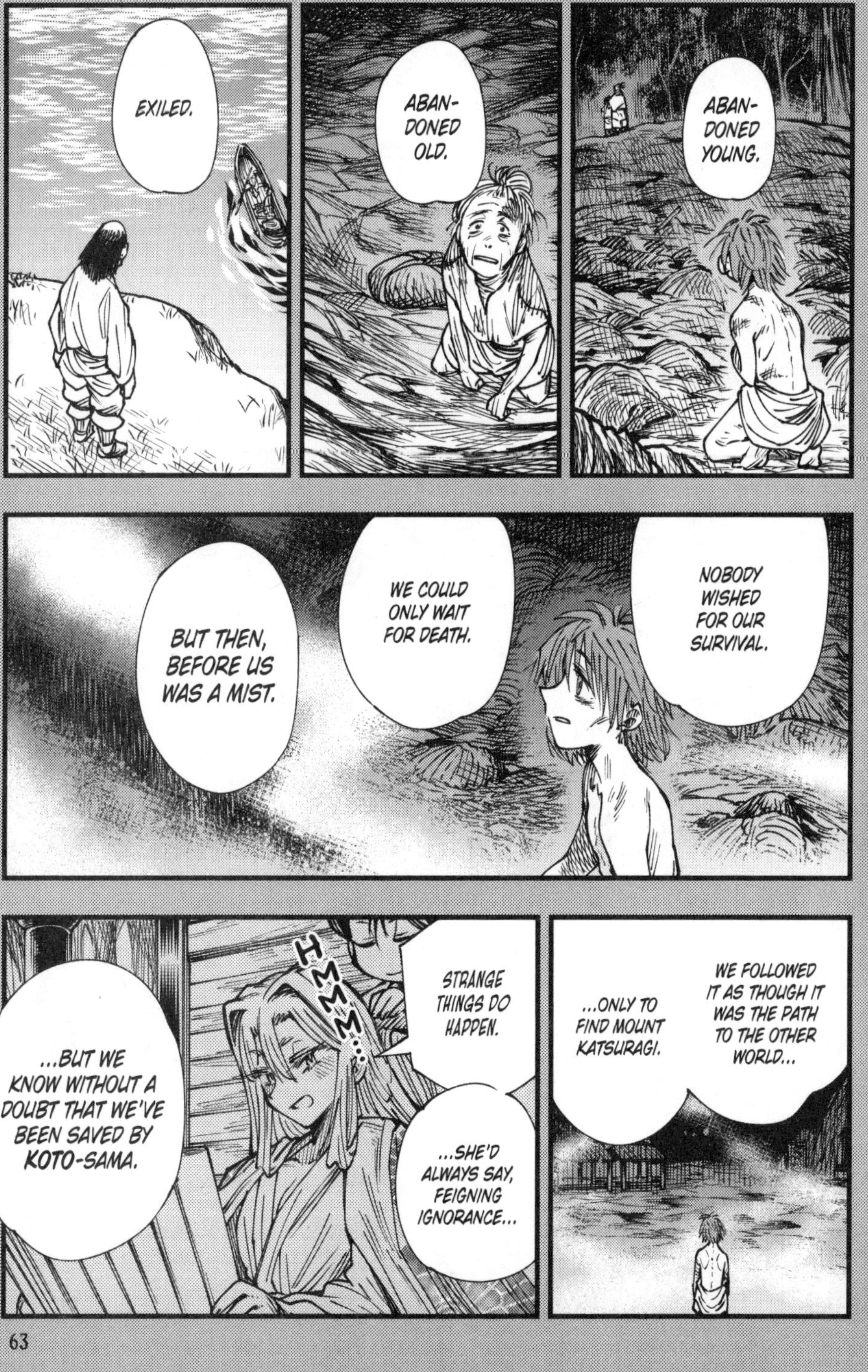
ABAN-DONED YOUNG.
ABAN-DONED OLD.
EXILED.
NOBODY WISHED FOR OUR SURVIVAL.
WE COULD ONLY WAIT FOR DEATH.
BUT THEN, BEFORE US WAS A MIST.
WE FOLLOWED IT AS THOUGH IT WAS THE PATH TO THE OTHER WORLD...
...ONLY TO FIND MOUNT KATSURAGI.
STRANGE THINGS DO HAPPEN.
HMMM...
...SHE'D ALWAYS SAY, FEIGNING IGNORANCE...
...BUT WE KNOW WITHOUT A DOUBT THAT WE'VE BEEN SAVED BY KOTO-SAMA.

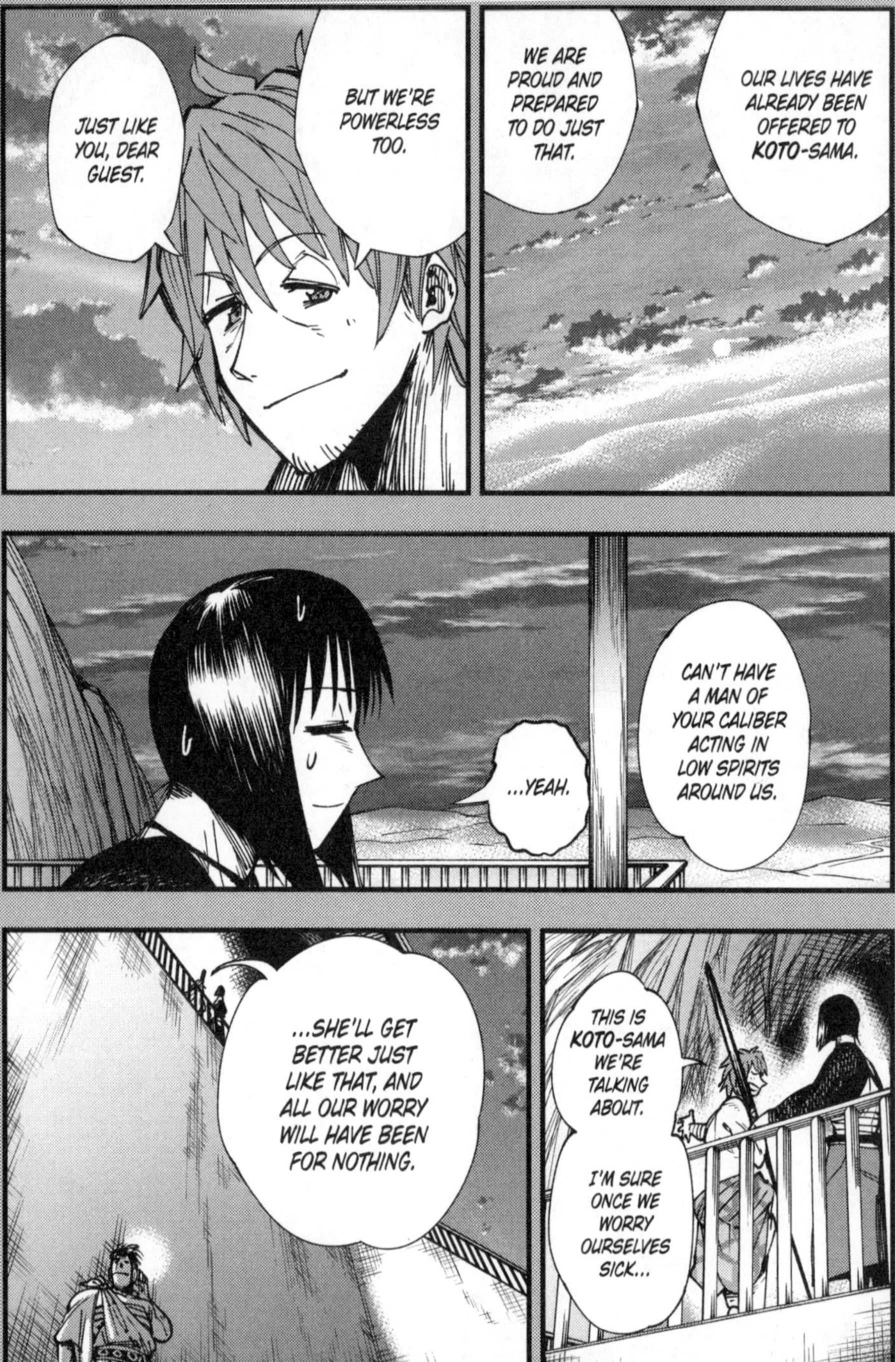
OUR LIVES HAVE ALREADY BEEN OFFERED TO **KOTO**-SAMA.
WE ARE PROUD AND PREPARED TO DO JUST THAT.
BUT WE'RE POWERLESS TOO.
JUST LIKE YOU, DEAR GUEST.
CAN'T HAVE A MAN OF YOUR CALIBER ACTING IN LOW SPIRITS AROUND US.
...YEAH.
THIS IS **KOTO**-SAMA WE'RE TALKING ABOUT.
I'M SURE ONCE WE WORRY OURSELVES SICK...
...SHE'LL GET BETTER JUST LIKE THAT, AND ALL OUR WORRY WILL HAVE BEEN FOR NOTHING.

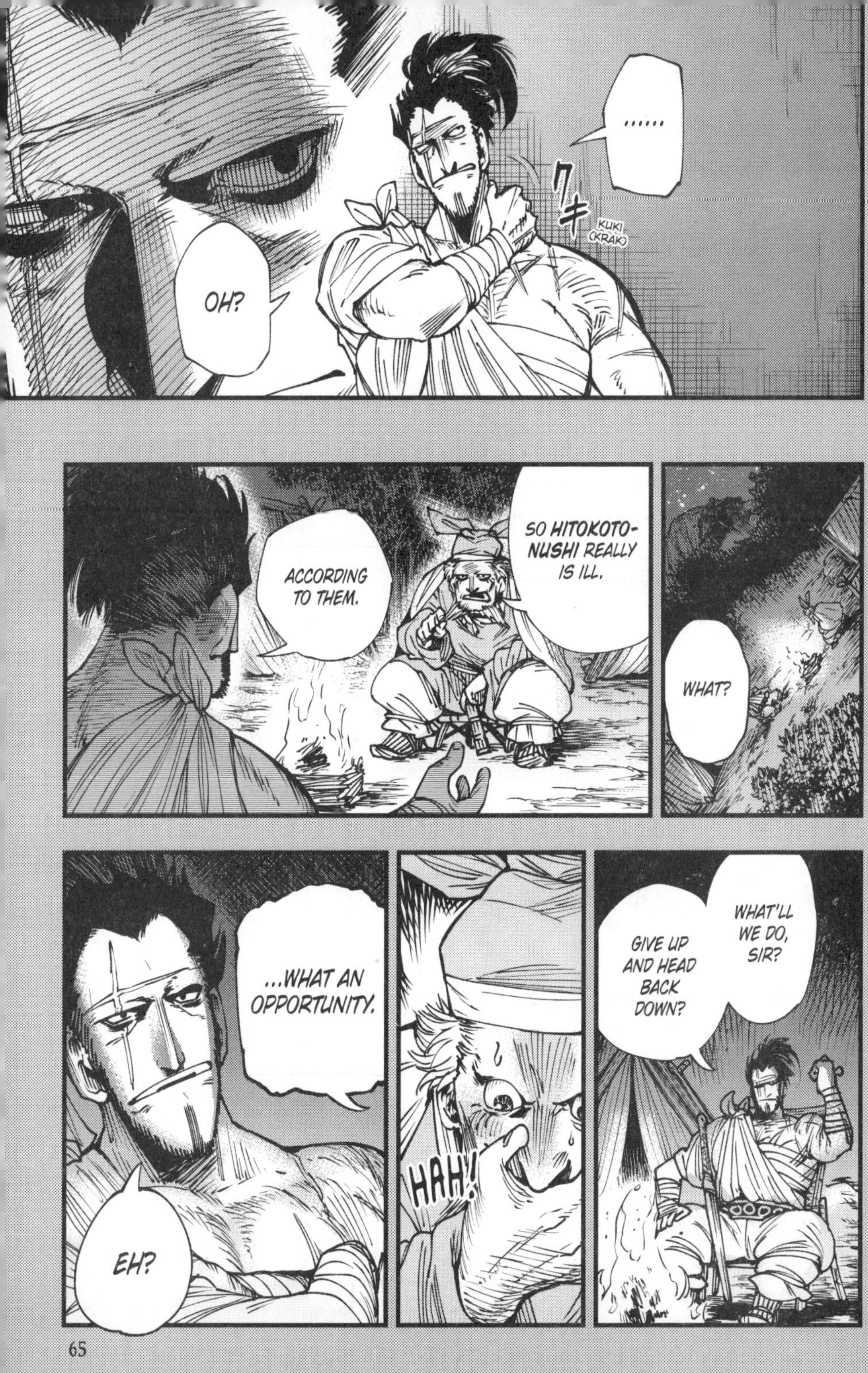
......
クキ
KUKI (KRAK)
OH?
WHAT?
SO HITOKOTO-NUSHI REALLY IS ILL.
ACCORDING TO THEM.
WHAT'LL WE DO, SIR?
GIVE UP AND HEAD BACK DOWN?
HAH!
...WHAT AN OPPORTUNITY.
EH?

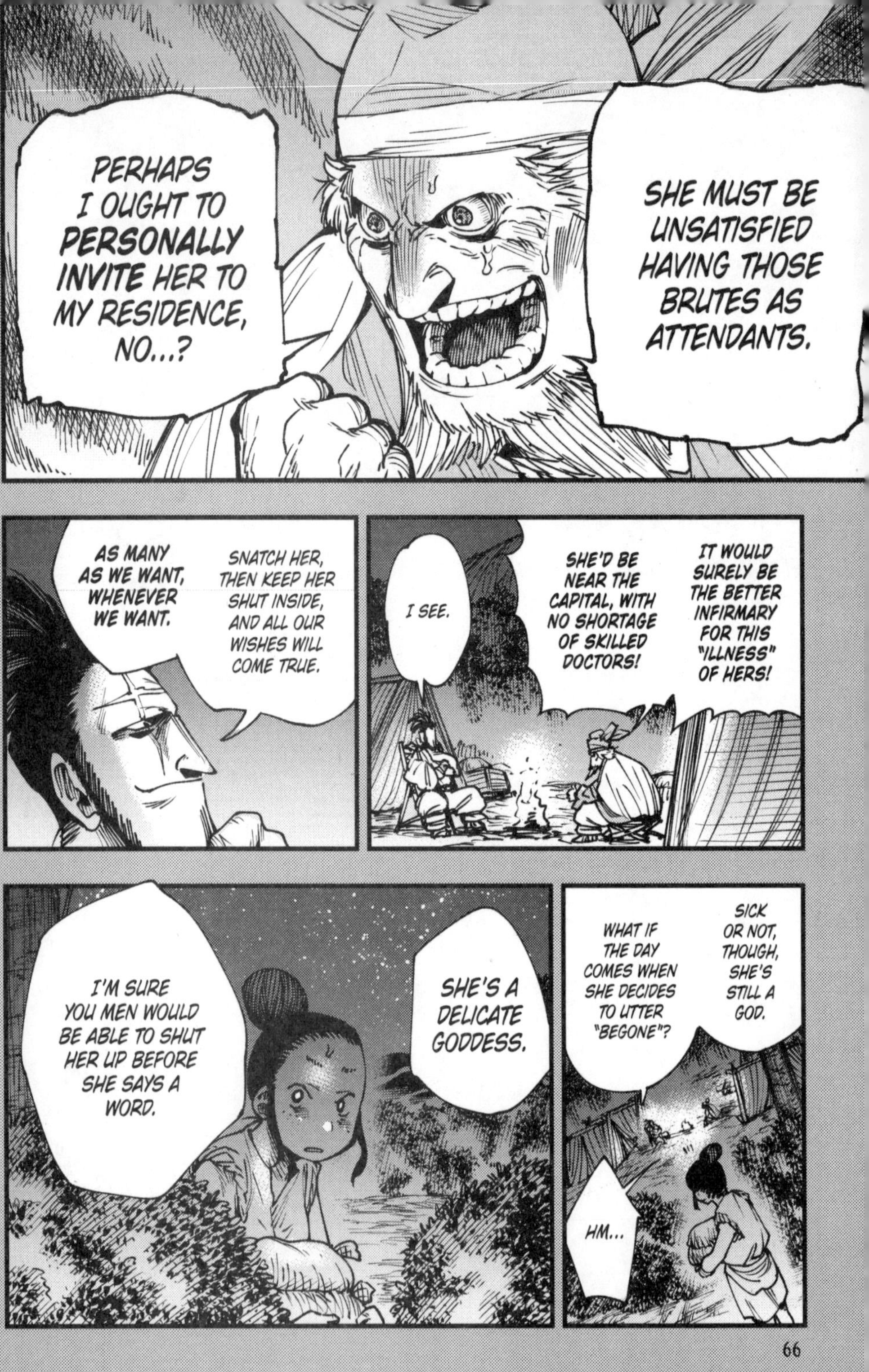
SHE MUST BE UNSATISFIED HAVING THOSE BRUTES AS ATTENDANTS.
PERHAPS I OUGHT TO PERSONALLY INVITE HER TO MY RESIDENCE, NO...?
IT WOULD SURELY BE THE BETTER INFIRMARY FOR THIS "ILLNESS" OF HERS!
SHE'D BE NEAR THE CAPITAL, WITH NO SHORTAGE OF SKILLED DOCTORS!
I SEE.
SNATCH HER, THEN KEEP HER SHUT INSIDE, AND ALL OUR WISHES WILL COME TRUE.
AS MANY AS WE WANT, WHENEVER WE WANT.
SICK OR NOT, THOUGH, SHE'S STILL A GOD.
WHAT IF THE DAY COMES WHEN SHE DECIDES TO UTTER "BEGONE"?
HM...
SHE'S A DELICATE GODDESS.
I'M SURE YOU MEN WOULD BE ABLE TO SHUT HER UP BEFORE SHE SAYS A WORD.

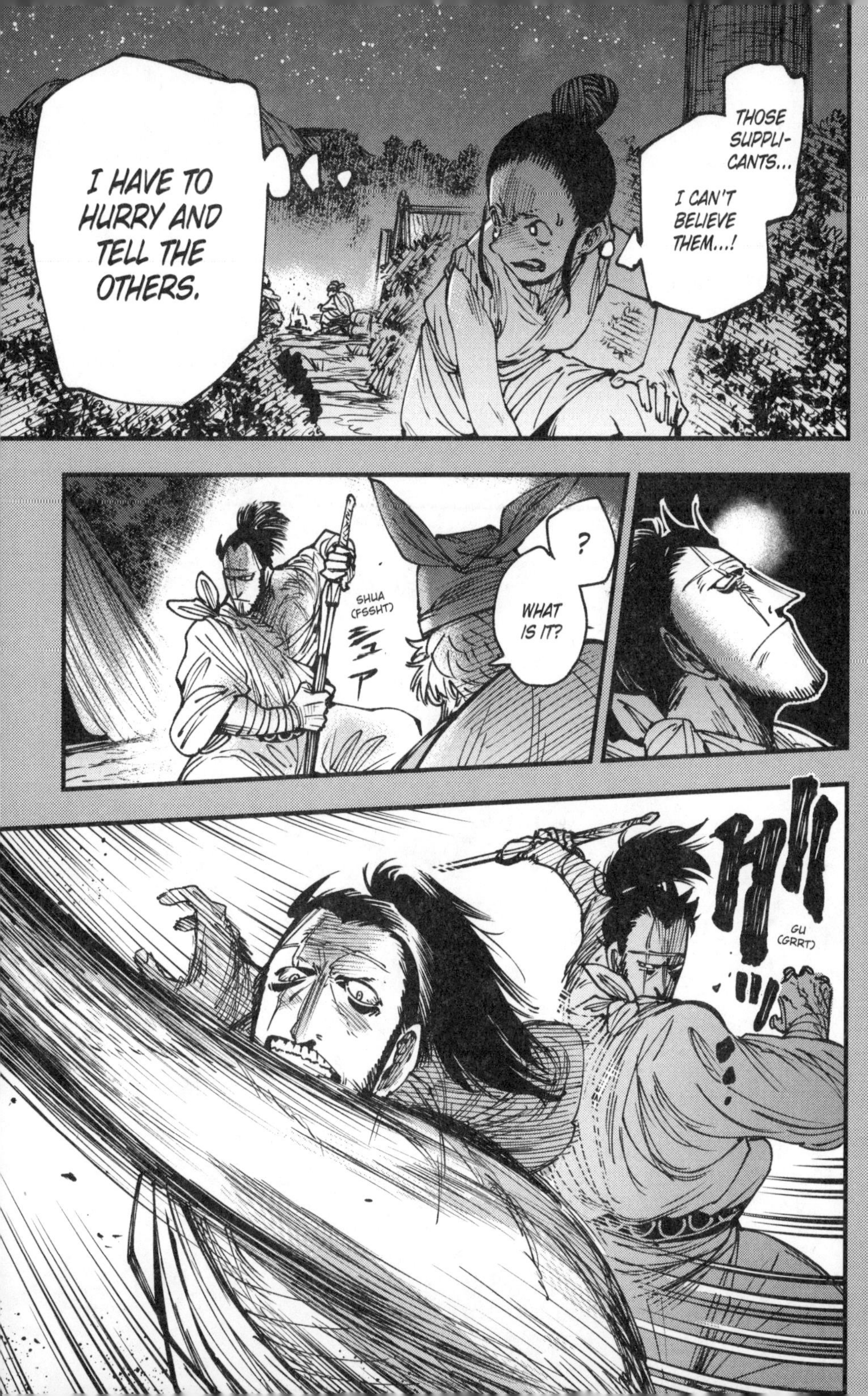
THOSE SUPPLI-CANTS...
I CAN'T BELIEVE THEM...!
I HAVE TO HURRY AND TELL THE OTHERS.
?
WHAT IS IT?
SHUA (FSSHT)
シュア
GU (GRRT)

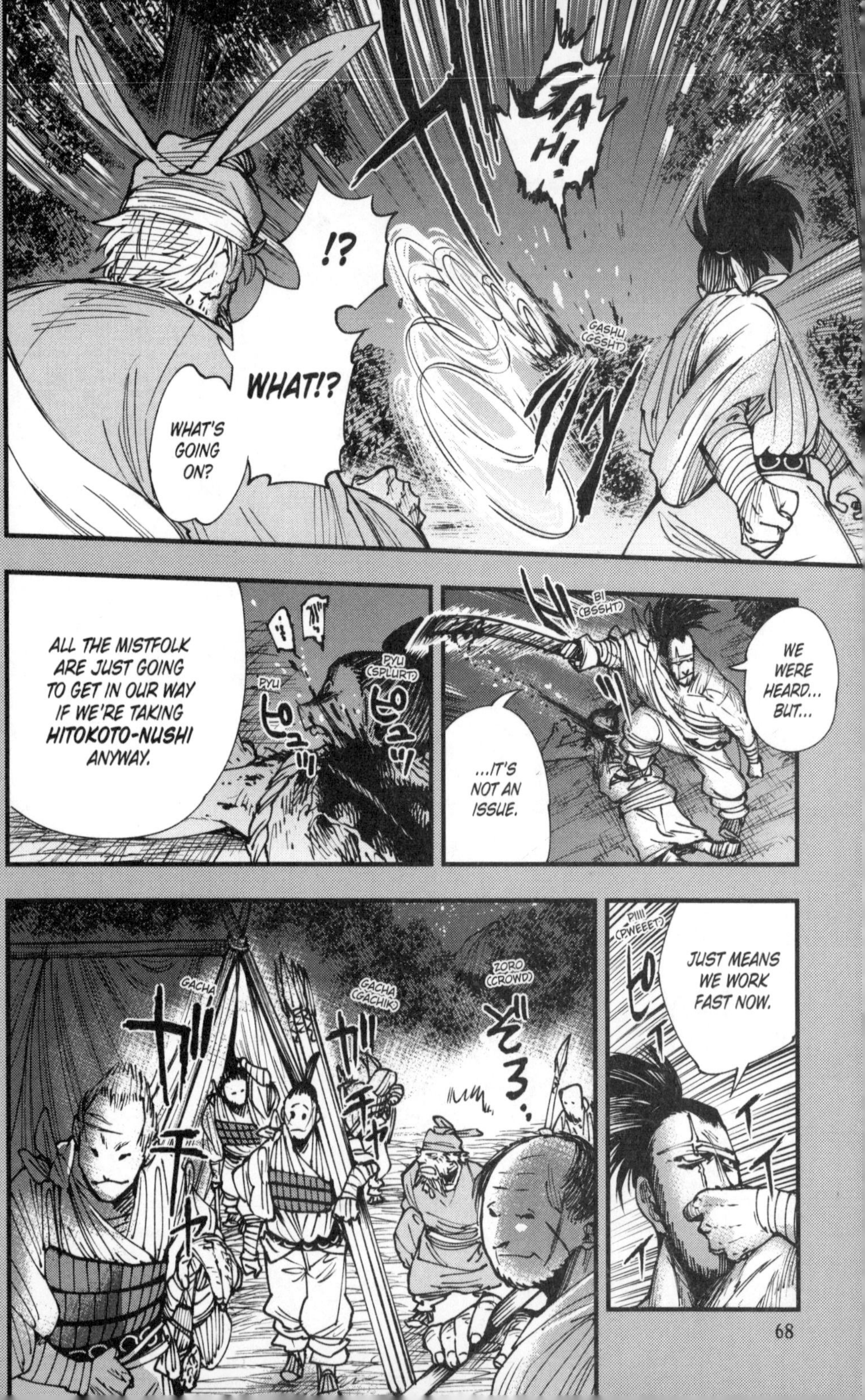
GAH!
GASHU (GSSHT)
!?
WHAT!?
WHAT'S GOING ON?
BI (BSSHT)
WE WERE HEARD... BUT...
...IT'S NOT AN ISSUE.
PYU (SPLURT)
PYU
ALL THE MISTFOLK ARE JUST GOING TO GET IN OUR WAY IF WE'RE TAKING HITOKOTO-NUSHI ANYWAY.
PIIII (PWEEET)
JUST MEANS WE WORK FAST NOW.
ZORO (CROWD)
GACHA (GACHIK)
GACHA

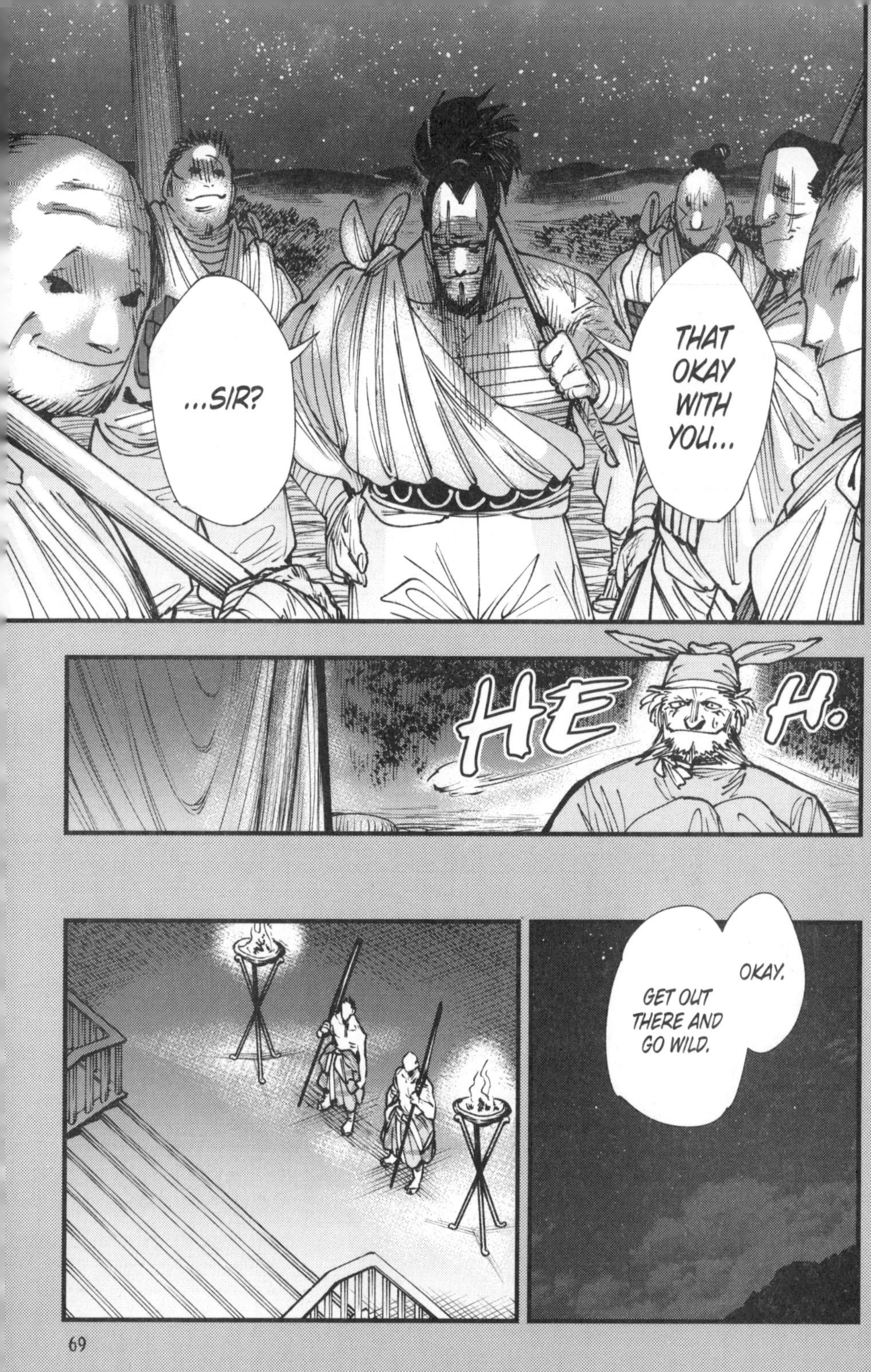
THAT OKAY WITH YOU...
...SIR?
HEH.
OKAY.
GET OUT THERE AND GO WILD.

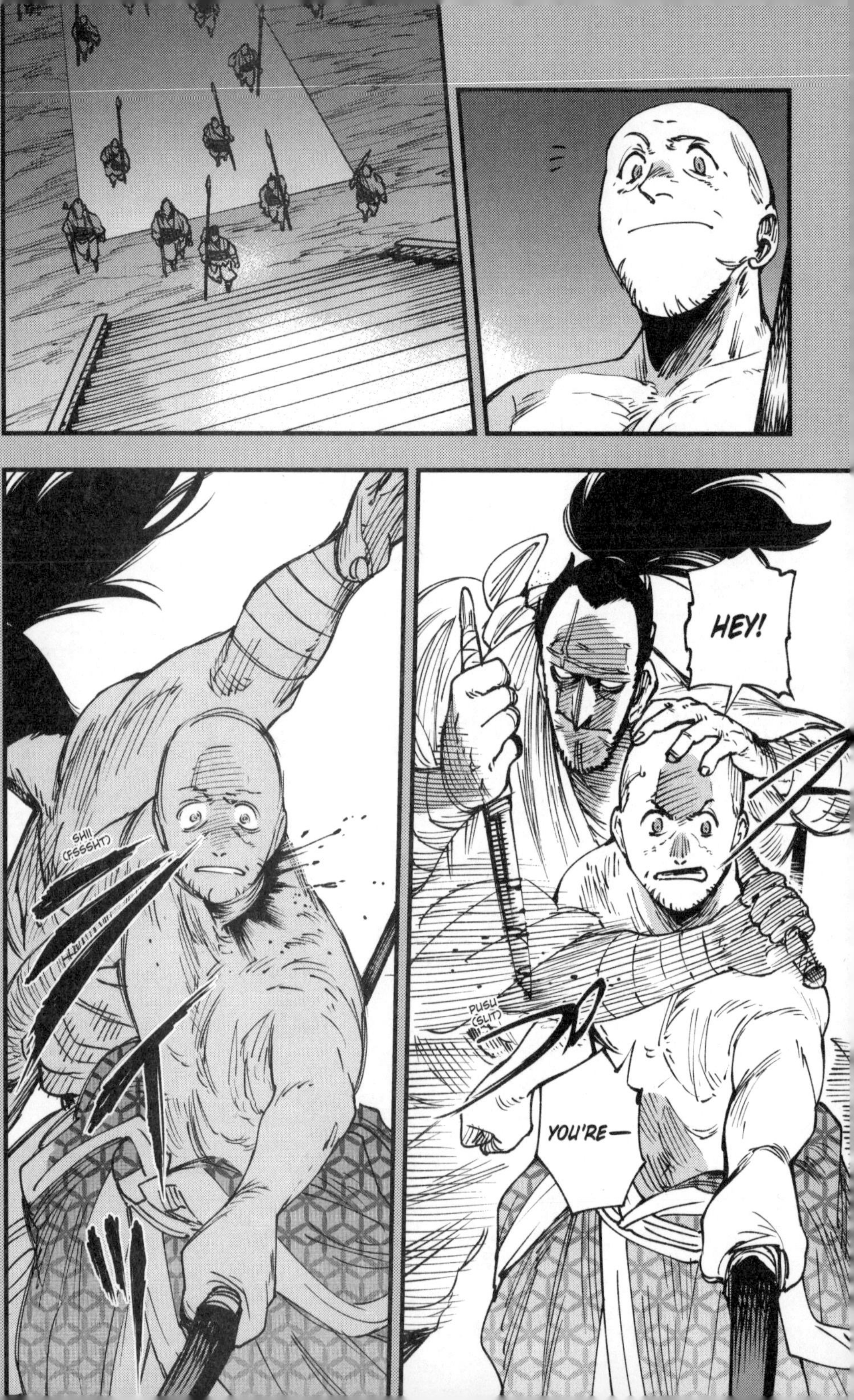
HEY!
PUSH (SLIT)
YOU'RE—
SHII (FSSSHT)

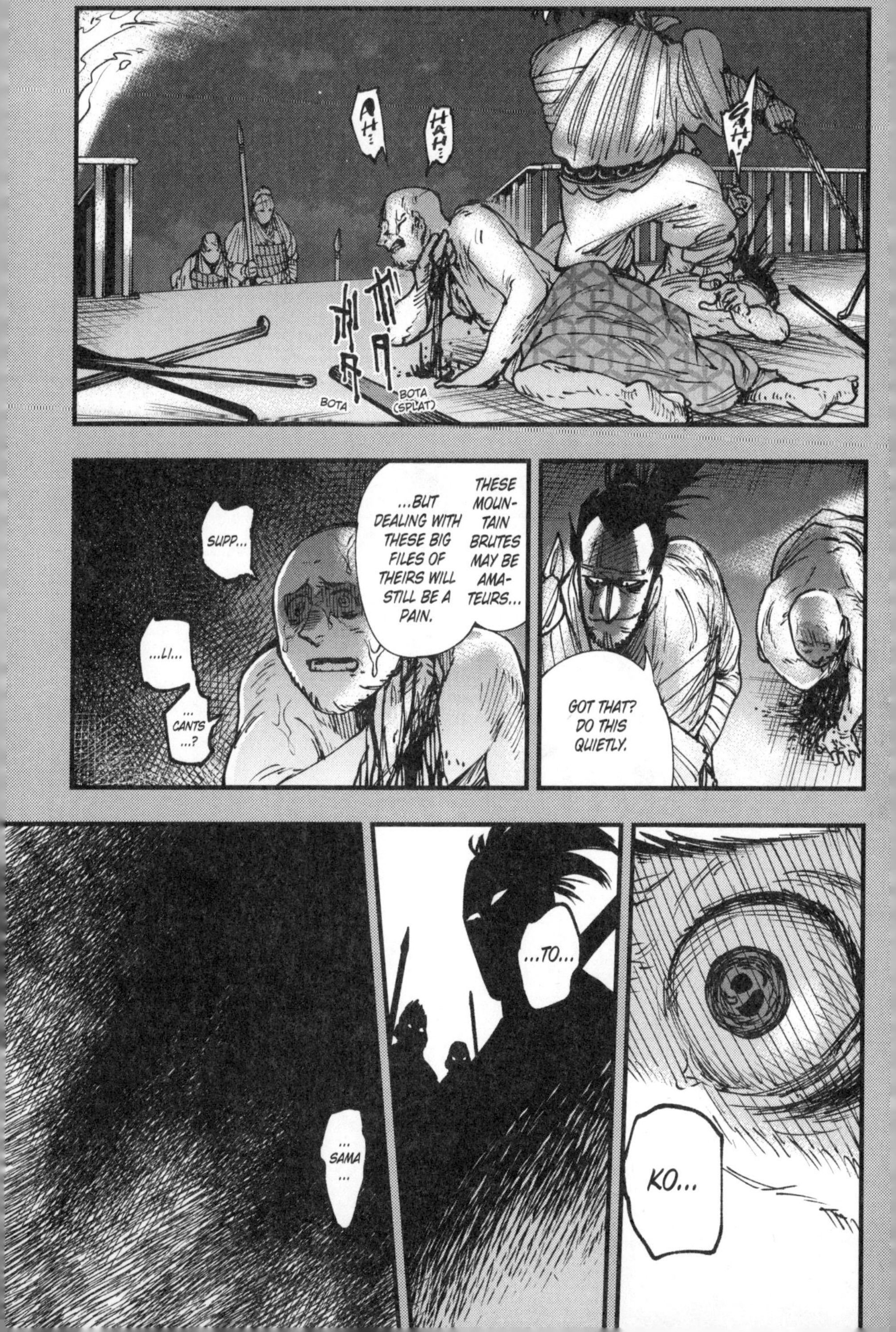
GAH!
HAH!...
AH!...
BOTA (SPLAT)
BOTA
GOT THAT? DO THIS QUIETLY.
THESE MOUNTAIN BRUTES MAY BE AMATEURS...
...BUT DEALING WITH THESE BIG FILES OF THEIRS WILL STILL BE A PAIN.
SUPP...
...LI...
...CANTS...?
KO...
...TO...
...SAMA...

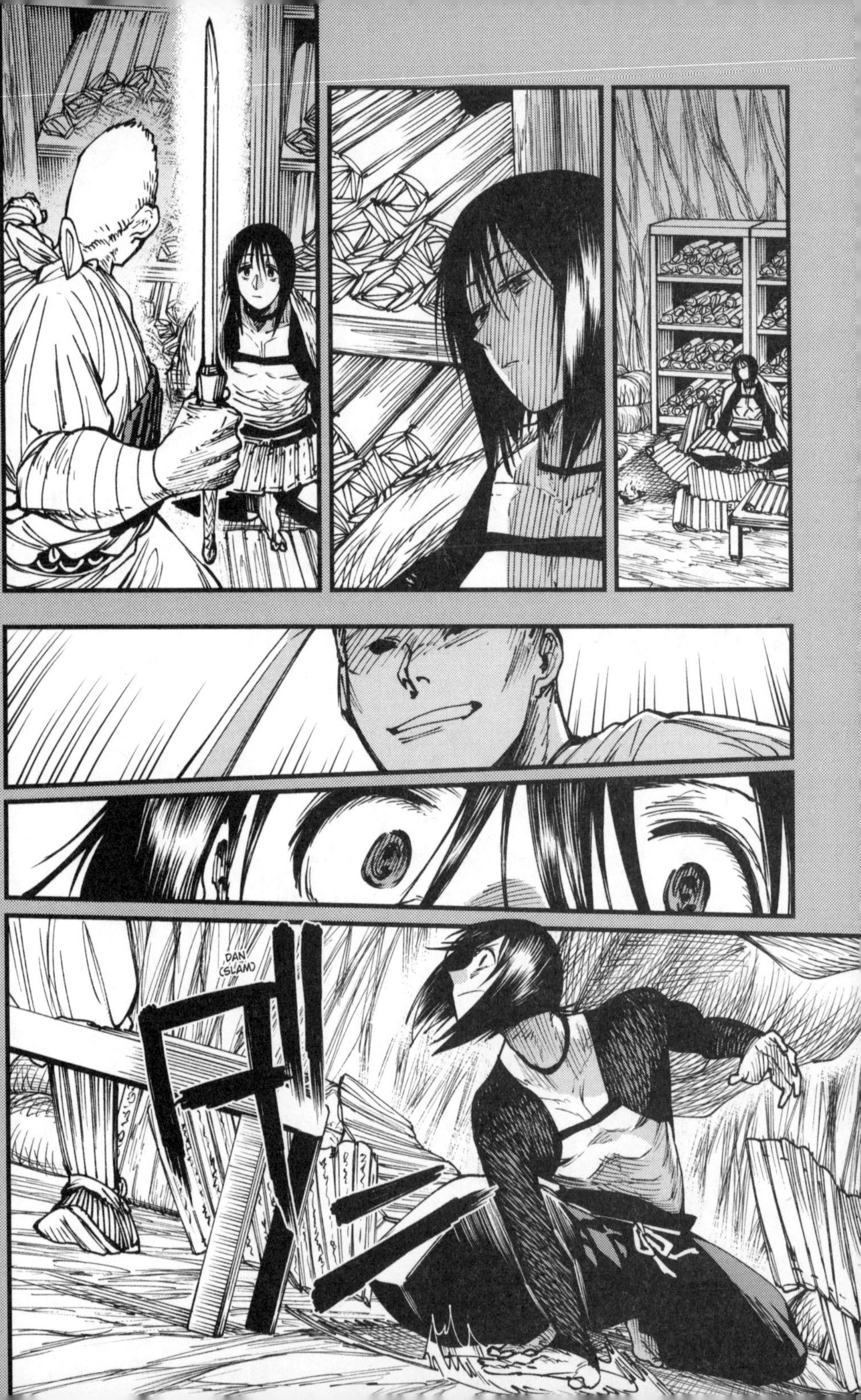
DAN
(SLAM)

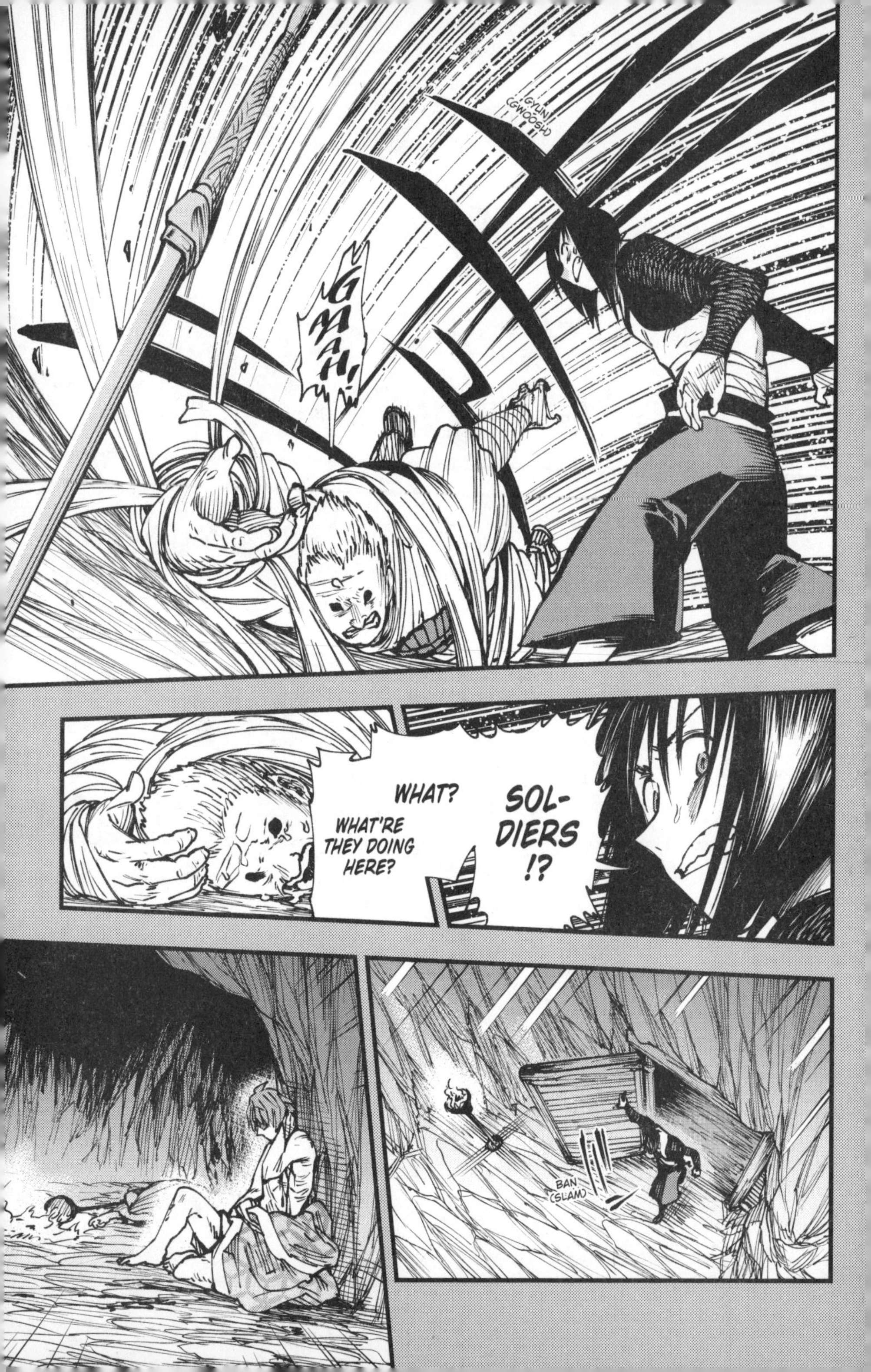

GYLUN! (GWOOSH)
NGMAH!
SOL-DIERS!?
WHAT?
WHAT'RE THEY DOING HERE?
BAN (SLAM)

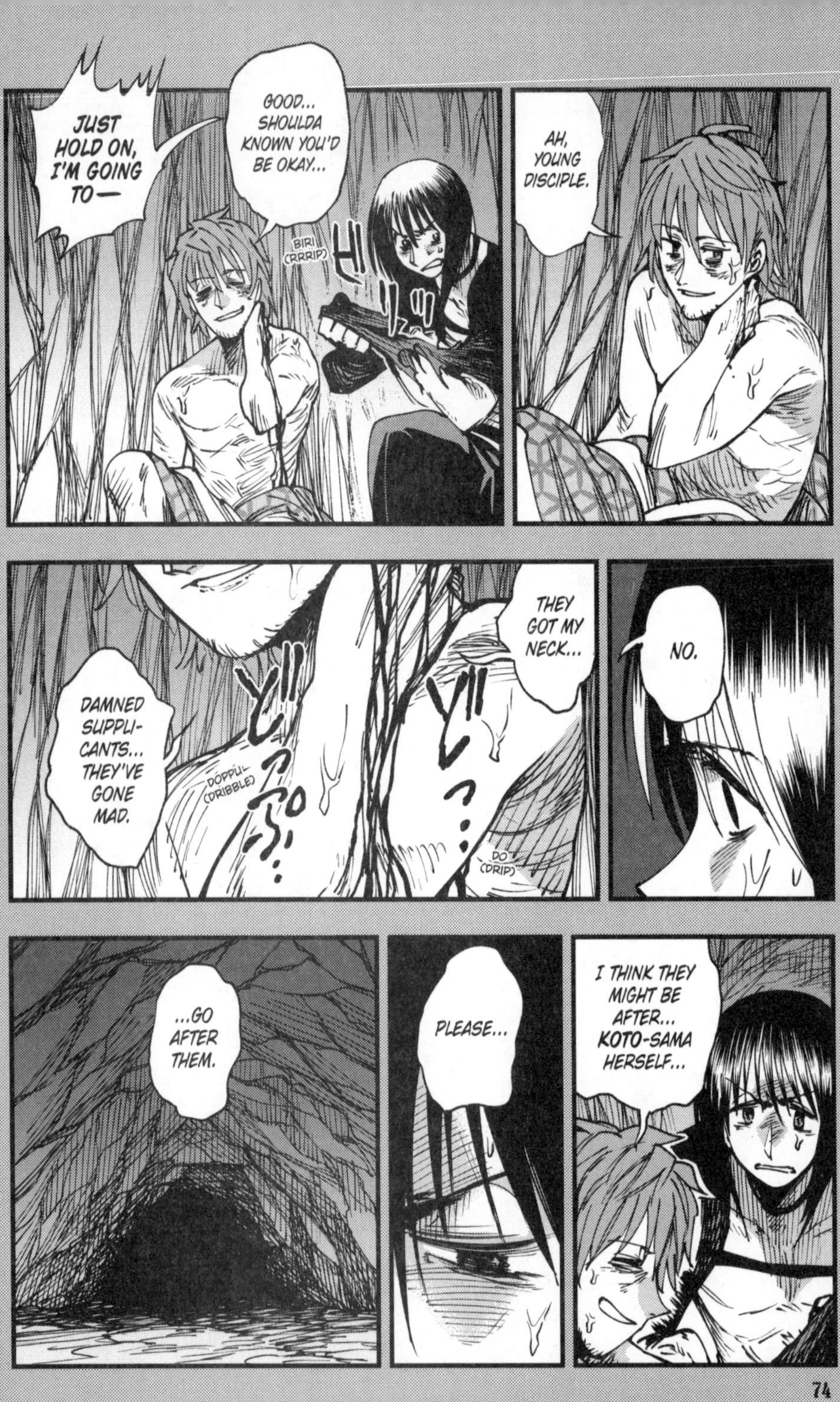
AH, YOUNG DISCIPLE.
GOOD... SHOULDA KNOWN YOU'D BE OKAY...
JUST HOLD ON, I'M GOING TO—
BIRI (RRRIP)
NO.
THEY GOT MY NECK...
DAMNED SUPPLI- CANTS... THEY'VE GONE MAD.
DOPPU (DRIBBLE)
DO (DRIP)
I THINK THEY MIGHT BE AFTER... KOTO-SAMA HERSELF...
PLEASE...
...GO AFTER THEM.

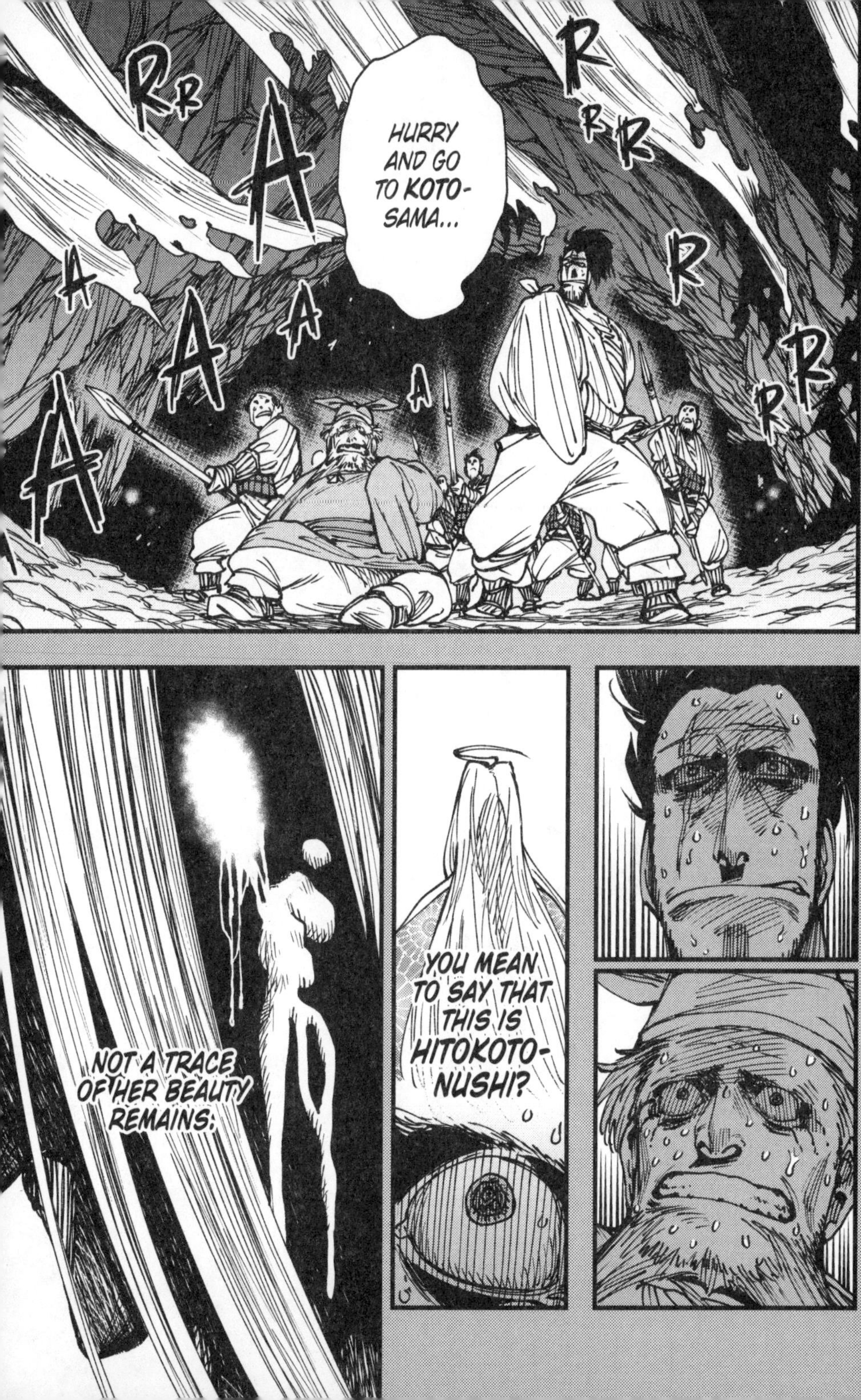
HURRY AND GO TO KOTO-SAMA...
YOU MEAN TO SAY THAT THIS IS HITOKOTO-NUSHI?
NOT A TRACE OF HER BEAUTY REMAINS.

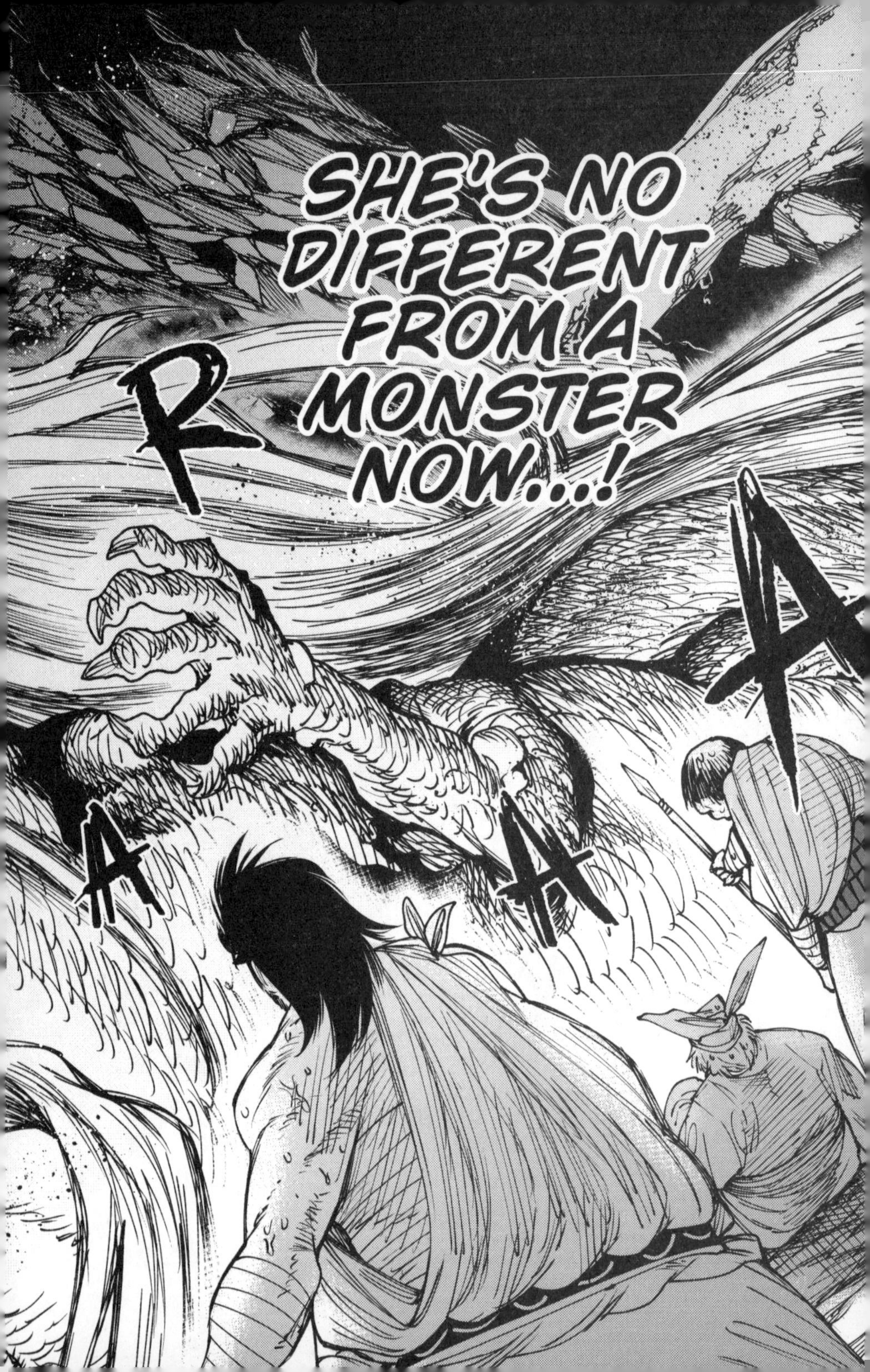
SHE'S NO DIFFERENT FROM A MONSTER NOW...!
RAAA

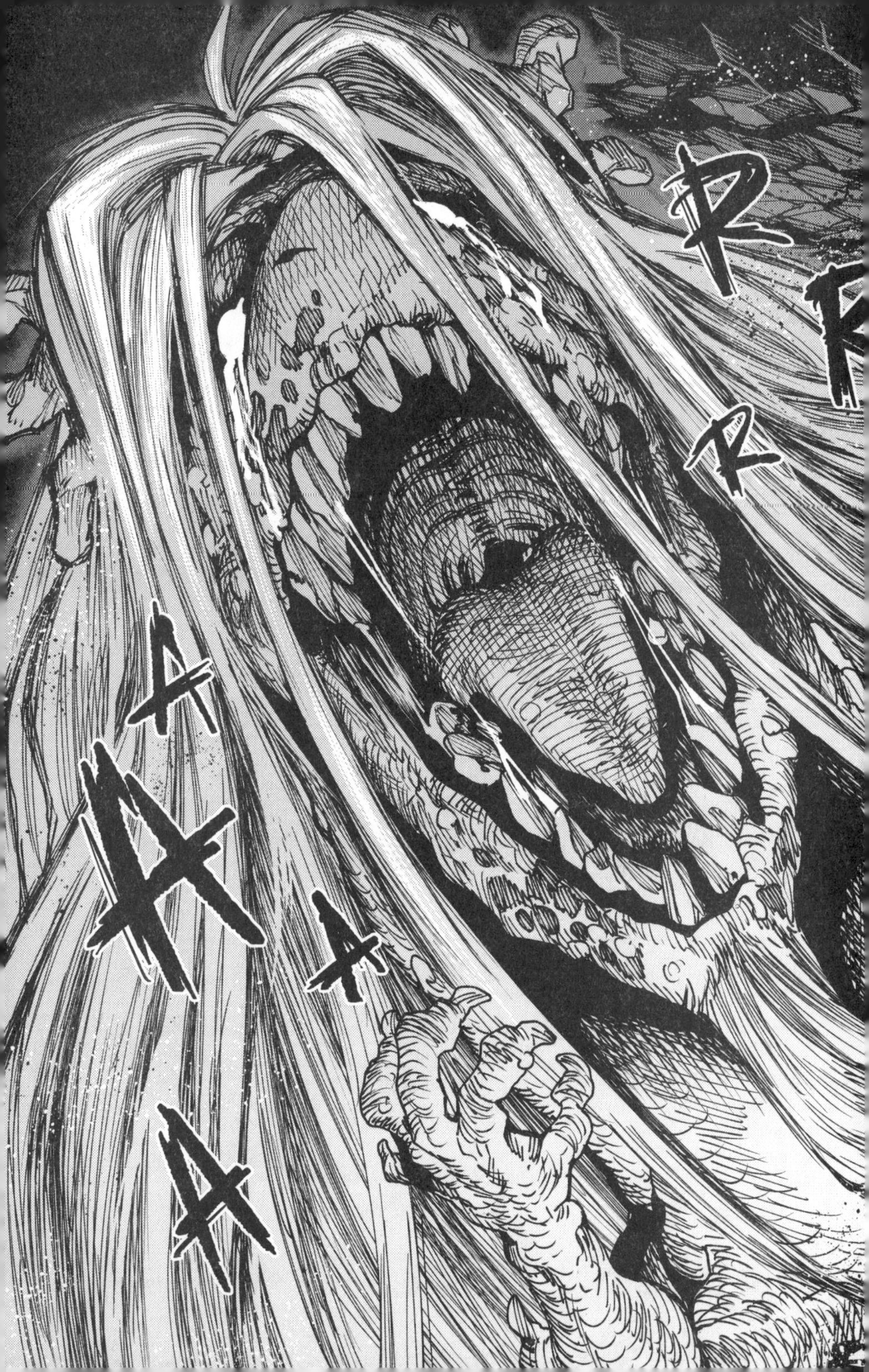
RRR
AAAA

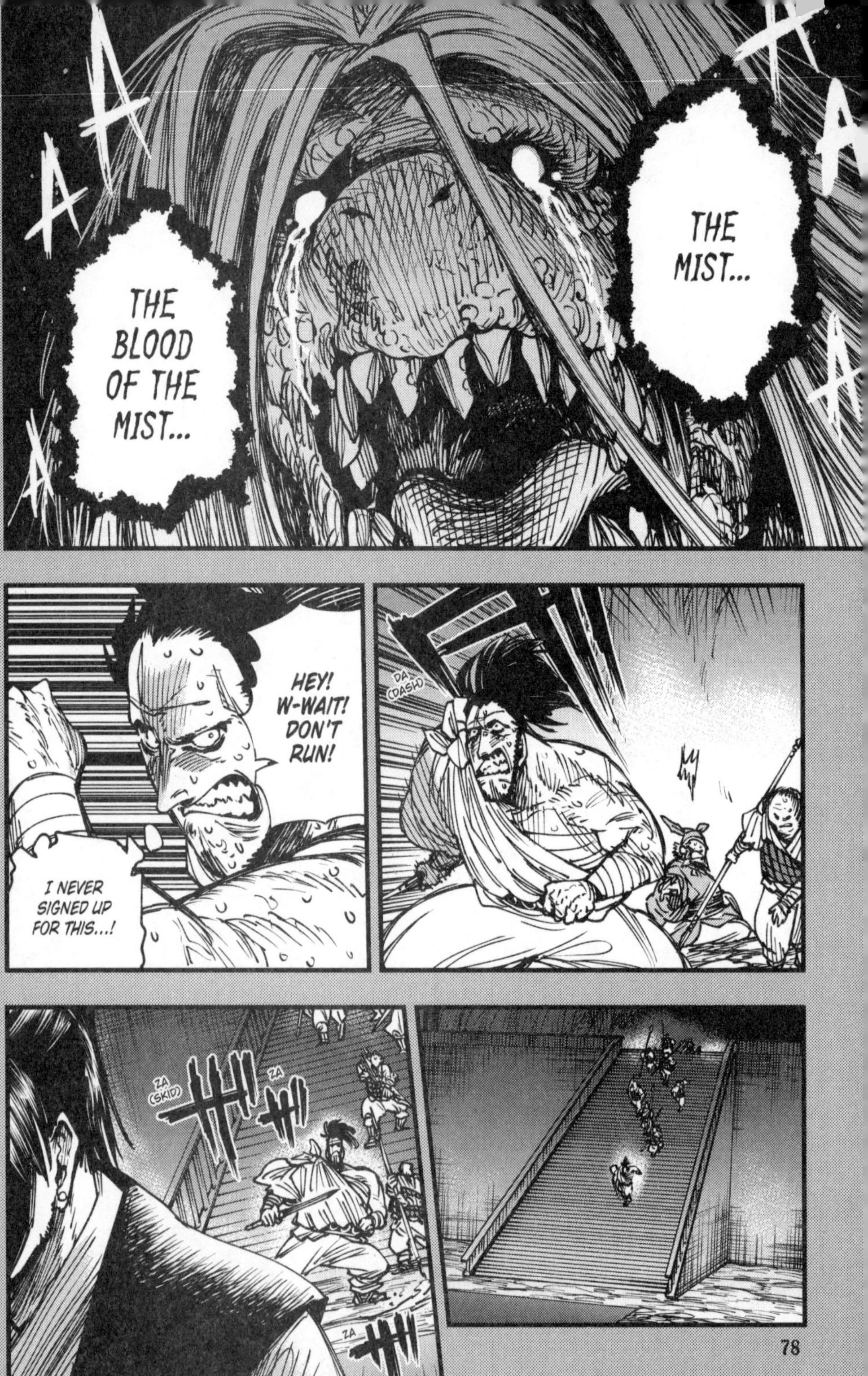
THE MIST...
THE BLOOD OF THE MIST...
DA (DASH)
HEY! W-WAIT! DON'T RUN!
I NEVER SIGNED UP FOR THIS...!
ZA (SKID)
ZA
ZA

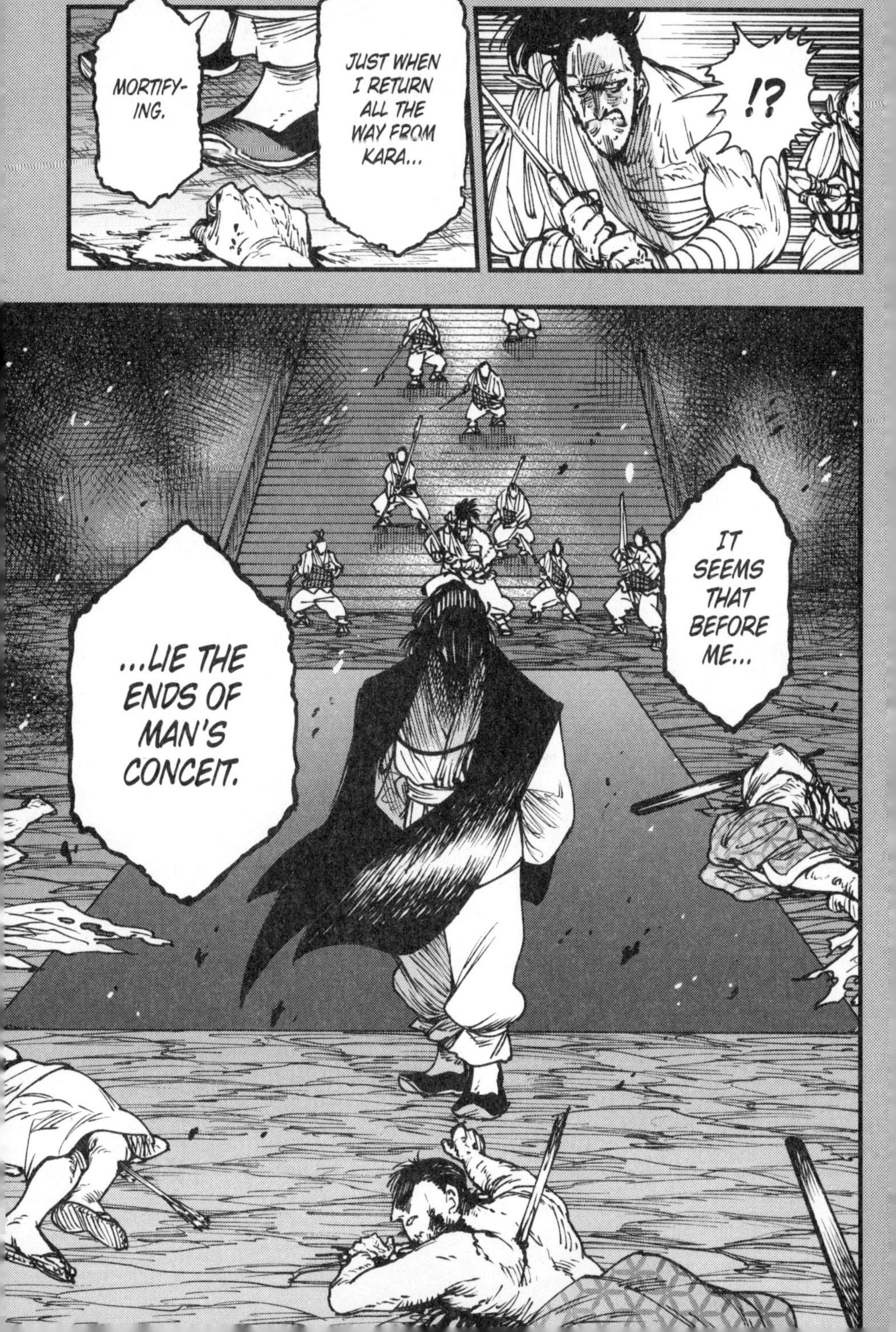
!?
JUST WHEN I RETURN ALL THE WAY FROM KARA...
MORTIFY-ING.
IT SEEMS THAT BEFORE ME...
...LIE THE ENDS OF MAN'S CONCEIT.

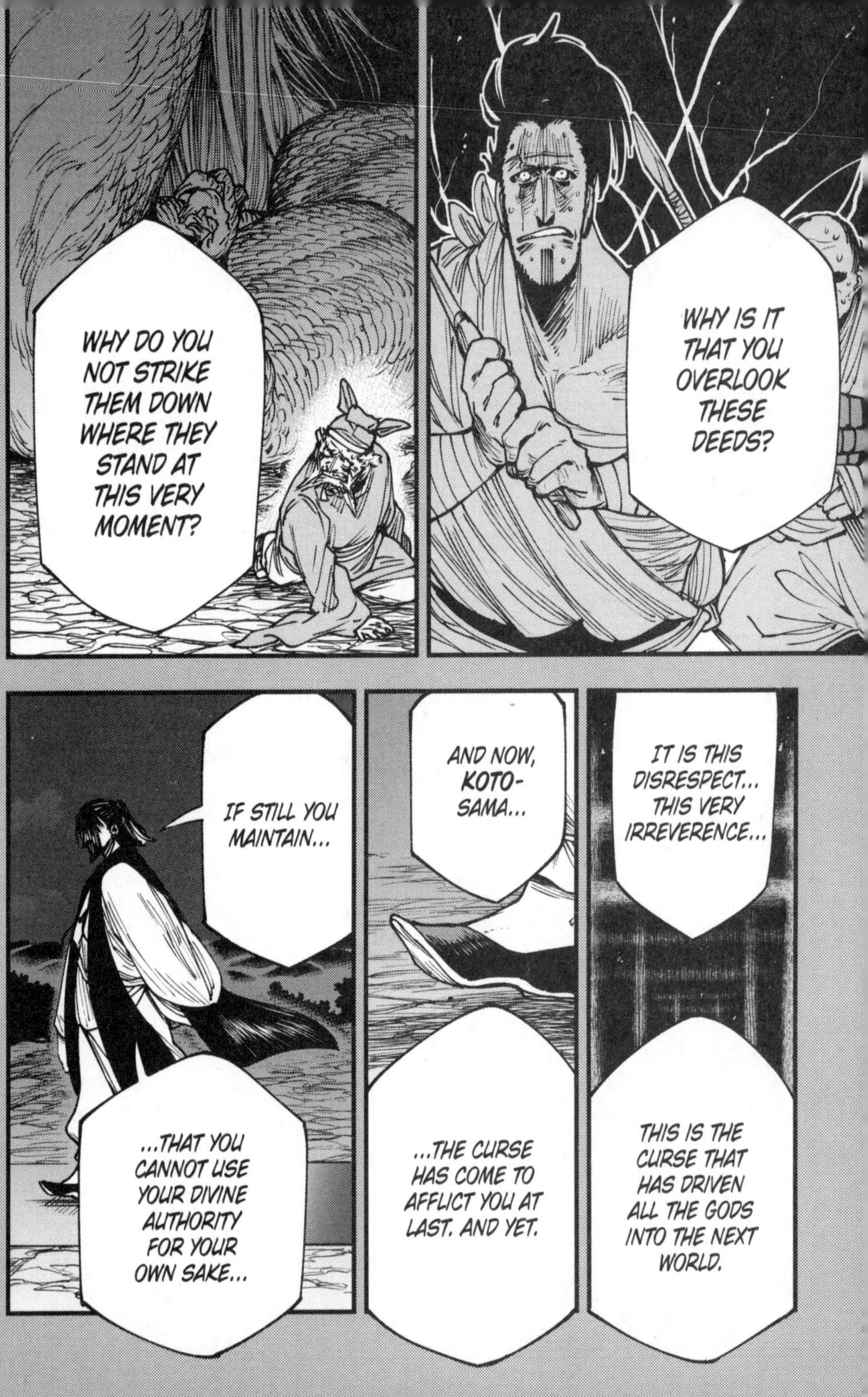
WHY IS IT THAT YOU OVERLOOK THESE DEEDS?
WHY DO YOU NOT STRIKE THEM DOWN WHERE THEY STAND AT THIS VERY MOMENT?
IT IS THIS DISRESPECT... THIS VERY IRREVERENCE...
THIS IS THE CURSE THAT HAS DRIVEN ALL THE GODS INTO THE NEXT WORLD.
AND NOW, KOTO-SAMA...
...THE CURSE HAS COME TO AFFLICT YOU AT LAST. AND YET.
IF STILL YOU MAINTAIN...
...THAT YOU CANNOT USE YOUR DIVINE AUTHORITY FOR YOUR OWN SAKE...

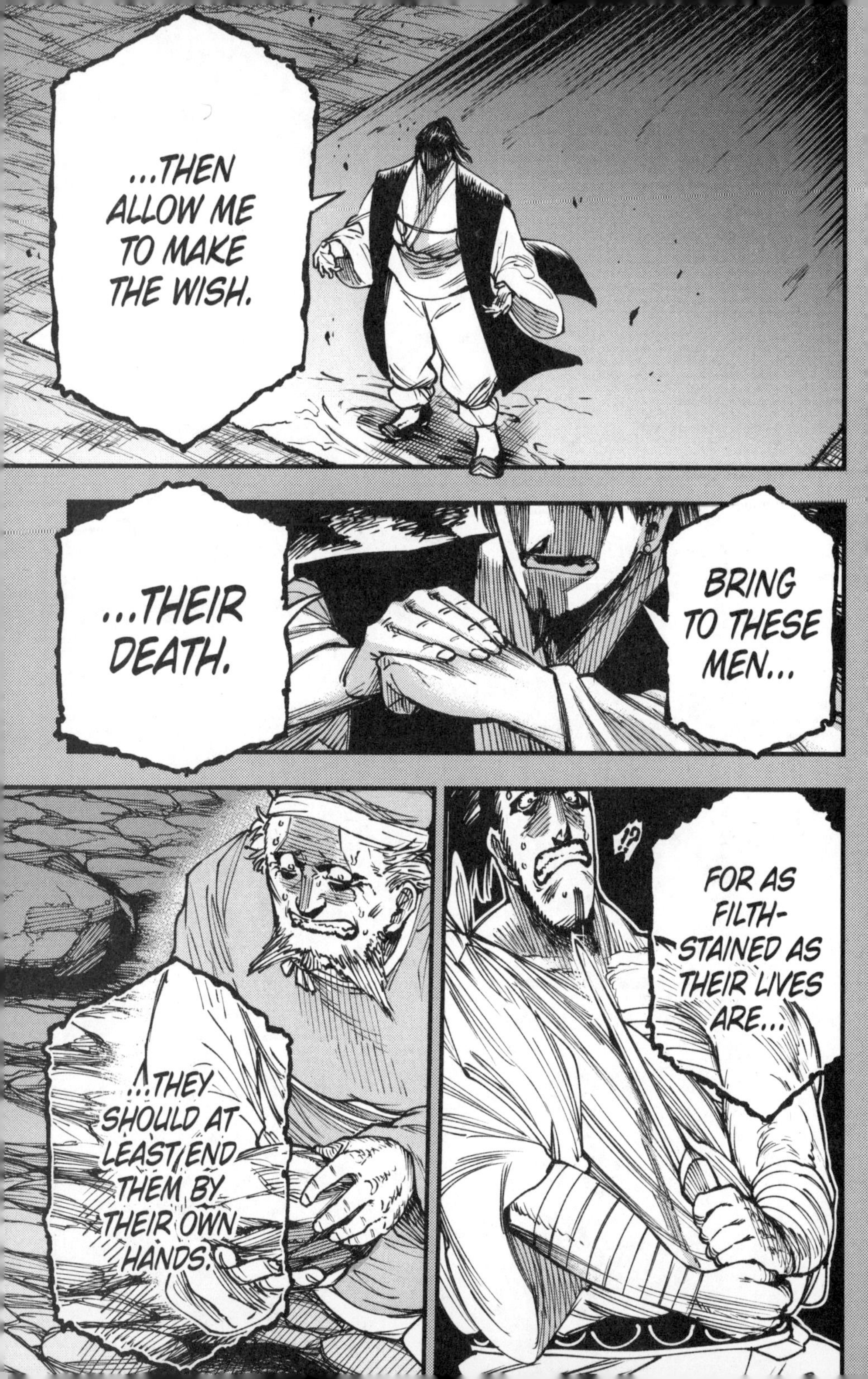
...THEN ALLOW ME TO MAKE THE WISH.
BRING TO THESE MEN...
...THEIR DEATH.
!?
FOR AS FILTH-STAINED AS THEIR LIVES ARE...
...THEY SHOULD AT LEAST END THEM BY THEIR OWN HANDS.

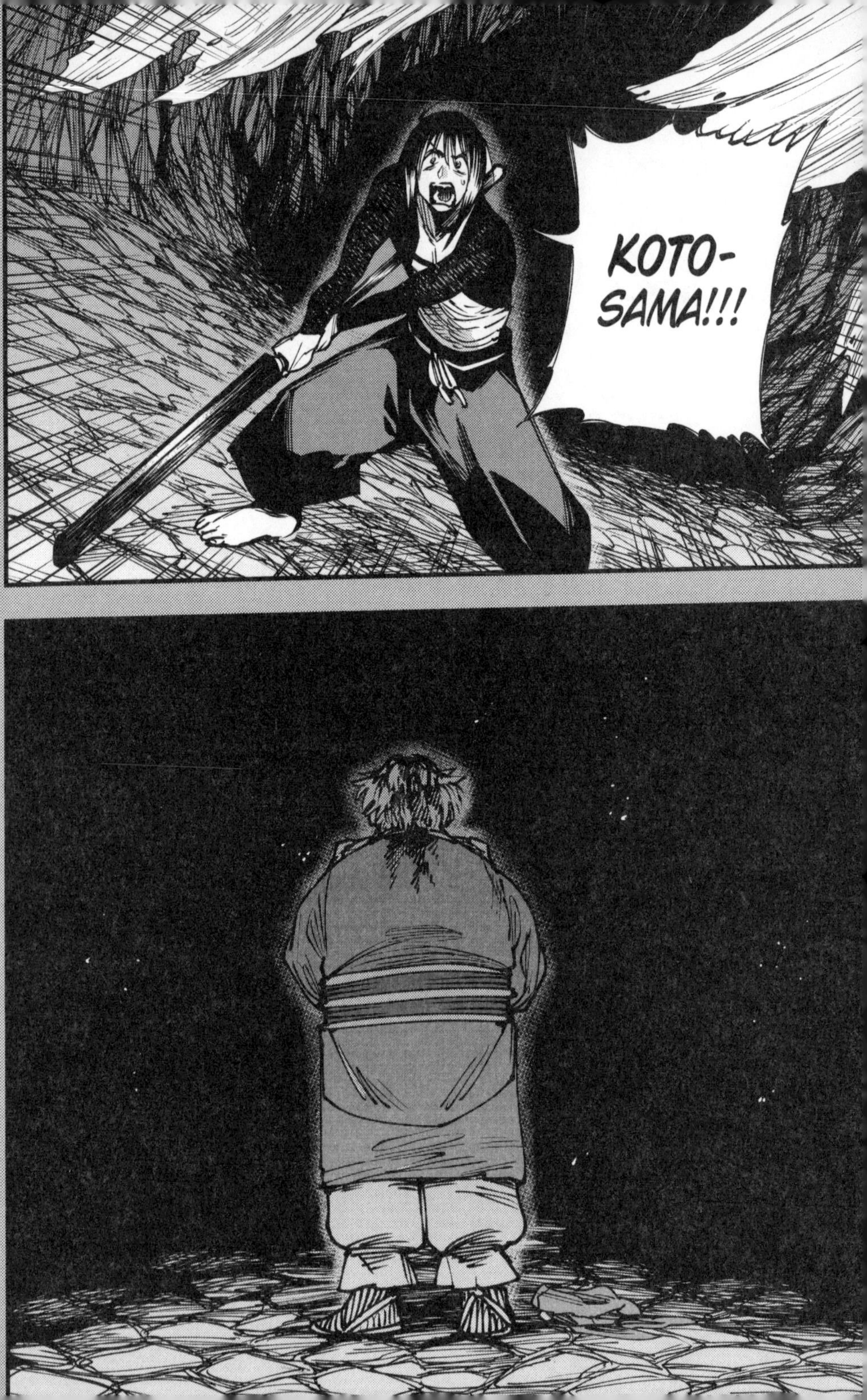
KOTO-
SAMA!!!

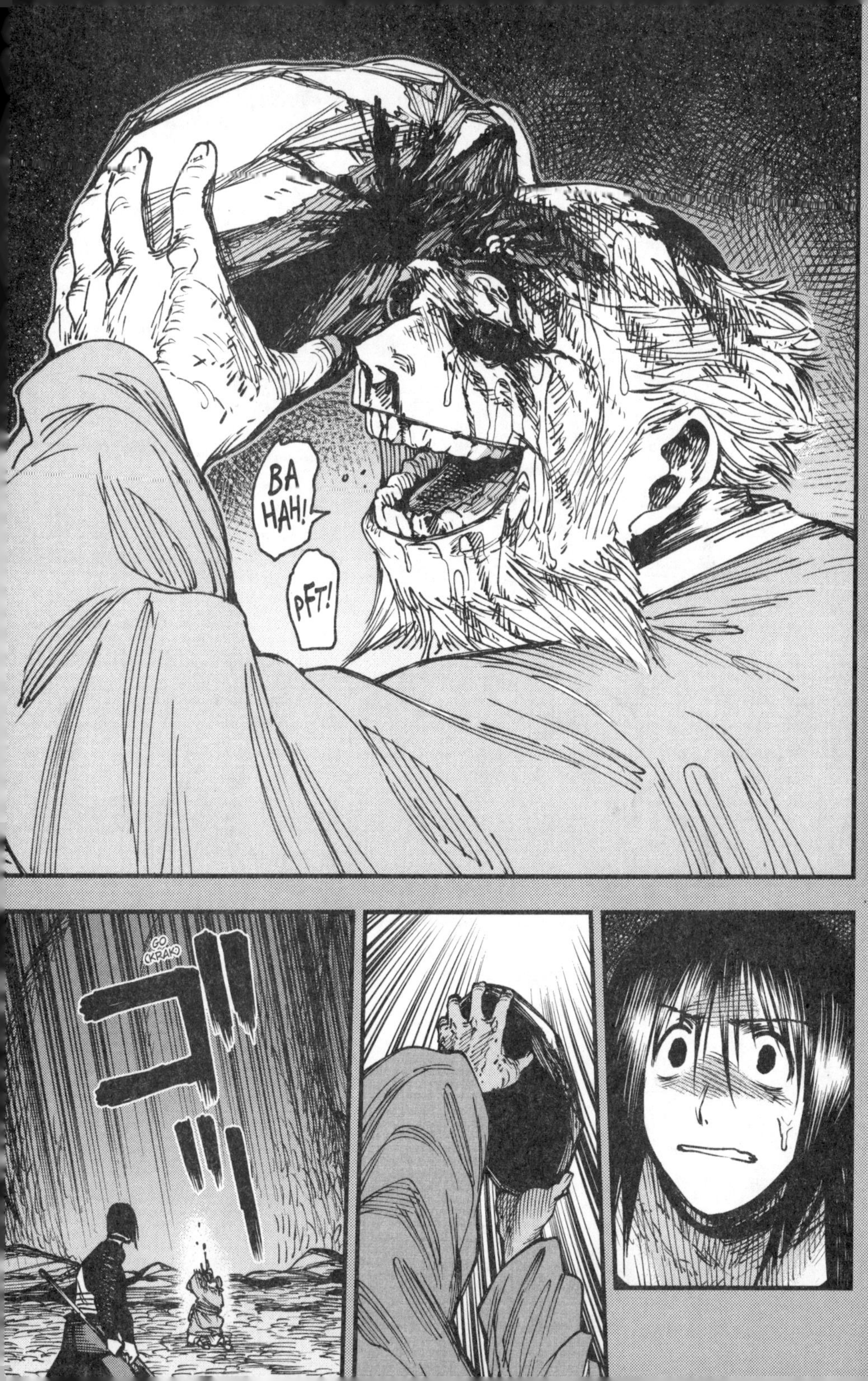
BA HAH!
PFT!
GO (KRAK)

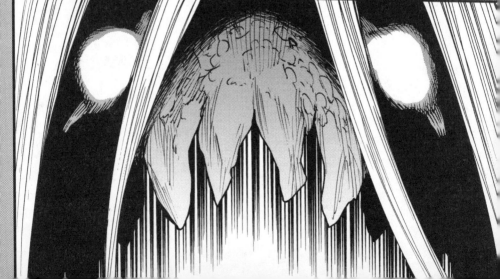

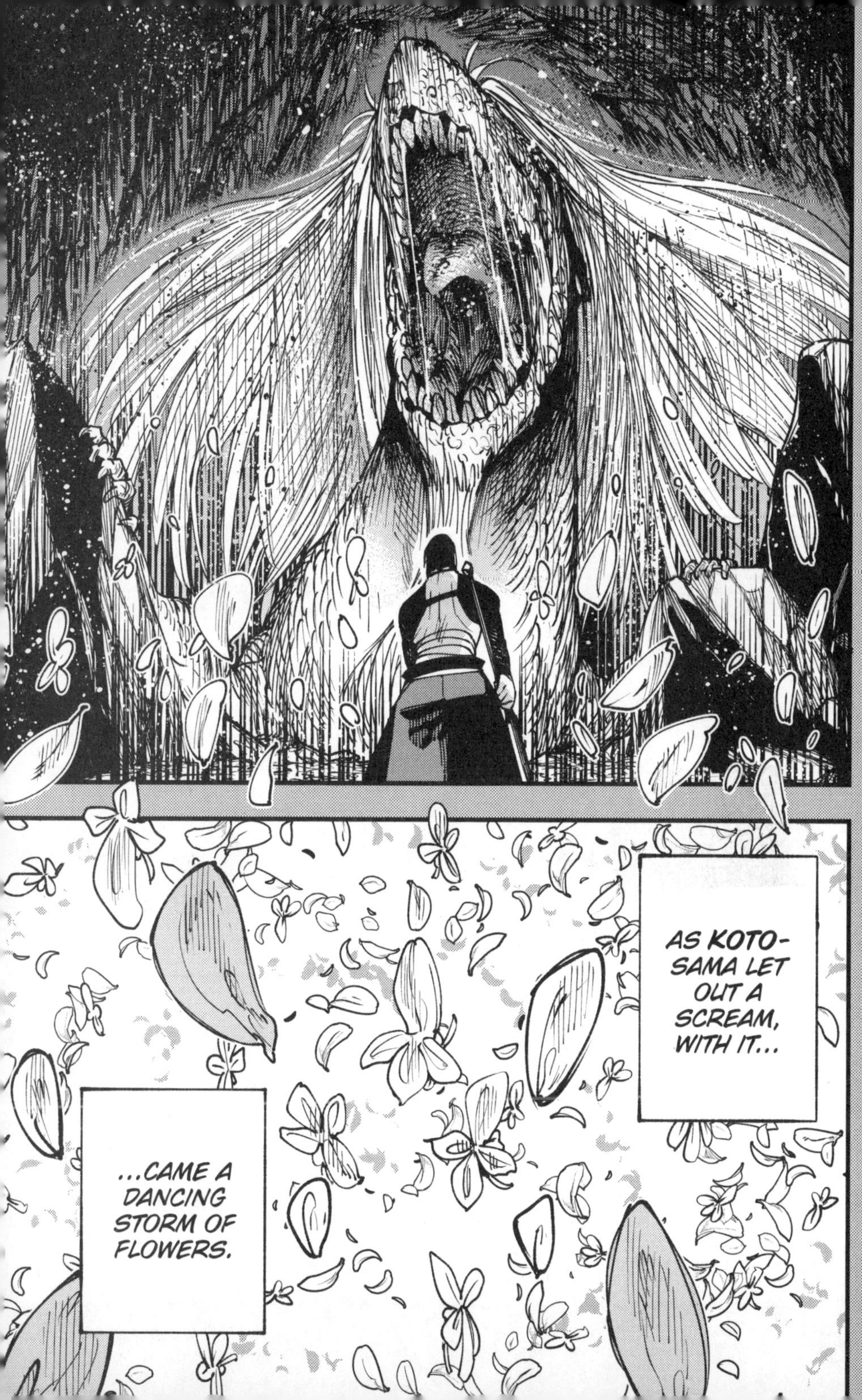
AS KOTO-SAMA LET OUT A SCREAM, WITH IT...
...CAME A DANCING STORM OF FLOWERS.

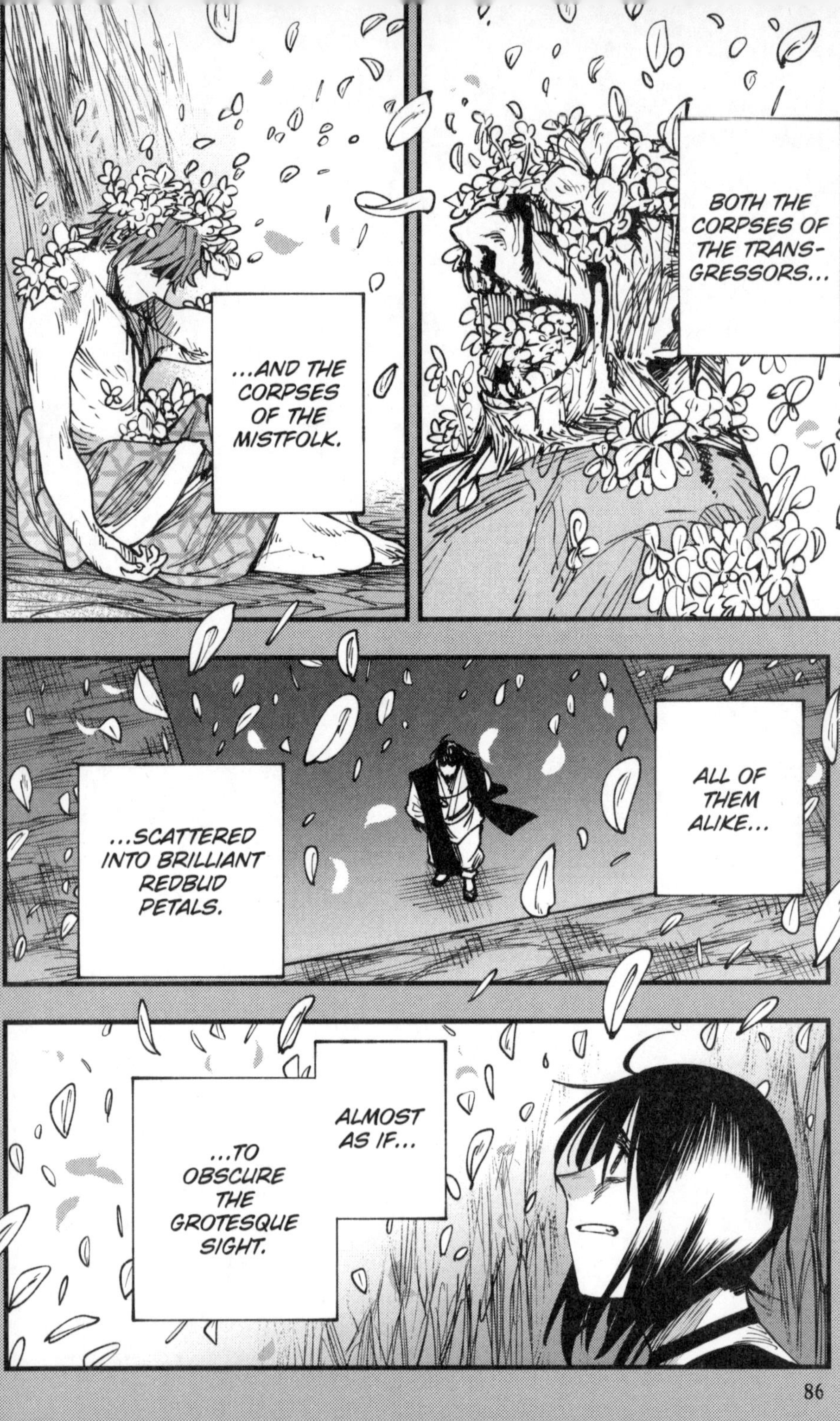
BOTH THE CORPSES OF THE TRANS-GRESSORS...
...AND THE CORPSES OF THE MISTFOLK.
ALL OF THEM ALIKE...
...SCATTERED INTO BRILLIANT REDBUD PETALS.
ALMOST AS IF...
...TO OBSCURE THE GROTESQUE SIGHT.

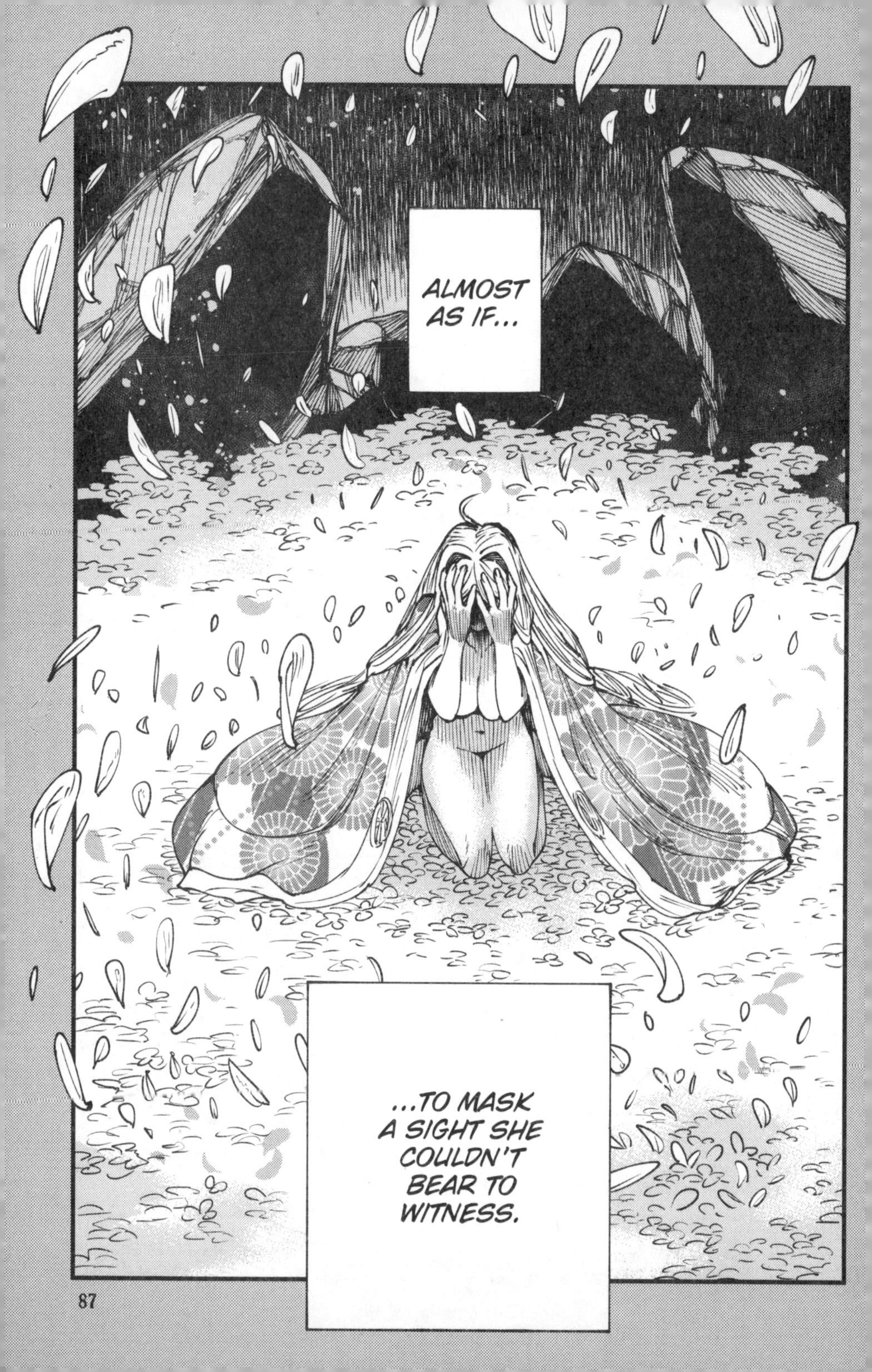
ALMOST AS IF...
...TO MASK A SIGHT SHE COULDN'T BEAR TO WITNESS.

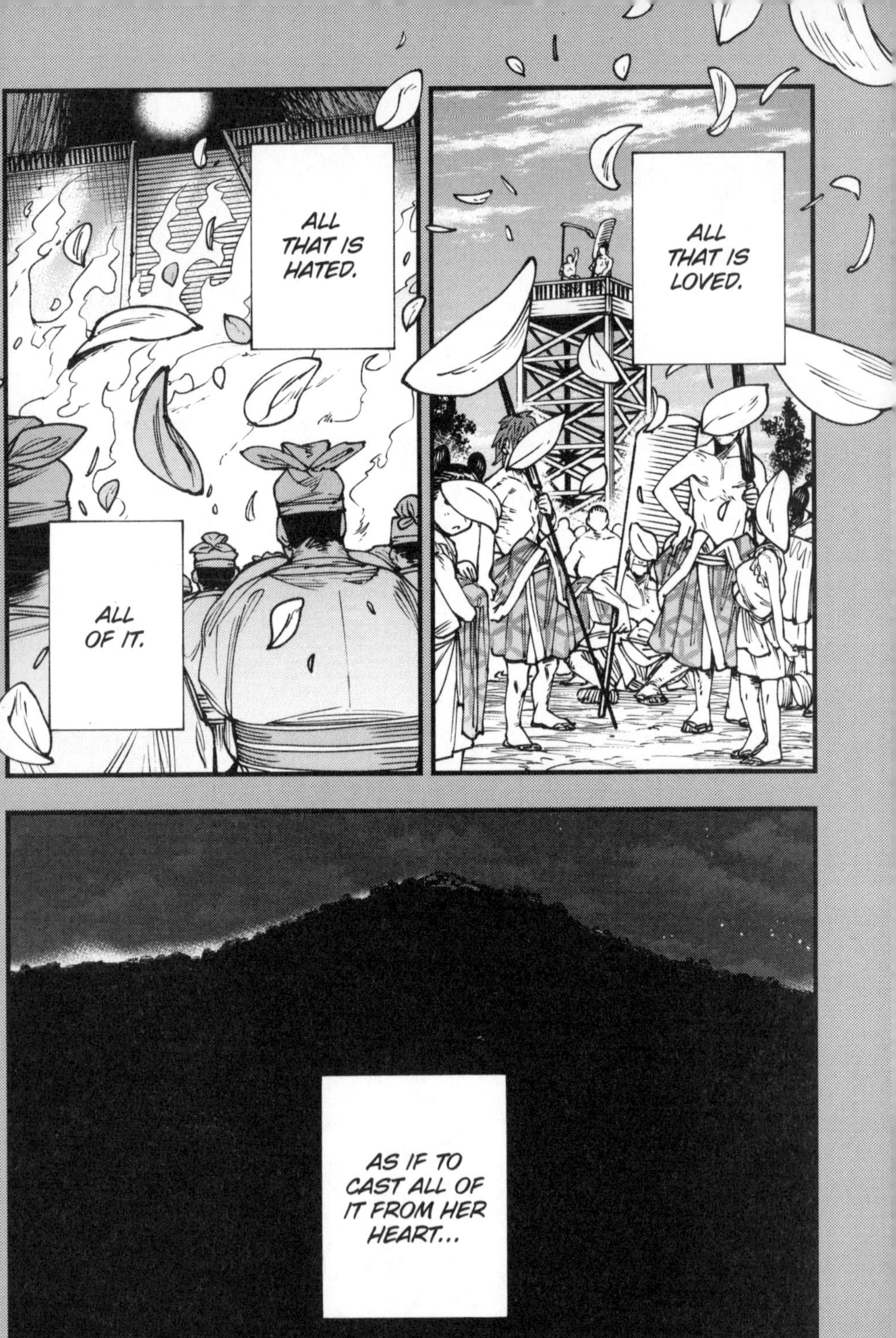
ALL THAT IS LOVED.
ALL THAT IS HATED.
ALL OF IT.
AS IF TO CAST ALL OF IT FROM HER HEART...

CHAPTER XIII ❤ END

RECORD OF DIVINE INSTRUMENTS

THE "MIST"

RARITY	BO (FIFTH-RATE)
CONVENIENCE	KOU (FIRST-RATE)
DANGER	BO (FIFTH-RATE)
SECRECY	TEI (FOURTH-RATE)
AMUSEMENT	HEI (THIRD-RATE)
OWNER	Hitokoto-Nushi-sama

NOTES — Hitokoto-Nushi-sama's former attendants. While gods who have been driven to the other world are attended by the dead who have traveled there themselves, it would make sense for the living to be Hitokoto-Nushi-sama's followers, as that is the world where she resides. They were those whose lives others would have seen ended. They were those who beckoned to Mount Katsuragi like mist, and like mist they vanished.

KOU is the highest rank given, followed by OTSU, HEI, TEI, and BO.

Touge Oni

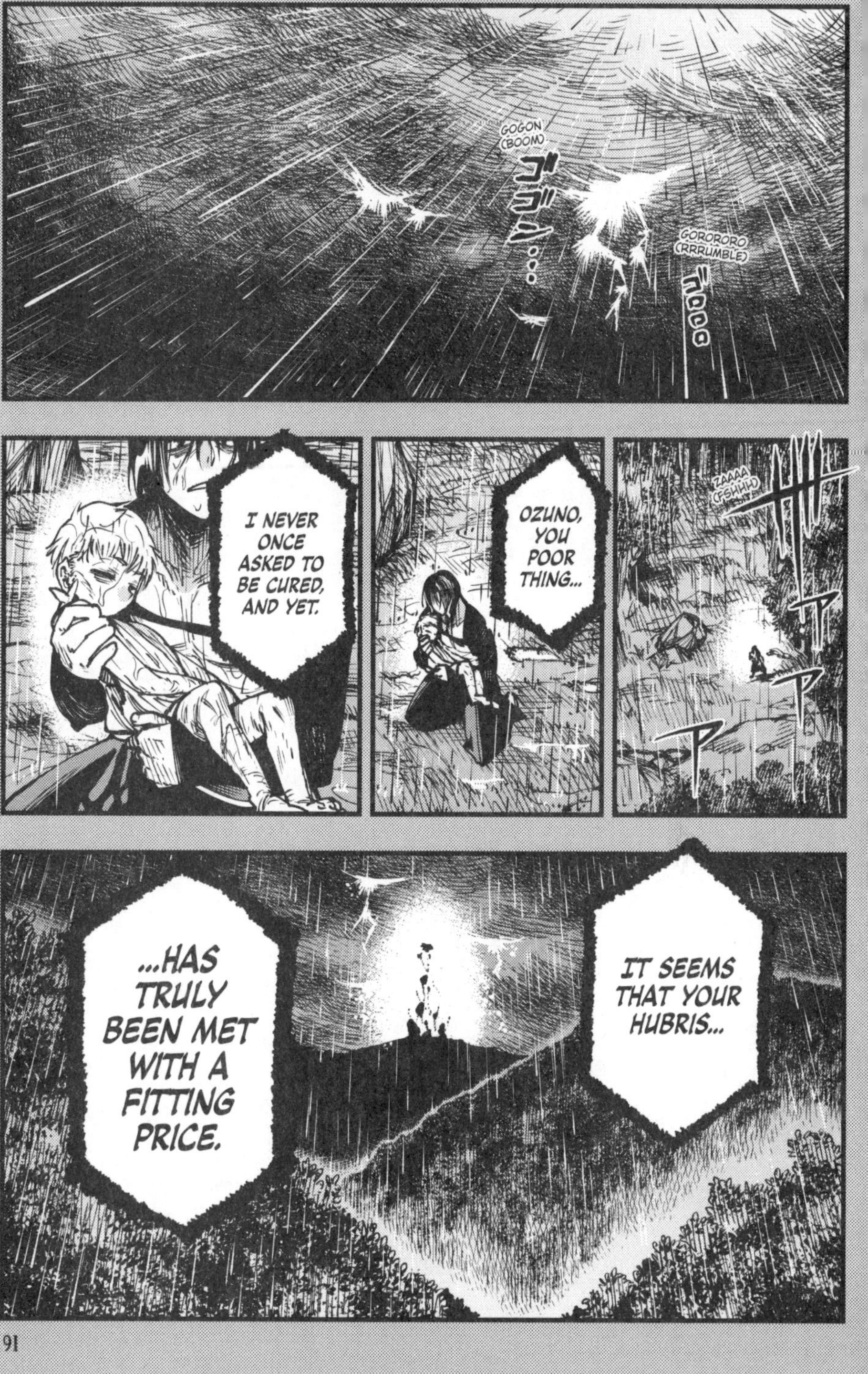
GOGON (BOOM)
ゴゴン…
GORORORO (RRRUMBLE)
ゴロロロ
ZAAAA (FSHHH)
ザァァァ
OZUNO, YOU POOR THING...
I NEVER ONCE ASKED TO BE CURED, AND YET.
IT SEEMS THAT YOUR HUBRIS...
...HAS TRULY BEEN MET WITH A FITTING PRICE.

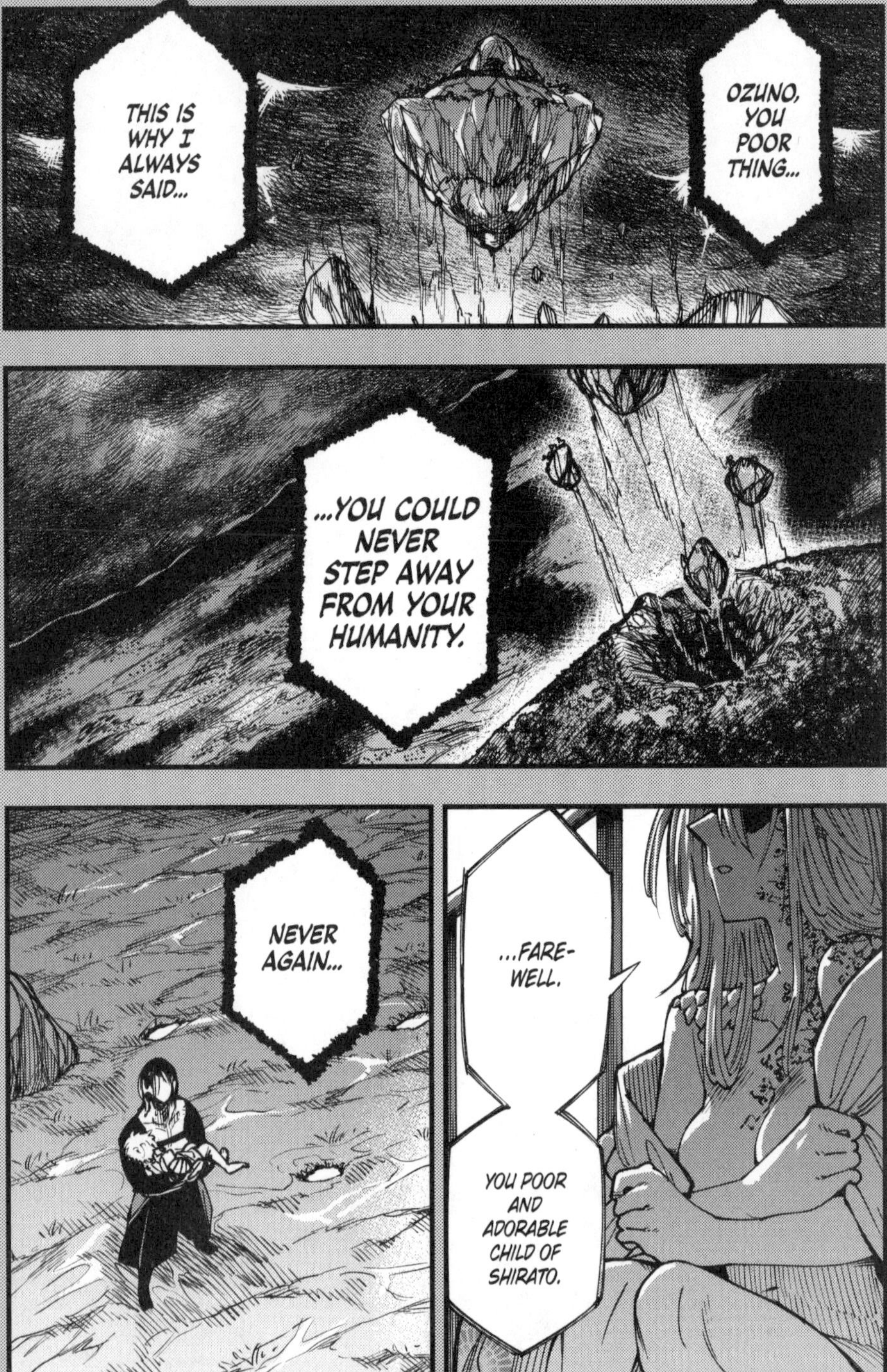
OZUNO, YOU POOR THING...
THIS IS WHY I ALWAYS SAID...
...YOU COULD NEVER STEP AWAY FROM YOUR HUMANITY.
...FARE-WELL.
YOU POOR AND ADORABLE CHILD OF SHIRATO.
NEVER AGAIN...

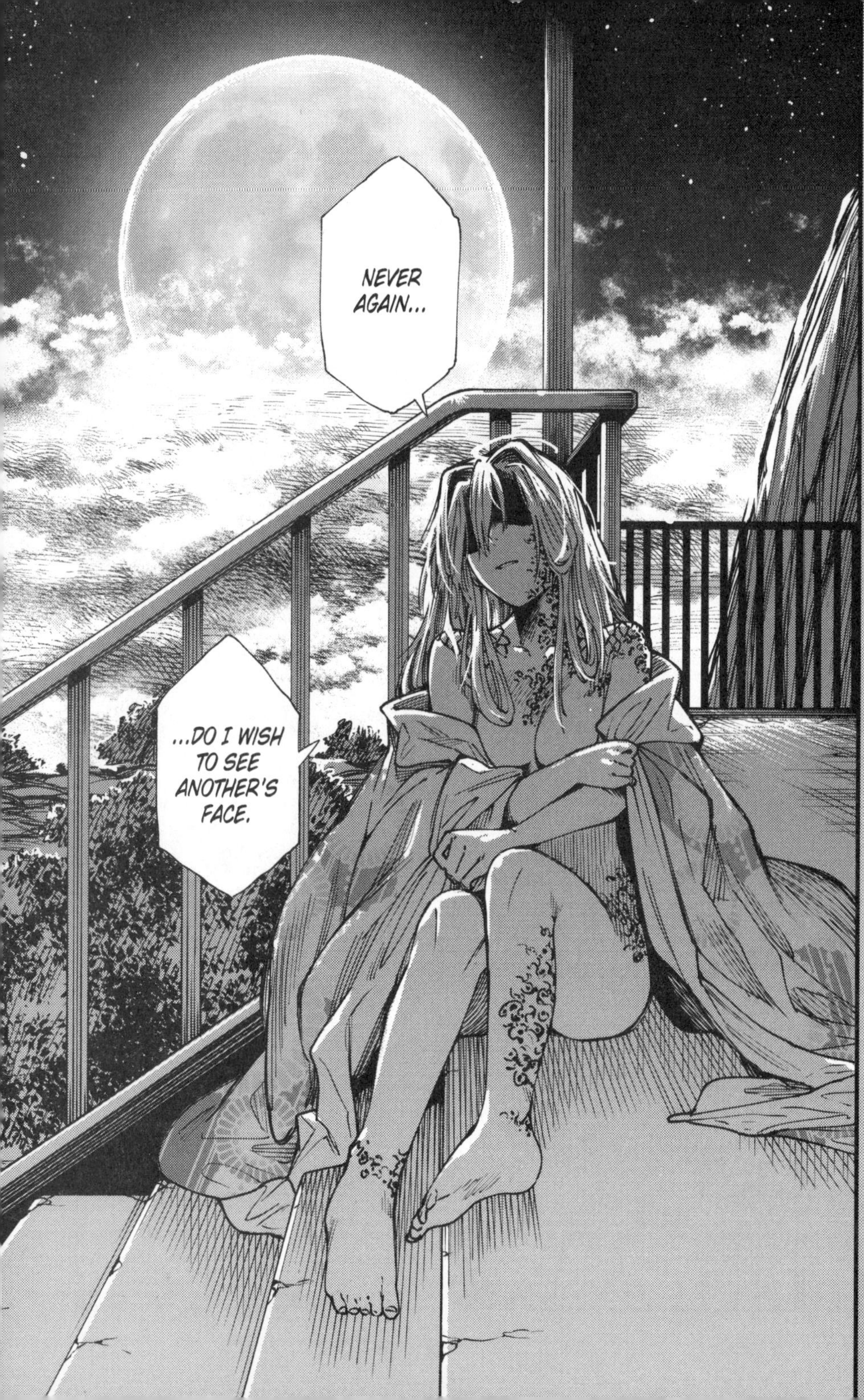
NEVER AGAIN...
...DO I WISH TO SEE ANOTHER'S FACE.

CHAPTER XIV TRAVEL THE STEPS

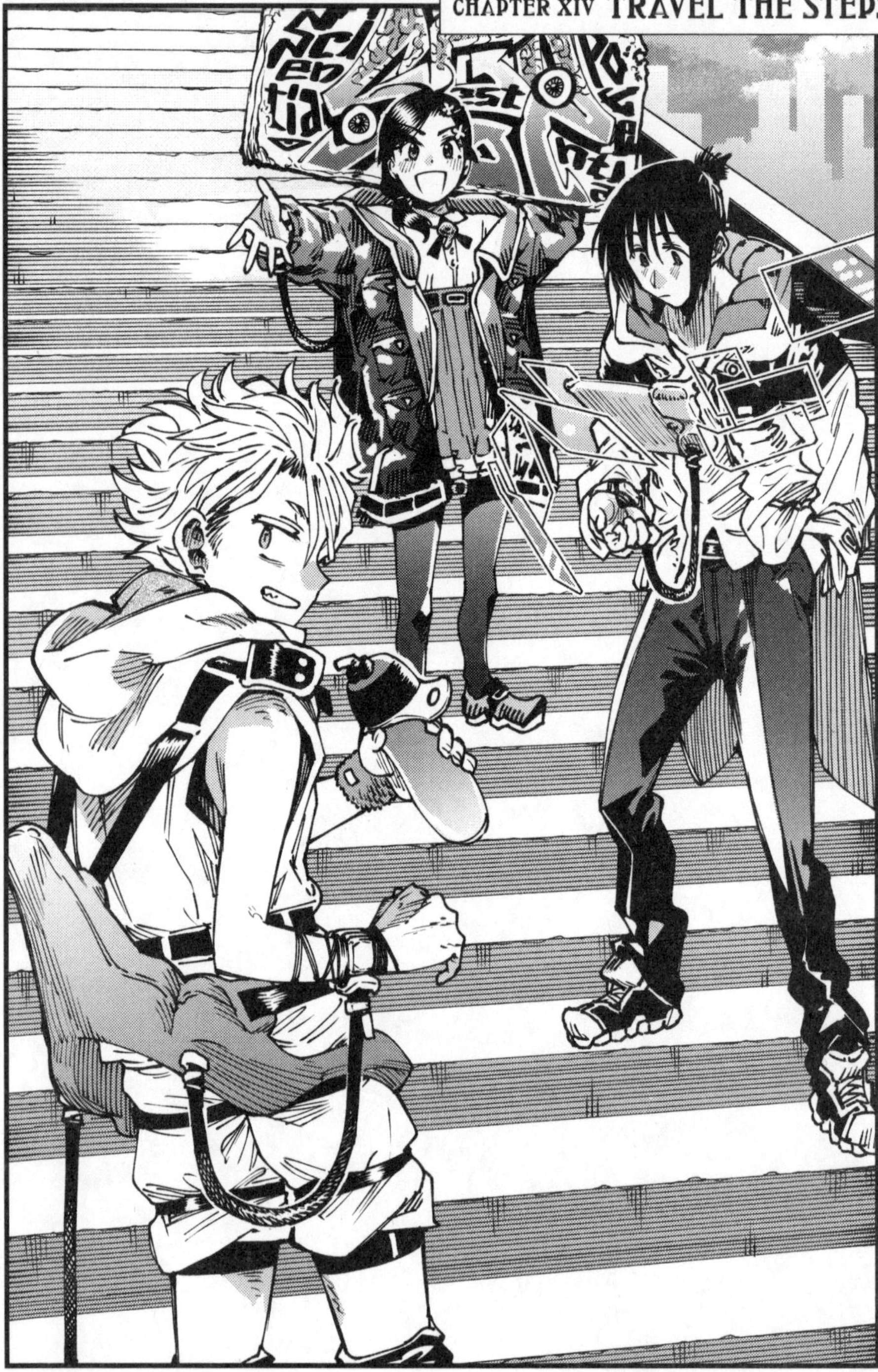

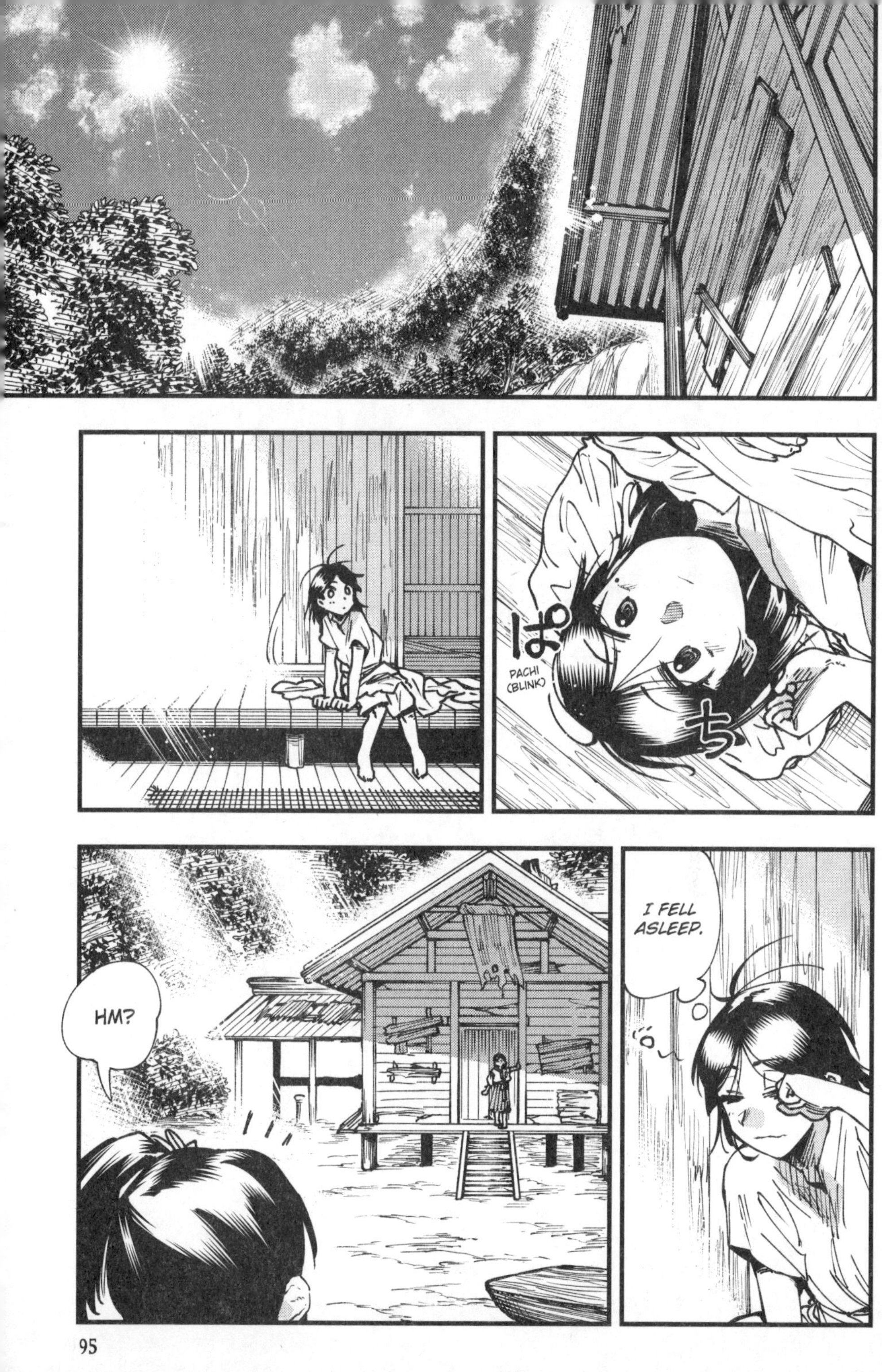
ぱち
PACHI (BLINK)
I FELL ASLEEP.
HM?

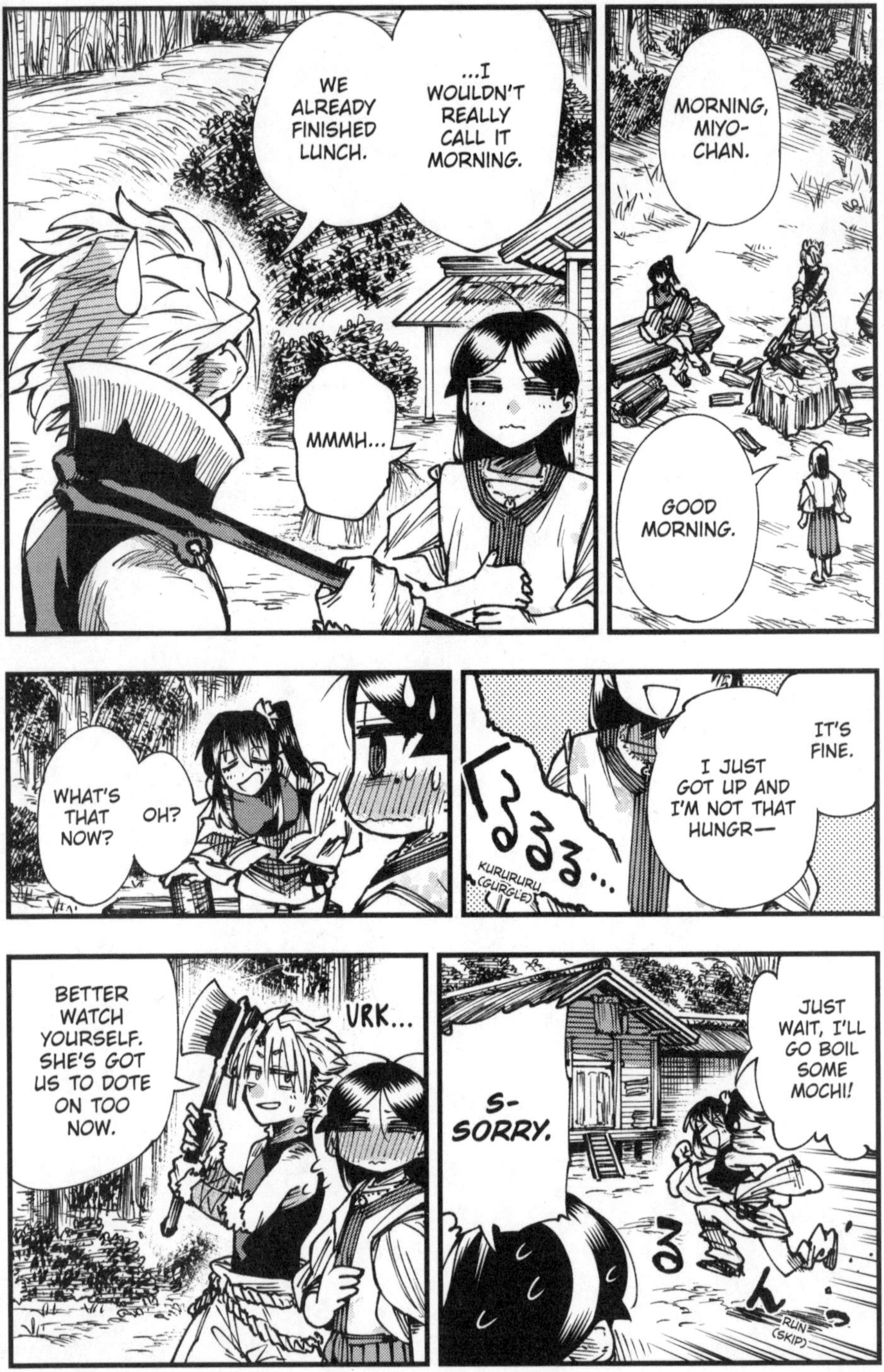
MORNING, MIYO-CHAN.
GOOD MORNING.
...I WOULDN'T REALLY CALL IT MORNING.
WE ALREADY FINISHED LUNCH.
MMMH...
IT'S FINE.
I JUST GOT UP AND I'M NOT THAT HUNGR—
くるるる...
KURURURU (GURGLE)
OH?
WHAT'S THAT NOW?
JUST WAIT, I'LL GO BOIL SOME MOCHI!
S-SORRY.
るんっ
RUN (SKIP)
URK...
BETTER WATCH YOURSELF. SHE'S GOT US TO DOTE ON TOO NOW.

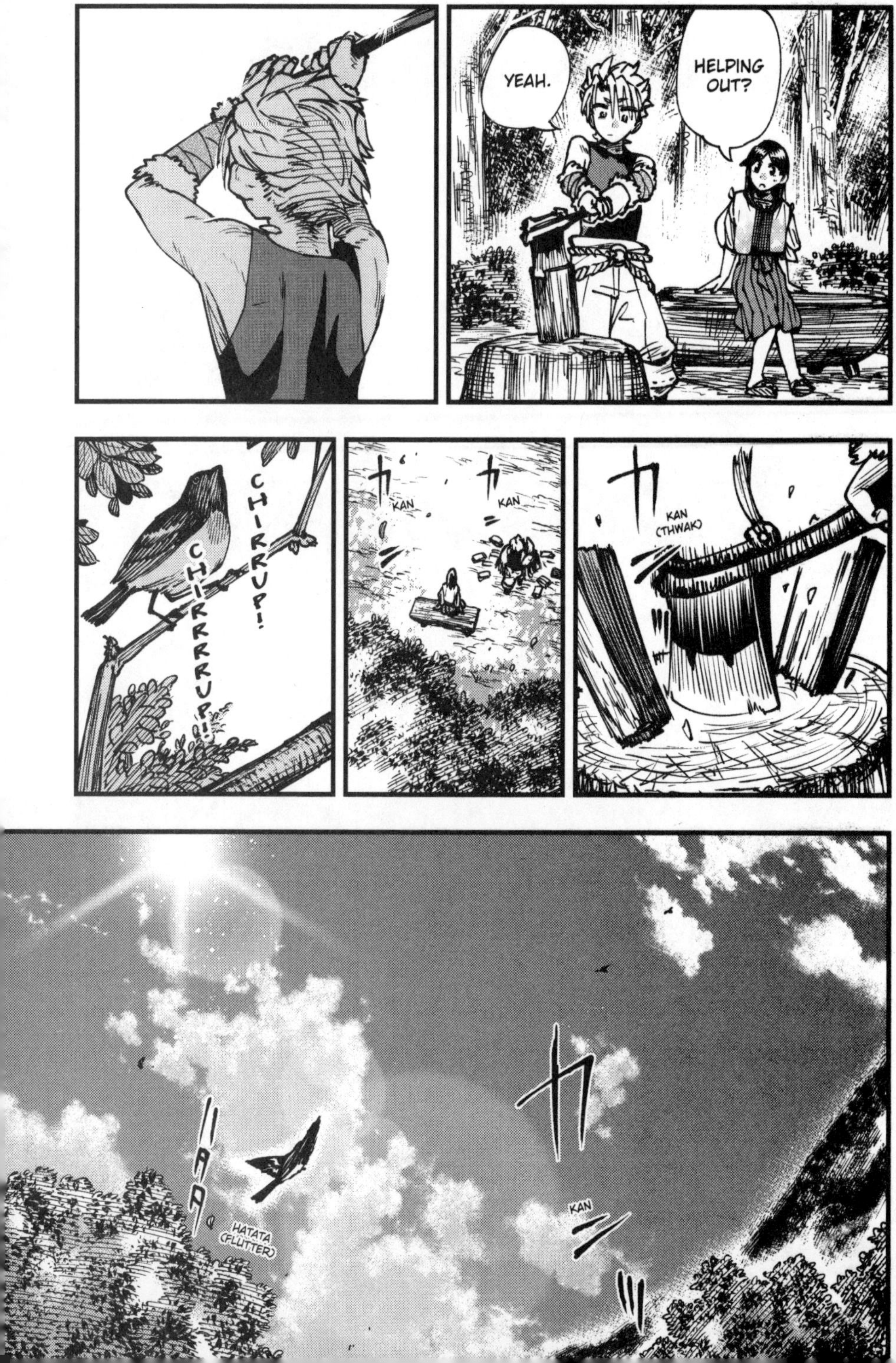
HELPING OUT?
YEAH.
KAN (THWAK)
KAN
KAN
CHIRRUP!
CHIRRRUP!
KAN
HATATA (FLUTTER)

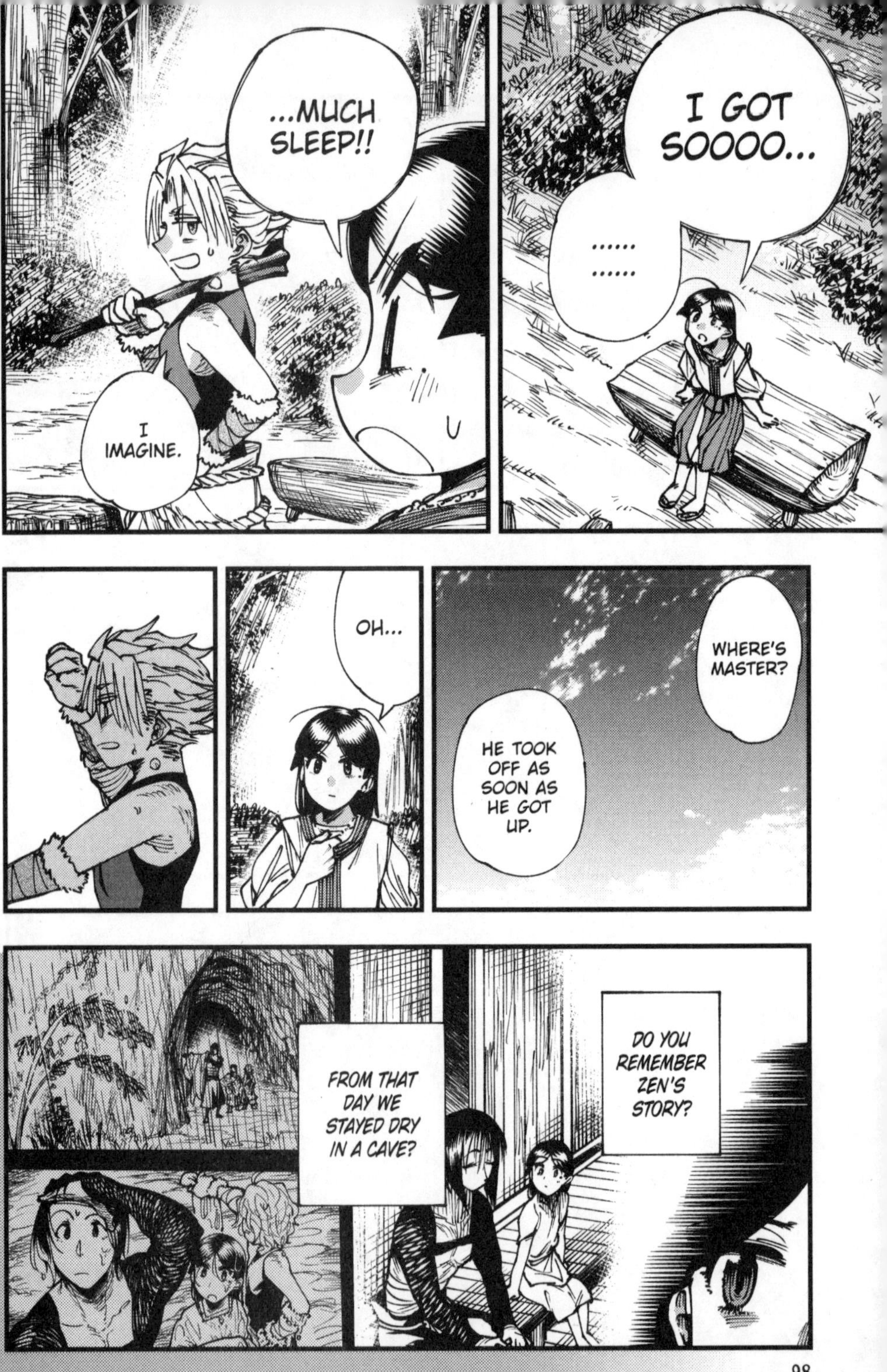
I GOT SOOOO...
......
......
...MUCH SLEEP!!
I IMAGINE.
WHERE'S MASTER?
HE TOOK OFF AS SOON AS HE GOT UP.
OH...
DO YOU REMEMBER ZEN'S STORY?
FROM THAT DAY WE STAYED DRY IN A CAVE?

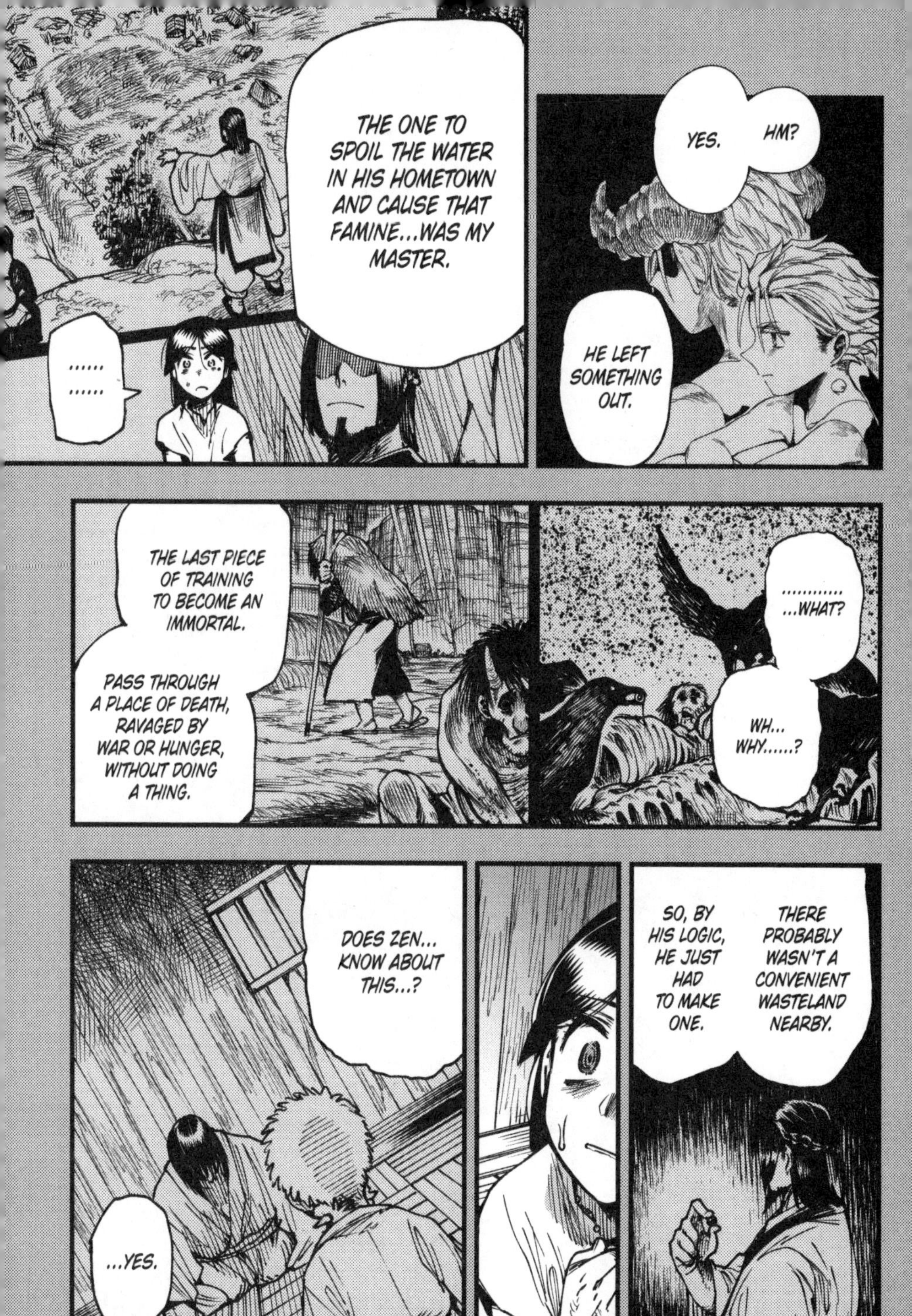
HM?
YES.
HE LEFT SOMETHING OUT.
THE ONE TO SPOIL THE WATER IN HIS HOMETOWN AND CAUSE THAT FAMINE...WAS MY MASTER.
....
....WHAT?
WH... WHY......?
THE LAST PIECE OF TRAINING TO BECOME AN IMMORTAL.
PASS THROUGH A PLACE OF DEATH, RAVAGED BY WAR OR HUNGER, WITHOUT DOING A THING.
THERE PROBABLY WASN'T A CONVENIENT WASTELAND NEARBY.
SO, BY HIS LOGIC, HE JUST HAD TO MAKE ONE.
DOES ZEN... KNOW ABOUT THIS...?
...YES.

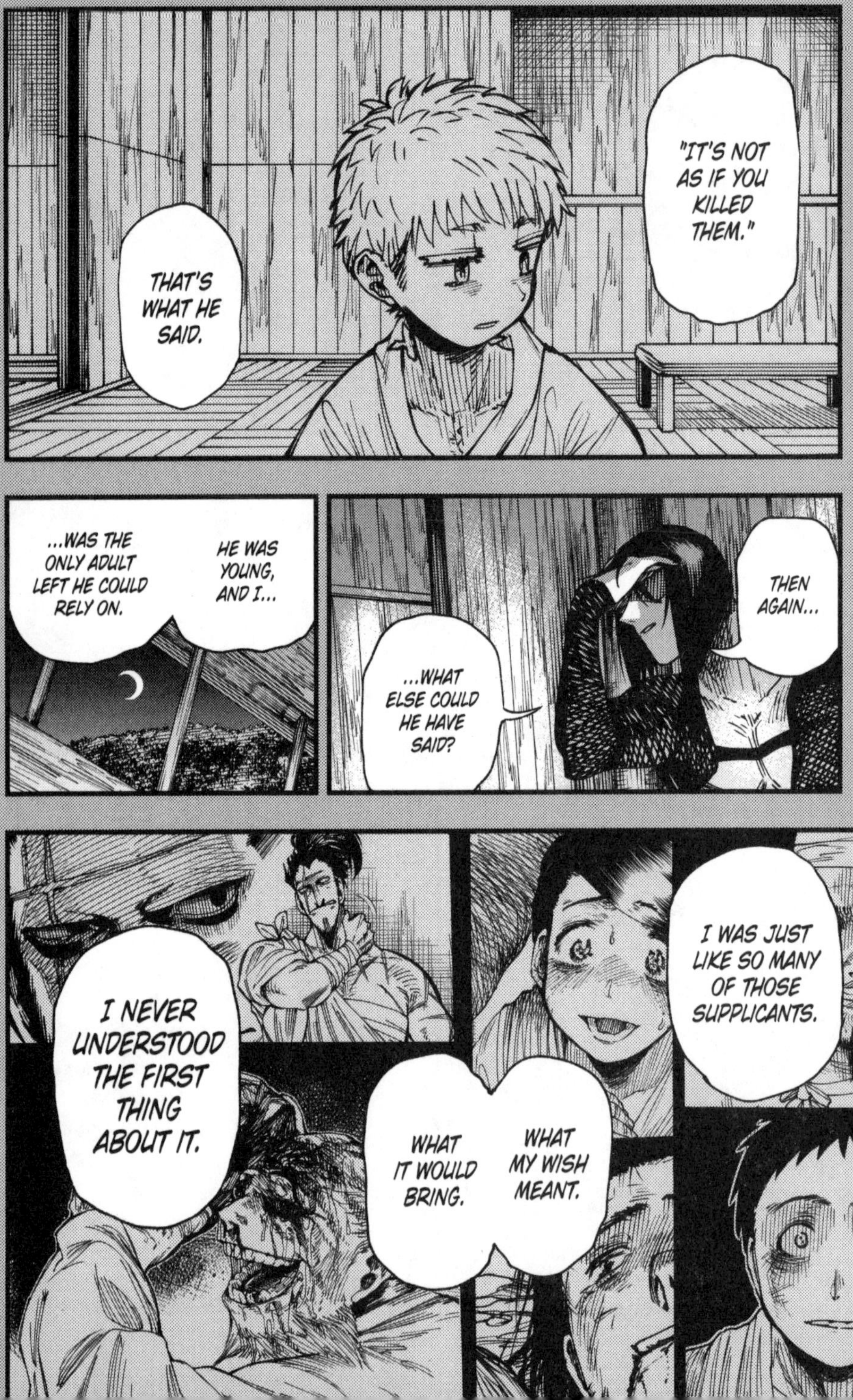
"IT'S NOT AS IF YOU KILLED THEM."
THAT'S WHAT HE SAID.
THEN AGAIN...
...WHAT ELSE COULD HE HAVE SAID?
HE WAS YOUNG, AND I...
...WAS THE ONLY ADULT LEFT HE COULD RELY ON.
I WAS JUST LIKE SO MANY OF THOSE SUPPLICANTS.
WHAT MY WISH MEANT.
WHAT IT WOULD BRING.
I NEVER UNDERSTOOD THE FIRST THING ABOUT IT.

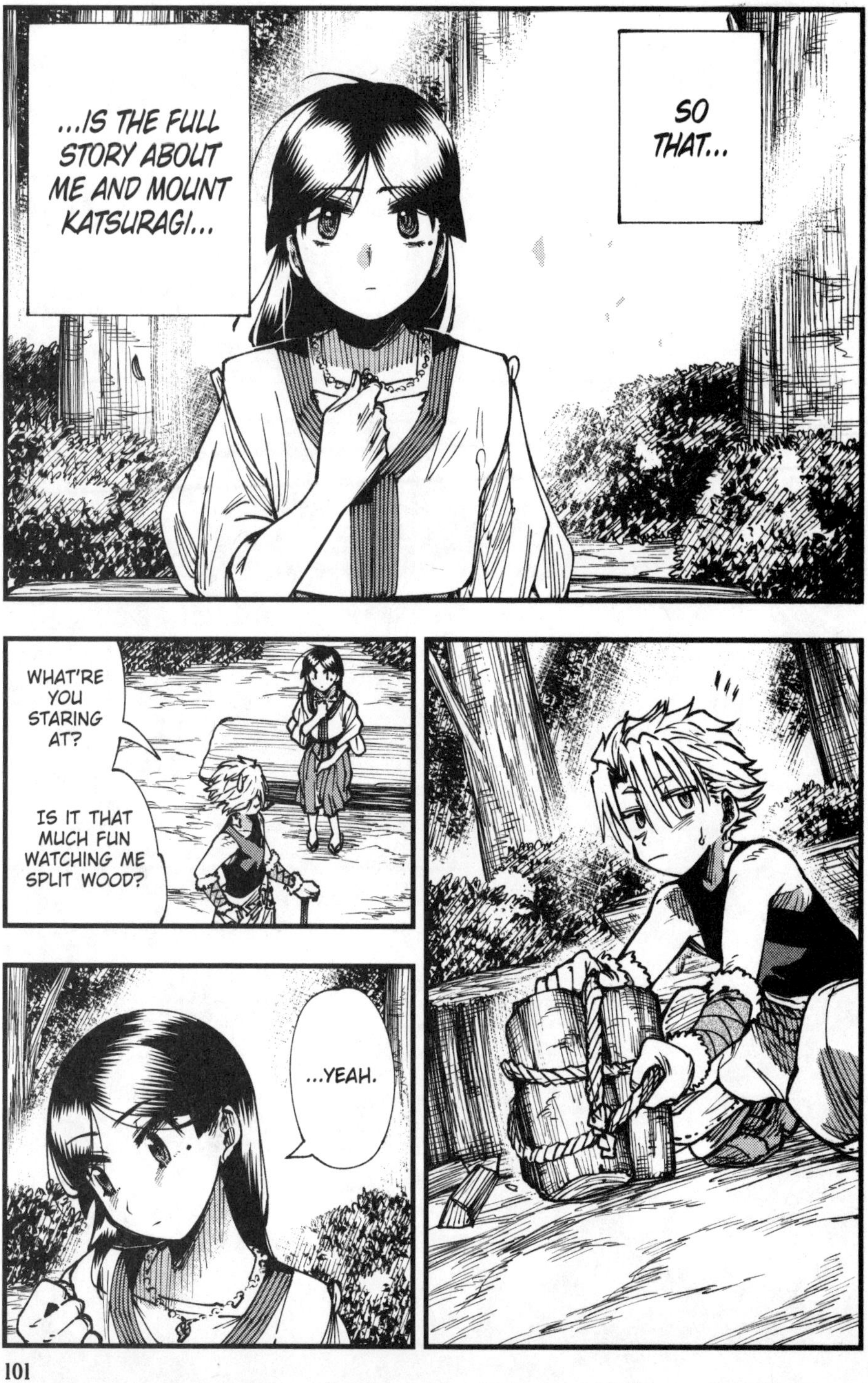
SO THAT...
...IS THE FULL STORY ABOUT ME AND MOUNT KATSURAGI...
WHAT'RE YOU STARING AT?
IS IT THAT MUCH FUN WATCHING ME SPLIT WOOD?
...YEAH.

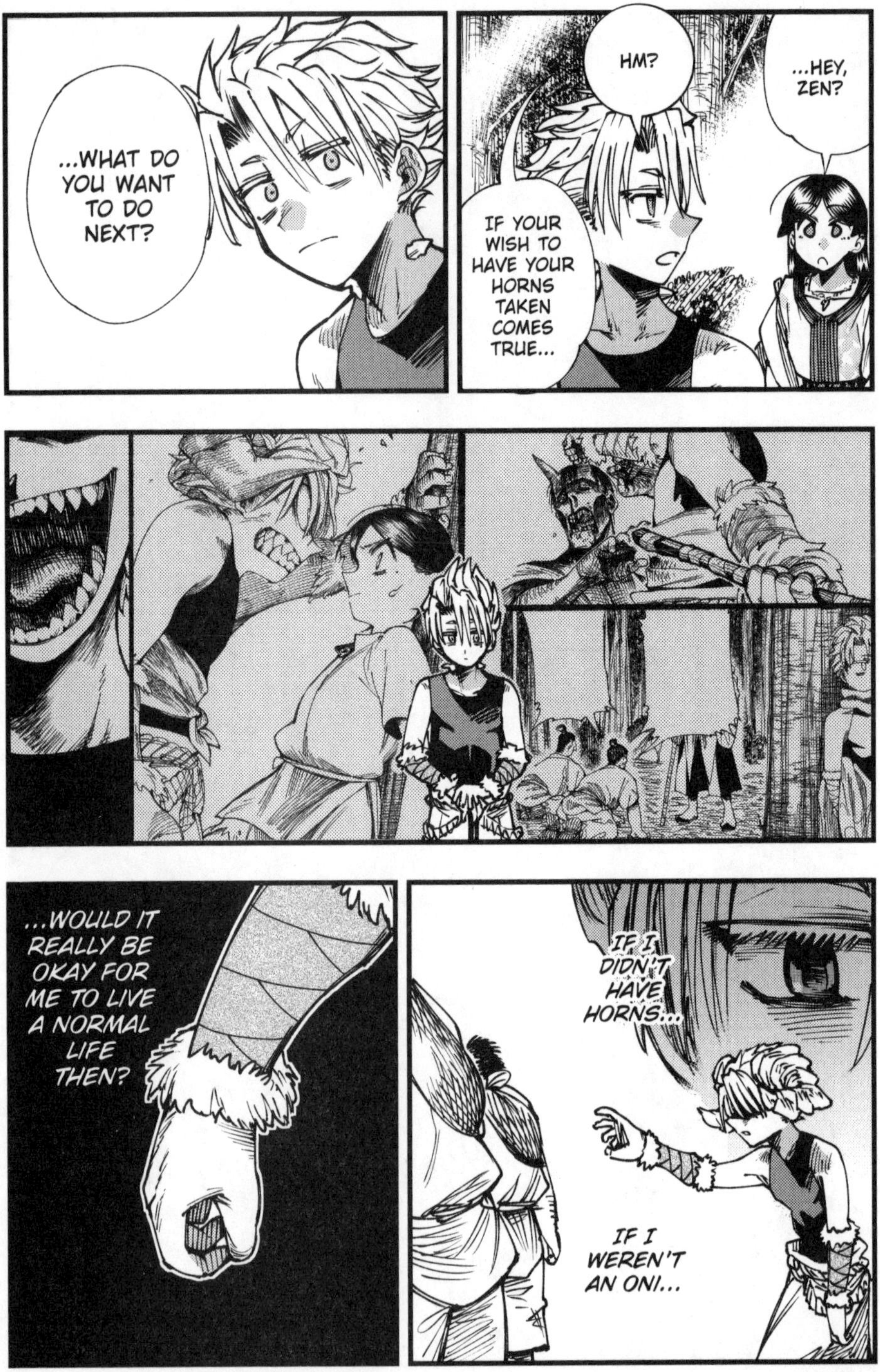
...HEY, ZEN?
HM?
IF YOUR WISH TO HAVE YOUR HORNS TAKEN COMES TRUE...
...WHAT DO YOU WANT TO DO NEXT?
IF I DIDN'T HAVE HORNS...
IF I WEREN'T AN ONI...
...WOULD IT REALLY BE OKAY FOR ME TO LIVE A NORMAL LIFE THEN?

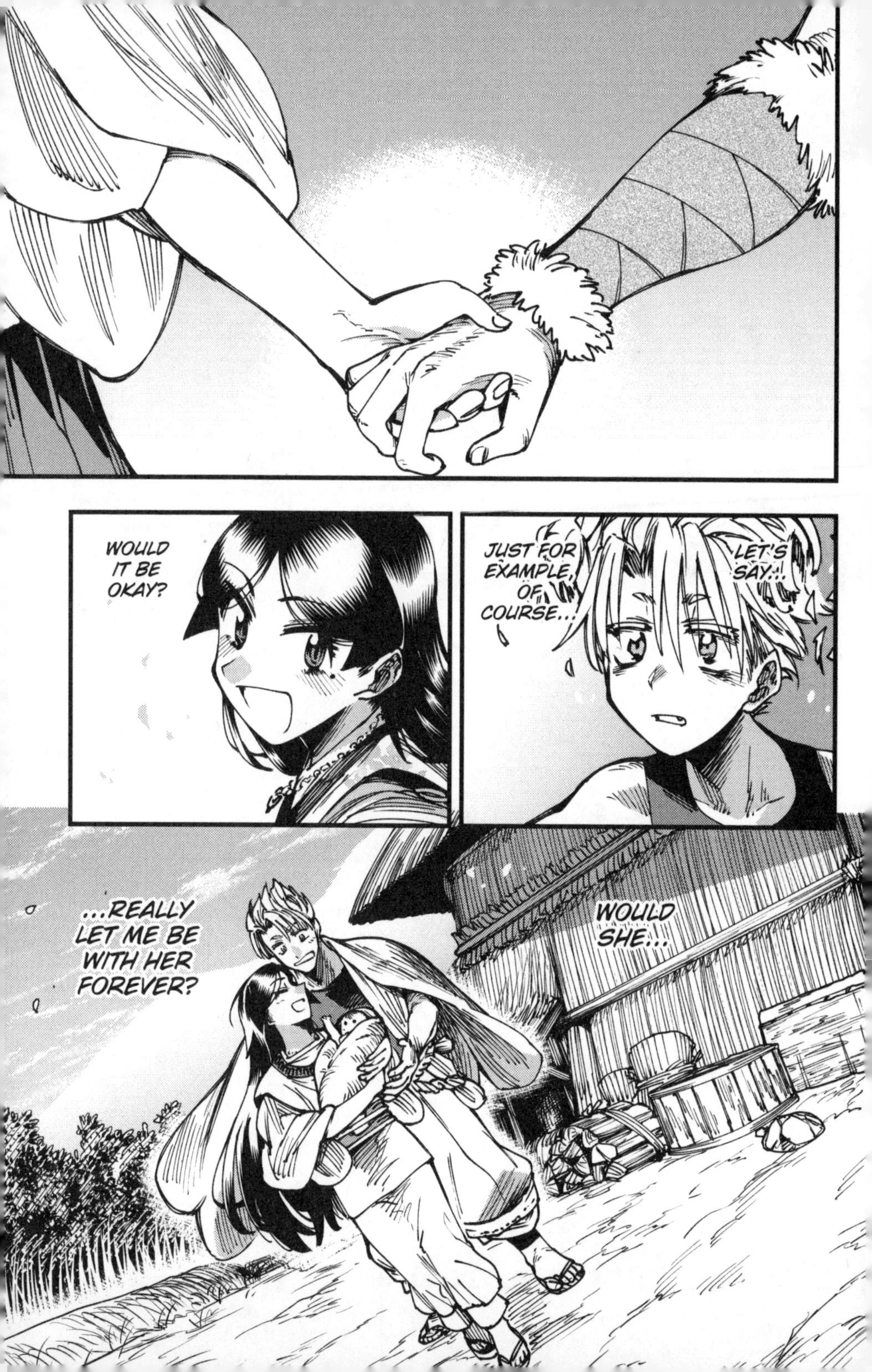
LET'S SAY...
JUST FOR EXAMPLE, OF COURSE...
WOULD IT BE OKAY?
WOULD SHE...
...REALLY LET ME BE WITH HER FOREVER?

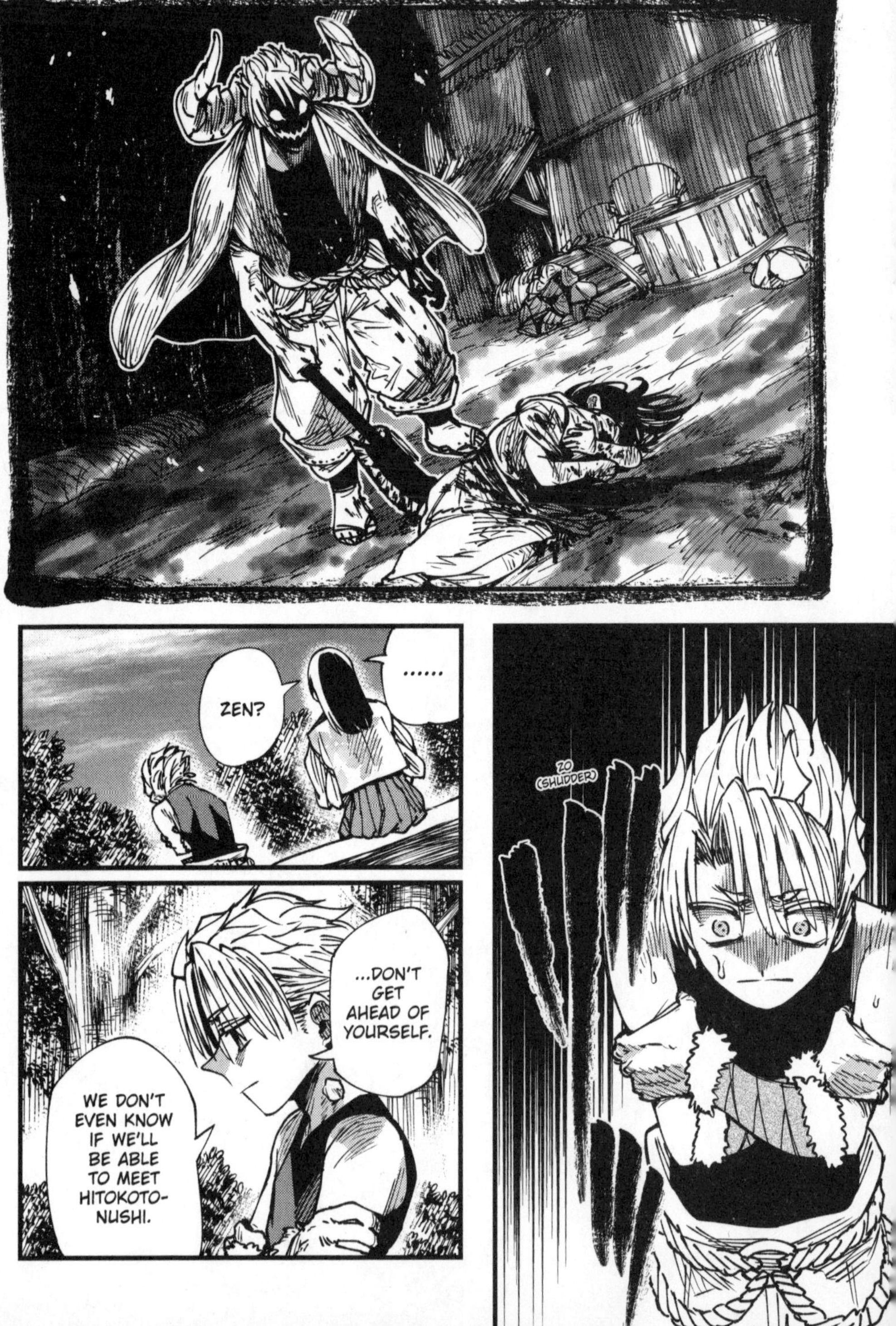
ZO (SHUDDER)
......
ZEN?
...DON'T GET AHEAD OF YOURSELF.
WE DON'T EVEN KNOW IF WE'LL BE ABLE TO MEET HITOKOTO-NUSHI.

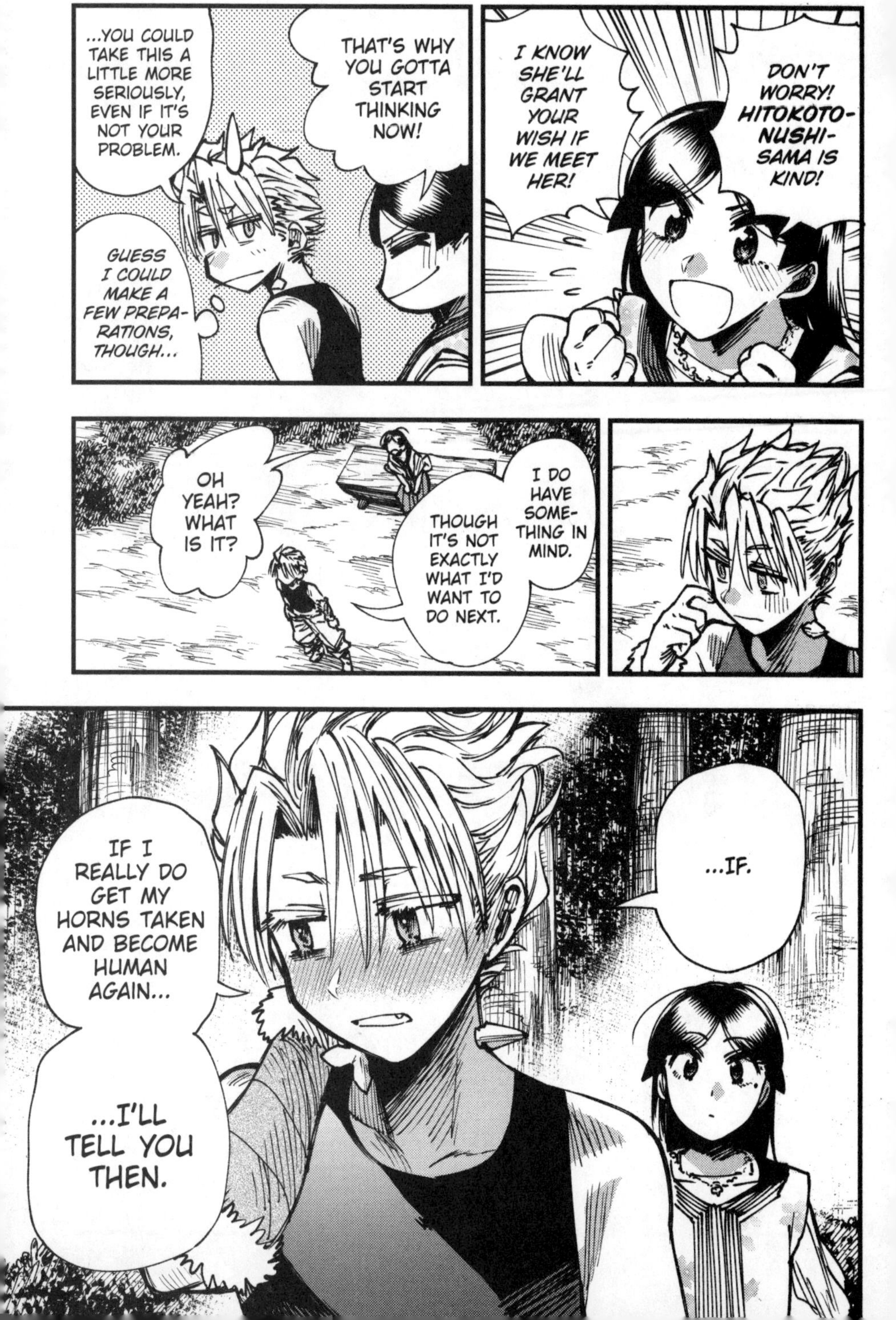
DON'T WORRY! HITOKOTO-NUSHI-SAMA IS KIND!
I KNOW SHE'LL GRANT YOUR WISH IF WE MEET HER!
THAT'S WHY YOU GOTTA START THINKING NOW!
...YOU COULD TAKE THIS A LITTLE MORE SERIOUSLY, EVEN IF IT'S NOT YOUR PROBLEM.
GUESS I COULD MAKE A FEW PREPARATIONS, THOUGH...
I DO HAVE SOMETHING IN MIND.
THOUGH IT'S NOT EXACTLY WHAT I'D WANT TO DO NEXT.
OH YEAH? WHAT IS IT?
...IF.
IF I REALLY DO GET MY HORNS TAKEN AND BECOME HUMAN AGAIN...
...I'LL TELL YOU THEN.

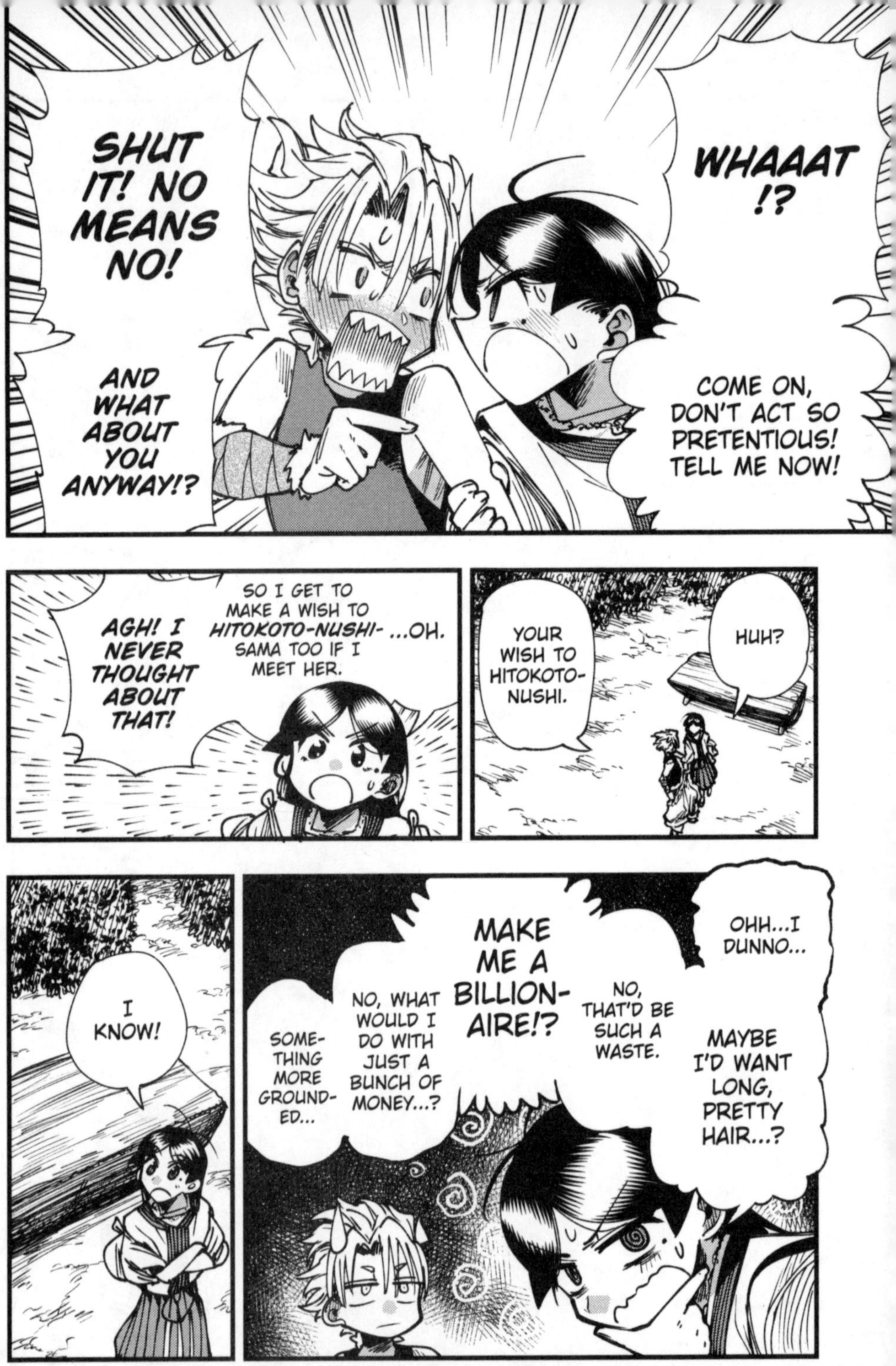
WHAAAT!?
COME ON, DON'T ACT SO PRETENTIOUS! TELL ME NOW!
SHUT IT! NO MEANS NO!
AND WHAT ABOUT YOU ANYWAY!?
HUH?
YOUR WISH TO HITOKOTO-NUSHI.
...OH.
SO I GET TO MAKE A WISH TO HITOKOTO-NUSHI-SAMA TOO IF I MEET HER.
AGH! I NEVER THOUGHT ABOUT THAT!
OHH...I DUNNO...
MAYBE I'D WANT LONG, PRETTY HAIR...?
NO, THAT'D BE SUCH A WASTE.
MAKE ME A BILLIONAIRE!?
NO, WHAT WOULD I DO WITH JUST A BUNCH OF MONEY...?
SOMETHING MORE GROUNDED...
I KNOW!

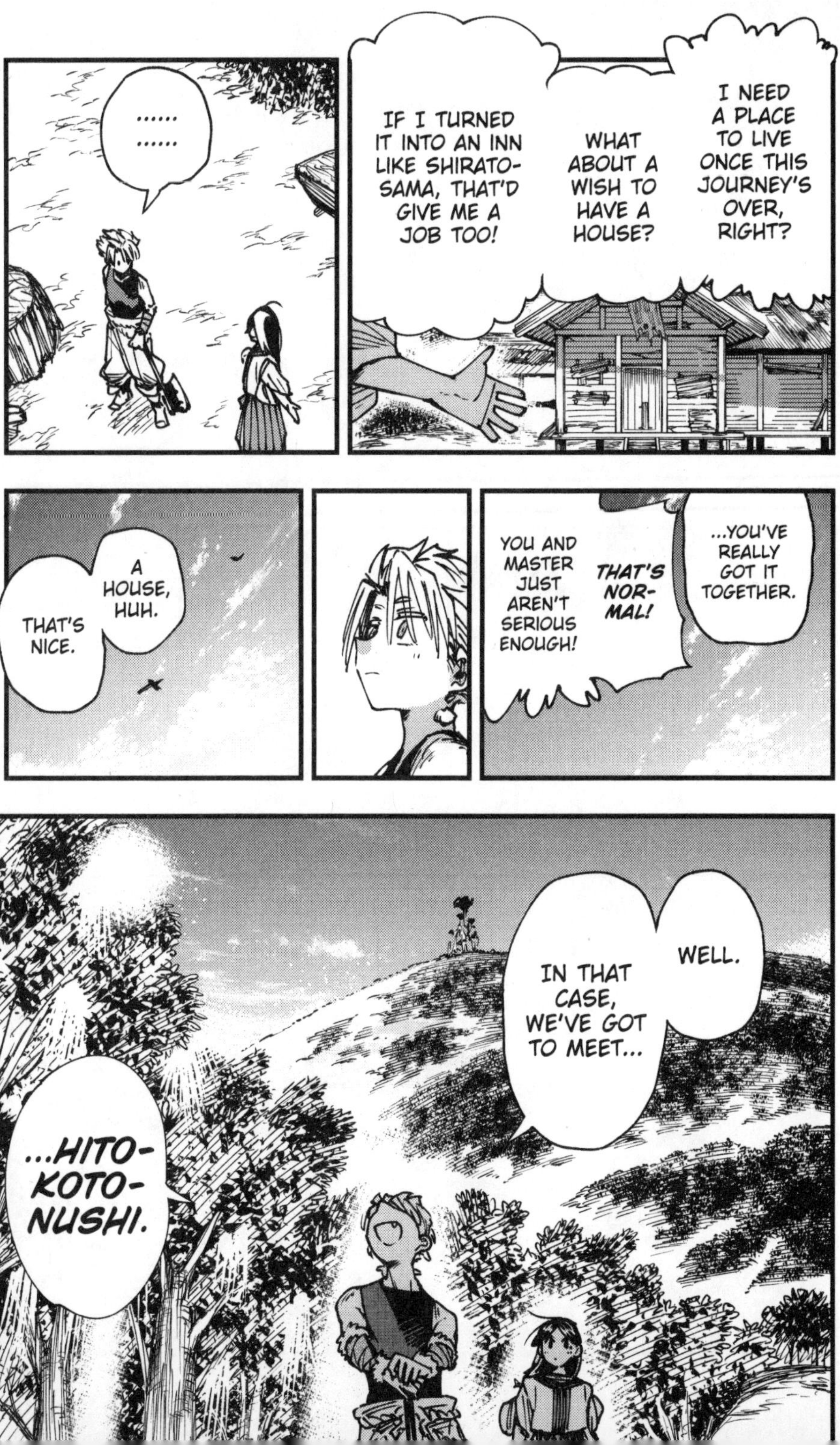
I NEED A PLACE TO LIVE ONCE THIS JOURNEY'S OVER, RIGHT?
WHAT ABOUT A WISH TO HAVE A HOUSE?
IF I TURNED IT INTO AN INN LIKE SHIRATO-SAMA, THAT'D GIVE ME A JOB TOO!
......
......
...YOU'VE REALLY GOT IT TOGETHER.
THAT'S NOR-MAL!
YOU AND MASTER JUST AREN'T SERIOUS ENOUGH!
A HOUSE, HUH.
THAT'S NICE.
WELL.
IN THAT CASE, WE'VE GOT TO MEET...
...HITO-KOTO-NUSHI.

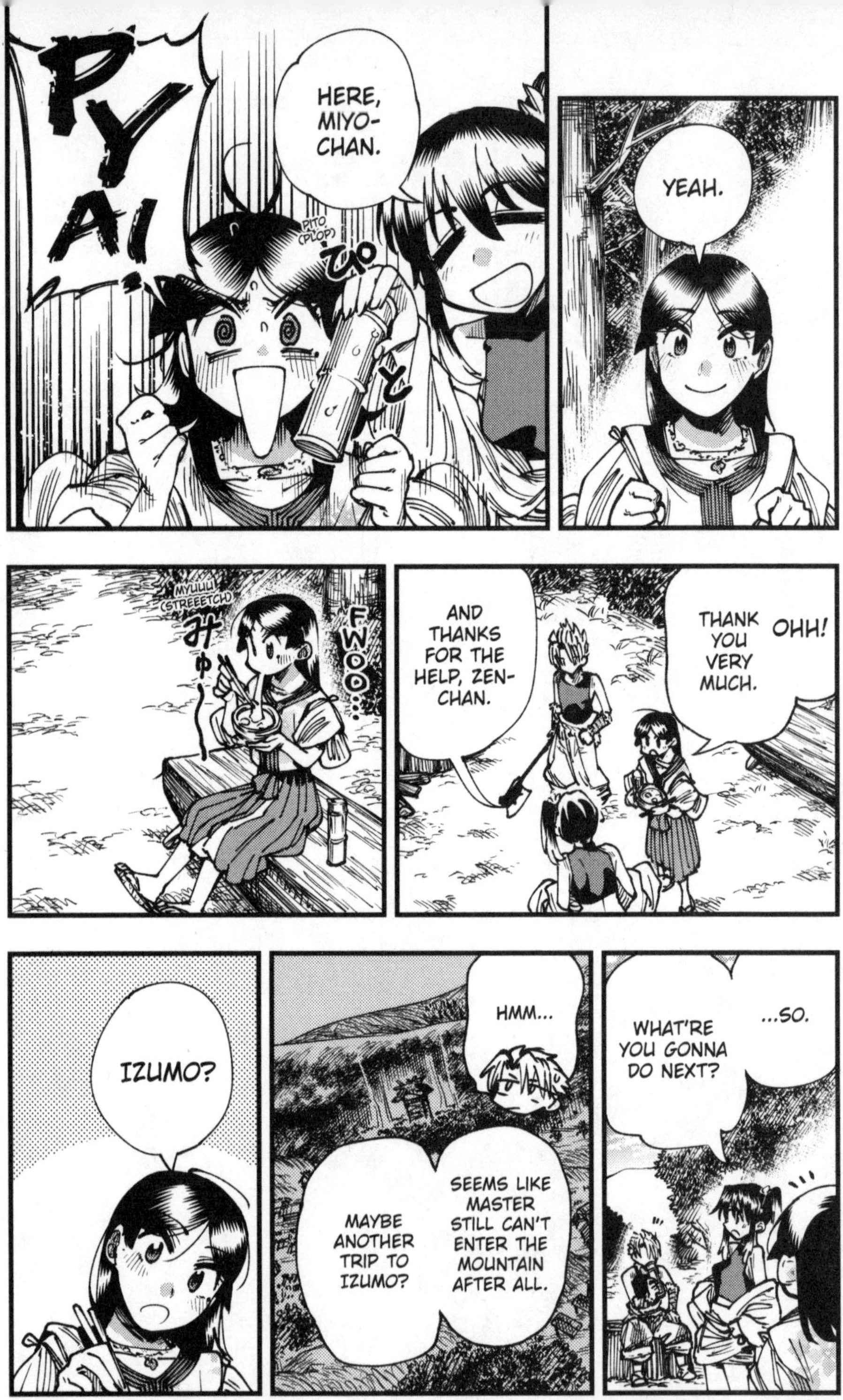
YEAH.
HERE, MIYO-CHAN.
PITO (PLOP)
ぴと
PYAI
THANK YOU VERY MUCH.
OHH!
AND THANKS FOR THE HELP, ZEN-CHAN.
MYUUU (STREEETCH)
みゅ〜
FWOO...
...SO.
WHAT'RE YOU GONNA DO NEXT?
HMM...
SEEMS LIKE MASTER STILL CAN'T ENTER THE MOUNTAIN AFTER ALL.
MAYBE ANOTHER TRIP TO IZUMO?
IZUMO?

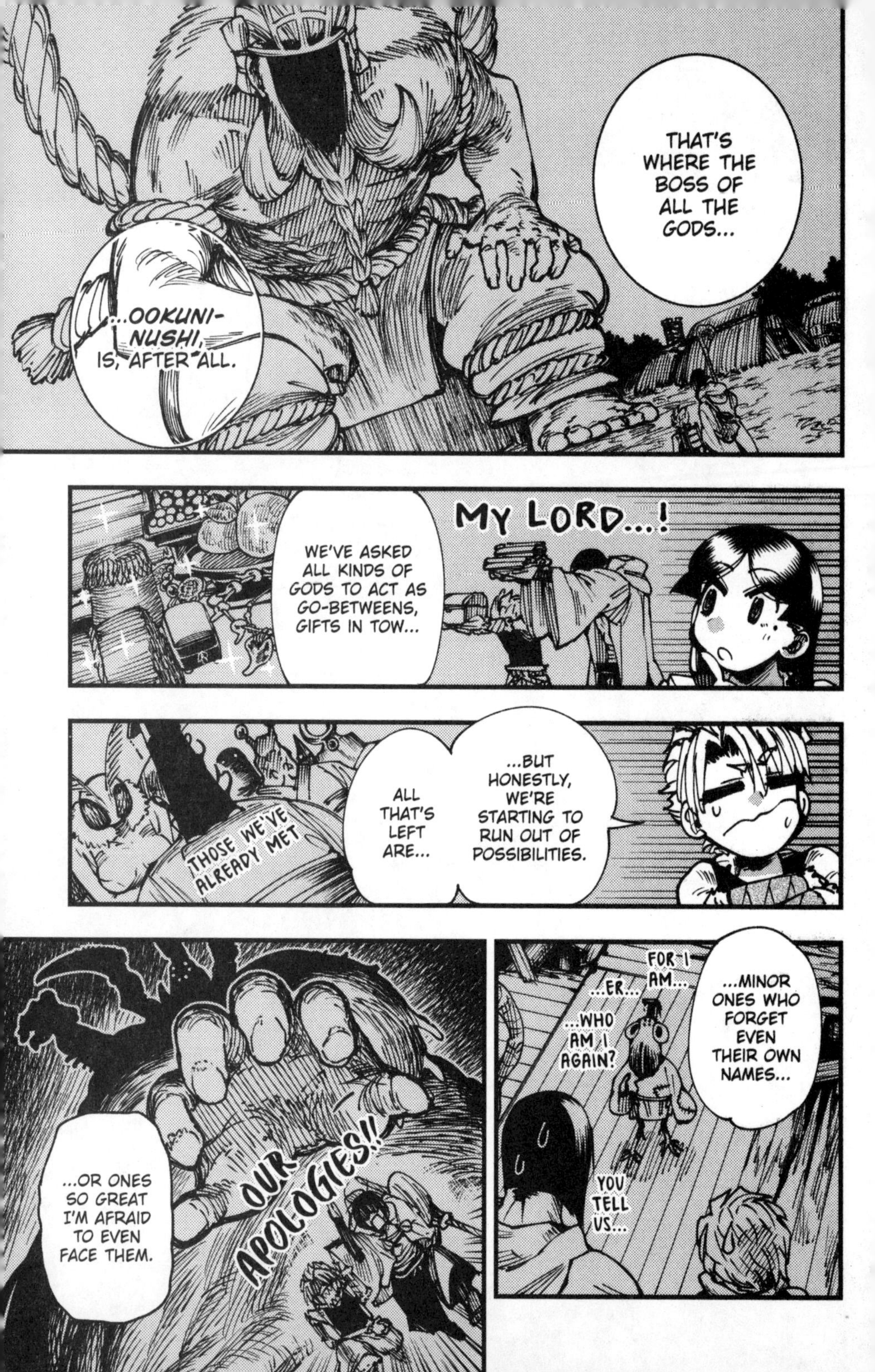
THAT'S WHERE THE BOSS OF ALL THE GODS...
...OOKUNI-NUSHI, IS, AFTER ALL.
MY LORD...!
WE'VE ASKED ALL KINDS OF GODS TO ACT AS GO-BETWEENS, GIFTS IN TOW...
...BUT HONESTLY, WE'RE STARTING TO RUN OUT OF POSSIBILITIES.
ALL THAT'S LEFT ARE...
THOSE WE'VE ALREADY MET
...MINOR ONES WHO FORGET EVEN THEIR OWN NAMES...
FOR I AM...
...ER...
...WHO AM I AGAIN?
YOU TELL US...
...OR ONES SO GREAT I'M AFRAID TO EVEN FACE THEM.
OUR APOLOGIES!!

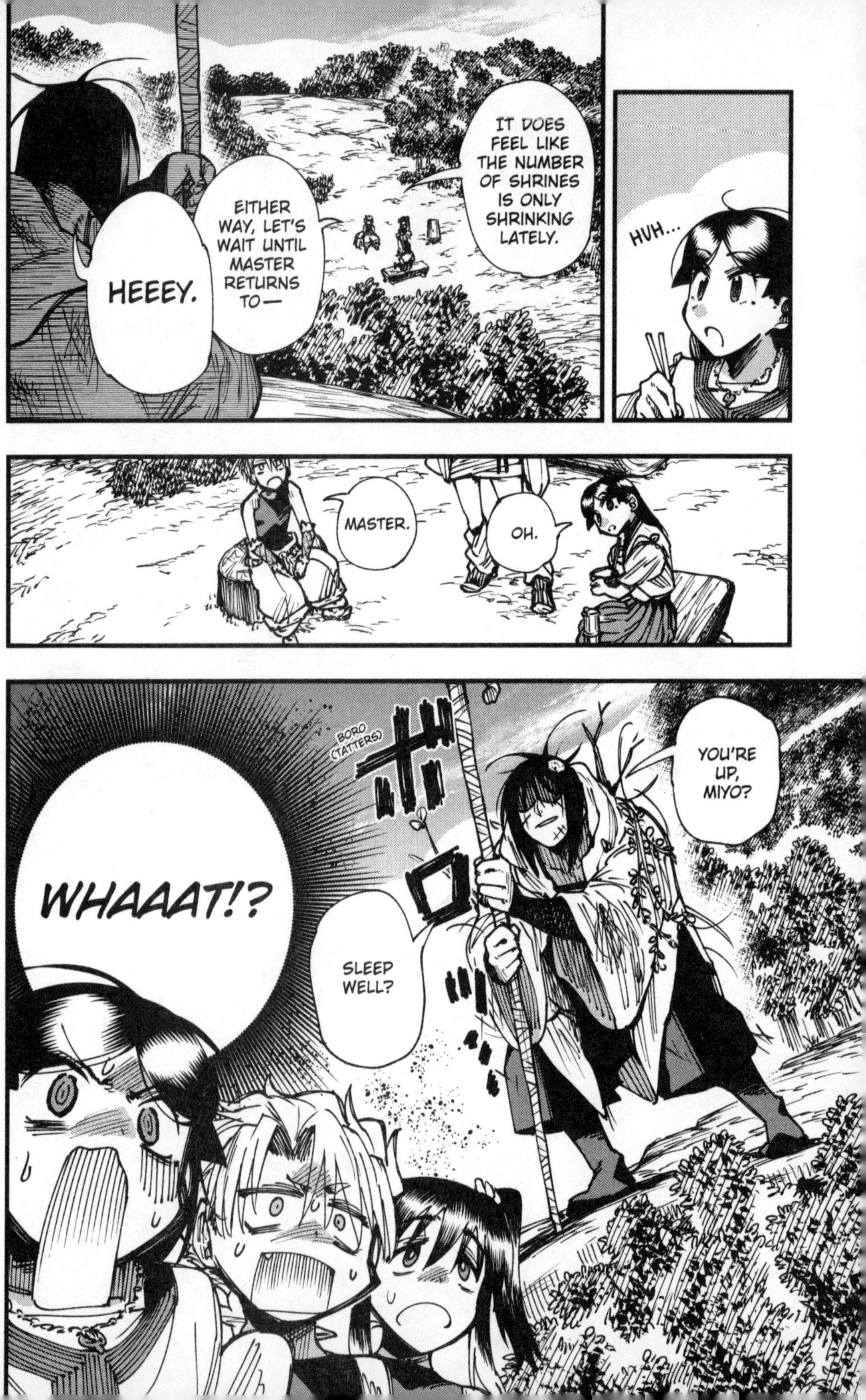
HUH...
IT DOES FEEL LIKE THE NUMBER OF SHRINES IS ONLY SHRINKING LATELY.
EITHER WAY, LET'S WAIT UNTIL MASTER RETURNS TO—
HEEEY.
OH.
MASTER.
YOU'RE UP, MIYO?
BORO (TATTERS)
SLEEP WELL?
WHAAAT!?

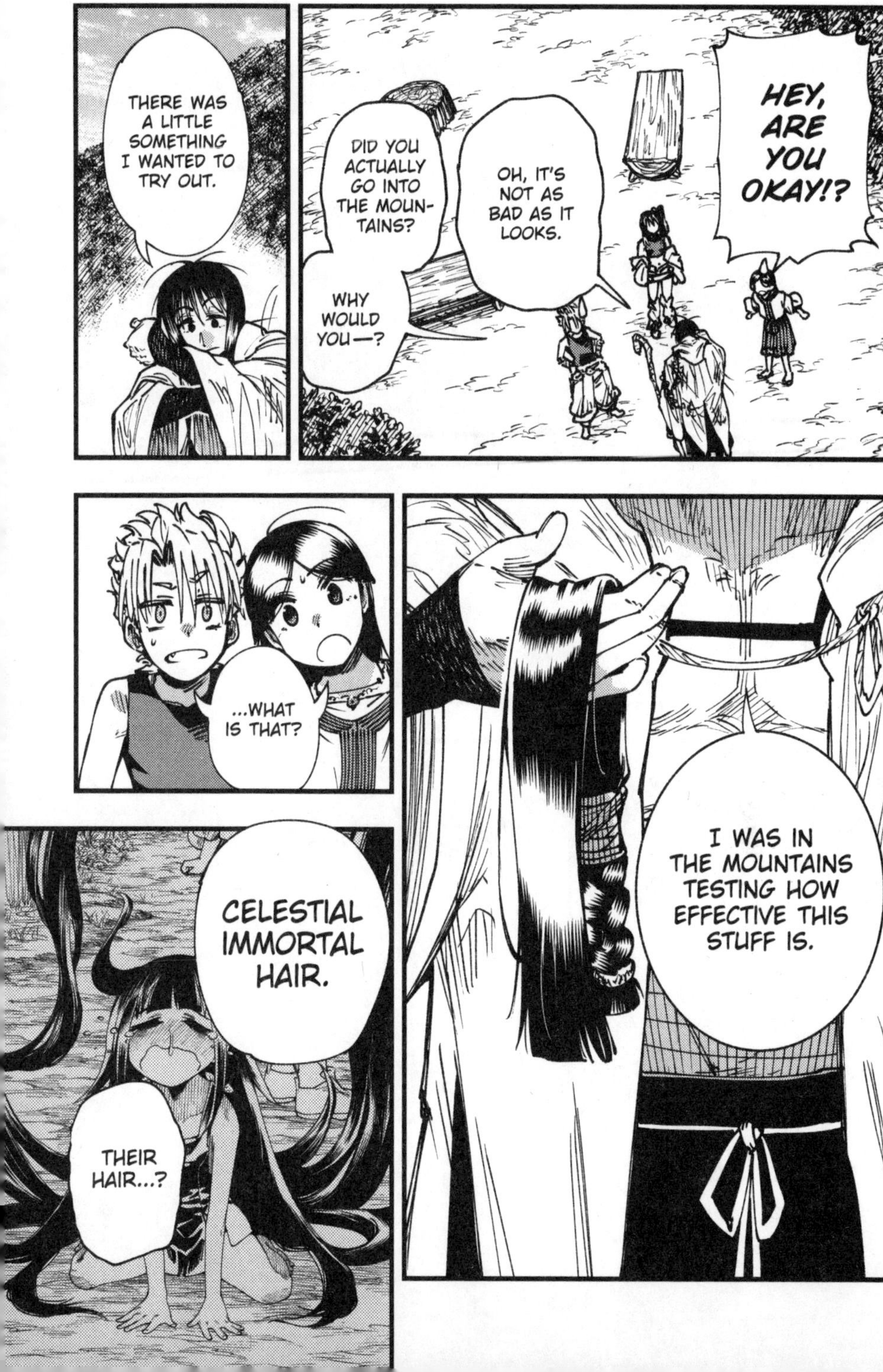
HEY, ARE YOU OKAY!?
OH, IT'S NOT AS BAD AS IT LOOKS.
DID YOU ACTUALLY GO INTO THE MOUN-TAINS?
WHY WOULD YOU—?
THERE WAS A LITTLE SOMETHING I WANTED TO TRY OUT.
I WAS IN THE MOUNTAINS TESTING HOW EFFECTIVE THIS STUFF IS.
...WHAT IS THAT?
CELESTIAL IMMORTAL HAIR.
THEIR HAIR...?

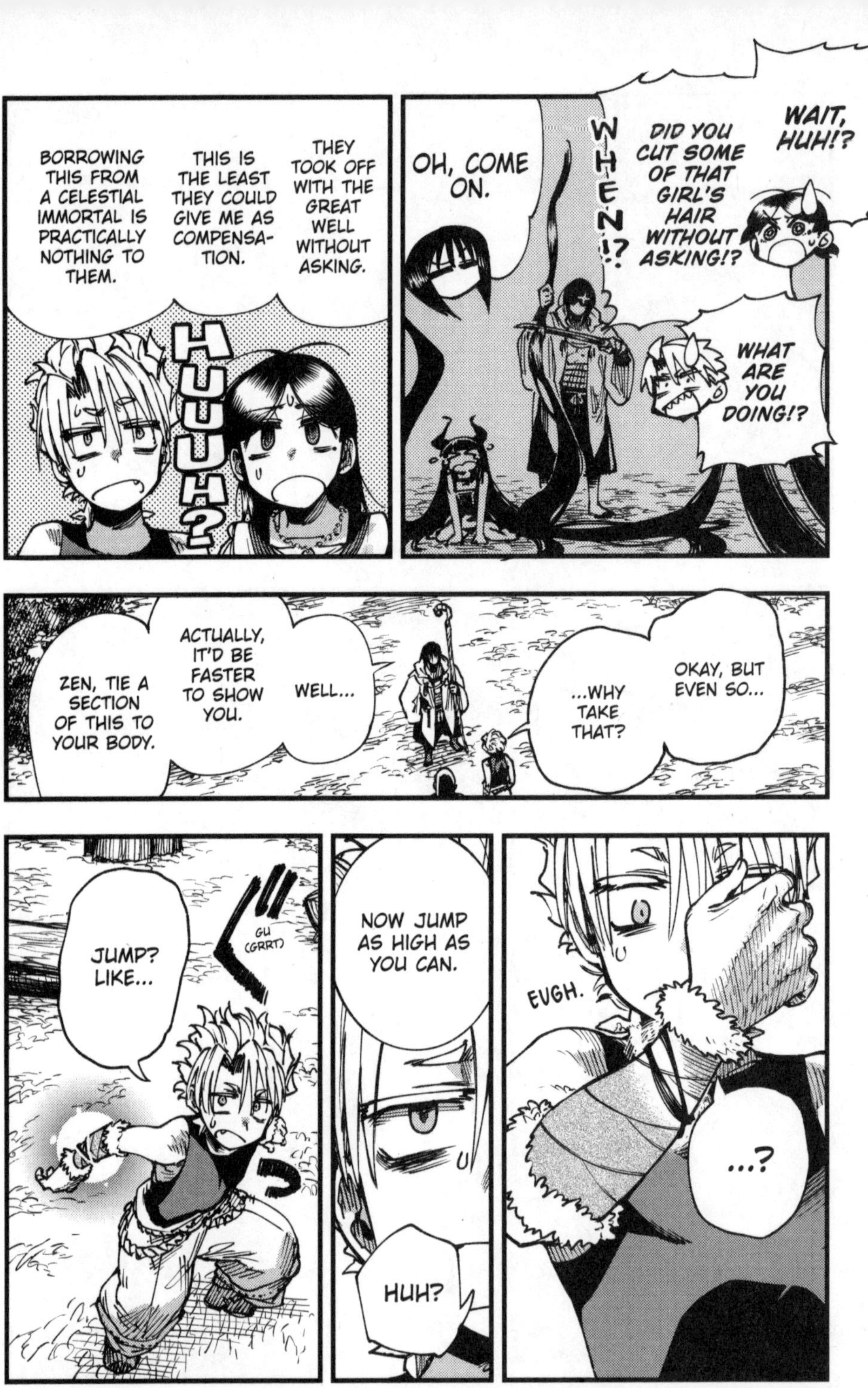

WAIT, HUH!?
DID YOU CUT SOME OF THAT GIRL'S HAIR WITHOUT ASKING!?
WHEN!?
WHAT ARE YOU DOING!?
OH, COME ON.
THEY TOOK OFF WITH THE GREAT WELL WITHOUT ASKING.
THIS IS THE LEAST THEY COULD GIVE ME AS COMPENSATION.
BORROWING THIS FROM A CELESTIAL IMMORTAL IS PRACTICALLY NOTHING TO THEM.
HUUUH?
OKAY, BUT EVEN SO...
...WHY TAKE THAT?
WELL...
ACTUALLY, IT'D BE FASTER TO SHOW YOU.
ZEN, TIE A SECTION OF THIS TO YOUR BODY.
EUGH.
...?
NOW JUMP AS HIGH AS YOU CAN.
HUH?
GU (GRRT)
JUMP? LIKE...

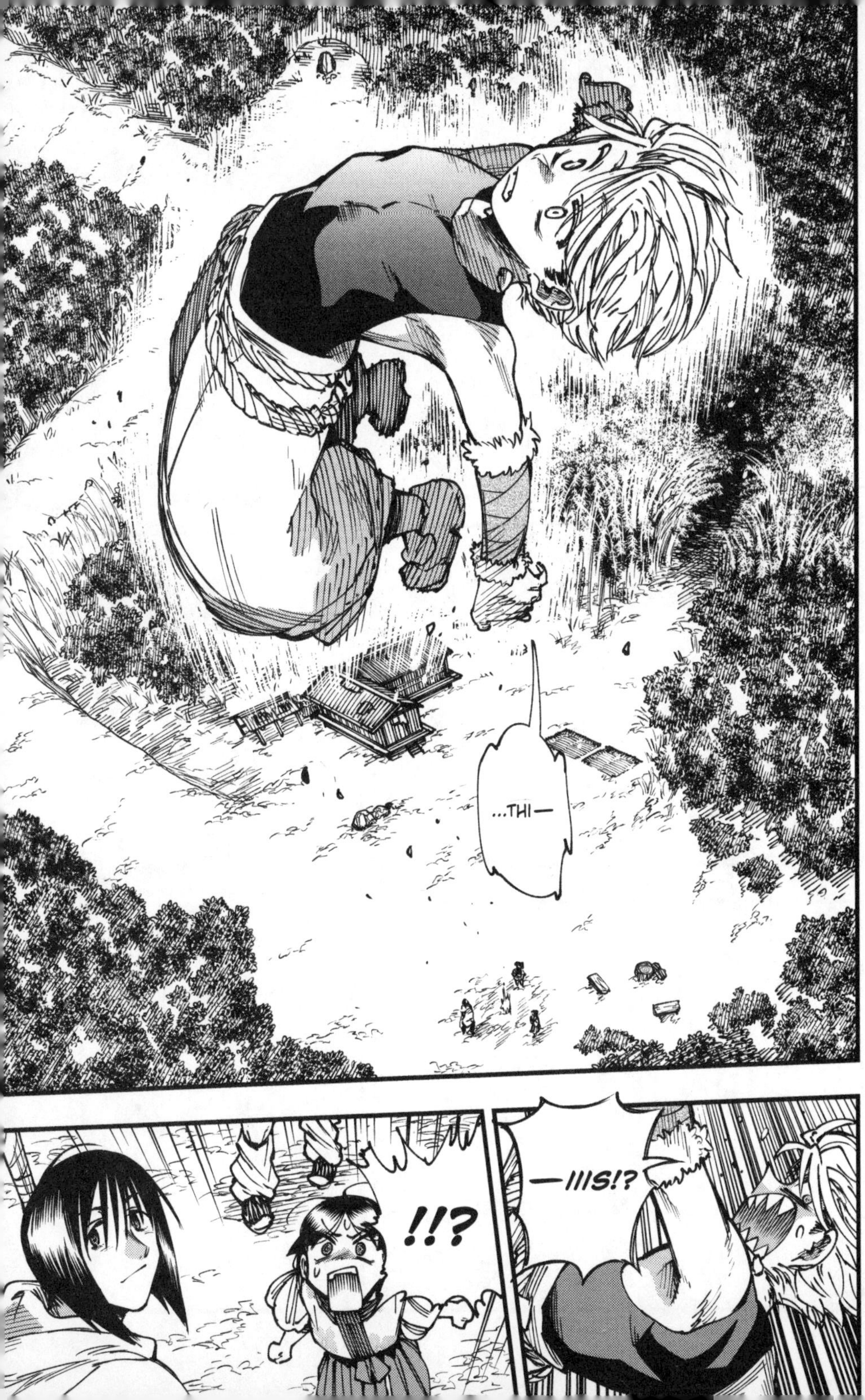
...THI—
—IIIS!?
!!?

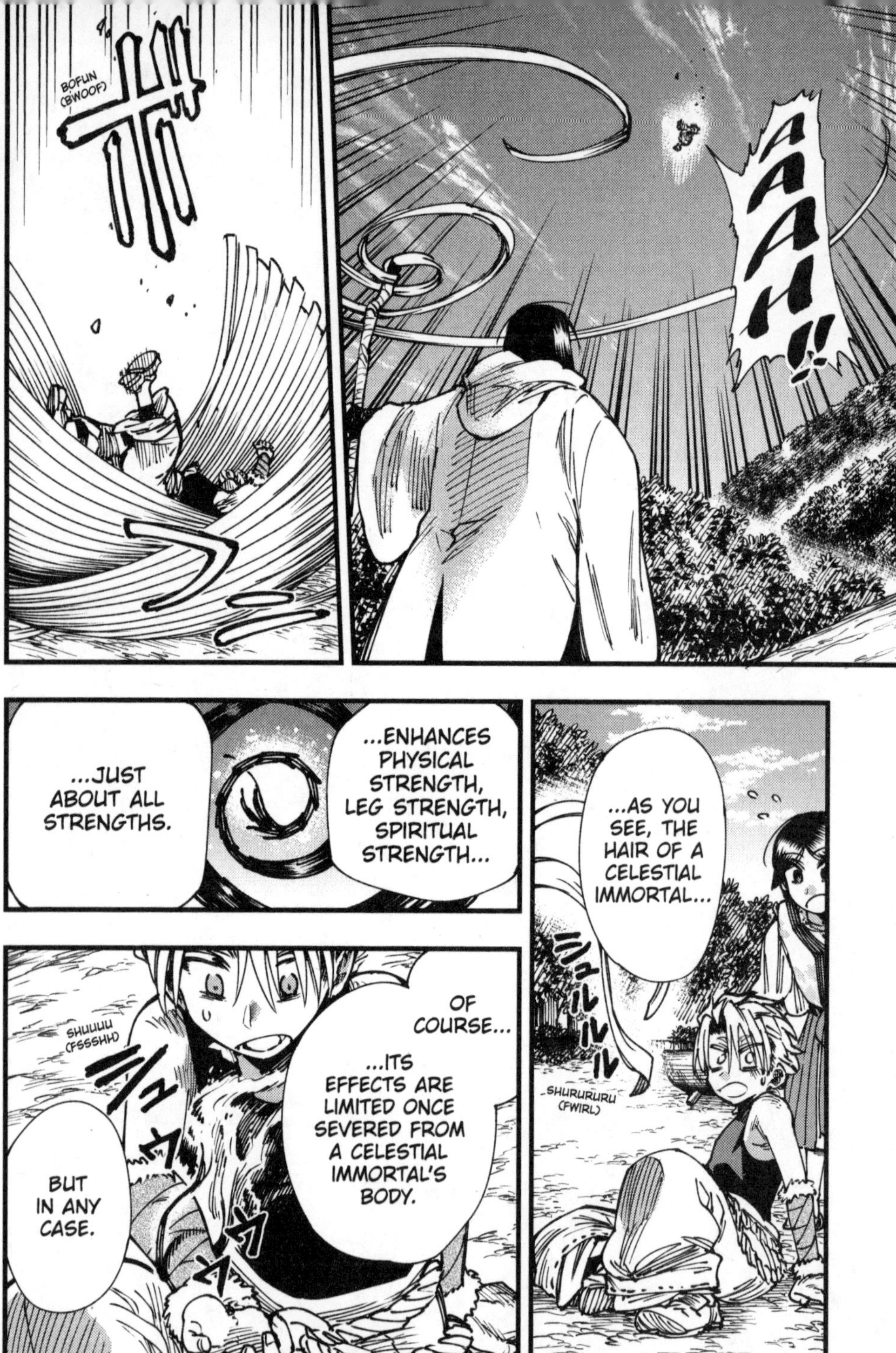
AAAH!!
BOFUN (BWOOF)
...AS YOU SEE, THE HAIR OF A CELESTIAL IMMORTAL...
SHURURURU (FWIRL)
...ENHANCES PHYSICAL STRENGTH, LEG STRENGTH, SPIRITUAL STRENGTH...
...JUST ABOUT ALL STRENGTHS.
OF COURSE...
...ITS EFFECTS ARE LIMITED ONCE SEVERED FROM A CELESTIAL IMMORTAL'S BODY.
SHUUUU (FSSSHH)
BUT IN ANY CASE.

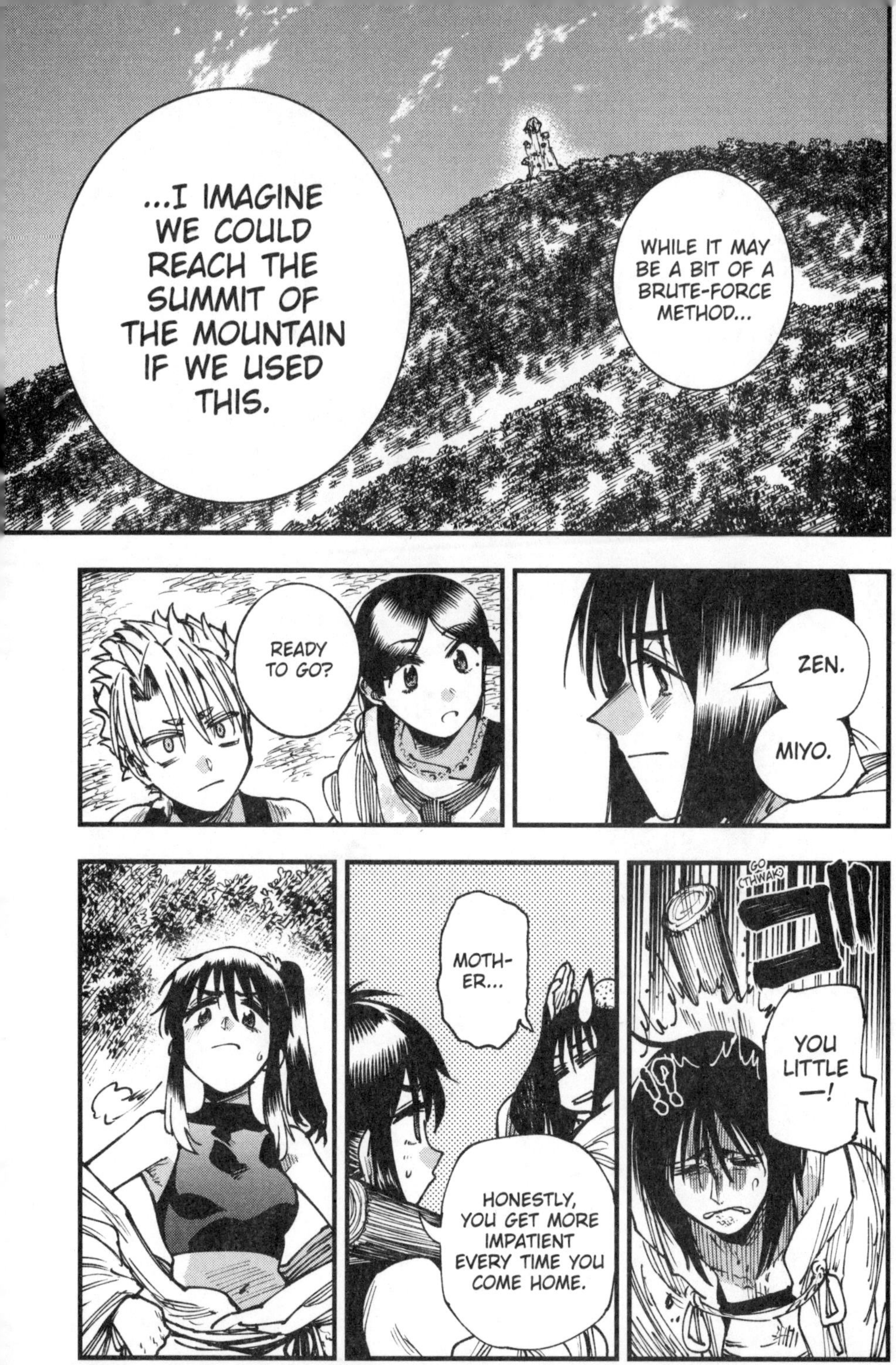
WHILE IT MAY BE A BIT OF A BRUTE-FORCE METHOD...
...I IMAGINE WE COULD REACH THE SUMMIT OF THE MOUNTAIN IF WE USED THIS.
ZEN.
MIYO.
READY TO GO?
GO (THWAK)
YOU LITTLE—!
MOTHER...
HONESTLY, YOU GET MORE IMPATIENT EVERY TIME YOU COME HOME.

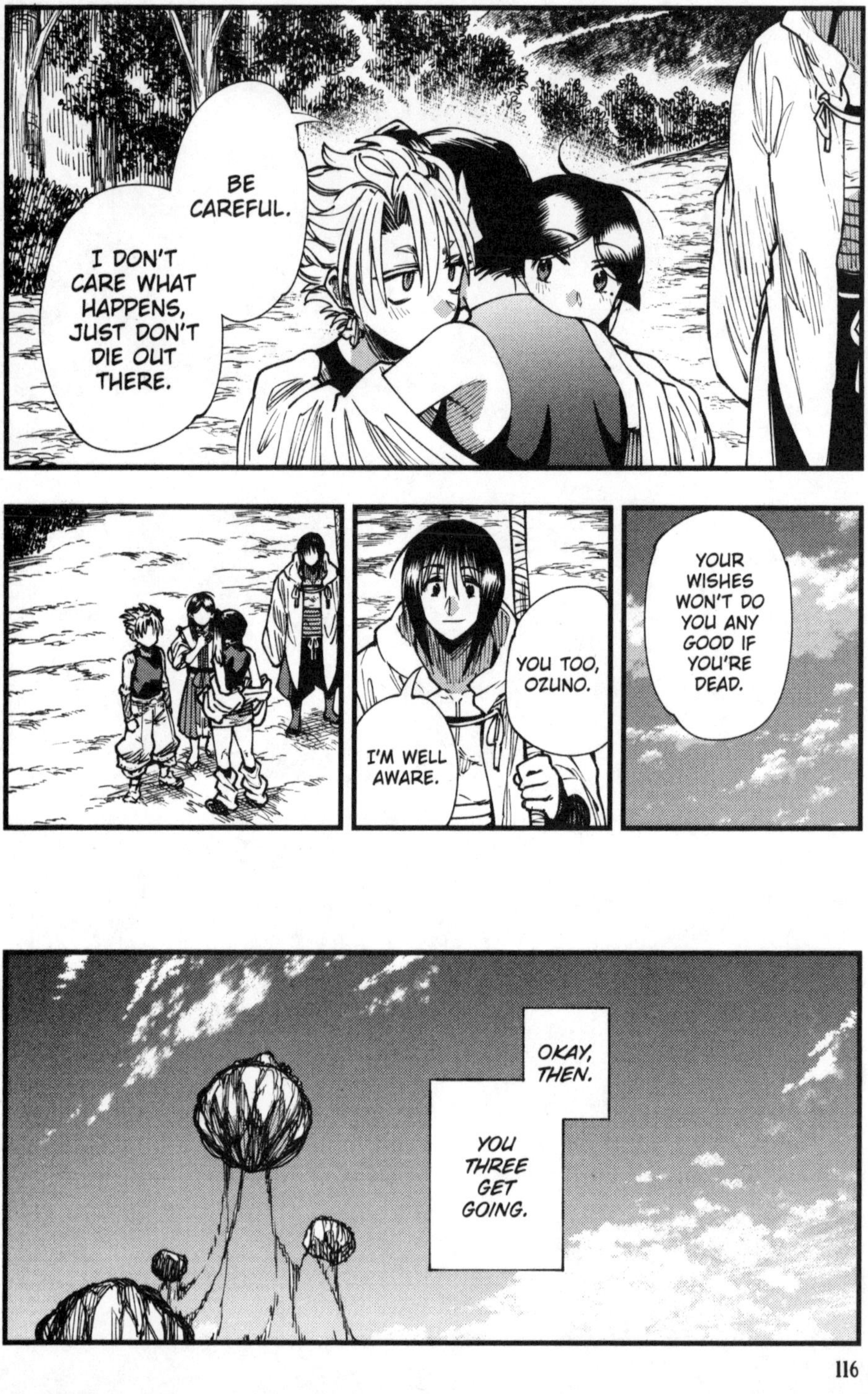
BE CAREFUL.
I DON'T CARE WHAT HAPPENS, JUST DON'T DIE OUT THERE.
YOUR WISHES WON'T DO YOU ANY GOOD IF YOU'RE DEAD.
YOU TOO, OZUNO.
I'M WELL AWARE.
OKAY, THEN.
YOU THREE GET GOING.

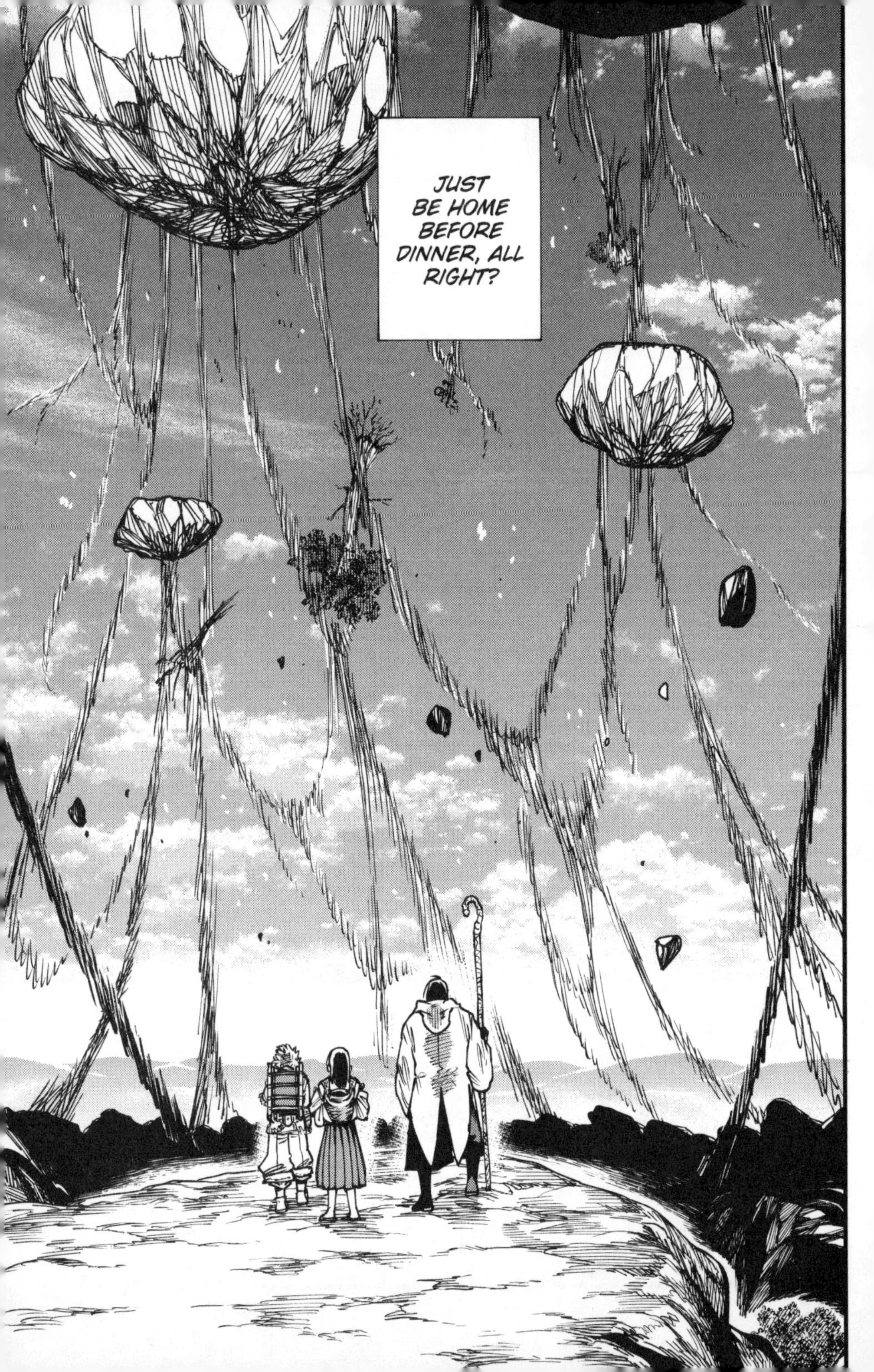
JUST BE HOME BEFORE DINNER, ALL RIGHT?

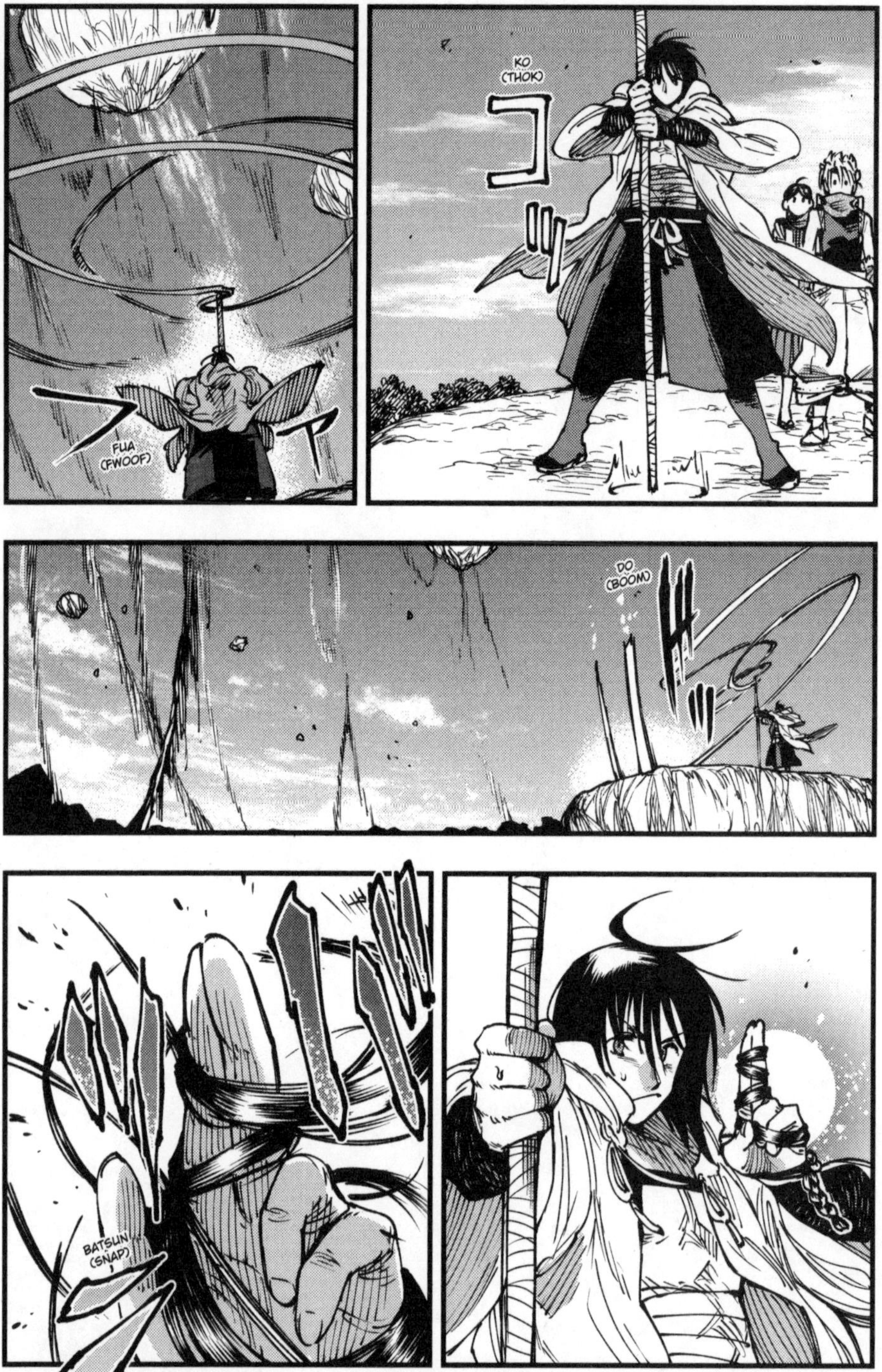
KO
(THOK)
FUA
(FWOOF)
DO
(BOOM)
BATSUN
(SNAP)

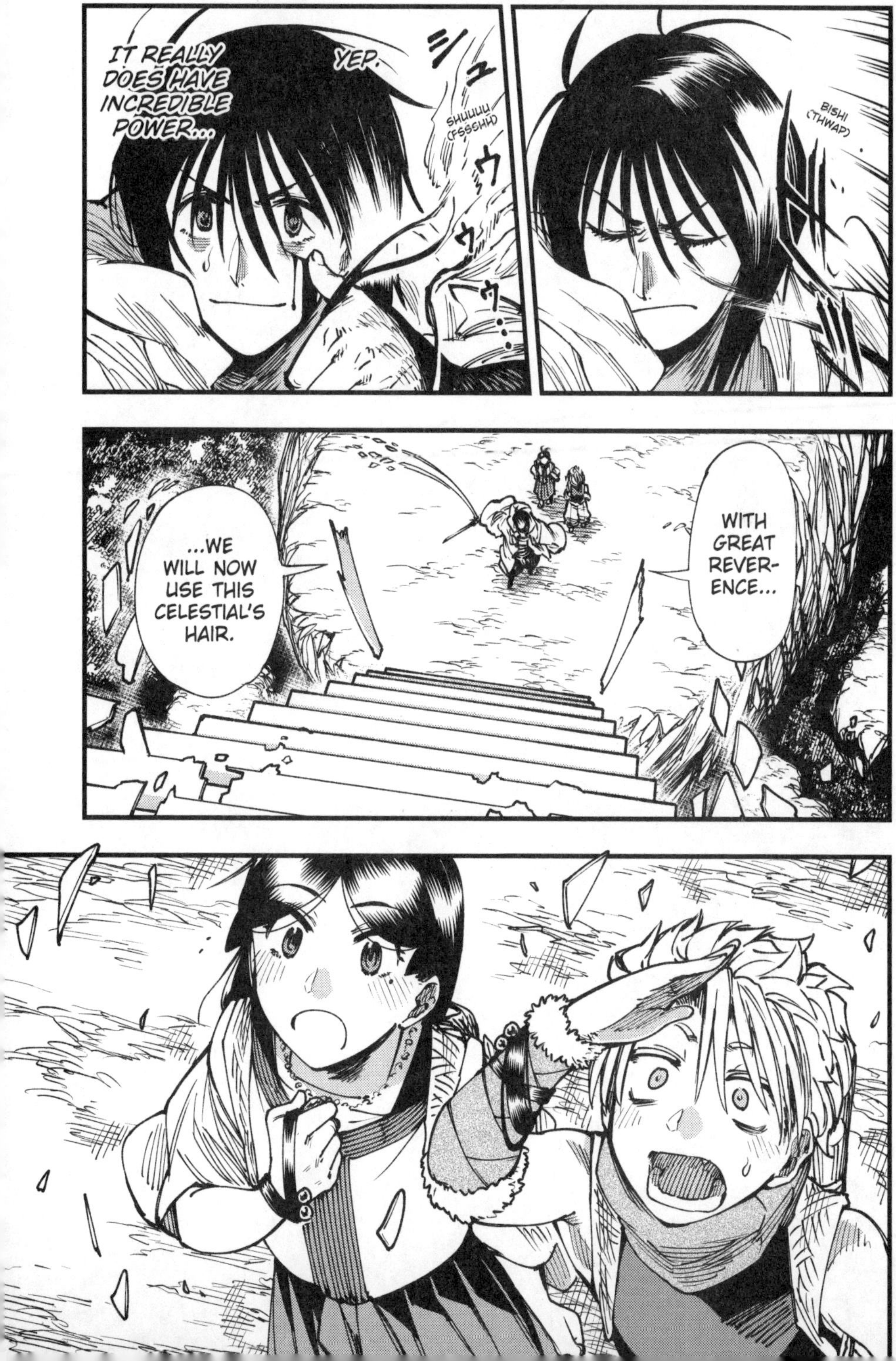
BISHI (THWAP)
シュウウウ…
SHUUUU (FSSSHH)
YEP.
IT REALLY DOES HAVE INCREDIBLE POWER...
WITH GREAT REVER-ENCE...
...WE WILL NOW USE THIS CELESTIAL'S HAIR.

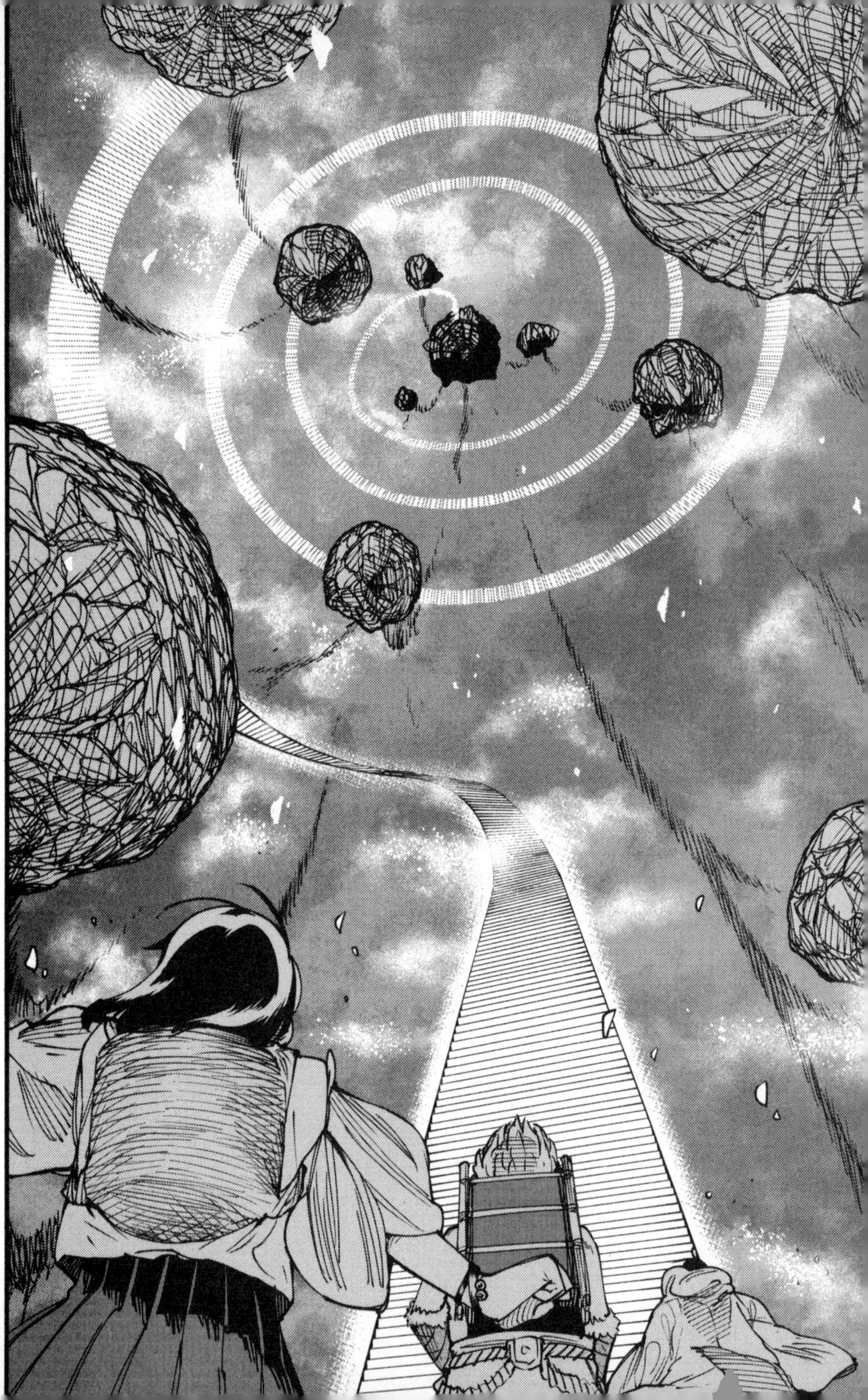

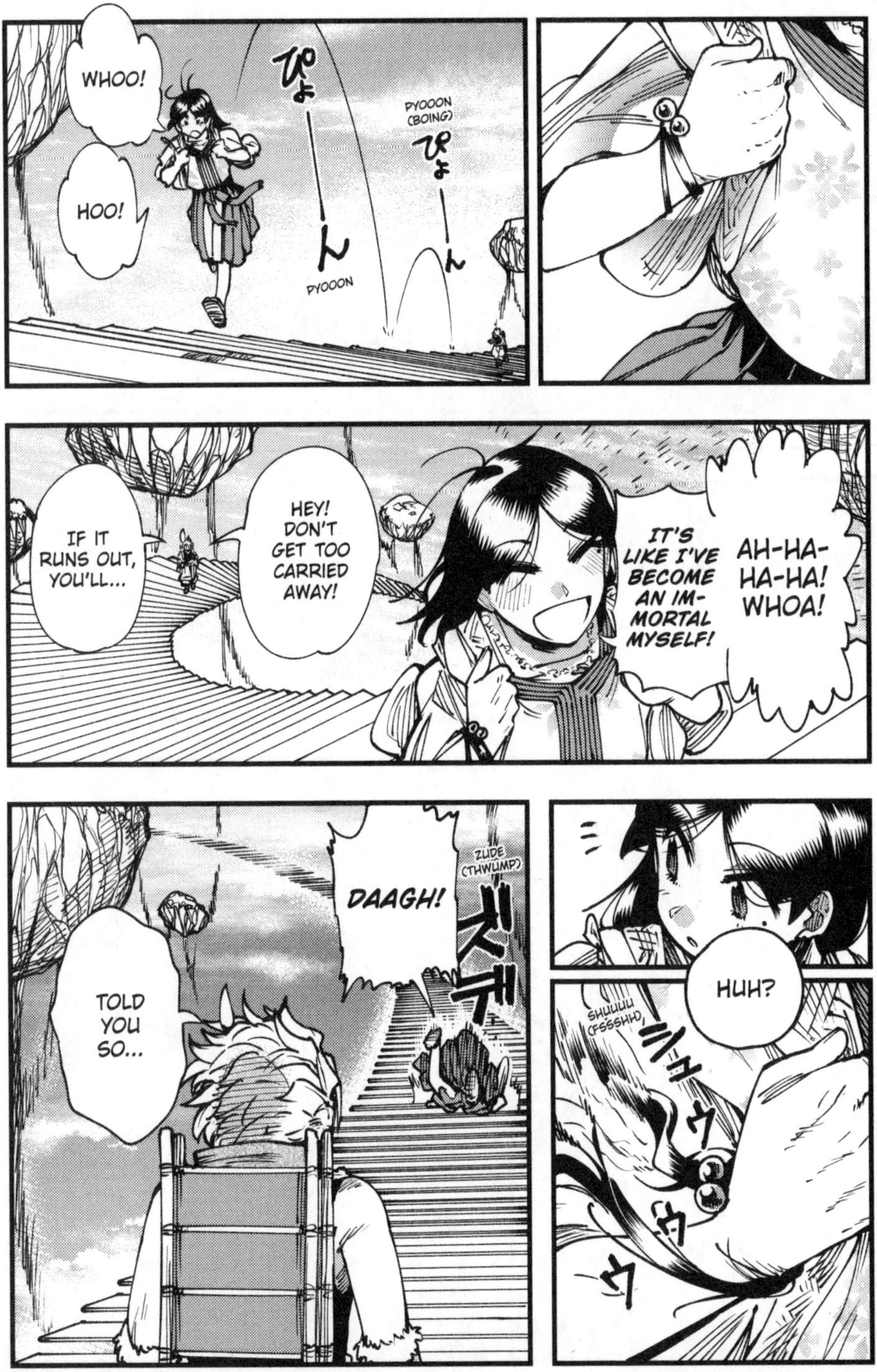
PYOOON (BOING)
ぴょーん
ぴょーん
PYOOON
WHOO!
HOO!
AH-HA-HA-HA! WHOA!
IT'S LIKE I'VE BECOME AN IMMORTAL MYSELF!
HEY! DON'T GET TOO CARRIED AWAY!
IF IT RUNS OUT, YOU'LL...
HUH?
SHUUUU (FSSSHH)
シュウウウ
ZUDE (THWUMP)
ズデ
DAAGH!
TOLD YOU SO...

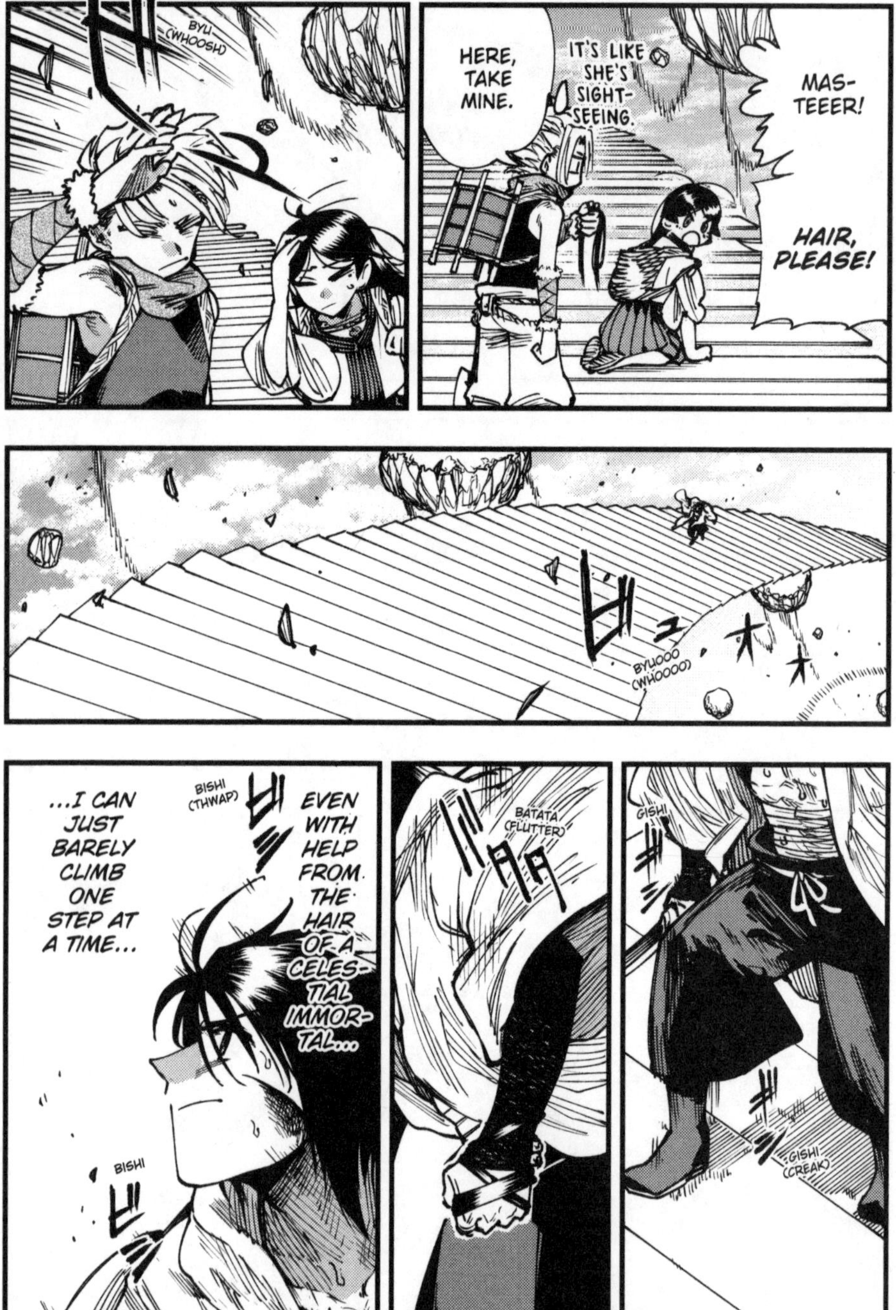
MAS-TEEER!
HAIR, PLEASE!
IT'S LIKE SHE'S SIGHT-SEEING.
HERE, TAKE MINE.
BYU (WHOOSH)
BYUOOO (WHOOOO)
GISHI
GISHI (CREAK)
BATATA (FLUTTER)
EVEN WITH HELP FROM THE HAIR OF A CELES-TIAL IMMOR-TAL...
BISHI (THWAP)
...I CAN JUST BARELY CLIMB ONE STEP AT A TIME...
BISHI

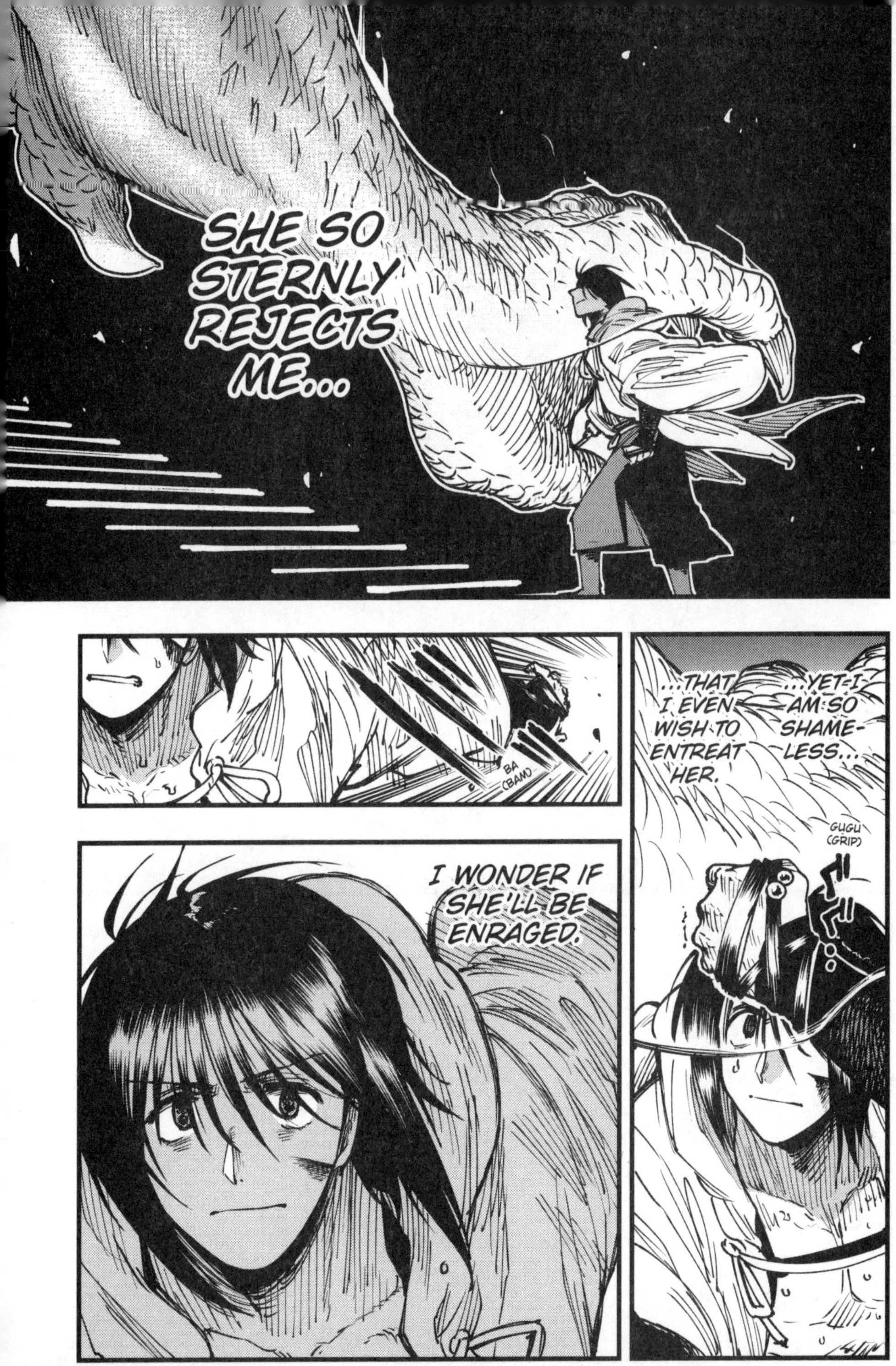
SHE SO STERNLY REJECTS ME...
...YET I AM SO SHAMELESS...
...THAT I EVEN WISH TO ENTREAT HER.
GUGU (GRIP)
BA (BAM)
I WONDER IF SHE'LL BE ENRAGED.

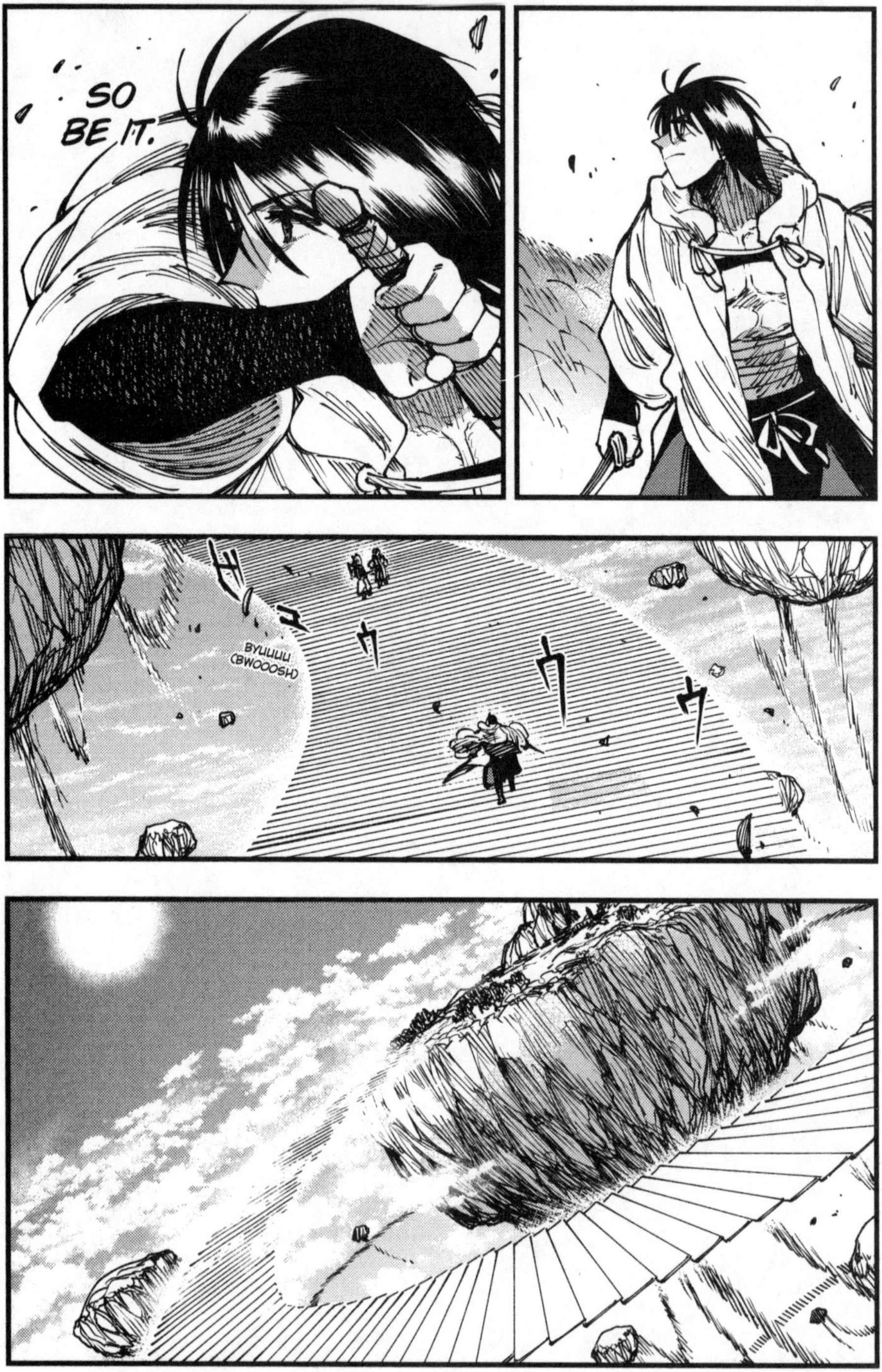
SO BE IT.
BYUUUU (BWOOOSH)

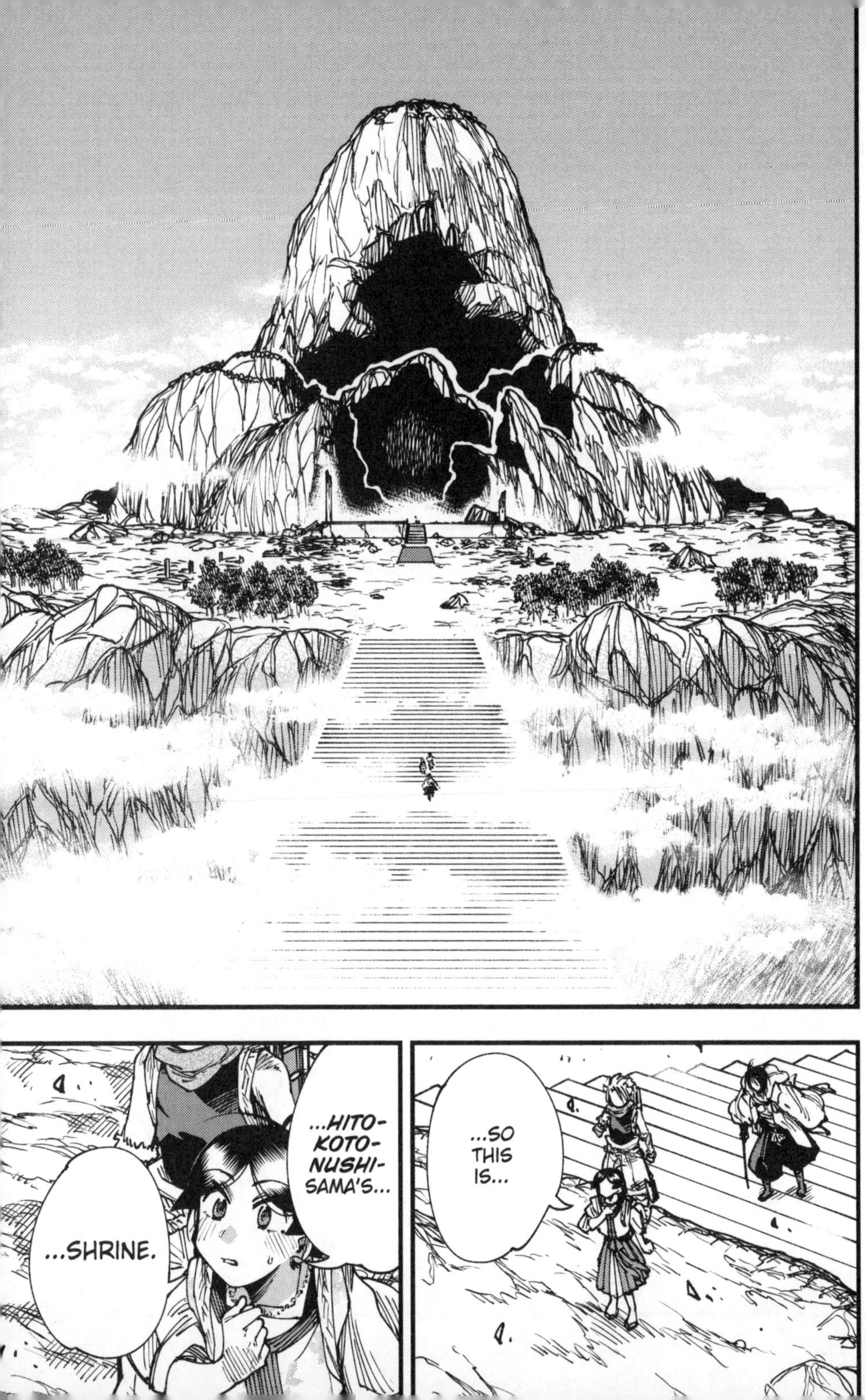
...SO THIS IS...
...HITO-KOTO-NUSHI-SAMA'S...
...SHRINE.

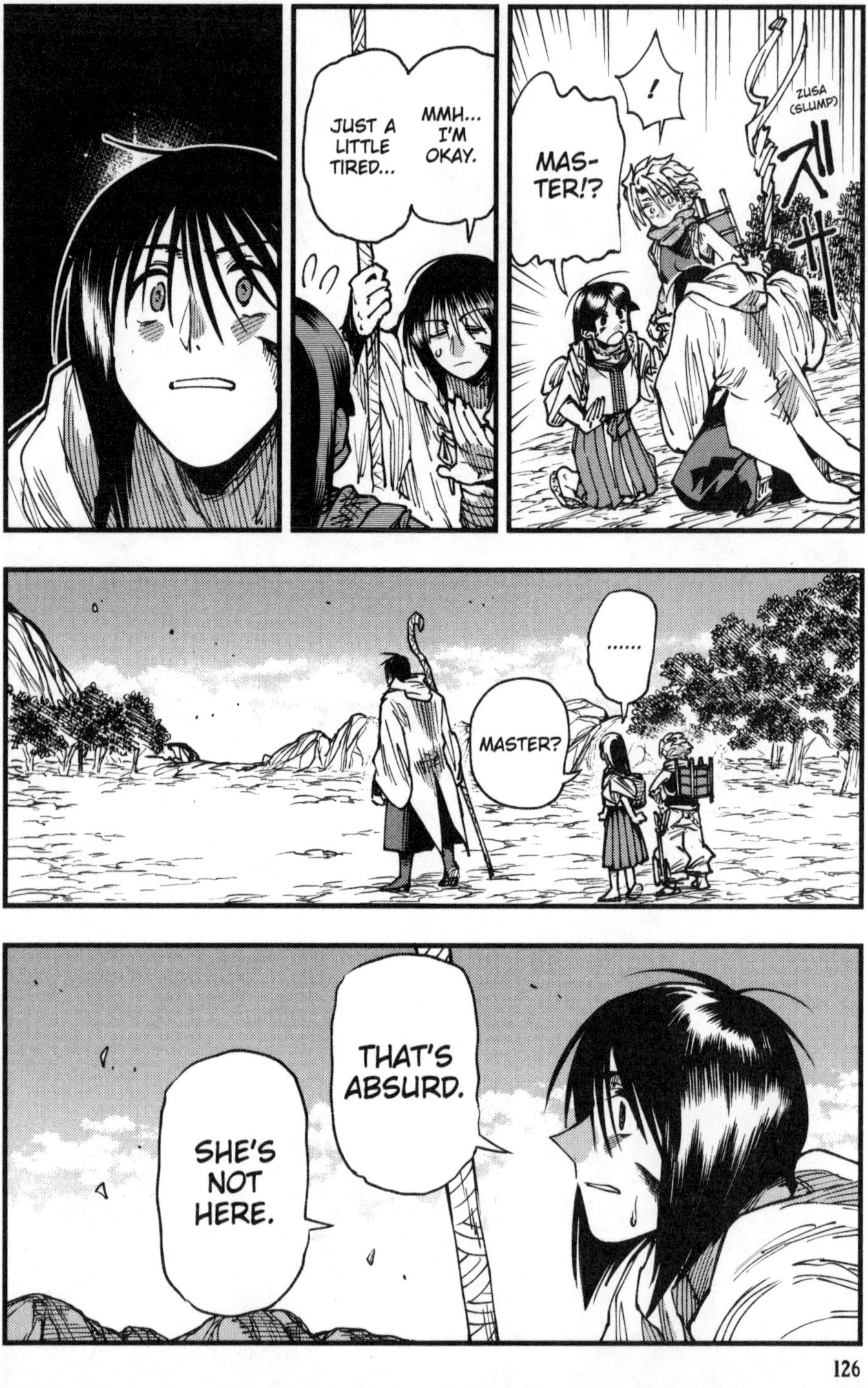
ZUSA (SLUMP)
!
MAS-TER!?
MMH... I'M OKAY.
JUST A LITTLE TIRED...
......
MASTER?
THAT'S ABSURD.
SHE'S NOT HERE.

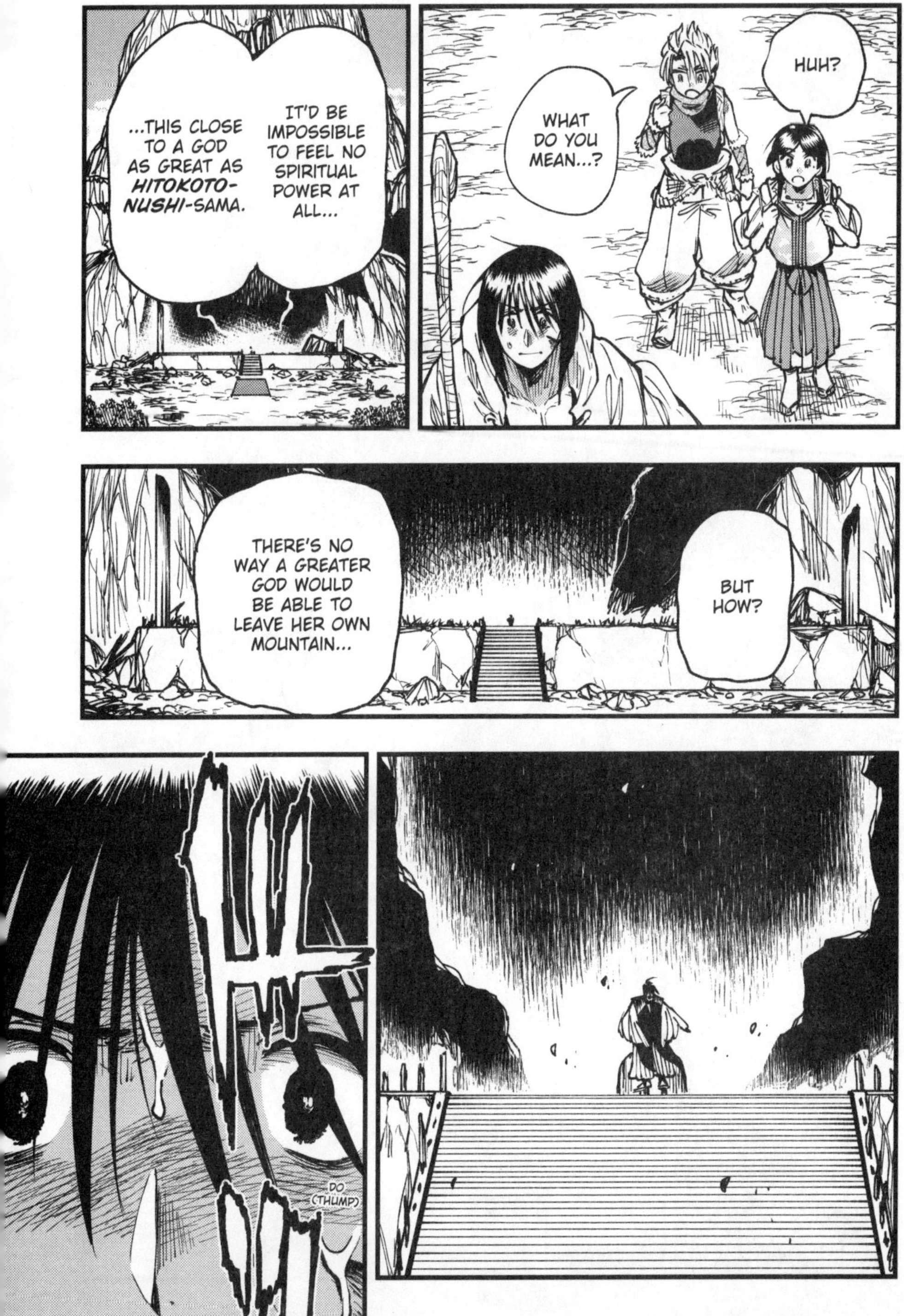
HUH?
WHAT DO YOU MEAN...?
IT'D BE IMPOSSIBLE TO FEEL NO SPIRITUAL POWER AT ALL...
...THIS CLOSE TO A GOD AS GREAT AS HITOKOTO-NUSHI-SAMA.
BUT HOW?
THERE'S NO WAY A GREATER GOD WOULD BE ABLE TO LEAVE HER OWN MOUNTAIN...
DO (THUMP)

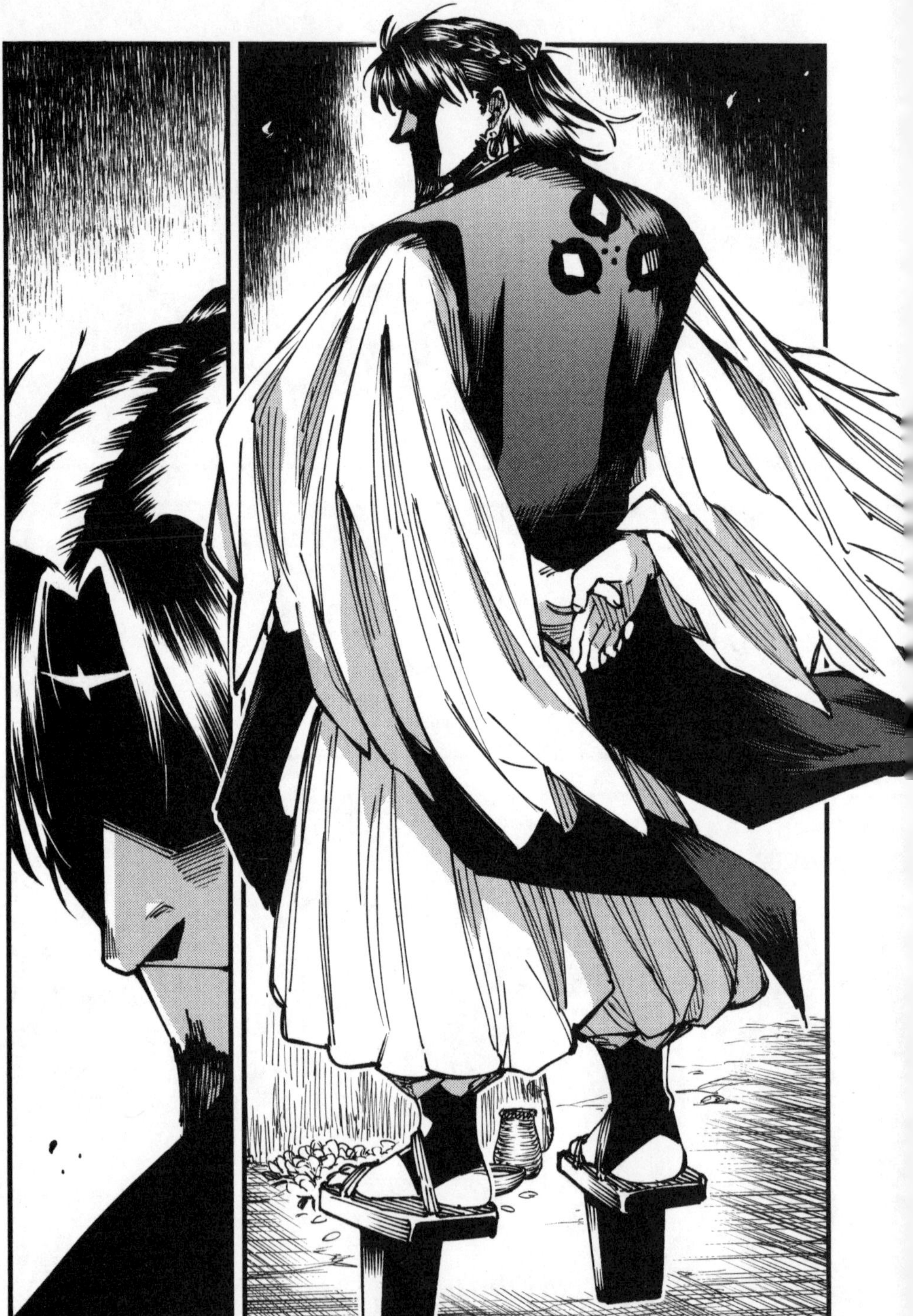

HN!

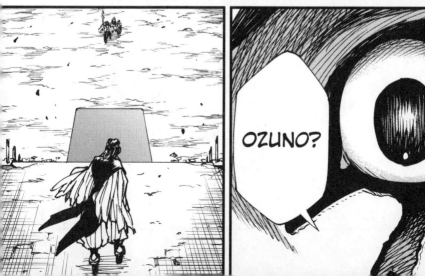

OZUNO?

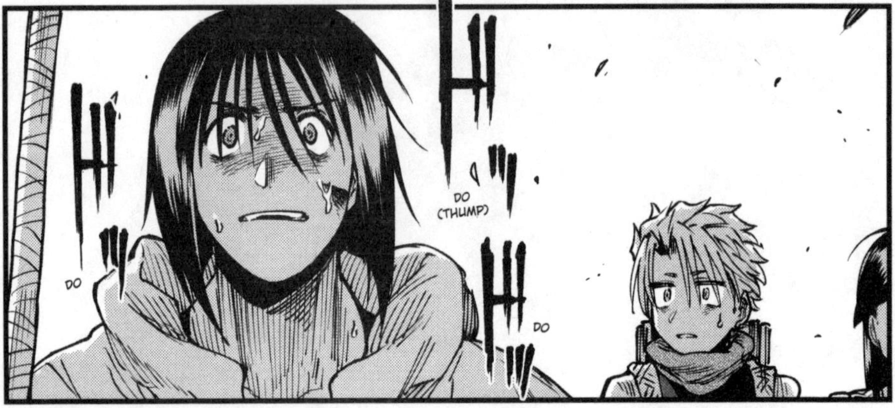
DO
(THUMP)
DO
DO

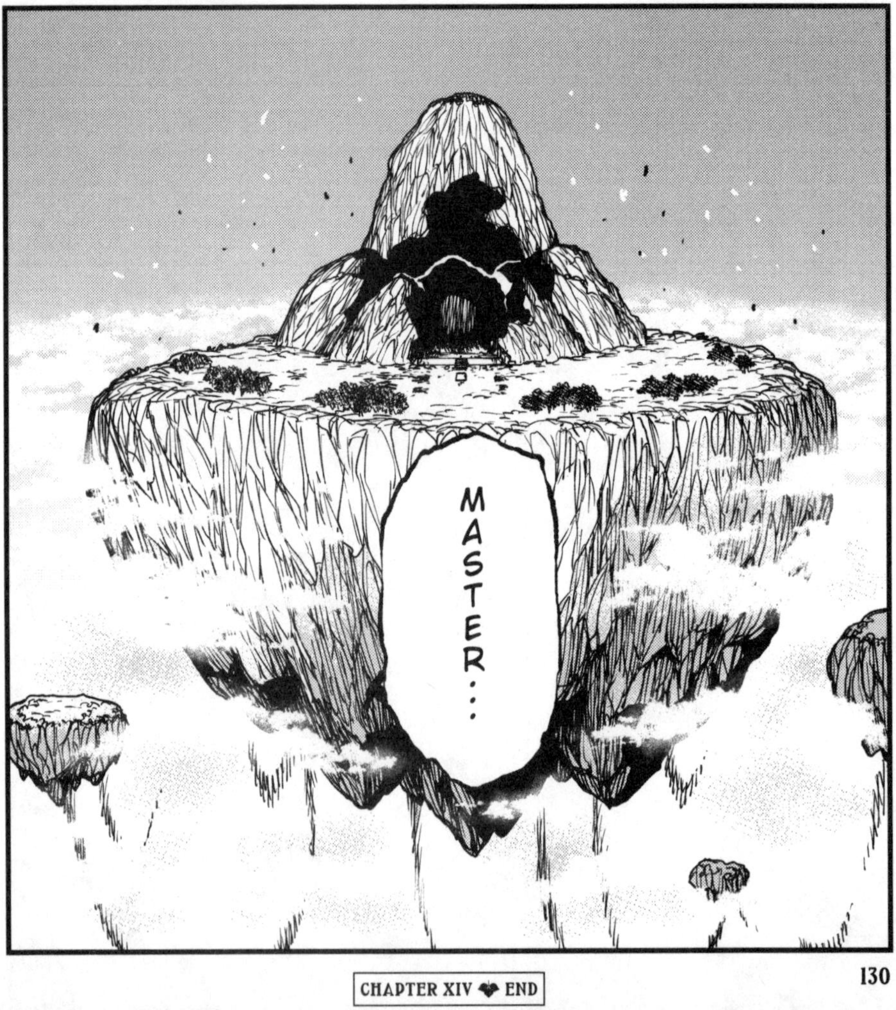
MASTER...

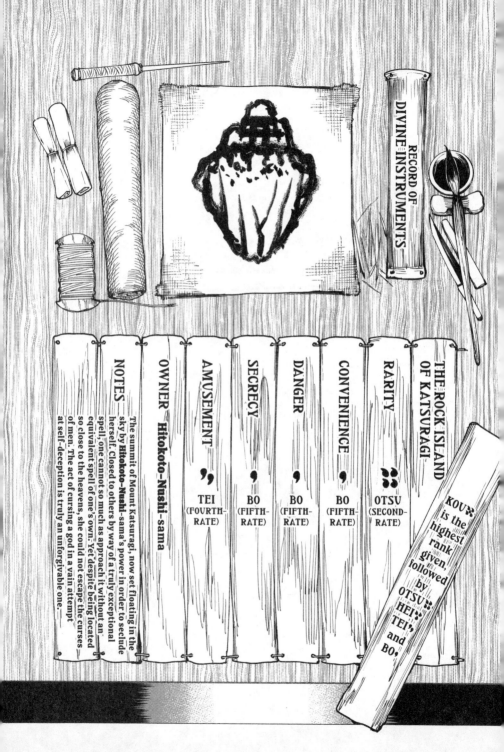

THE ROCK ISLAND OF KATSURAGI

RARITY	OTSU (SECOND-RATE)	,,
CONVENIENCE	BO (FIFTH-RATE)	,
DANGER	BO (FIFTH-RATE)	,
SECRECY	BO (FIFTH-RATE)	,
AMUSEMENT	TEI (FOURTH-RATE)	,,

OWNER **Hitokoto-Nushi-sama**

NOTES The summit of Mount Katsuragi, now set floating in the sky by **Hitokoto-Nushi**-sama's power in order to seclude herself. Closed to others by way of a truly exceptional spell, one cannot so much as approach it without an equivalent spell of one's own. Yet despite being located so close to the heavens, she could not escape the curses of men. The act of cursing a god in a vain attempt at self-deception is truly an unforgivable one.

KOU is the highest rank given, followed by OTSU, HEI, TEI, and BO.

Touge Oni

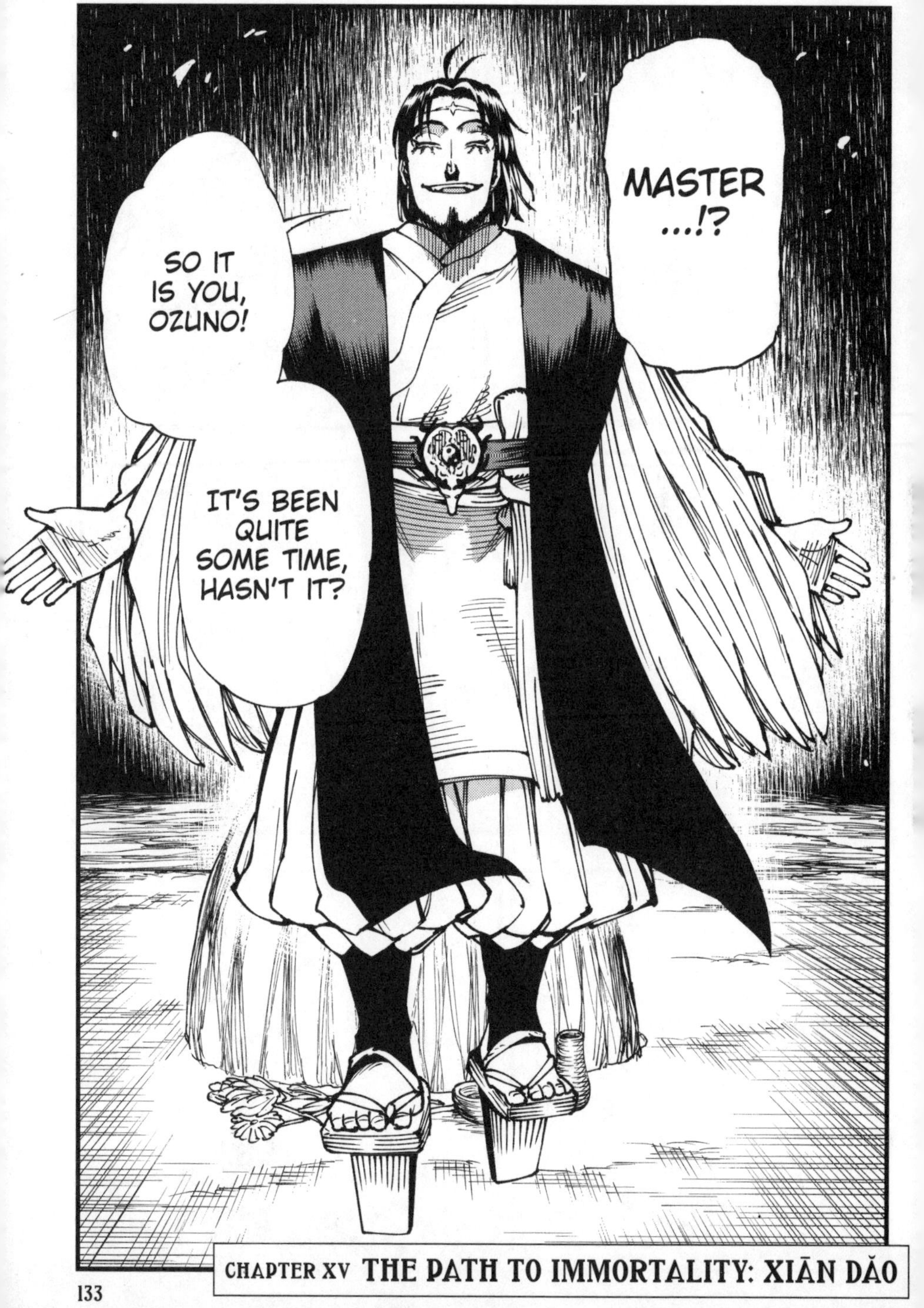
MASTER ...!?
SO IT IS YOU, OZUNO!
IT'S BEEN QUITE SOME TIME, HASN'T IT?

CHAPTER XV THE PATH TO IMMORTALITY: XIĀN DǍO

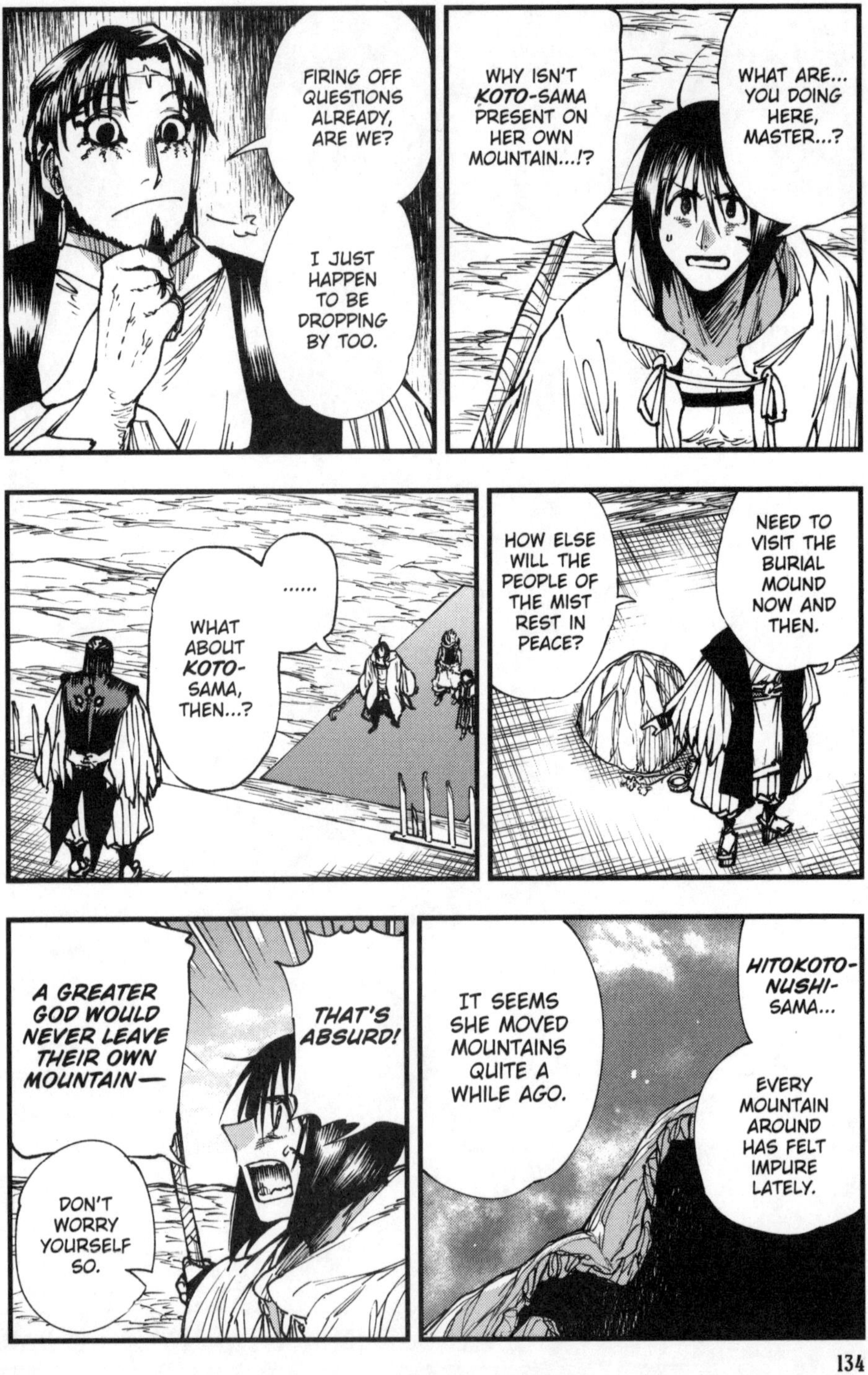
WHAT ARE... YOU DOING HERE, MASTER...?
WHY ISN'T KOTO-SAMA PRESENT ON HER OWN MOUNTAIN...!?
FIRING OFF QUESTIONS ALREADY, ARE WE?
I JUST HAPPEN TO BE DROPPING BY TOO.
NEED TO VISIT THE BURIAL MOUND NOW AND THEN.
HOW ELSE WILL THE PEOPLE OF THE MIST REST IN PEACE?
......
WHAT ABOUT KOTO-SAMA, THEN...?
HITOKOTO-NUSHI-SAMA...
EVERY MOUNTAIN AROUND HAS FELT IMPURE LATELY.
IT SEEMS SHE MOVED MOUNTAINS QUITE A WHILE AGO.
THAT'S ABSURD!
A GREATER GOD WOULD NEVER LEAVE THEIR OWN MOUNTAIN—
DON'T WORRY YOURSELF SO.

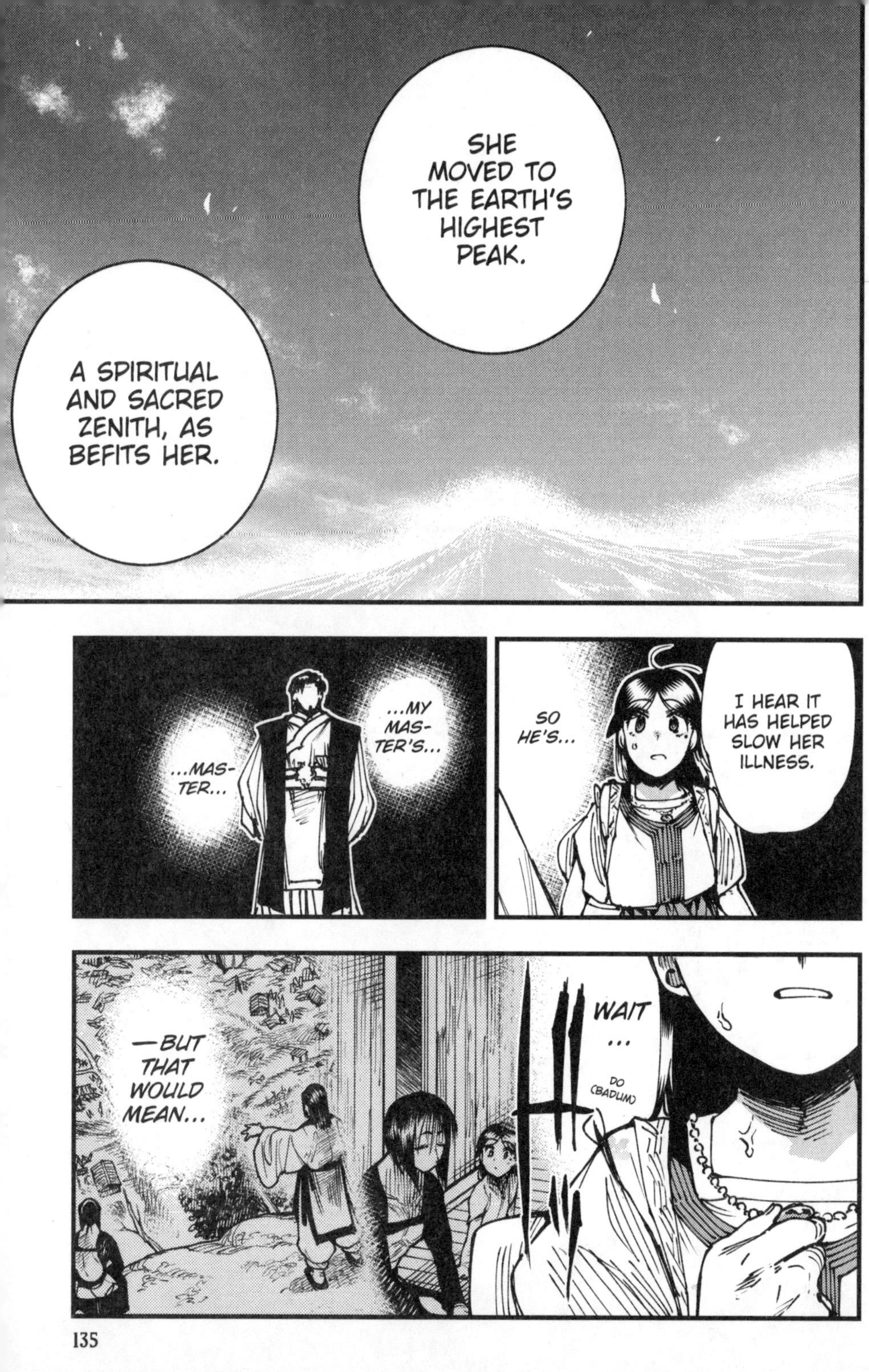
SHE MOVED TO THE EARTH'S HIGHEST PEAK.
A SPIRITUAL AND SACRED ZENITH, AS BEFITS HER.
I HEAR IT HAS HELPED SLOW HER ILLNESS.
SO HE'S...
...MY MASTER'S...
...MASTER...
WAIT ...
DO (BADUM)
—BUT THAT WOULD MEAN...

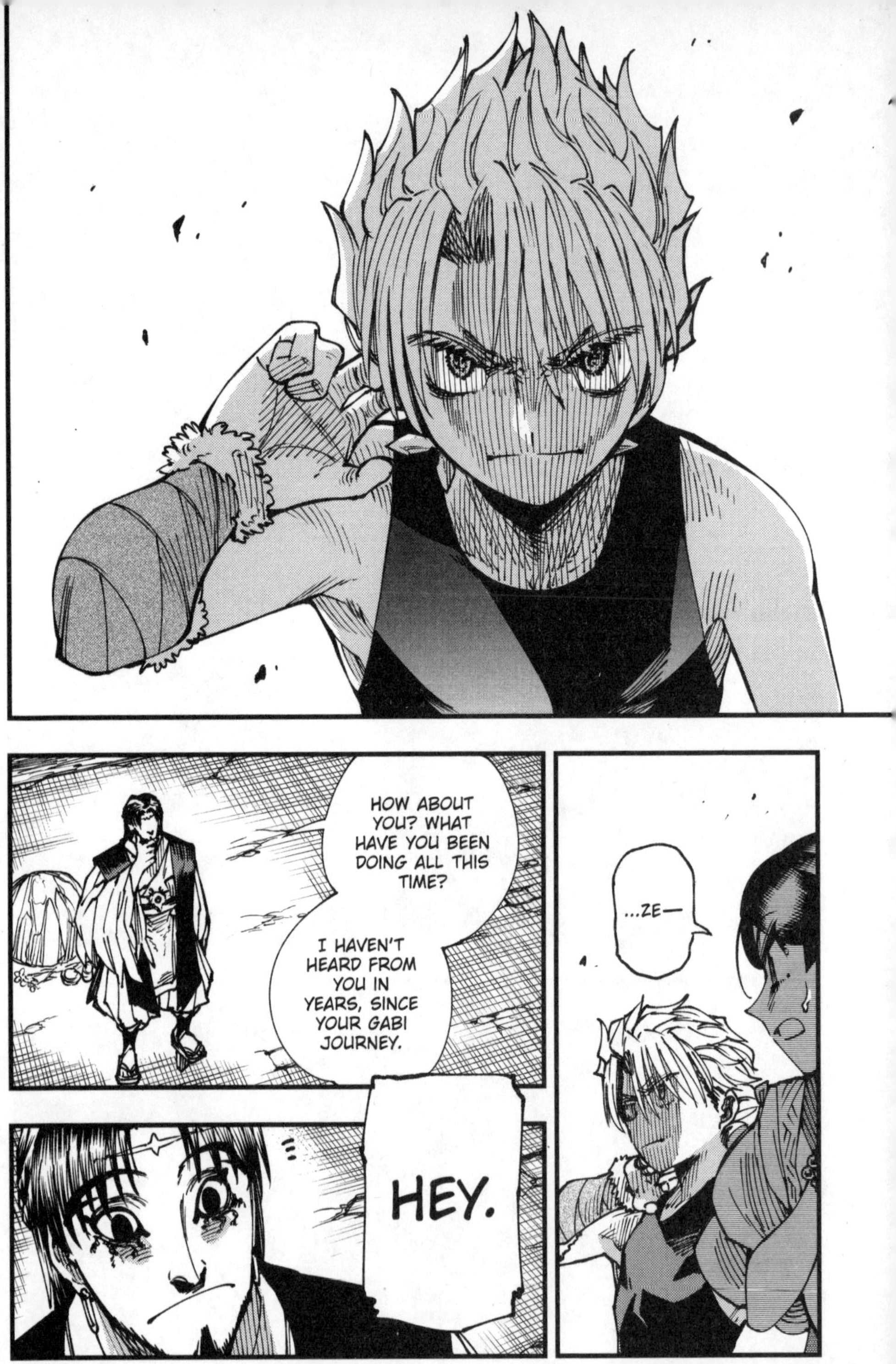
...ZE—
HOW ABOUT YOU? WHAT HAVE YOU BEEN DOING ALL THIS TIME?
I HAVEN'T HEARD FROM YOU IN YEARS, SINCE YOUR GABI JOURNEY.
HEY.

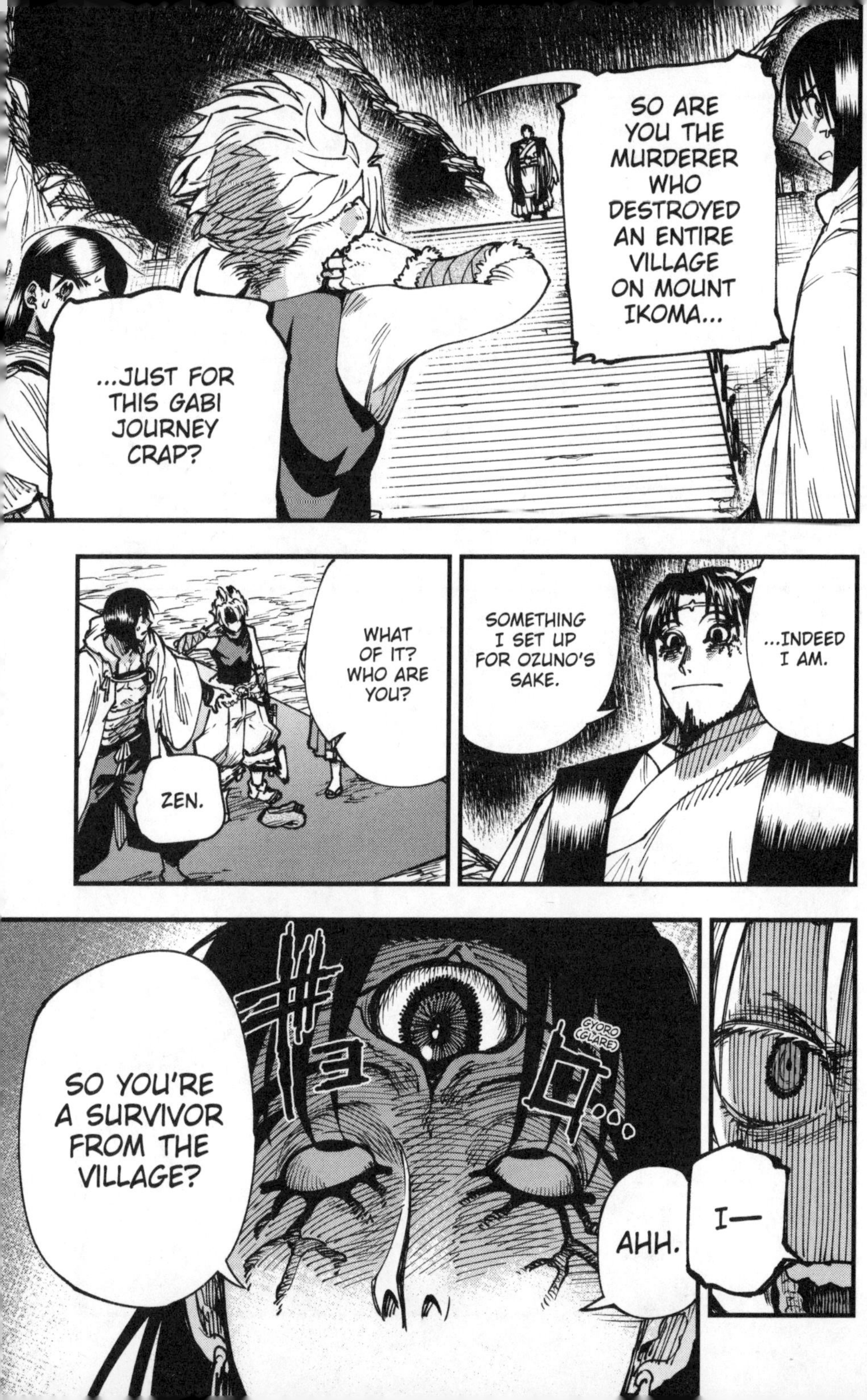
SO ARE YOU THE MURDERER WHO DESTROYED AN ENTIRE VILLAGE ON MOUNT IKOMA...
...JUST FOR THIS GABI JOURNEY CRAP?
...INDEED I AM.
SOMETHING I SET UP FOR OZUNO'S SAKE.
WHAT OF IT? WHO ARE YOU?
ZEN.
I—
GYORO (GLARE)
AHH.
SO YOU'RE A SURVIVOR FROM THE VILLAGE?

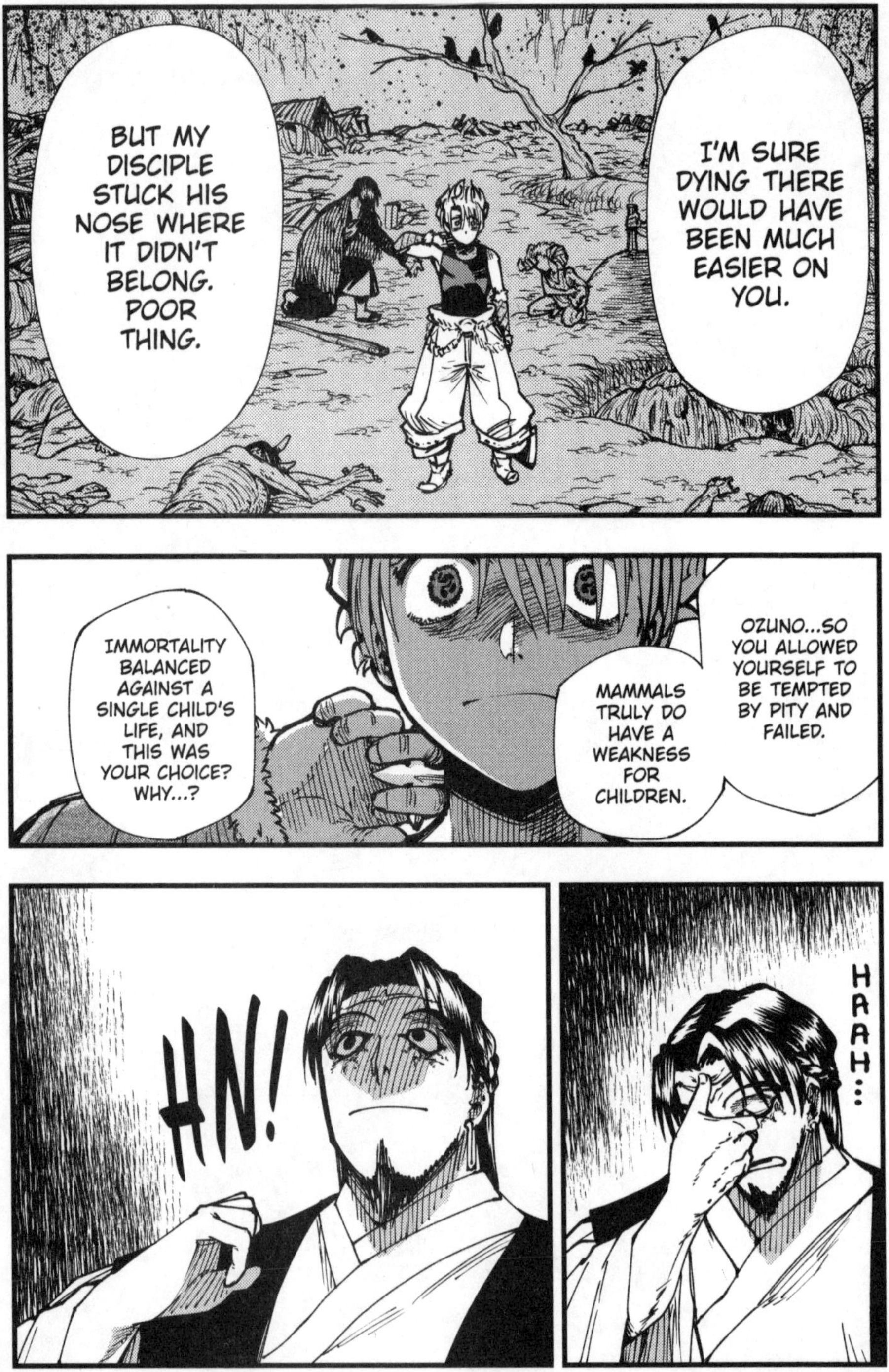
I'M SURE DYING THERE WOULD HAVE BEEN MUCH EASIER ON YOU.
BUT MY DISCIPLE STUCK HIS NOSE WHERE IT DIDN'T BELONG. POOR THING.
OZUNO...SO YOU ALLOWED YOURSELF TO BE TEMPTED BY PITY AND FAILED.
MAMMALS TRULY DO HAVE A WEAKNESS FOR CHILDREN.
IMMORTALITY BALANCED AGAINST A SINGLE CHILD'S LIFE, AND THIS WAS YOUR CHOICE? WHY...?
HAAH...
HN!

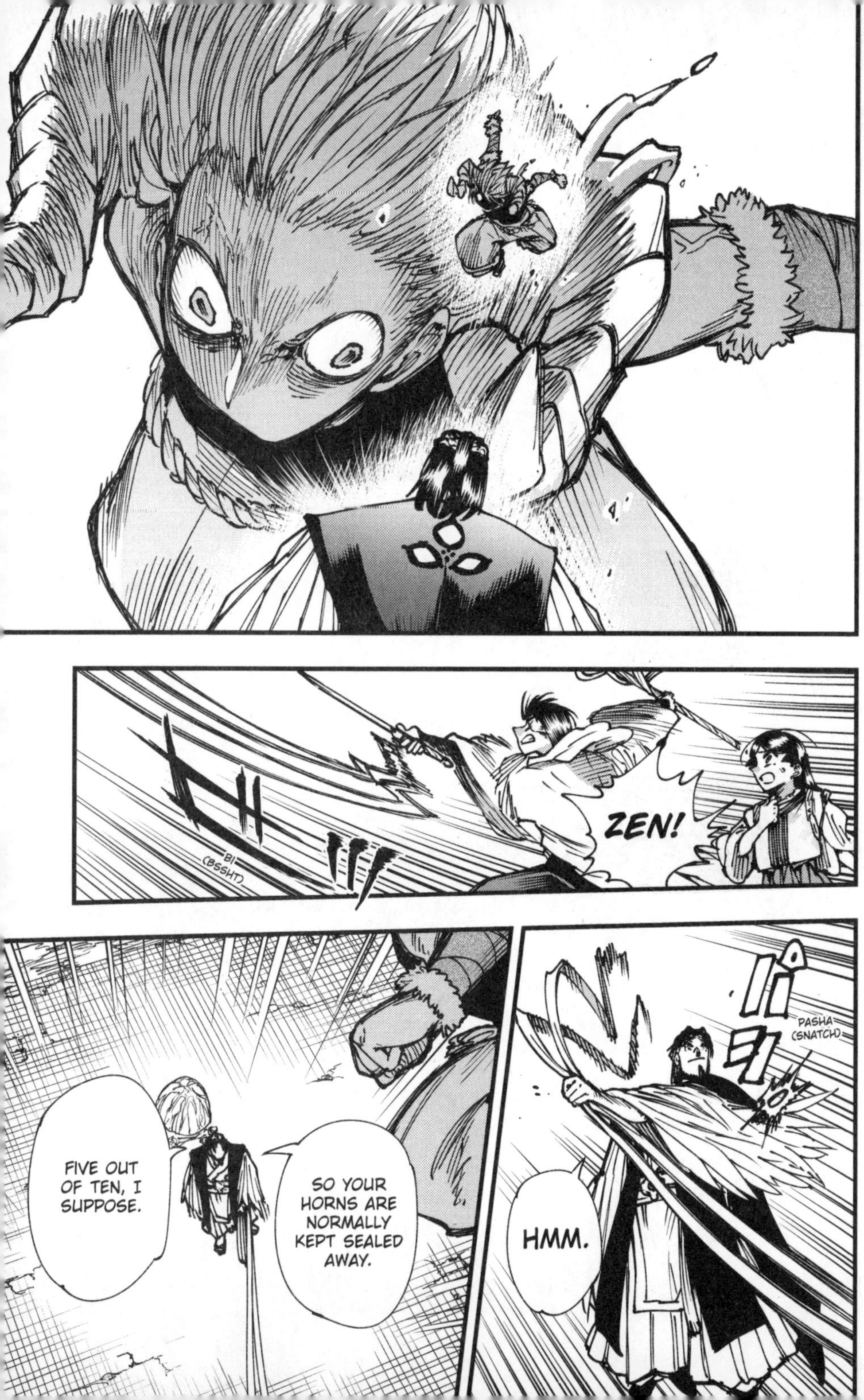
ZEN!
BI
(BSSHT)
PASHA
(SNATCH)
HMM.
SO YOUR HORNS ARE NORMALLY KEPT SEALED AWAY.
FIVE OUT OF TEN, I SUPPOSE.

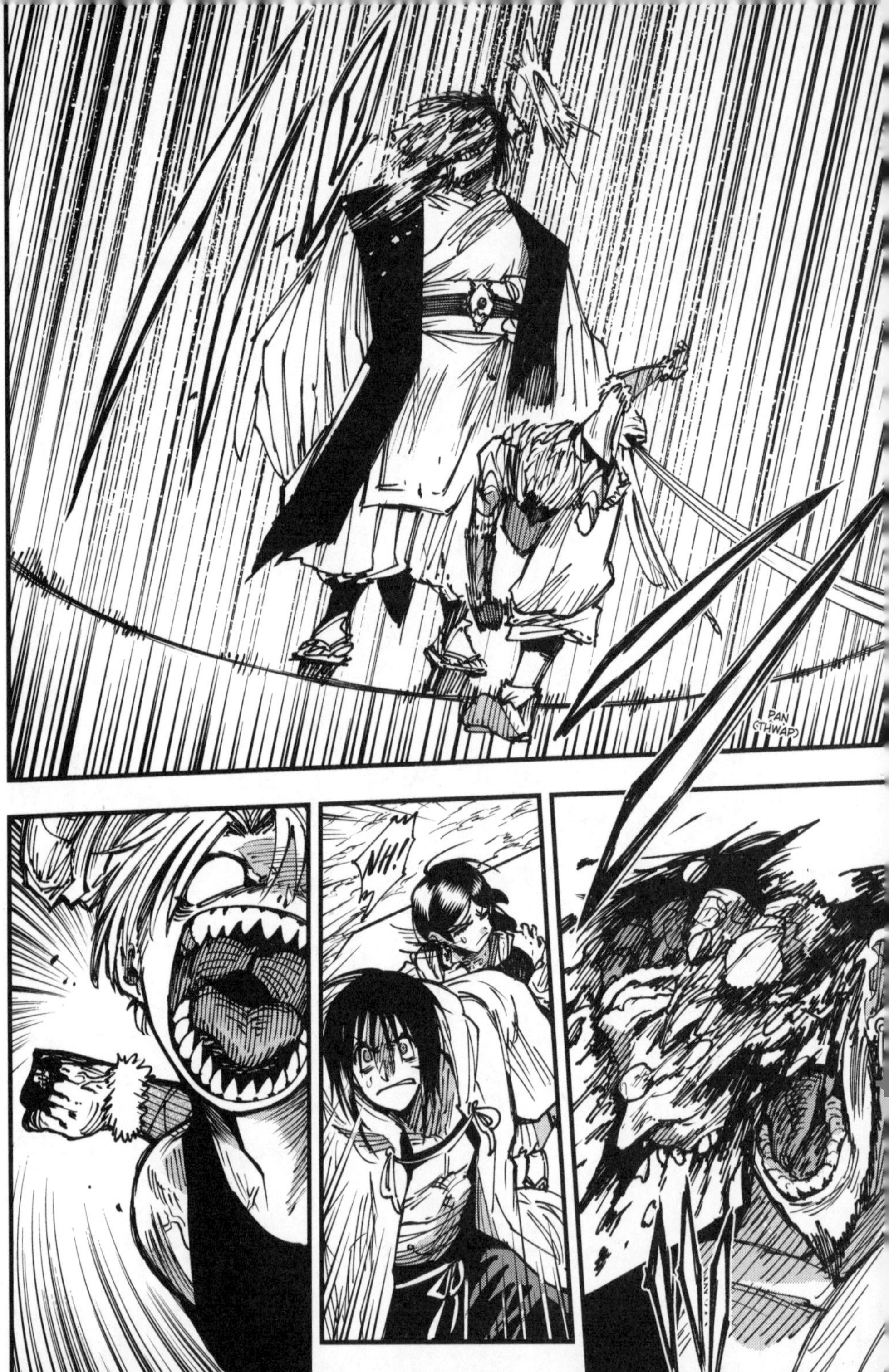
PAN
(THWAP)
NH!

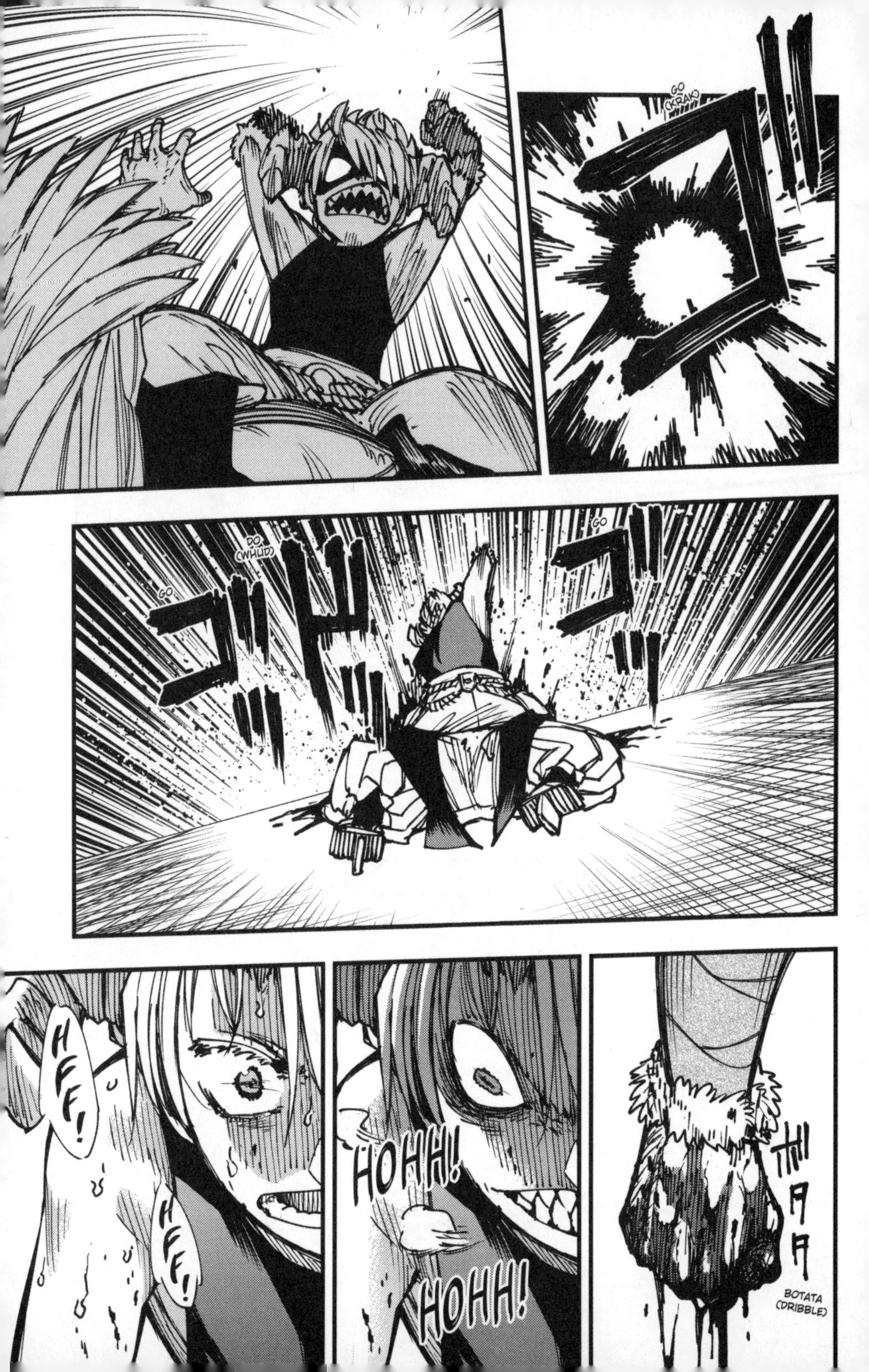

GO (KRAK)
GO
DO (WHUD)
GO
BOTATA (DRIBBLE)
HOHH!
HOHH!
HFF!
HFF!

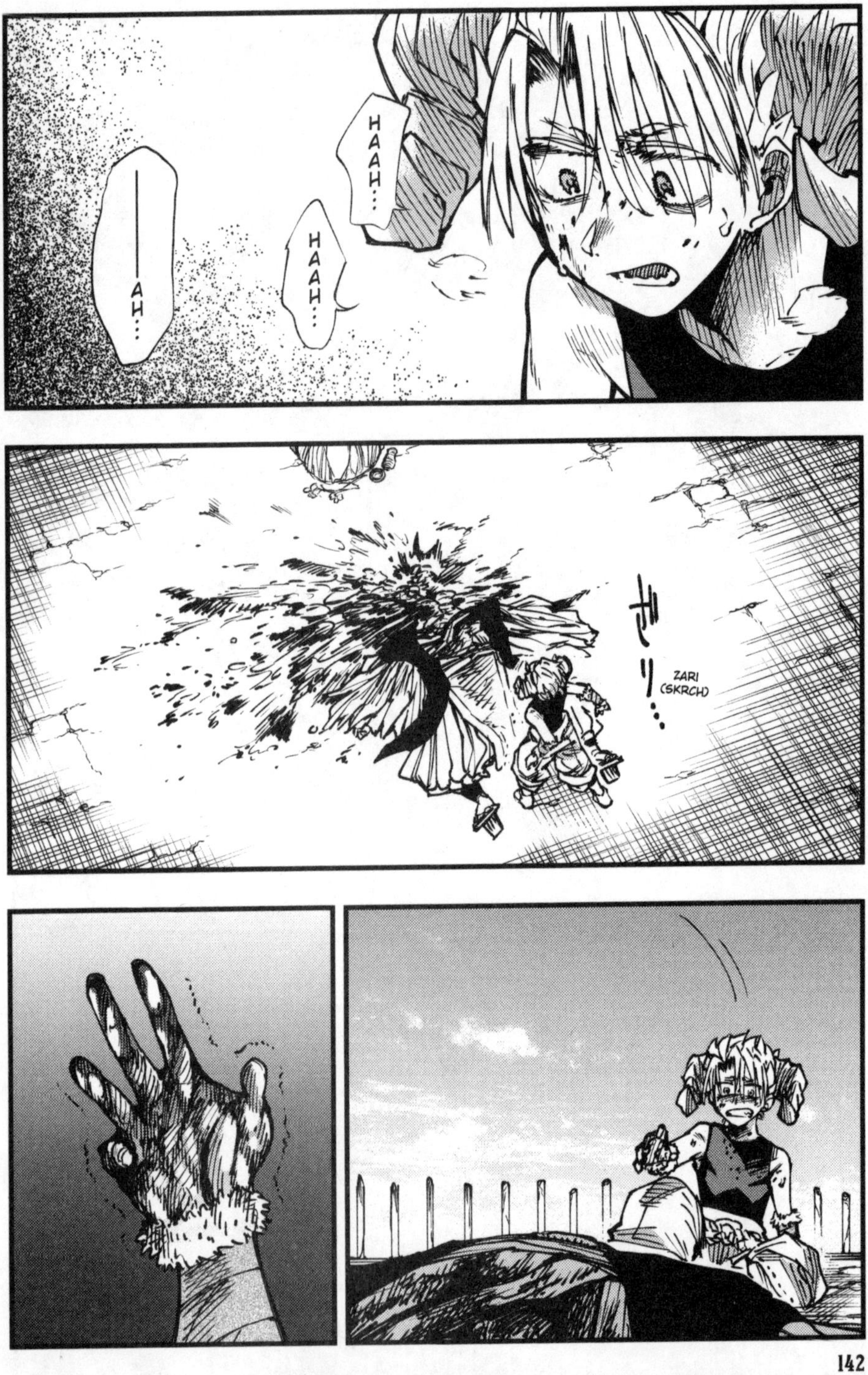
HAAAH...
HAAAH...
——AH...
ザリ…
ZARI (SKRCH)

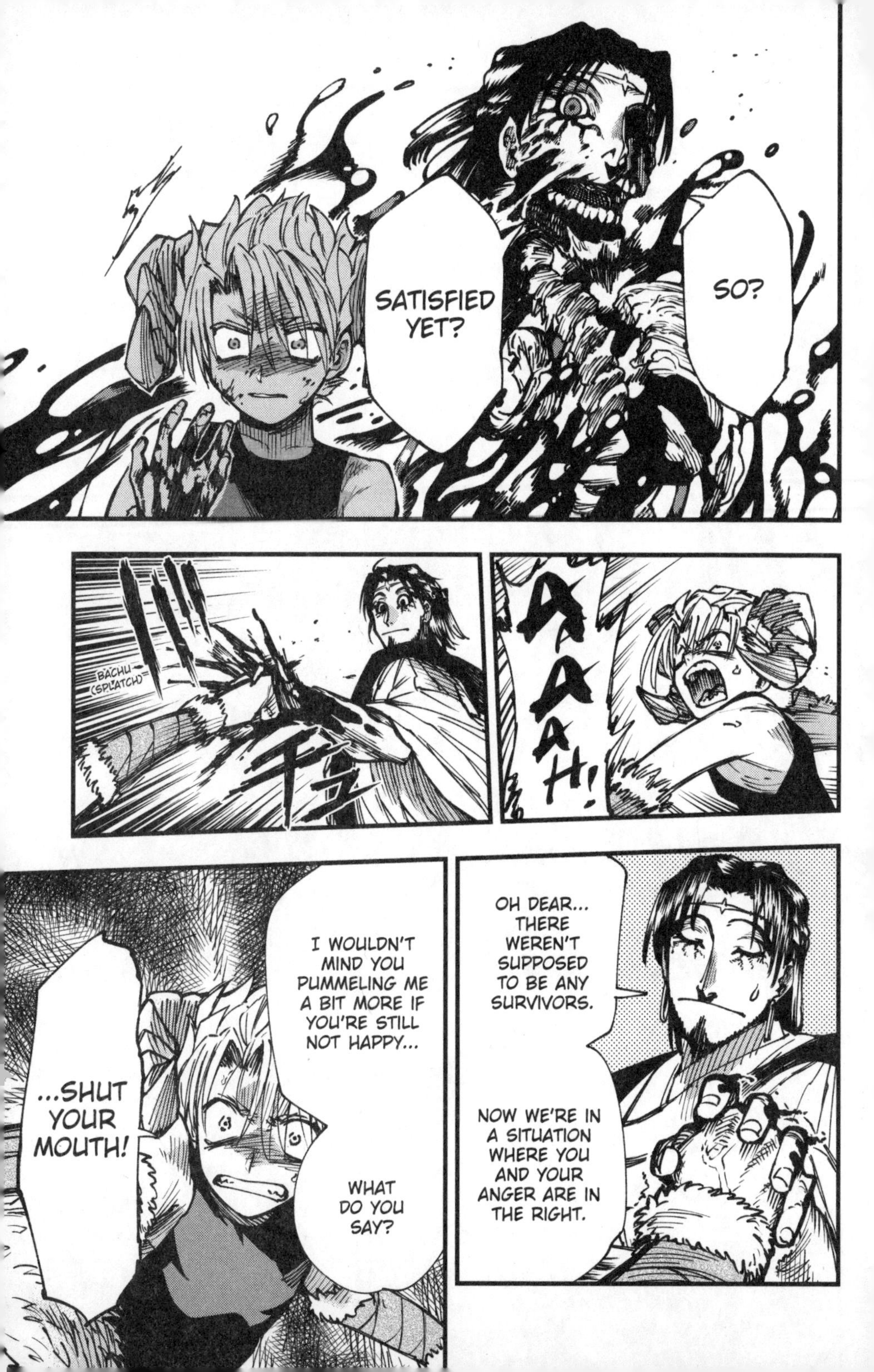
SO?
SATISFIED YET?
AAAAAH!
BACHU (SPLATCH)
OH DEAR... THERE WEREN'T SUPPOSED TO BE ANY SURVIVORS.
NOW WE'RE IN A SITUATION WHERE YOU AND YOUR ANGER ARE IN THE RIGHT.
I WOULDN'T MIND YOU PUMMELING ME A BIT MORE IF YOU'RE STILL NOT HAPPY...
WHAT DO YOU SAY?
...SHUT YOUR MOUTH!

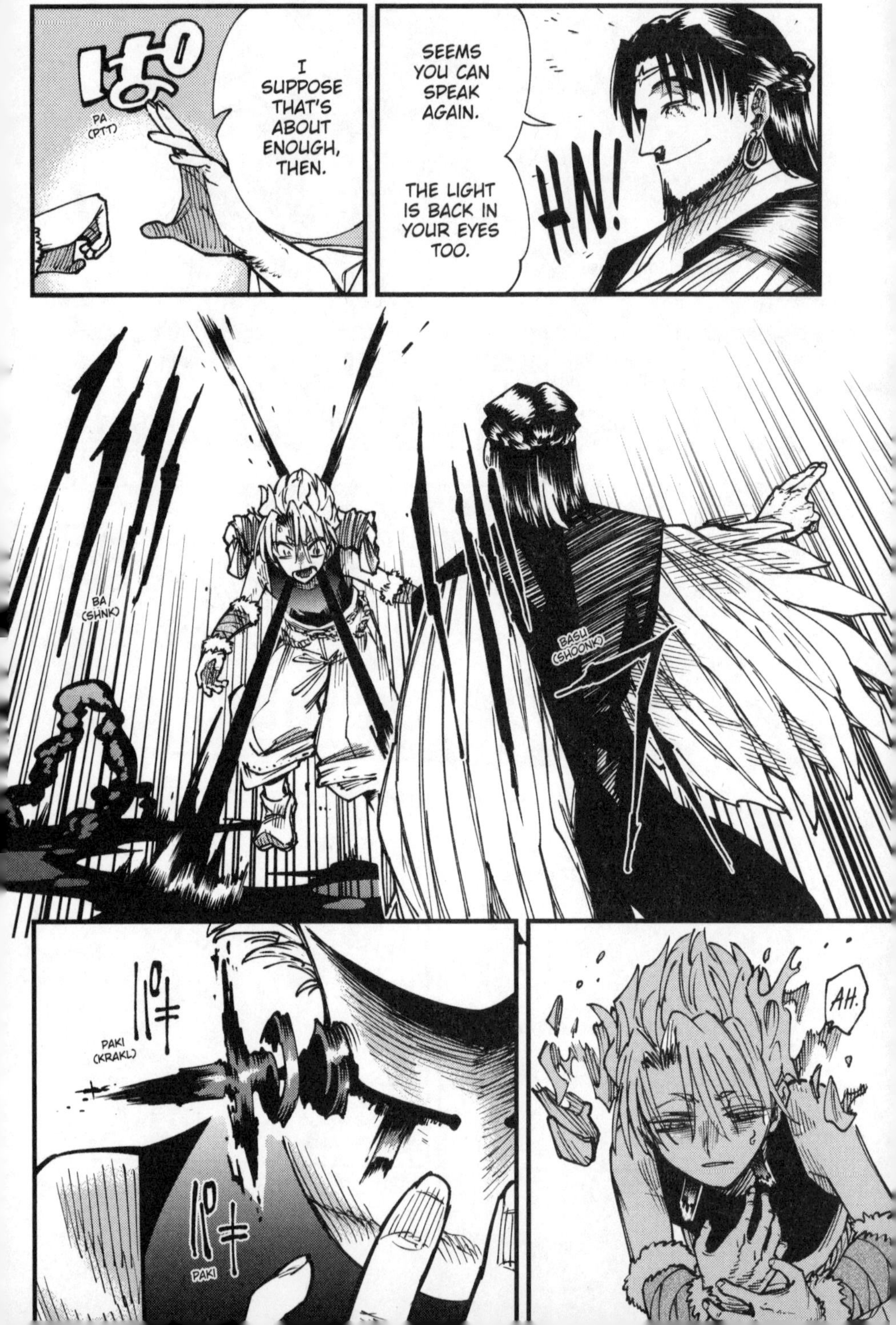
SEEMS YOU CAN SPEAK AGAIN.
THE LIGHT IS BACK IN YOUR EYES TOO.
HN!
I SUPPOSE THAT'S ABOUT ENOUGH, THEN.
PA (PTT)
BASU (SHOONK)
BA (SHNK)
AH.
PAKI (KRAKL)
パキ
PAKI

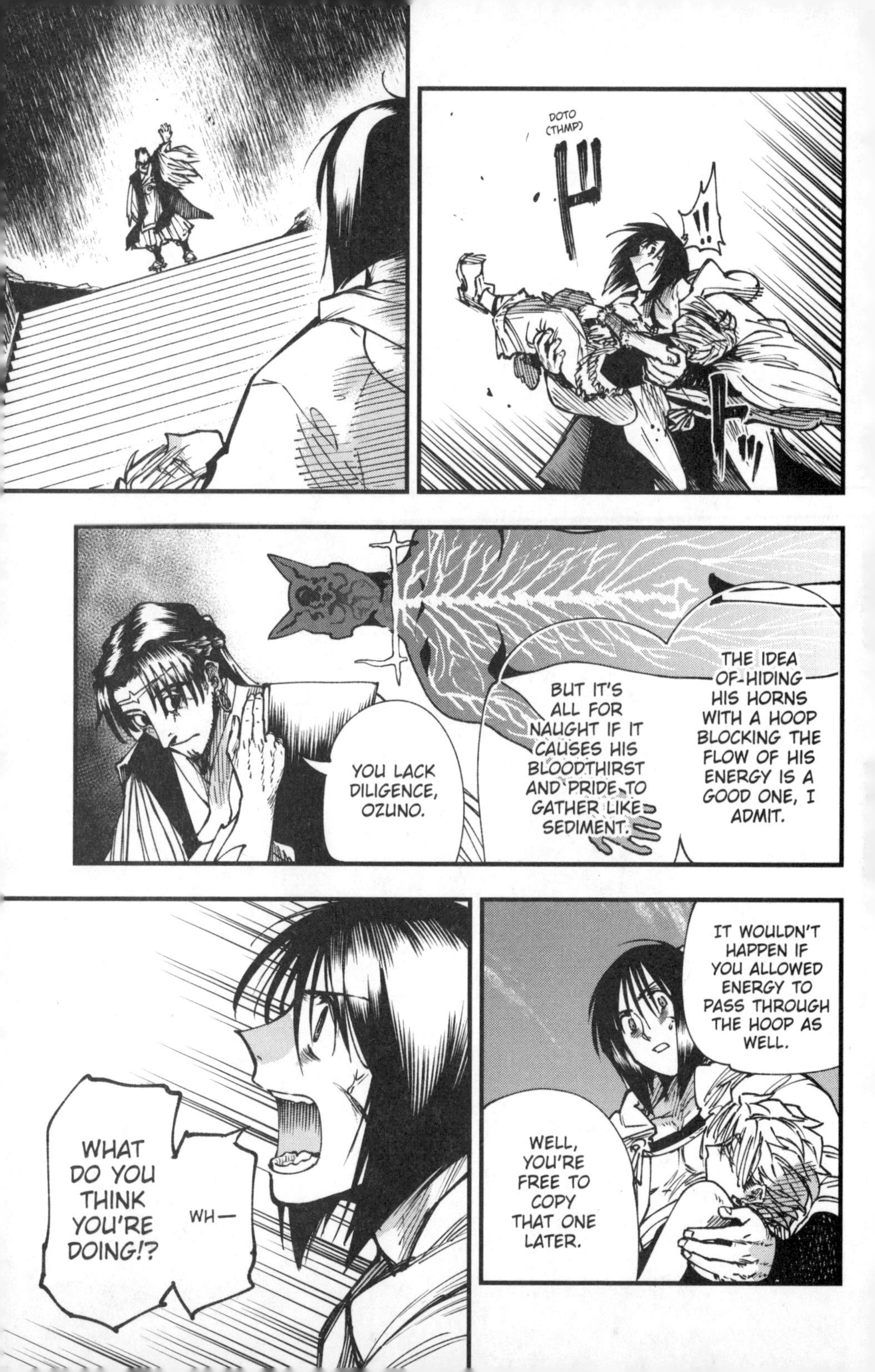
DOTO (THMP)
!!
THE IDEA OF HIDING HIS HORNS WITH A HOOP BLOCKING THE FLOW OF HIS ENERGY IS A GOOD ONE, I ADMIT.
BUT IT'S ALL FOR NAUGHT IF IT CAUSES HIS BLOODTHIRST AND PRIDE TO GATHER LIKE SEDIMENT.
YOU LACK DILIGENCE, OZUNO.
IT WOULDN'T HAPPEN IF YOU ALLOWED ENERGY TO PASS THROUGH THE HOOP AS WELL.
WELL, YOU'RE FREE TO COPY THAT ONE LATER.
WH—
WHAT DO YOU THINK YOU'RE DOING!?

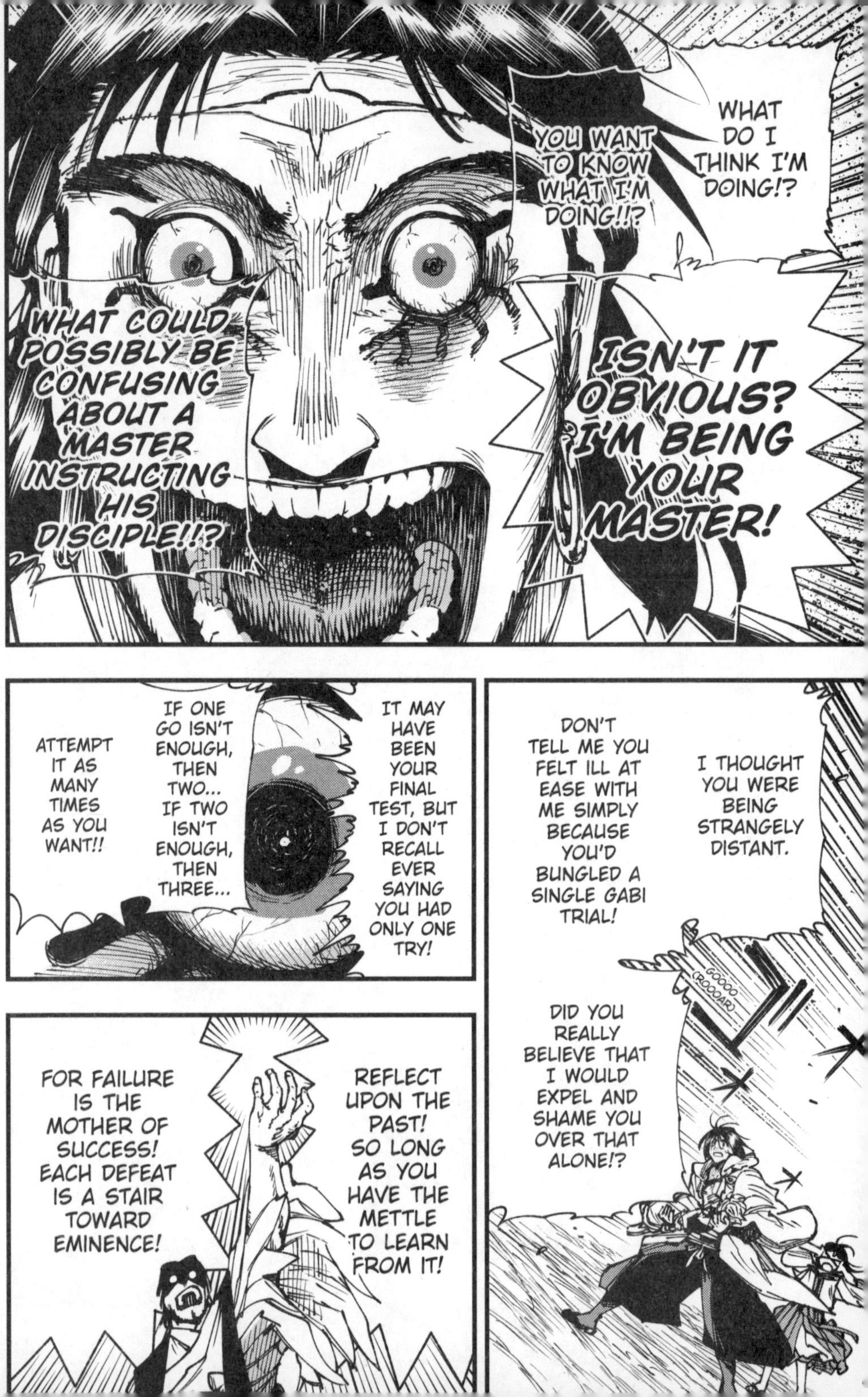
WHAT DO I THINK I'M DOING!?
YOU WANT TO KNOW WHAT I'M DOING!!?
ISN'T IT OBVIOUS? I'M BEING YOUR MASTER!
WHAT COULD POSSIBLY BE CONFUSING ABOUT A MASTER INSTRUCTING HIS DISCIPLE!!?
I THOUGHT YOU WERE BEING STRANGELY DISTANT.
DON'T TELL ME YOU FELT ILL AT EASE WITH ME SIMPLY BECAUSE YOU'D BUNGLED A SINGLE GABI TRIAL!
GOOOO (ROOOAR)
DID YOU REALLY BELIEVE THAT I WOULD EXPEL AND SHAME YOU OVER THAT ALONE!?
IT MAY HAVE BEEN YOUR FINAL TEST, BUT I DON'T RECALL EVER SAYING YOU HAD ONLY ONE TRY!
IF ONE GO ISN'T ENOUGH, THEN TWO... IF TWO ISN'T ENOUGH, THEN THREE...
ATTEMPT IT AS MANY TIMES AS YOU WANT!!
REFLECT UPON THE PAST! SO LONG AS YOU HAVE THE METTLE TO LEARN FROM IT!
FOR FAILURE IS THE MOTHER OF SUCCESS! EACH DEFEAT IS A STAIR TOWARD EMINENCE!

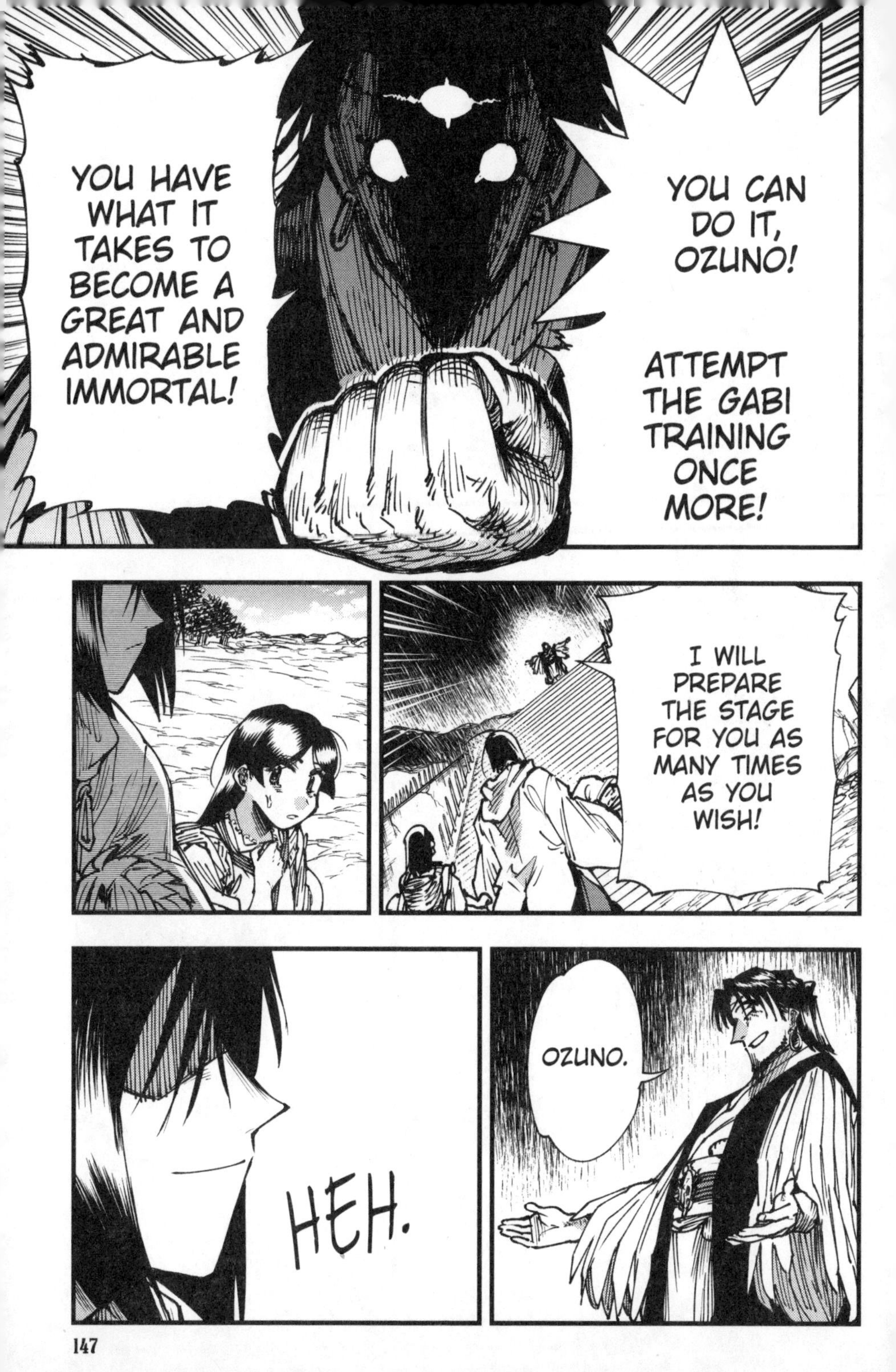
YOU CAN DO IT, OZUNO!
ATTEMPT THE GABI TRAINING ONCE MORE!
YOU HAVE WHAT IT TAKES TO BECOME A GREAT AND ADMIRABLE IMMORTAL!
I WILL PREPARE THE STAGE FOR YOU AS MANY TIMES AS YOU WISH!
OZUNO.
HEH.

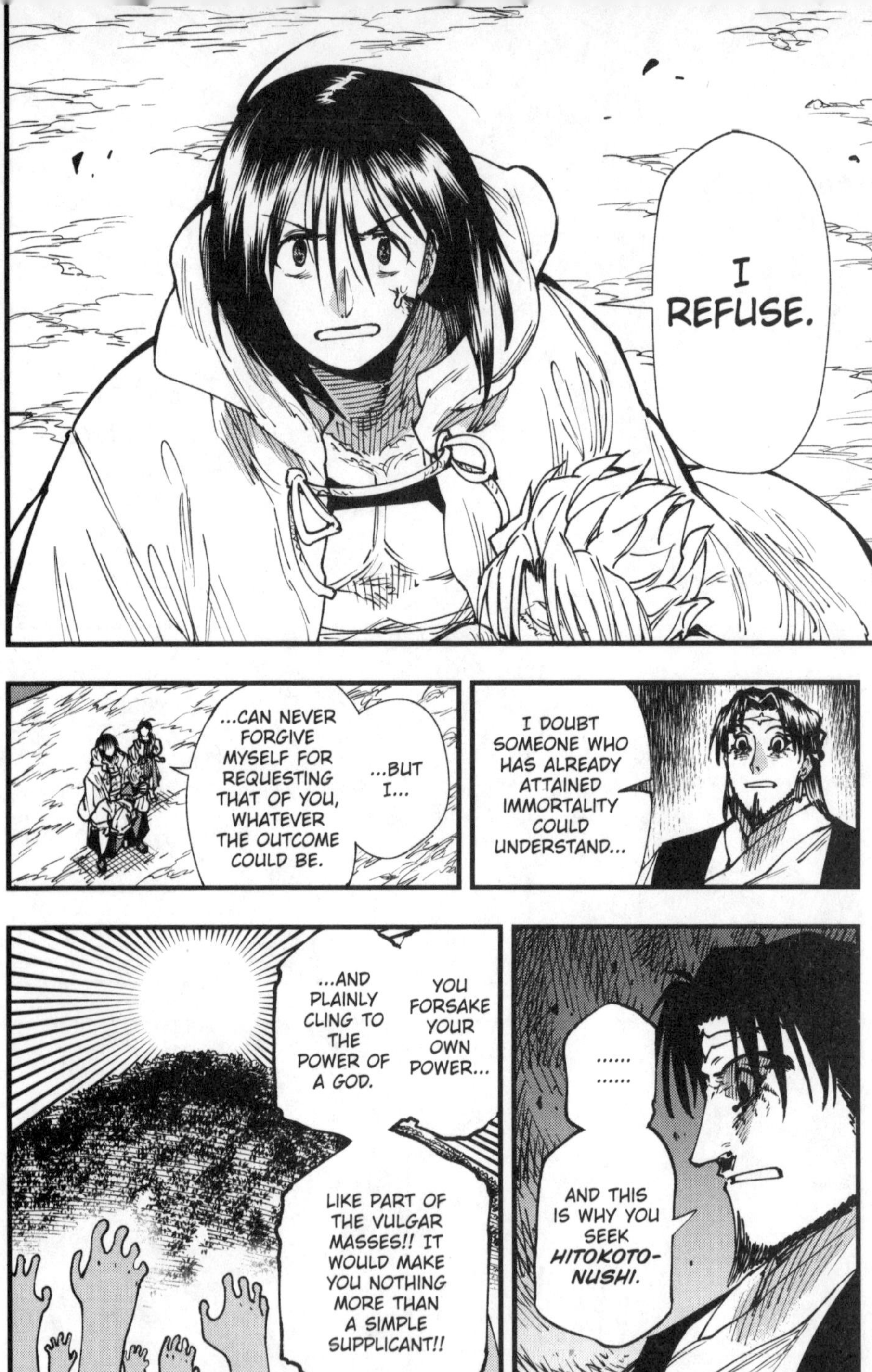
I REFUSE.
I DOUBT SOMEONE WHO HAS ALREADY ATTAINED IMMORTALITY COULD UNDERSTAND...
...BUT I...
...CAN NEVER FORGIVE MYSELF FOR REQUESTING THAT OF YOU, WHATEVER THE OUTCOME COULD BE.
......
......
AND THIS IS WHY YOU SEEK *HITOKOTO-NUSHI*.
YOU FORSAKE YOUR OWN POWER...
...AND PLAINLY CLING TO THE POWER OF A GOD.
LIKE PART OF THE VULGAR MASSES!! IT WOULD MAKE YOU NOTHING MORE THAN A SIMPLE SUPPLICANT!!

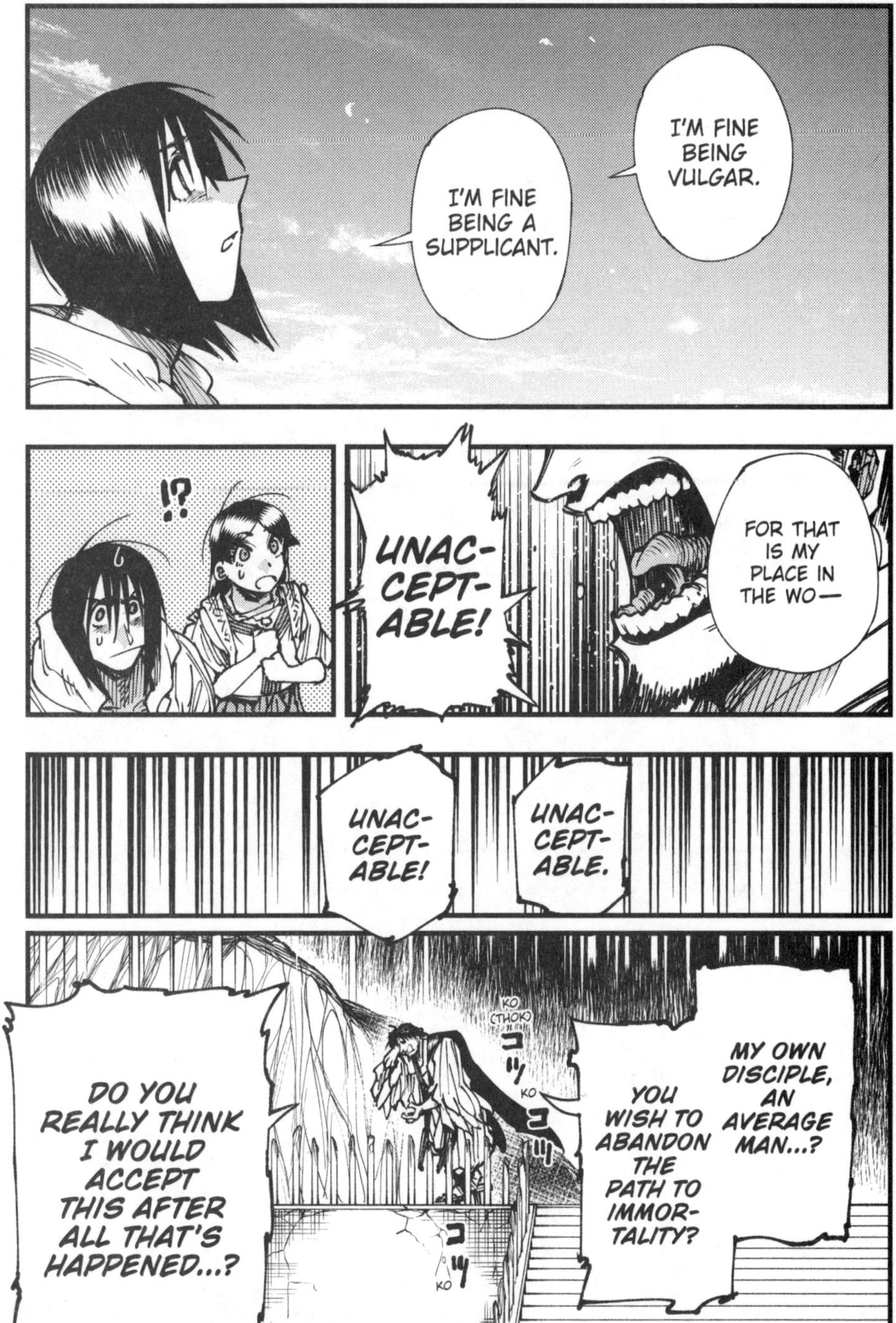
I'M FINE BEING VULGAR.
I'M FINE BEING A SUPPLICANT.
FOR THAT IS MY PLACE IN THE WO—
UNAC-CEPT-ABLE!
!?
UNAC-CEPT-ABLE.
UNAC-CEPT-ABLE!
MY OWN DISCIPLE, AN AVERAGE MAN...?
YOU WISH TO ABANDON THE PATH TO IMMOR-TALITY?
KO (THOK)
KO
KO
DO YOU REALLY THINK I WOULD ACCEPT THIS AFTER ALL THAT'S HAPPENED...?

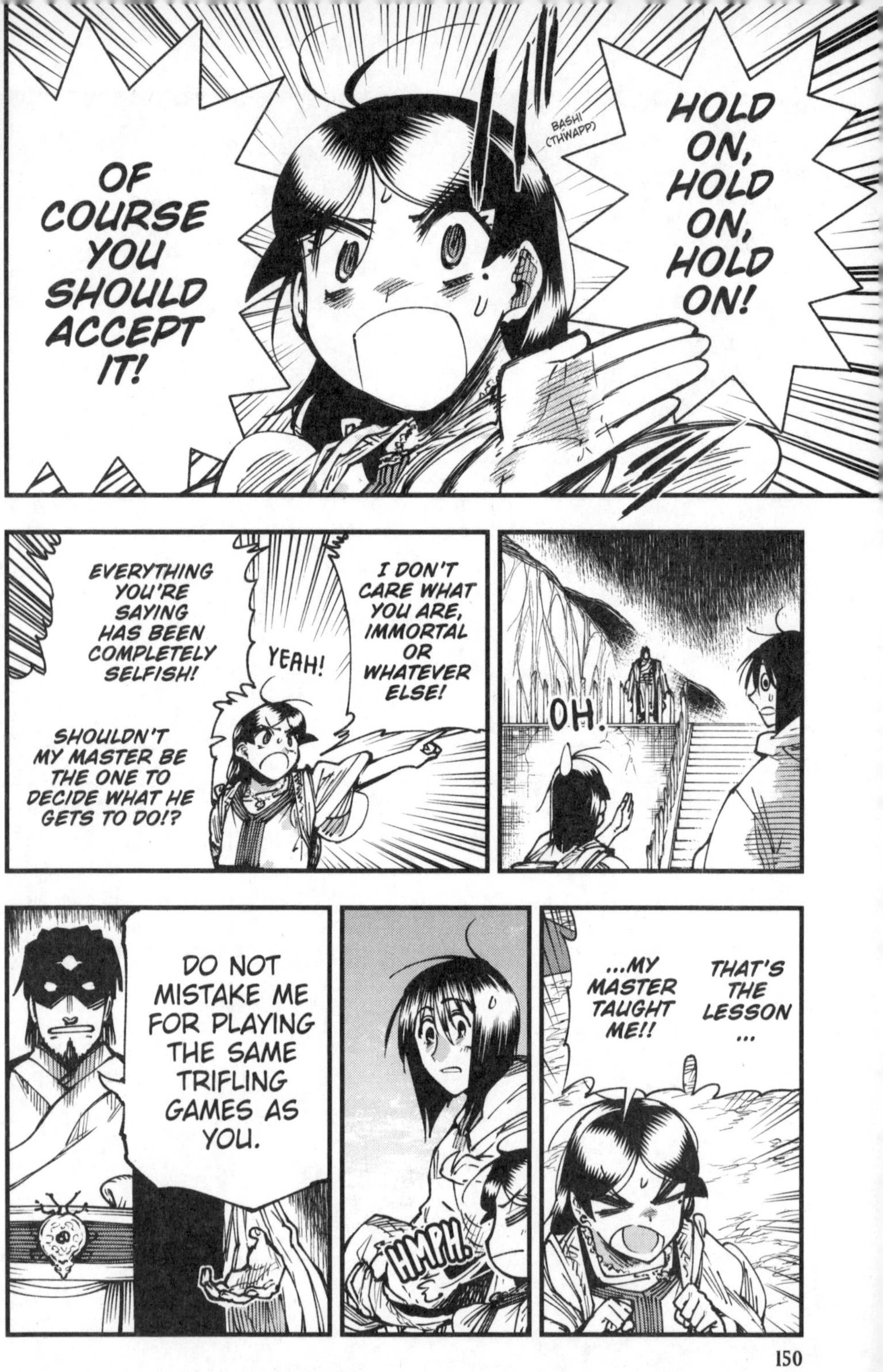
HOLD ON, HOLD ON, HOLD ON!
BASHI (THWAPP)
OF COURSE YOU SHOULD ACCEPT IT!
OH.
I DON'T CARE WHAT YOU ARE, IMMORTAL OR WHATEVER ELSE!
YEAH!
EVERYTHING YOU'RE SAYING HAS BEEN COMPLETELY SELFISH!
SHOULDN'T MY MASTER BE THE ONE TO DECIDE WHAT HE GETS TO DO!?
THAT'S THE LESSON ...
...MY MASTER TAUGHT ME!!
HMPH.
DO NOT MISTAKE ME FOR PLAYING THE SAME TRIFLING GAMES AS YOU.

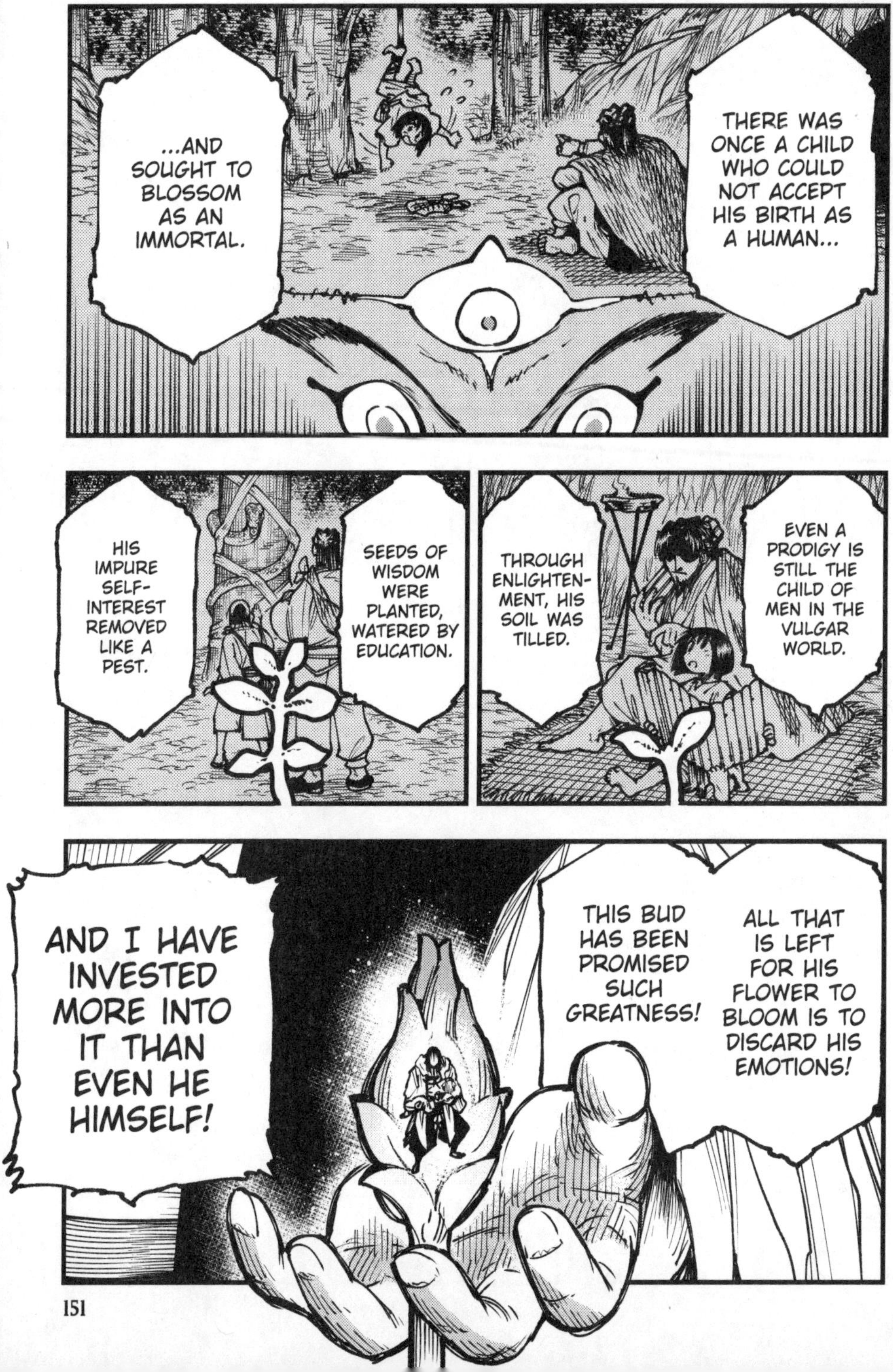
THERE WAS ONCE A CHILD WHO COULD NOT ACCEPT HIS BIRTH AS A HUMAN...
...AND SOUGHT TO BLOSSOM AS AN IMMORTAL.
EVEN A PRODIGY IS STILL THE CHILD OF MEN IN THE VULGAR WORLD.
THROUGH ENLIGHTEN-MENT, HIS SOIL WAS TILLED.
SEEDS OF WISDOM WERE PLANTED, WATERED BY EDUCATION.
HIS IMPURE SELF-INTEREST REMOVED LIKE A PEST.
ALL THAT IS LEFT FOR HIS FLOWER TO BLOOM IS TO DISCARD HIS EMOTIONS!
THIS BUD HAS BEEN PROMISED SUCH GREATNESS!
AND I HAVE INVESTED MORE INTO IT THAN EVEN HE HIMSELF!

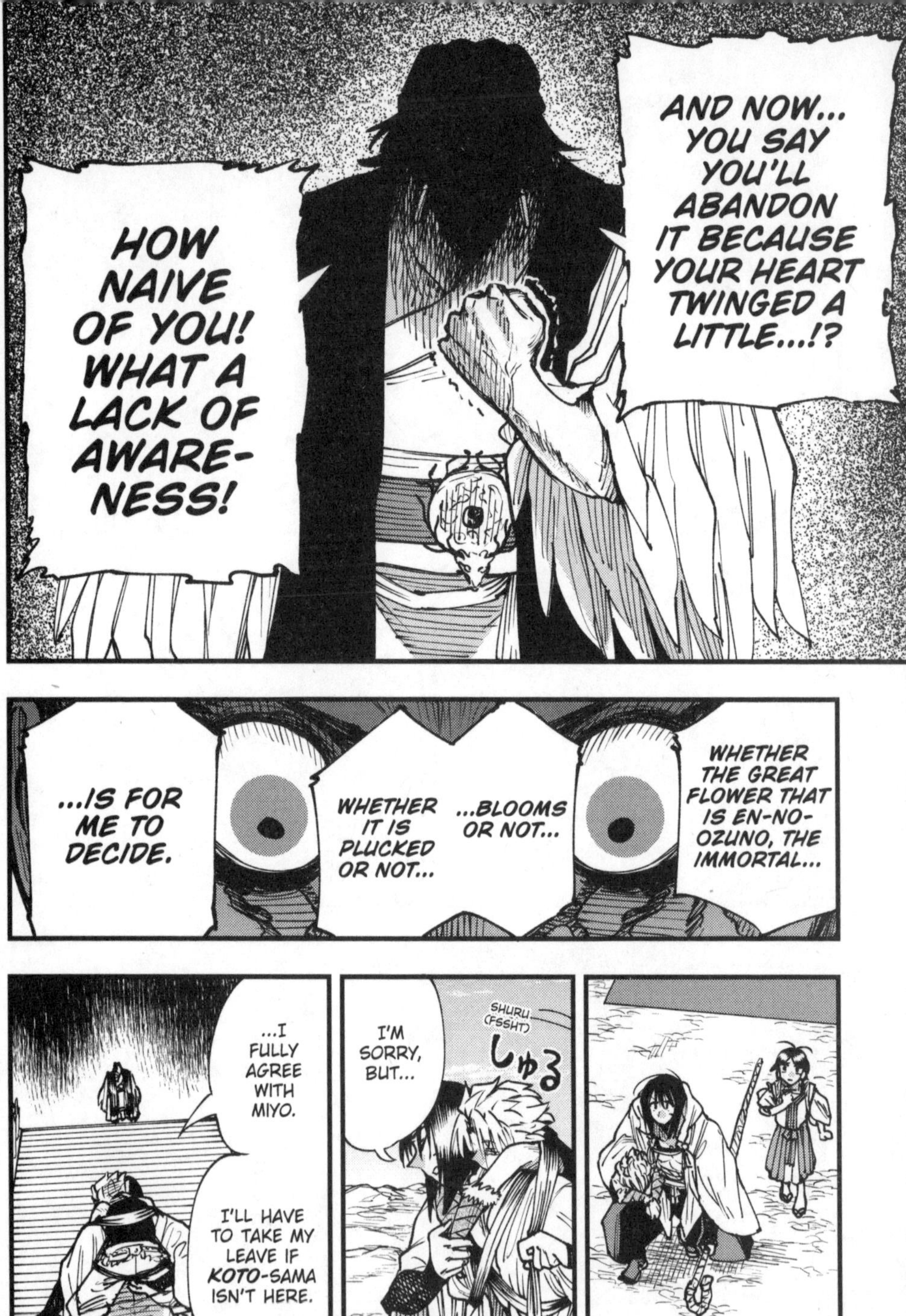
AND NOW... YOU SAY YOU'LL ABANDON IT BECAUSE YOUR HEART TWINGED A LITTLE...!?
HOW NAIVE OF YOU! WHAT A LACK OF AWARE-NESS!
WHETHER THE GREAT FLOWER THAT IS EN-NO-OZUNO, THE IMMORTAL...
...BLOOMS OR NOT...
WHETHER IT IS PLUCKED OR NOT...
...IS FOR ME TO DECIDE.
SHURU (FSSHT)
しゅる
I'M SORRY, BUT...
...I FULLY AGREE WITH MIYO.
I'LL HAVE TO TAKE MY LEAVE IF KOTO-SAMA ISN'T HERE.

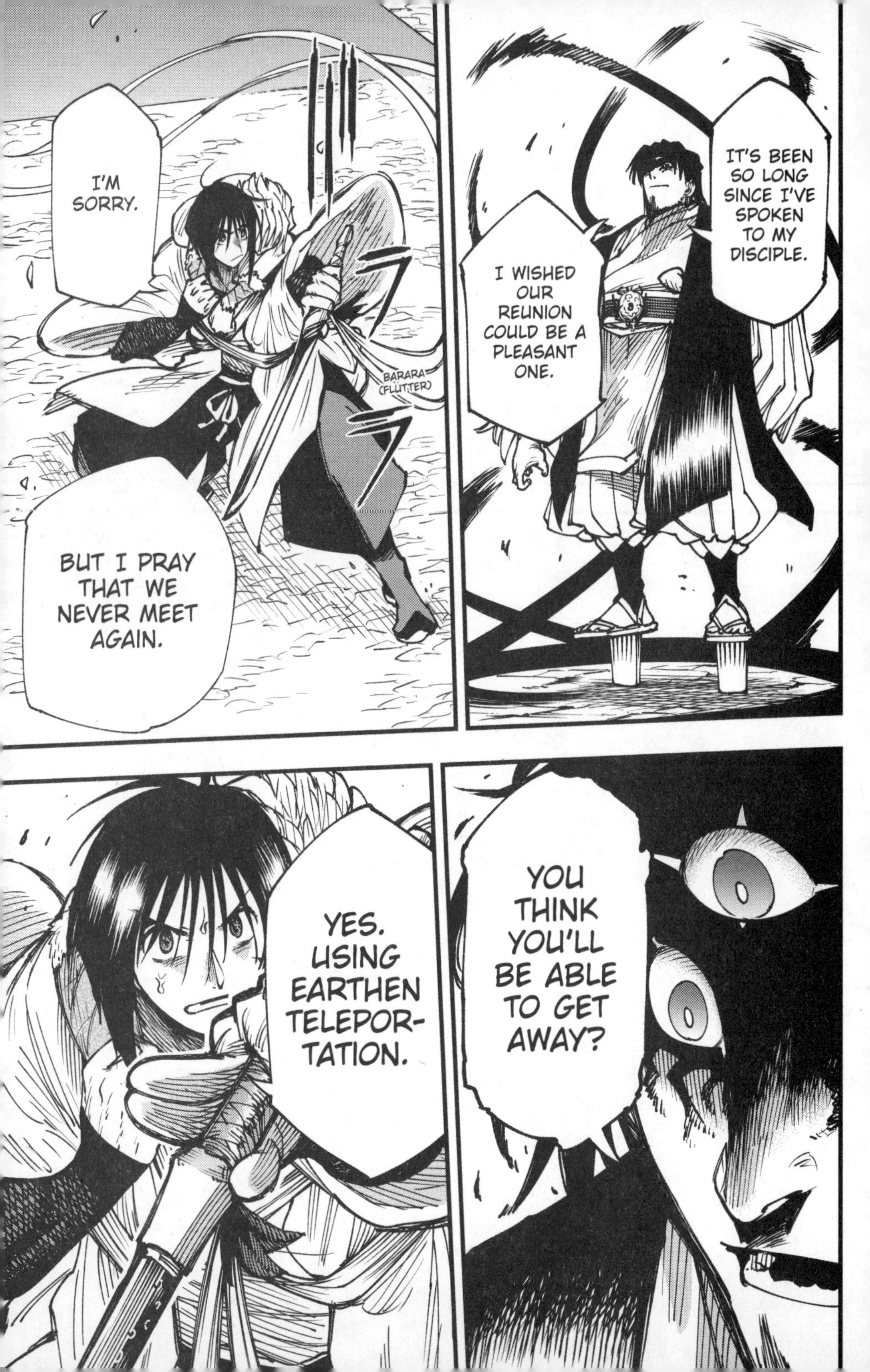
IT'S BEEN SO LONG SINCE I'VE SPOKEN TO MY DISCIPLE.
I WISHED OUR REUNION COULD BE A PLEASANT ONE.
I'M SORRY.
BARARA (FLUTTER)
BUT I PRAY THAT WE NEVER MEET AGAIN.
YOU THINK YOU'LL BE ABLE TO GET AWAY?
YES. USING EARTHEN TELEPOR-TATION.

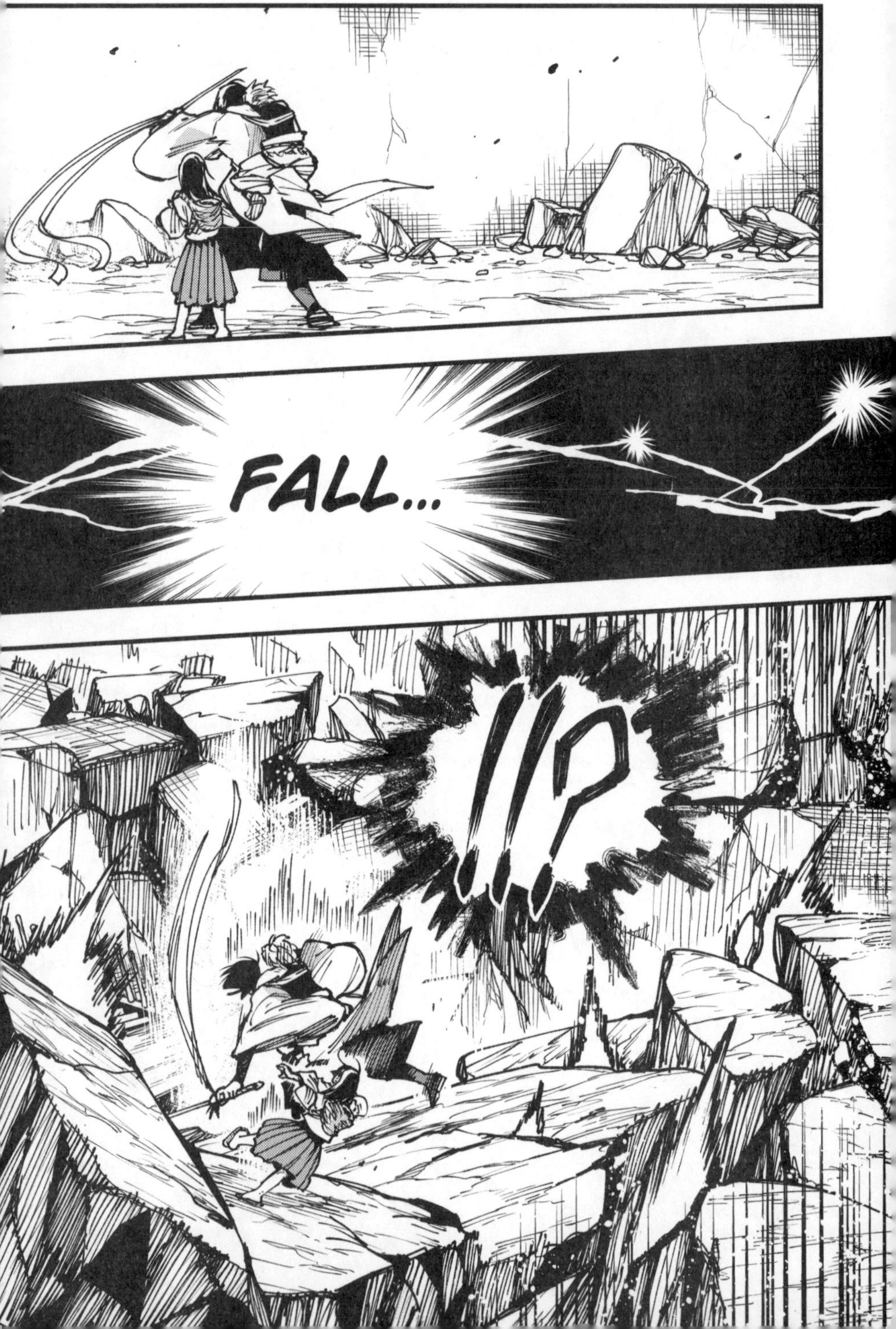
FALL...
!?

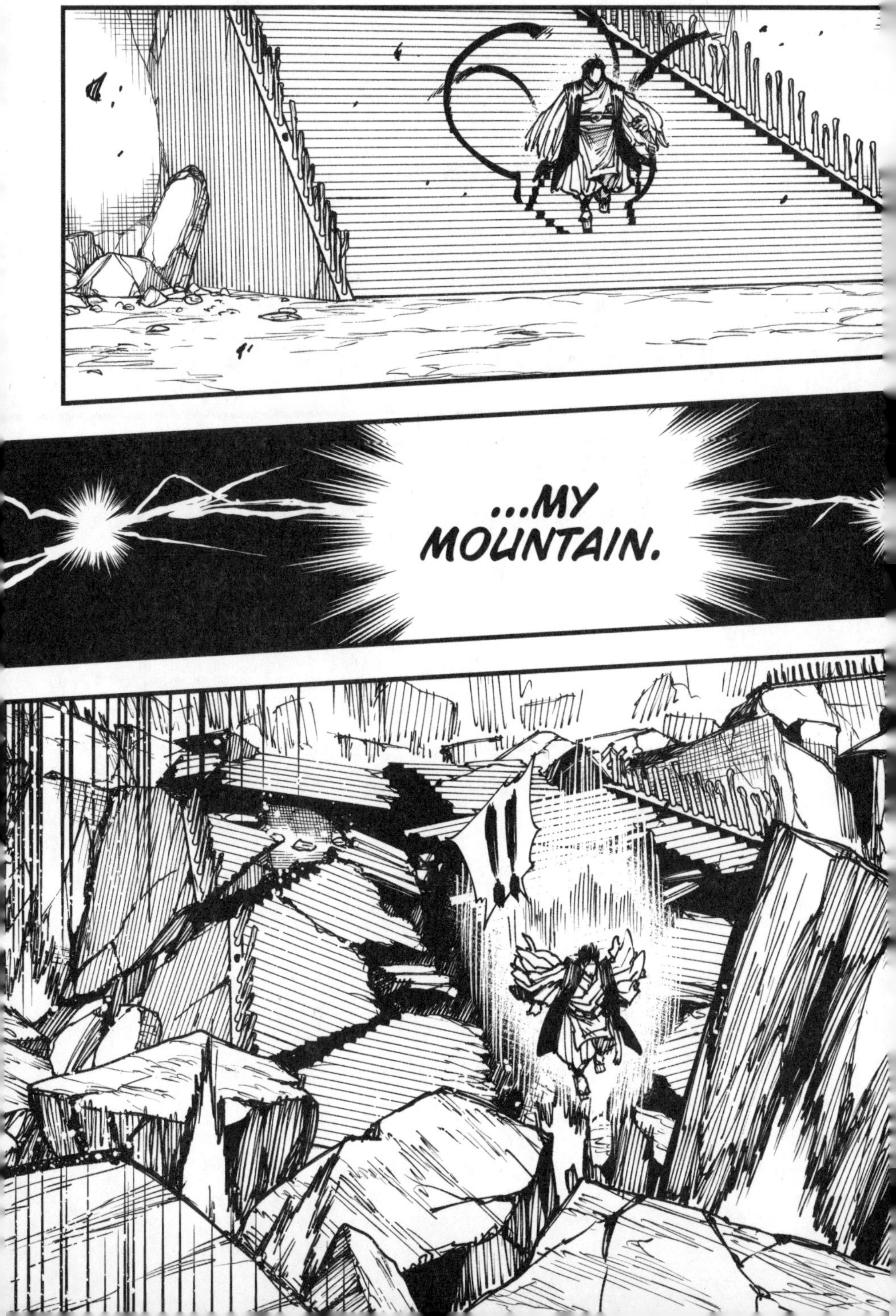
...MY MOUNTAIN.

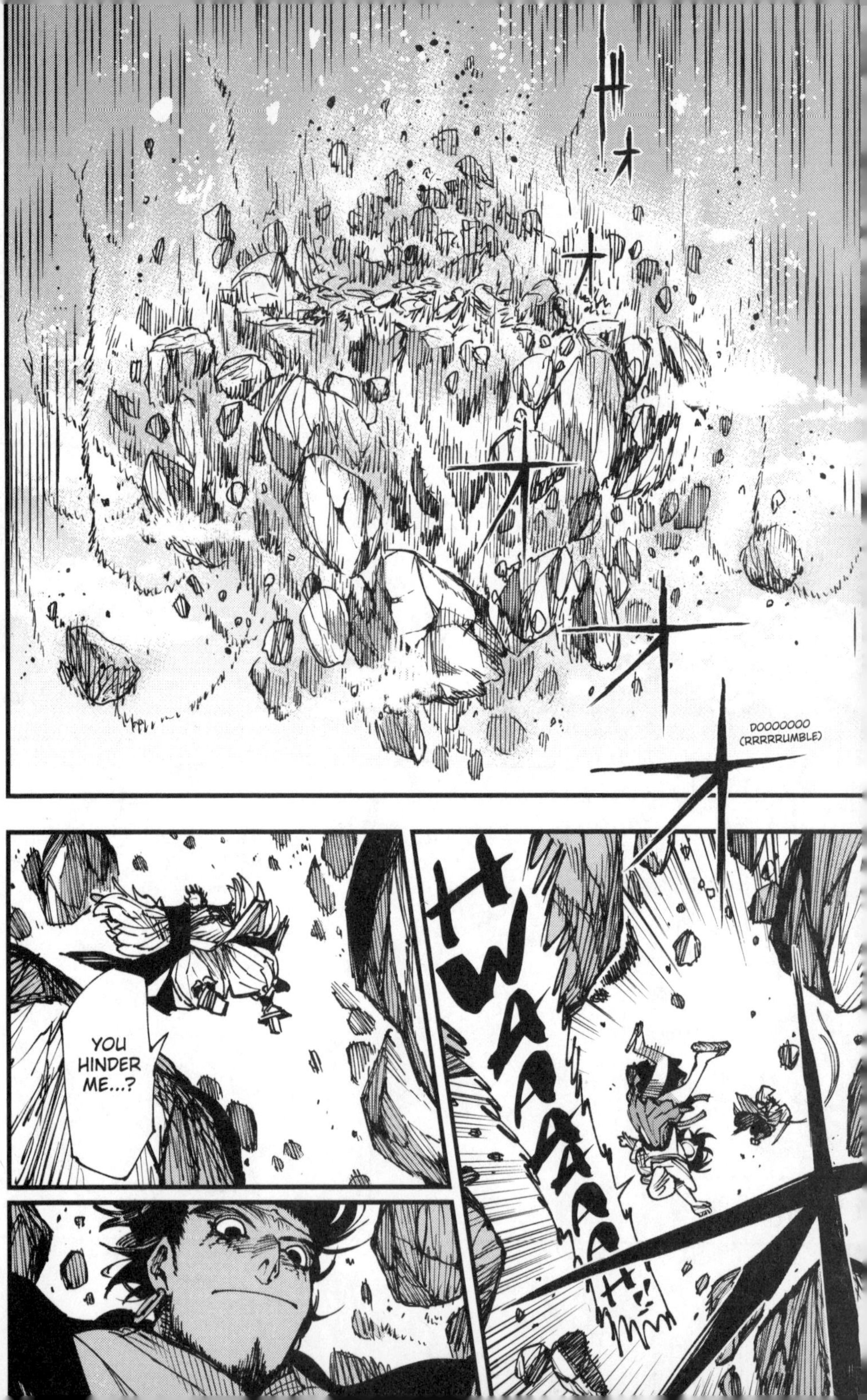
DOOOOOOO
(RRRRRUMBLE)
YOU HINDER ME...?

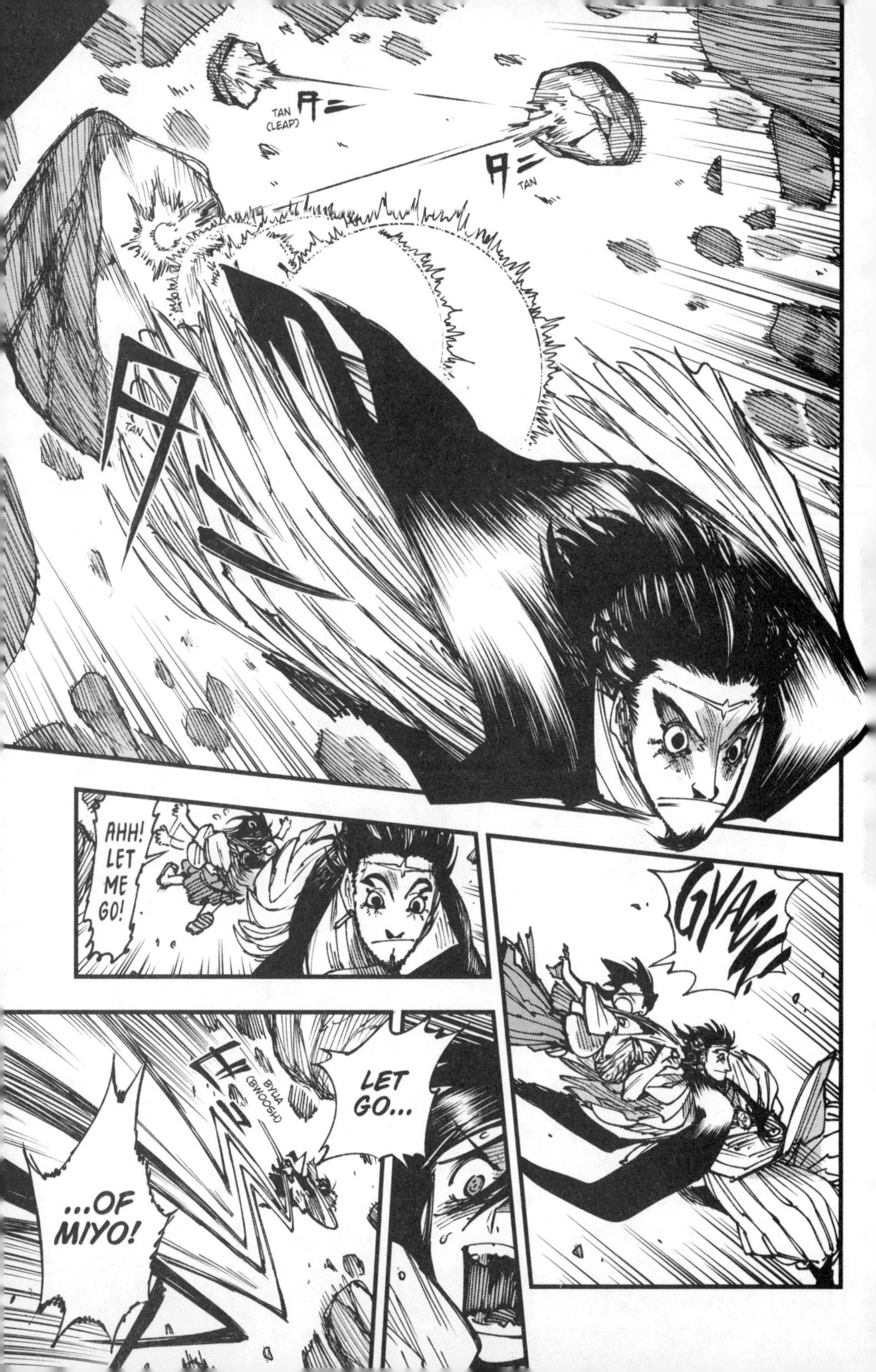
TAN (LEAP)
TAN
TAN
GYAAH!
AHH! LET ME GO!
BYUA (BWOOSH)
LET GO...
...OF MIYO!

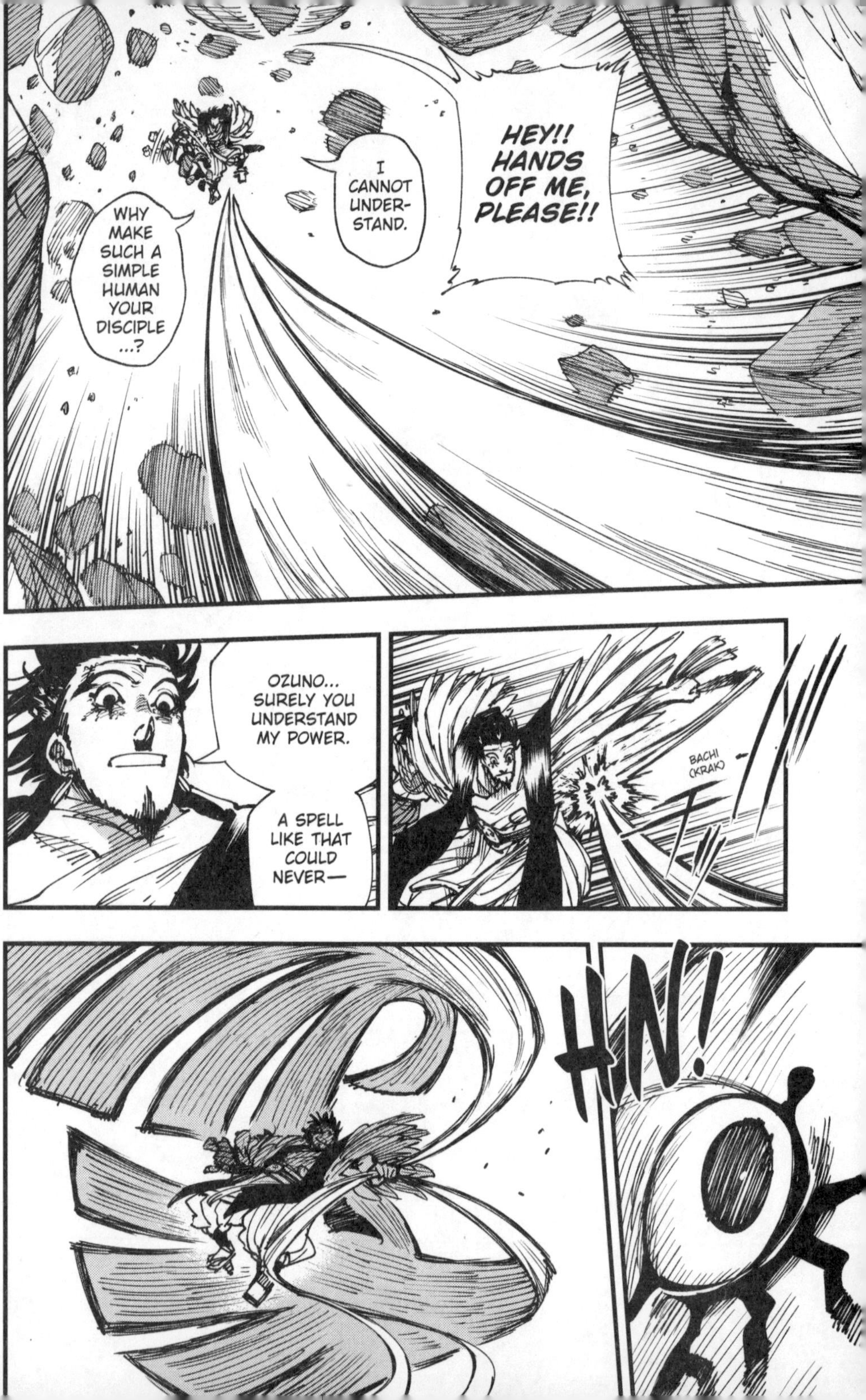
HEY!! HANDS OFF ME, PLEASE!!
I CANNOT UNDER-STAND.
WHY MAKE SUCH A SIMPLE HUMAN YOUR DISCIPLE ...?
BACHI (KRAK)
OZUNO... SURELY YOU UNDERSTAND MY POWER.
A SPELL LIKE THAT COULD NEVER—
HN!

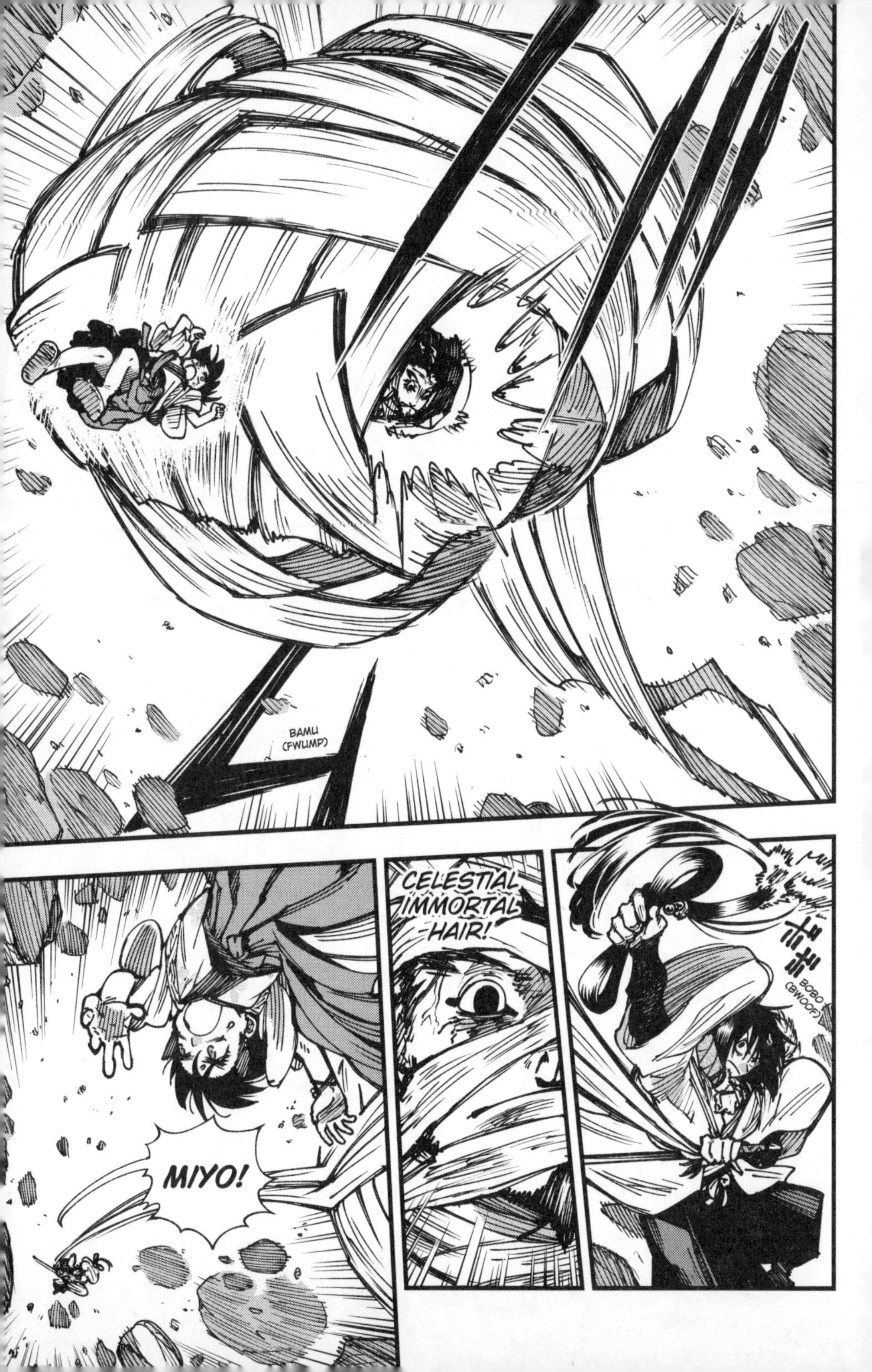
BAMU
(FWUMP)
BOBO
(BWOOF)
CELESTIAL IMMORTAL HAIR!
MIYO!

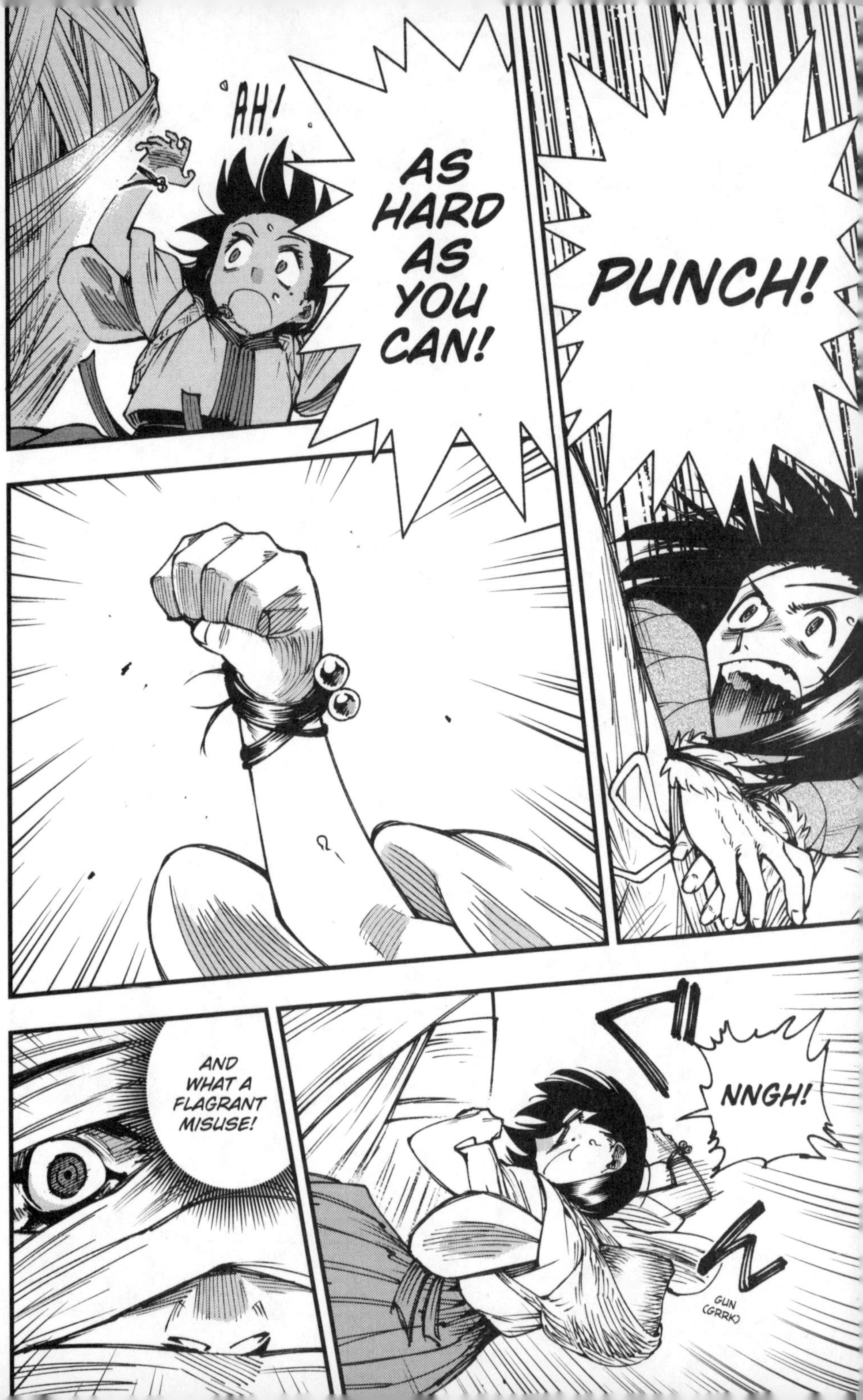
PUNCH!
AS HARD AS YOU CAN!
AH!
NNGH!
GUN (GRRK)
AND WHAT A FLAGRANT MISUSE!

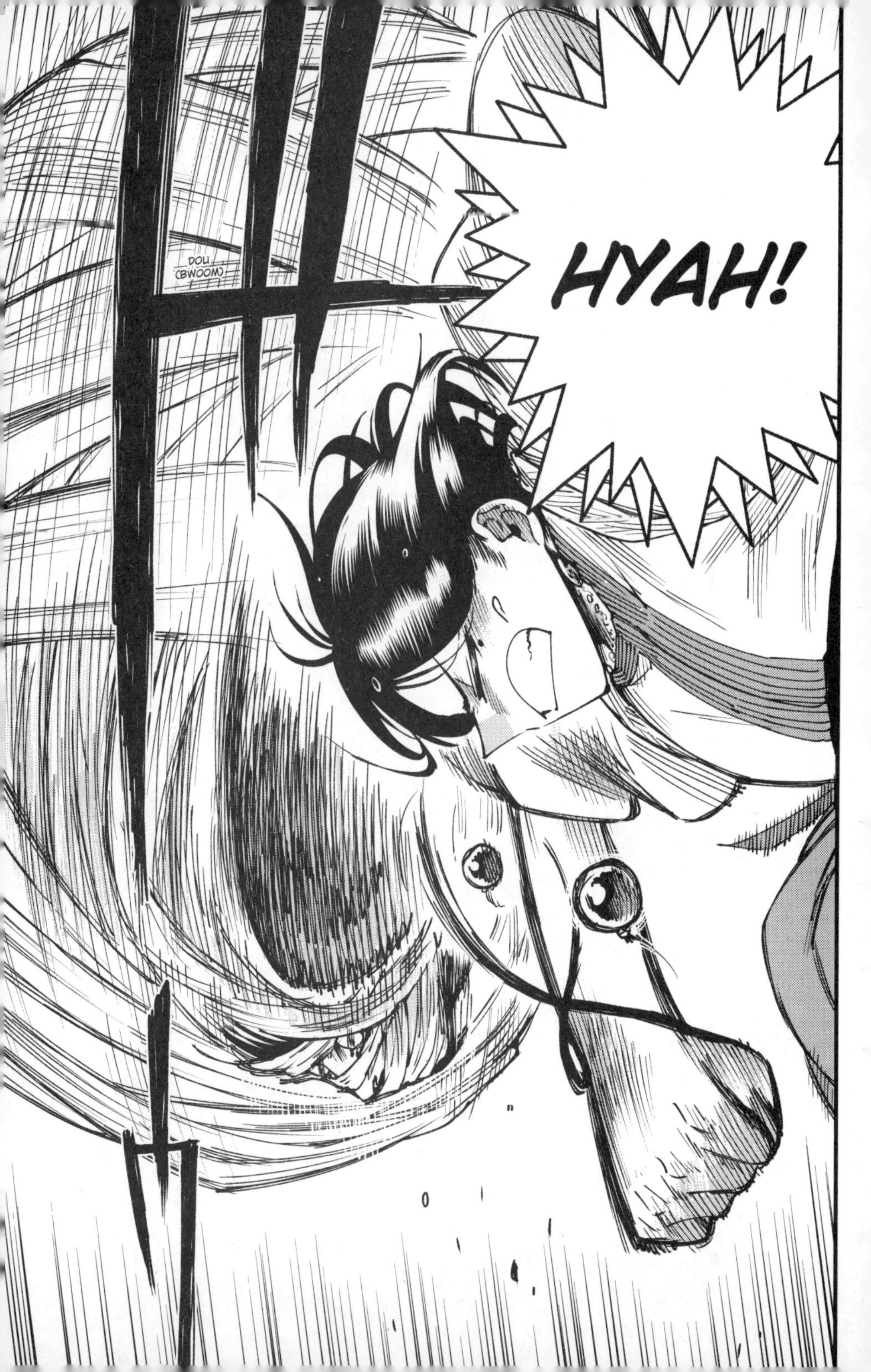
HYAH!
DOU
(BWOOM)

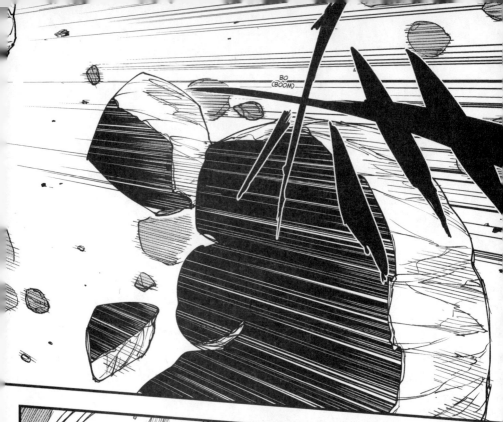

BO
(BOOM)

BUT NOW...

I-I'M SORRY...!

~~~~ ~~~....

THAT HAIR IS SCARY STUFF.

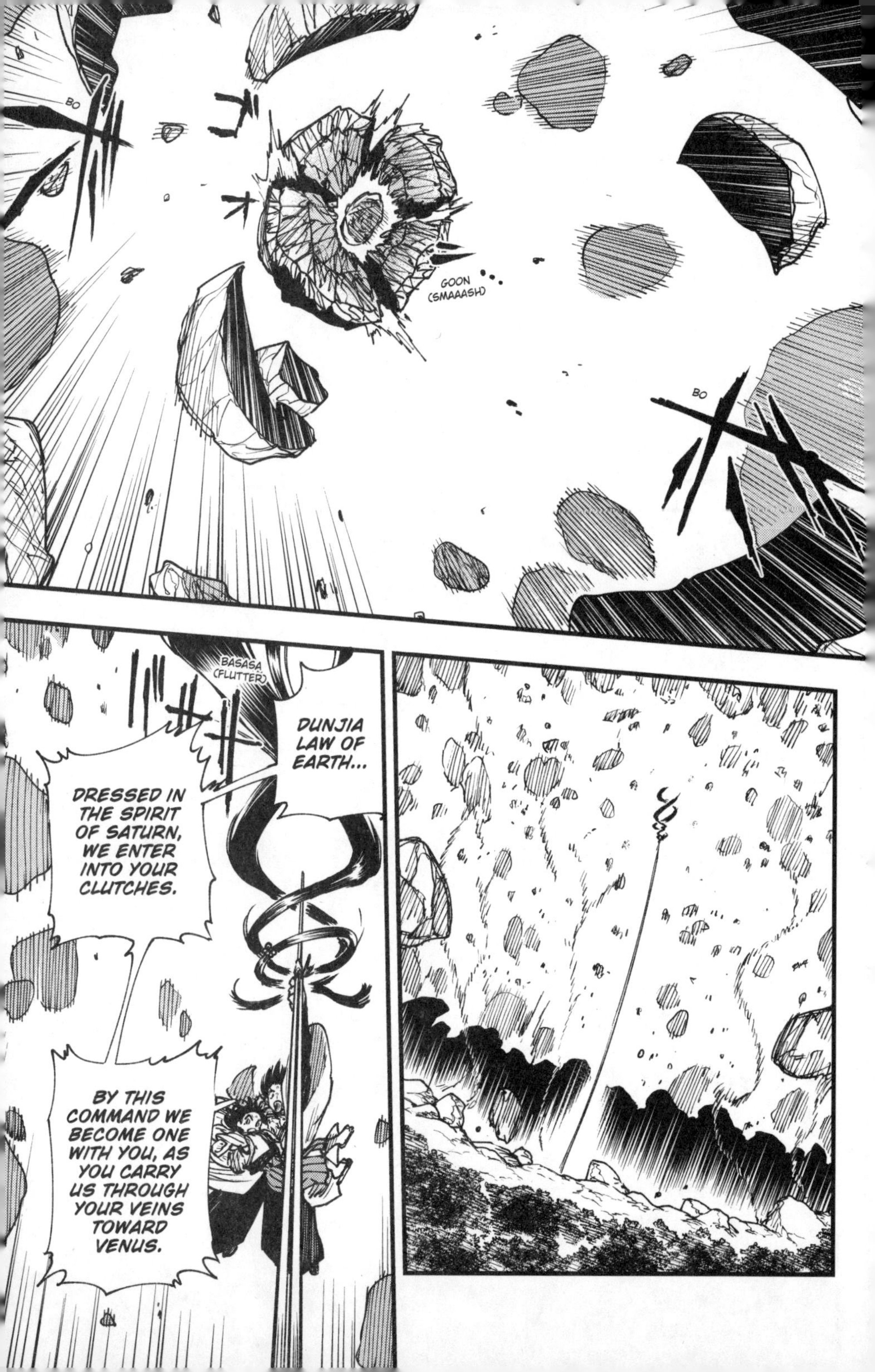
BO
GOON (SMAAASH)
BO
BASASA (FLUTTER)
DUNJIA LAW OF EARTH...
DRESSED IN THE SPIRIT OF SATURN, WE ENTER INTO YOUR CLUTCHES.
BY THIS COMMAND WE BECOME ONE WITH YOU, AS YOU CARRY US THROUGH YOUR VEINS TOWARD VENUS.

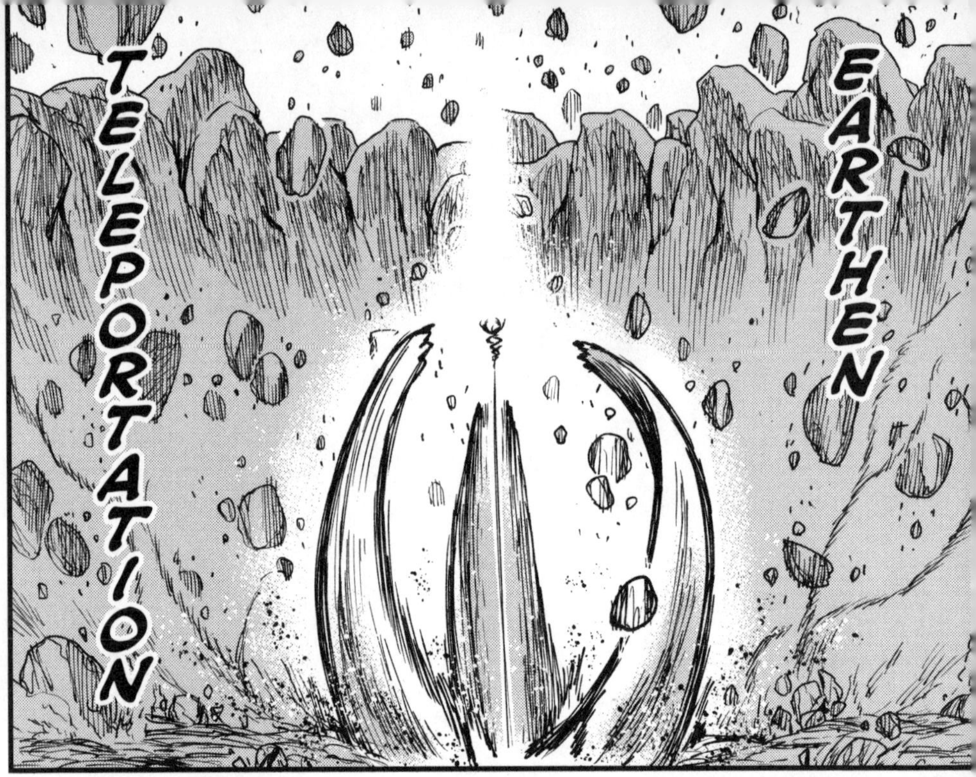
EARTHEN
TELEPORTATION
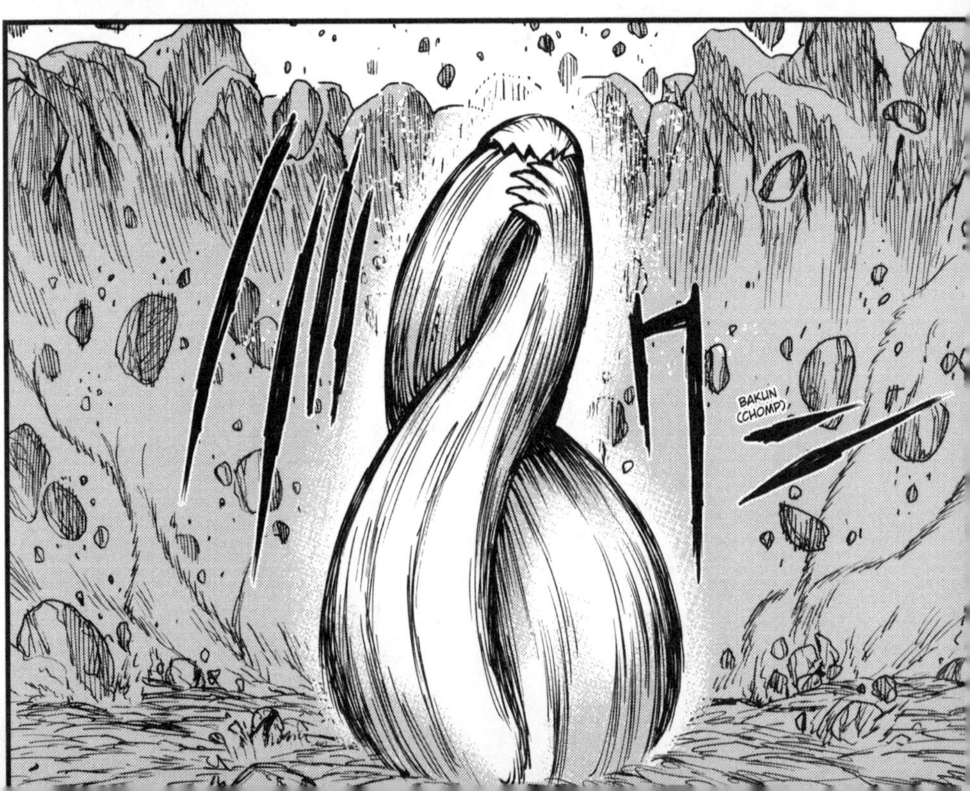
BAKUN (CHOMP)

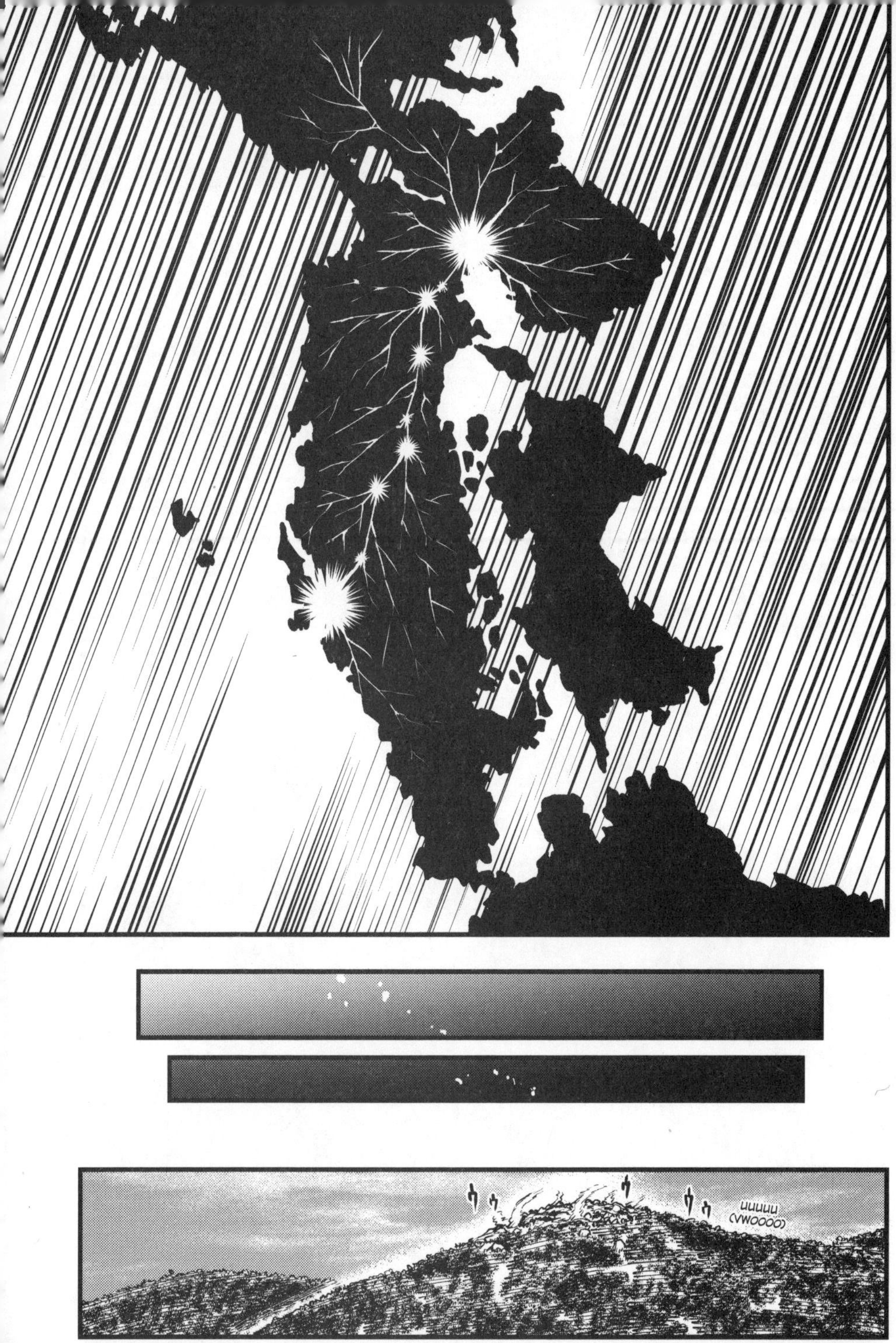
ウゥ
ウ
ウゥ
uuuuu
(VWOOOO)

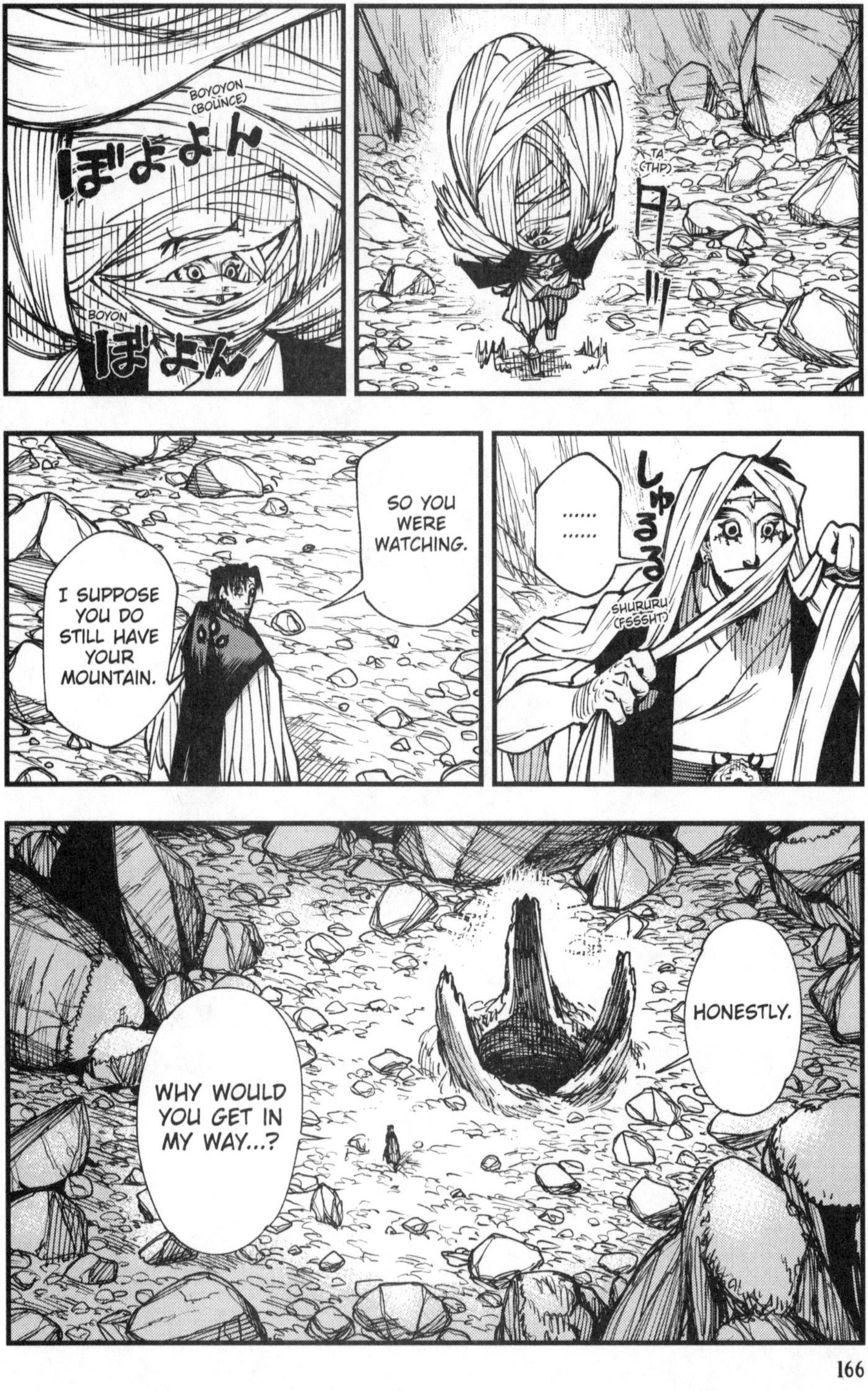
TA
(THP)
タッ
BOYOYON
(BOUNCE)
ぼよよん
BOYON
ぼよん
しゅるる
SHURURU
(FSSSHT)
......
......
SO YOU WERE WATCHING.
I SUPPOSE YOU DO STILL HAVE YOUR MOUNTAIN.
HONESTLY.
WHY WOULD YOU GET IN MY WAY...?

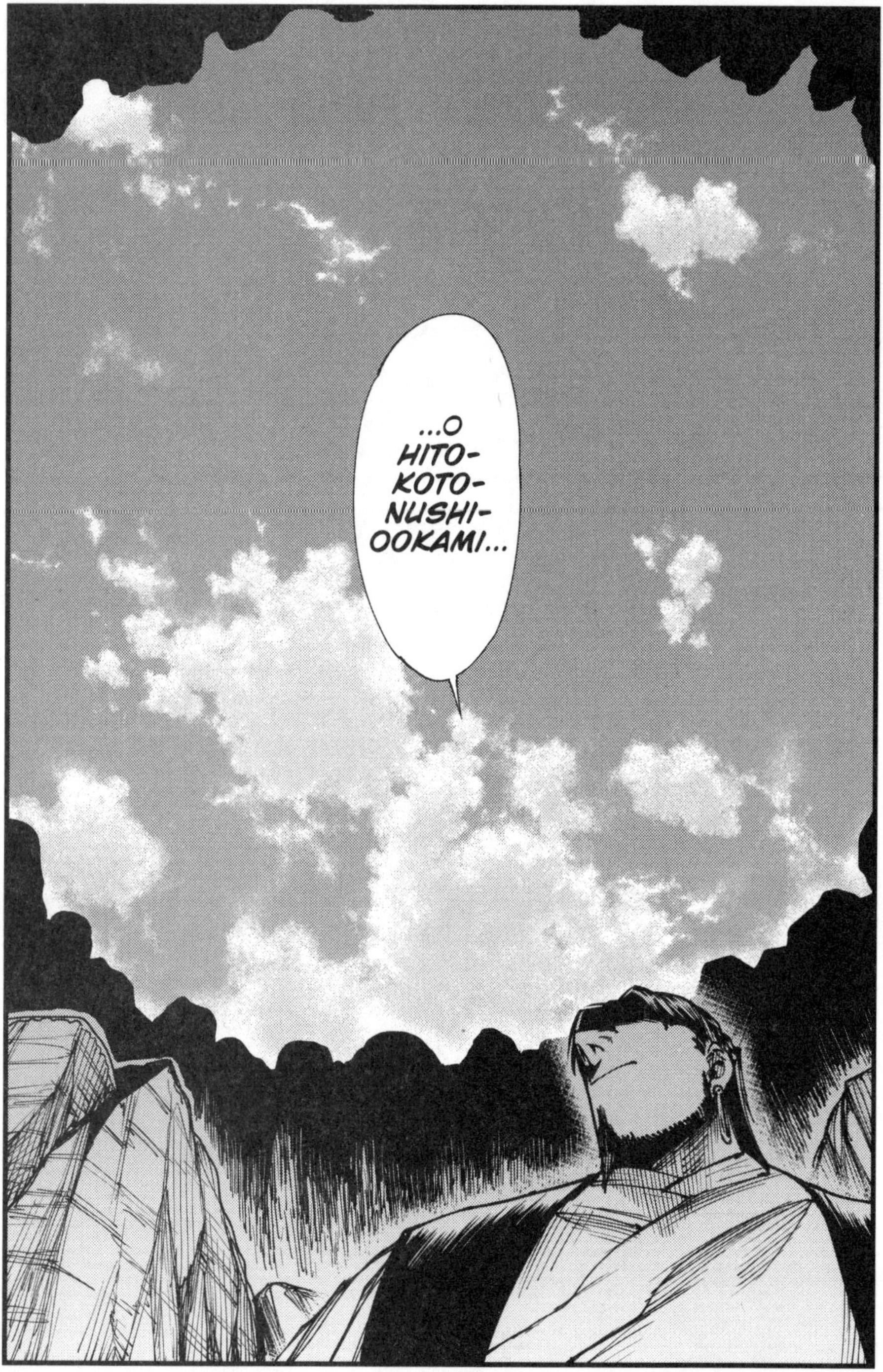
...O HITO-KOTO-NUSHI-OOKAMI...

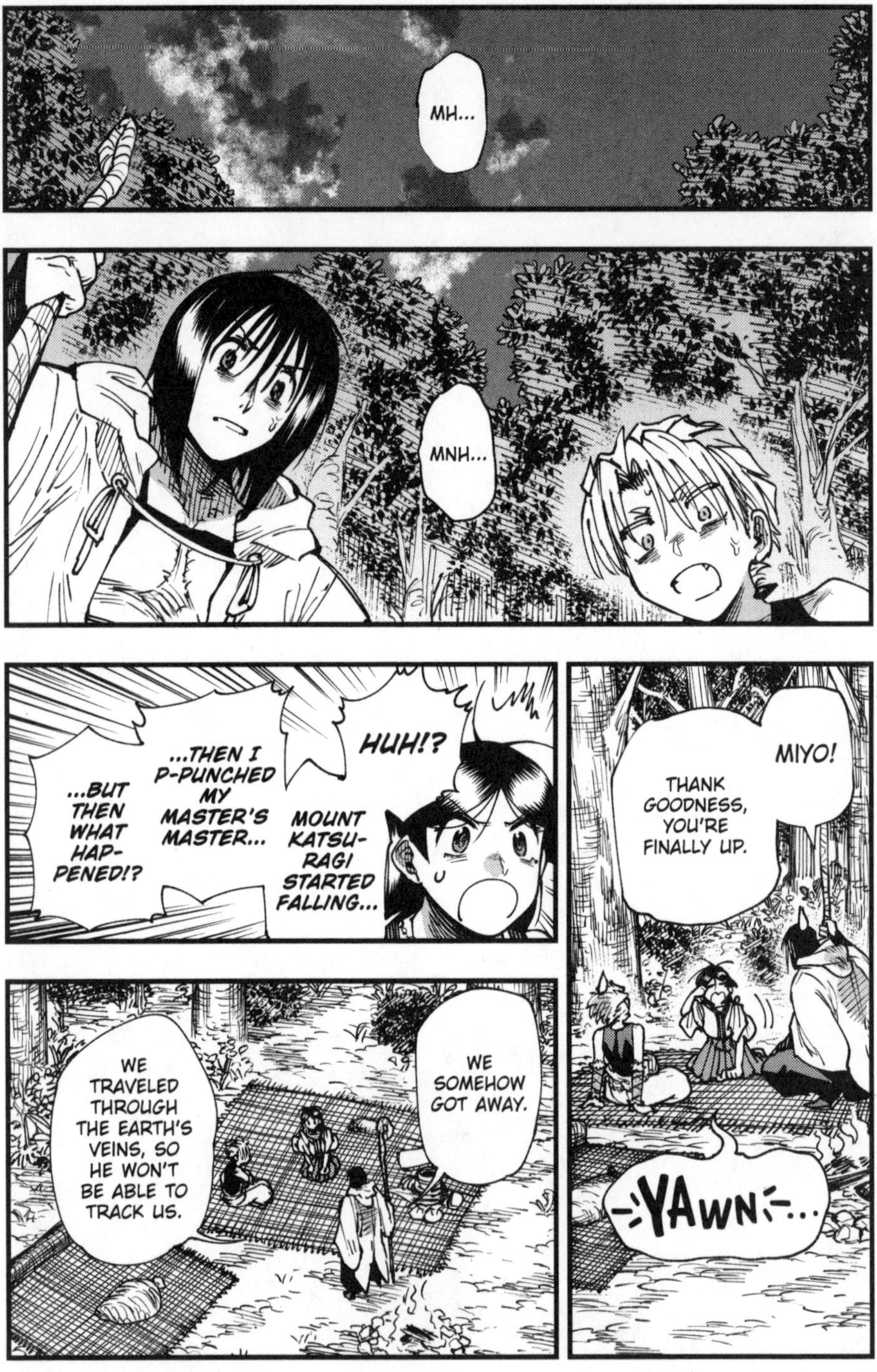
MH...
MNH...
MIYO! THANK GOODNESS, YOU'RE FINALLY UP.
YAWN...
HUH!?
MOUNT KATSURAGI STARTED FALLING...
...THEN I P-PUNCHED MY MASTER'S MASTER...
...BUT THEN WHAT HAPPENED!?
WE SOMEHOW GOT AWAY.
WE TRAVELED THROUGH THE EARTH'S VEINS, SO HE WON'T BE ABLE TO TRACK US.

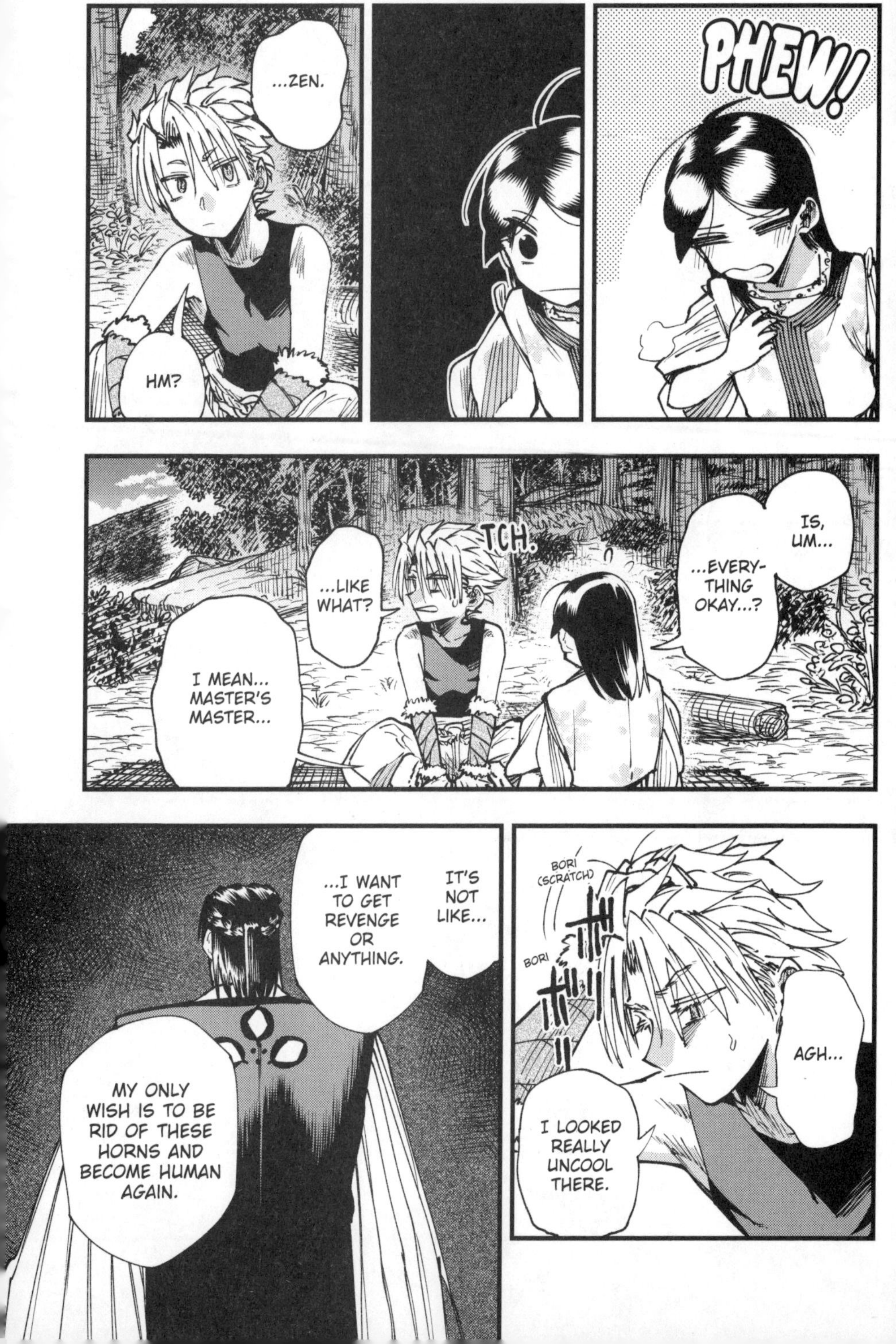
PHEW!
...ZEN.
HM?
IS, UM...
...EVERY-THING OKAY...?
TCH.
...LIKE WHAT?
I MEAN... MASTER'S MASTER...
BORI (SCRATCH)
BORI
AGH...
I LOOKED REALLY UNCOOL THERE.
IT'S NOT LIKE...
...I WANT TO GET REVENGE OR ANYTHING.
MY ONLY WISH IS TO BE RID OF THESE HORNS AND BECOME HUMAN AGAIN.

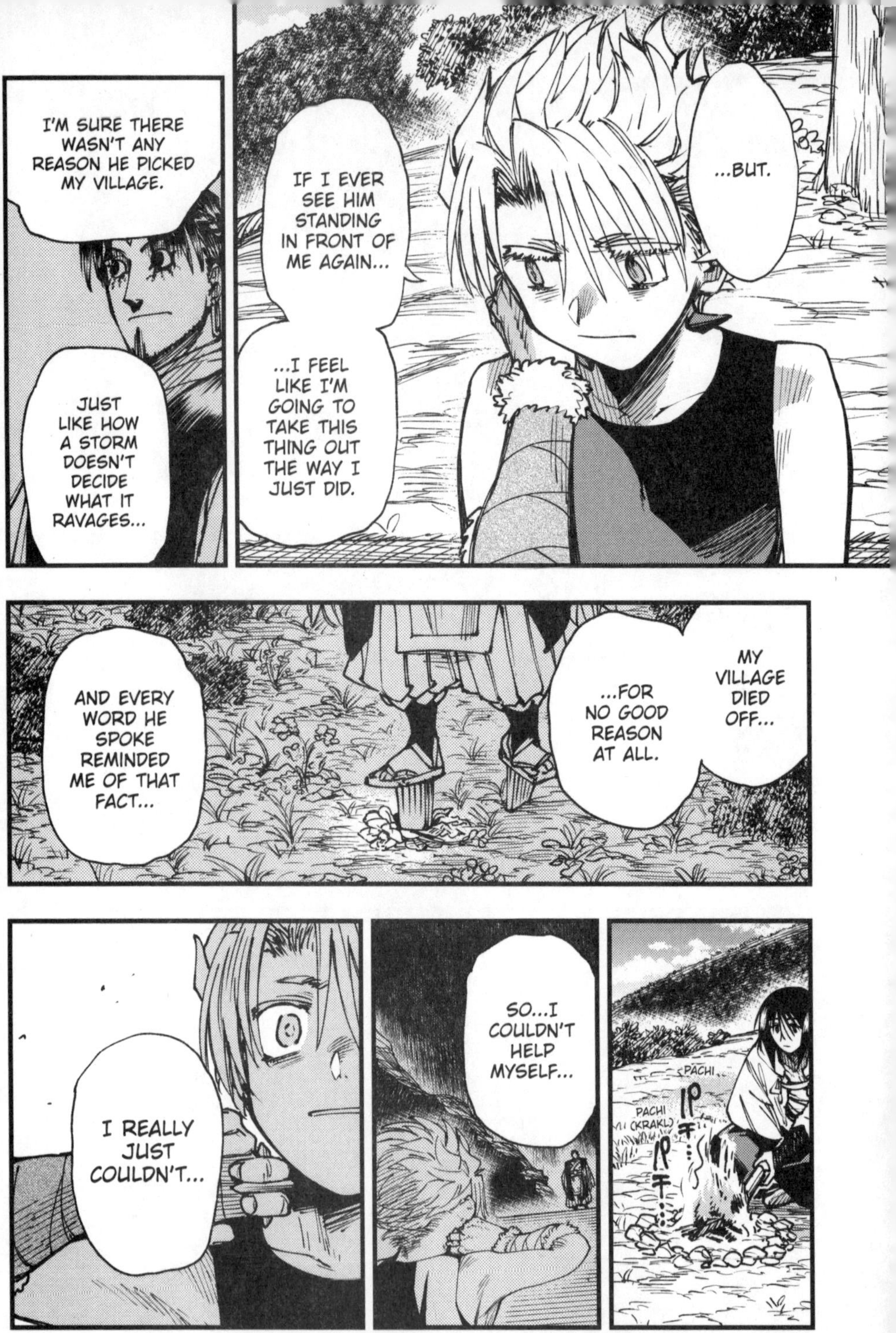
...BUT.
IF I EVER SEE HIM STANDING IN FRONT OF ME AGAIN...
...I FEEL LIKE I'M GOING TO TAKE THIS THING OUT THE WAY I JUST DID.
I'M SURE THERE WASN'T ANY REASON HE PICKED MY VILLAGE.
JUST LIKE HOW A STORM DOESN'T DECIDE WHAT IT RAVAGES...
MY VILLAGE DIED OFF...
...FOR NO GOOD REASON AT ALL.
AND EVERY WORD HE SPOKE REMINDED ME OF THAT FACT...
PACHI
パチ…
PACHI (KRAKL)
パチ…
SO...I COULDN'T HELP MYSELF...
I REALLY JUST COULDN'T...

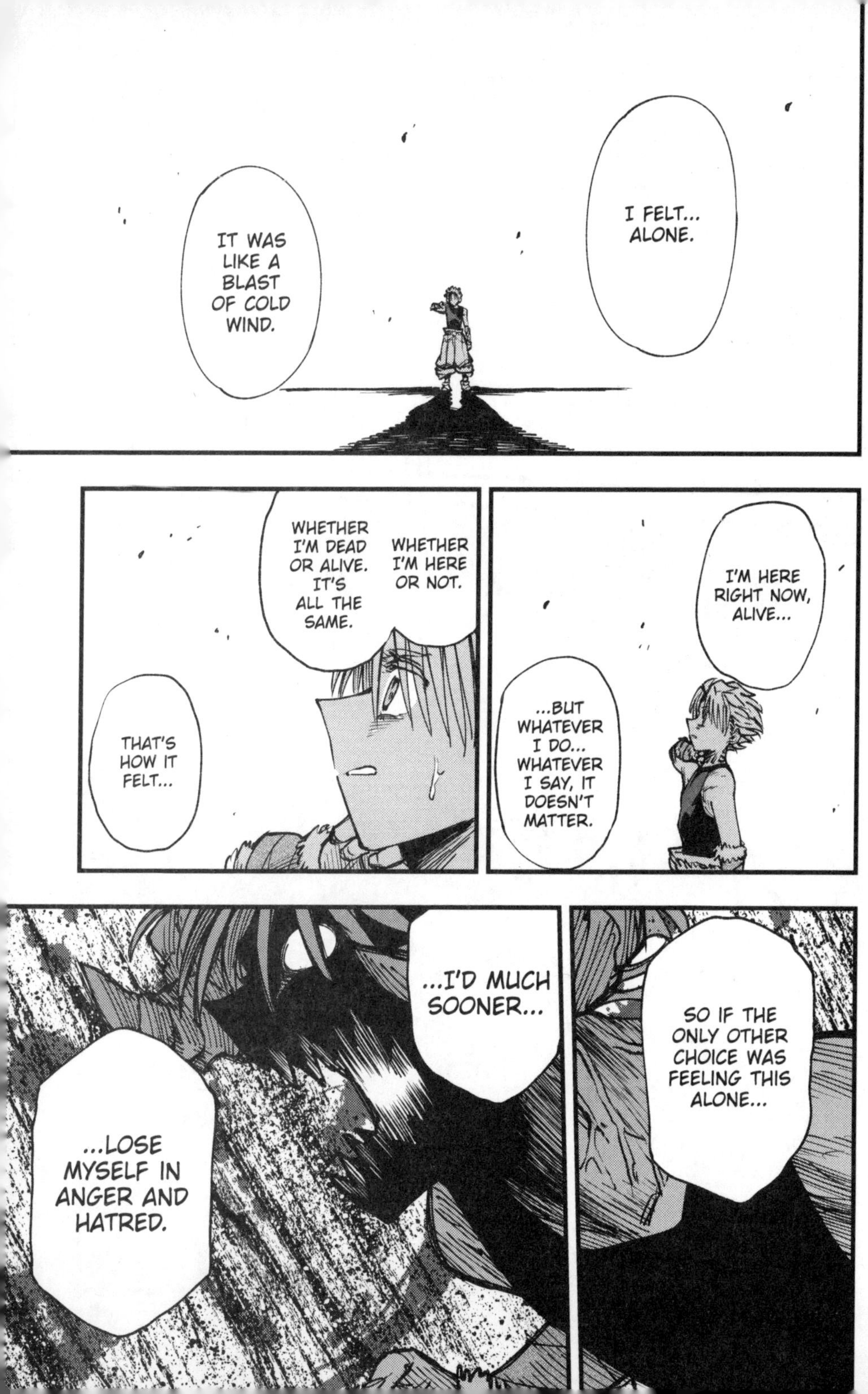
I FELT... ALONE.
IT WAS LIKE A BLAST OF COLD WIND.
I'M HERE RIGHT NOW, ALIVE...
...BUT WHATEVER I DO... WHATEVER I SAY, IT DOESN'T MATTER.
WHETHER I'M HERE OR NOT.
WHETHER I'M DEAD OR ALIVE. IT'S ALL THE SAME.
THAT'S HOW IT FELT...
SO IF THE ONLY OTHER CHOICE WAS FEELING THIS ALONE...
...I'D MUCH SOONER...
...LOSE MYSELF IN ANGER AND HATRED.

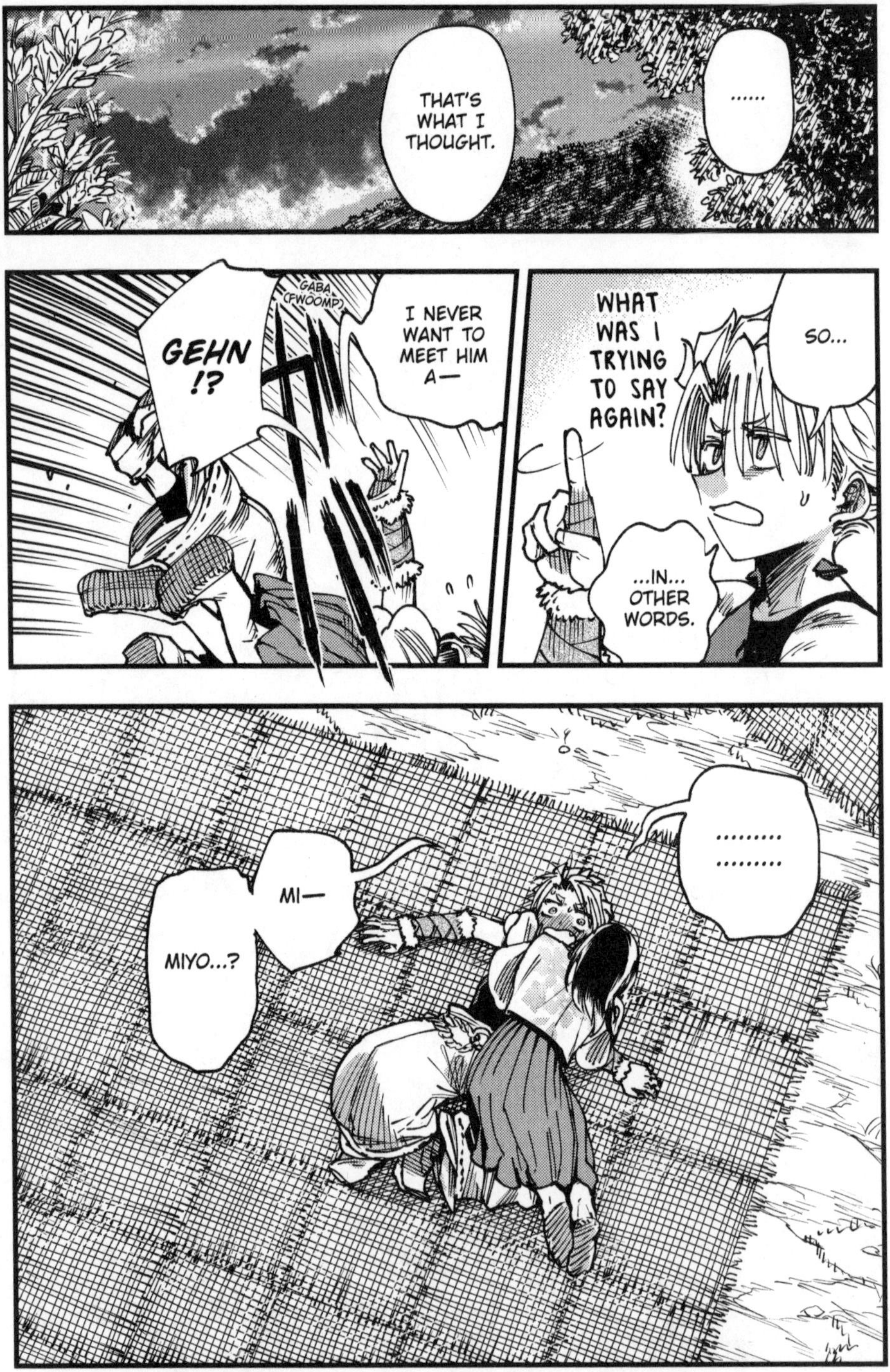
......
THAT'S WHAT I THOUGHT.
SO...
WHAT WAS I TRYING TO SAY AGAIN?
...IN... OTHER WORDS.
I NEVER WANT TO MEET HIM A—
GABA (FWOOMP)
GEHN !?
....
....
MI—
MIYO...?

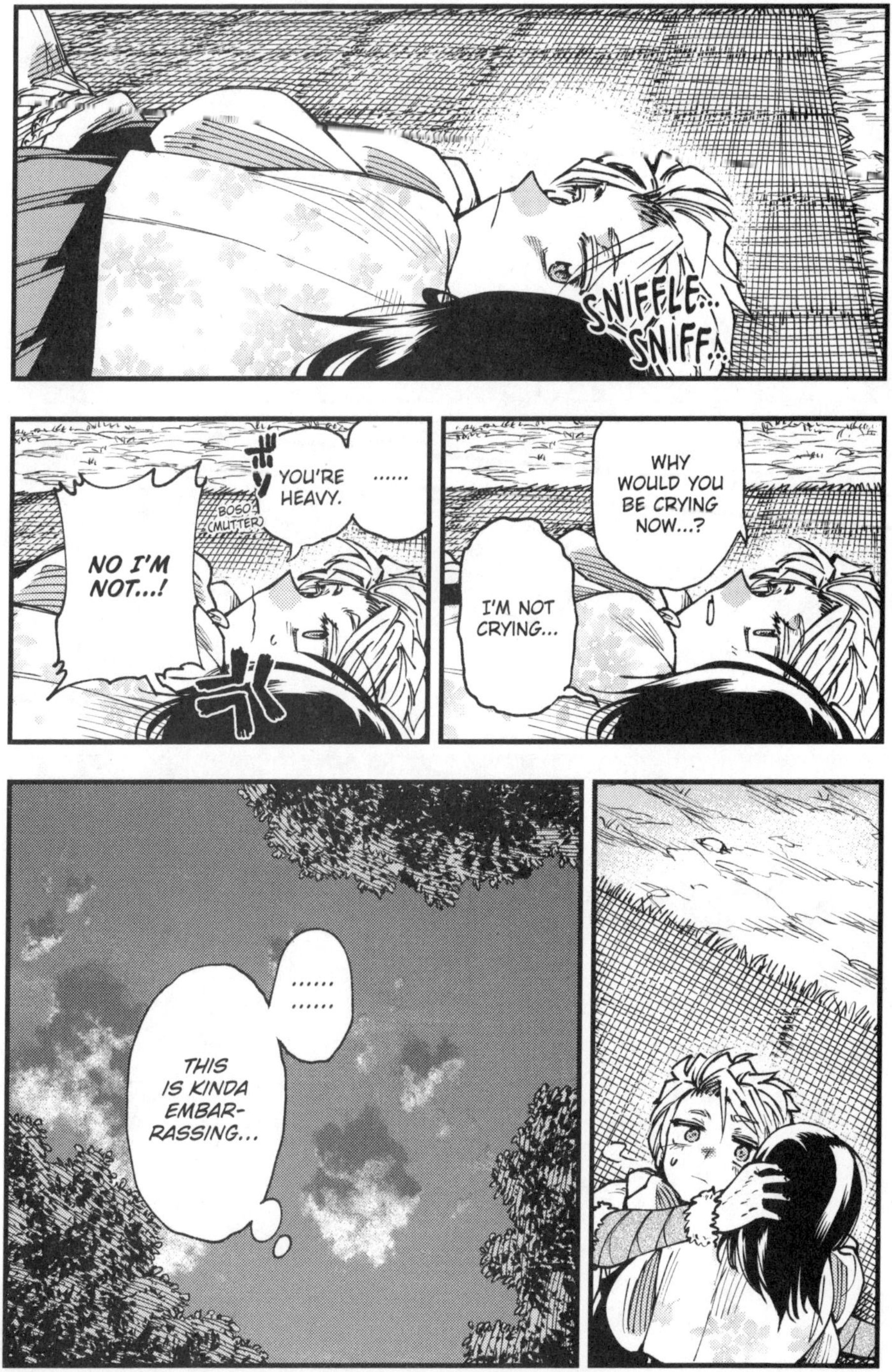
SNIFFLE...
SNIFF...
WHY WOULD YOU BE CRYING NOW...?
I'M NOT CRYING...
......
YOU'RE HEAVY.
BOSO (MUTTER)
NO I'M NOT...!
......
......
THIS IS KINDA EMBARRASSING...

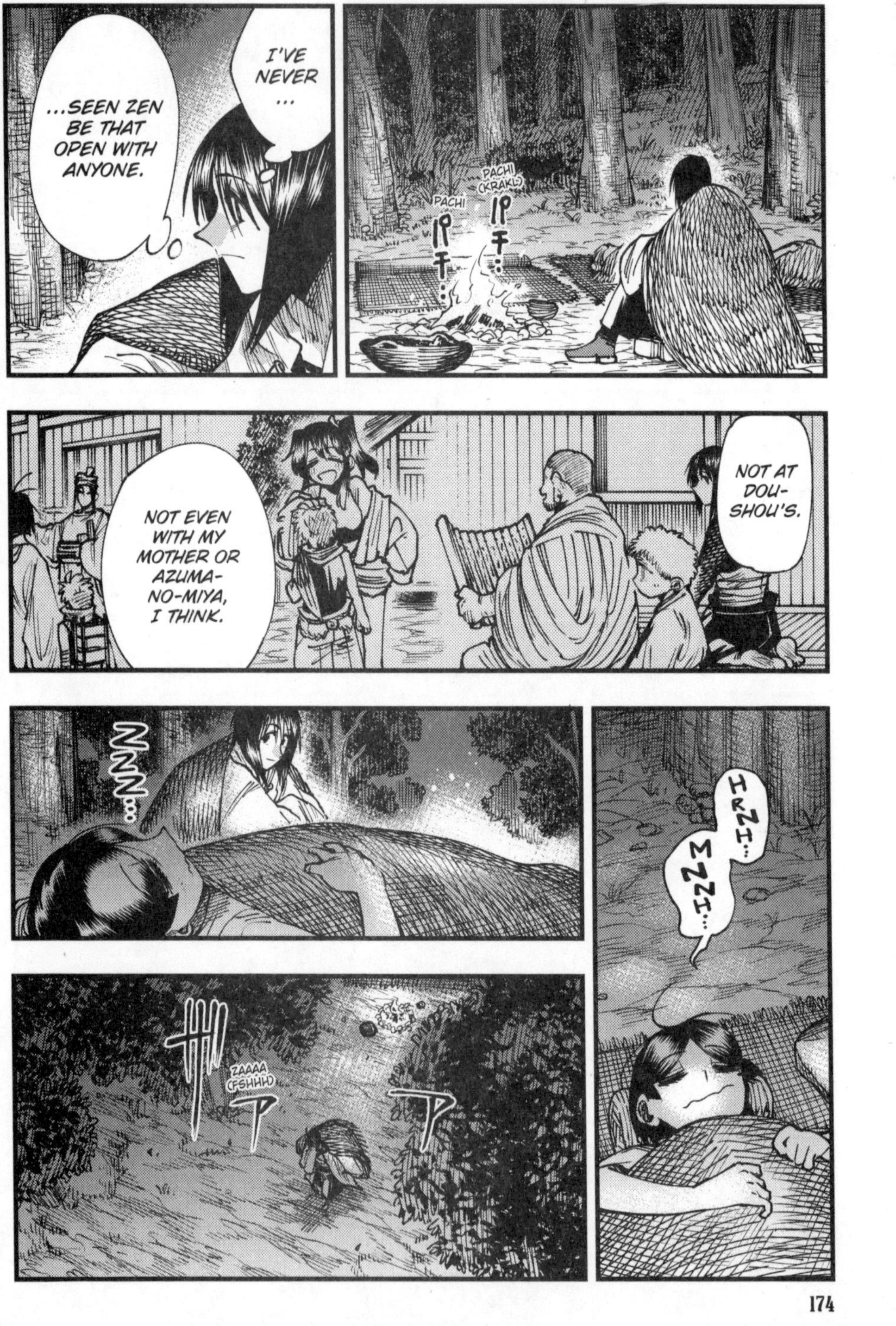

PACHI (KRAKL)
パチ…
PACHI
パチ…
I'VE NEVER ...
...SEEN ZEN BE THAT OPEN WITH ANYONE.
NOT AT DOU-SHOU'S.
NOT EVEN WITH MY MOTHER OR AZUMA-NO-MIYA, I THINK.
HRNH...
MNNH...
ZZZ...
ZAAAA (FSHHH)

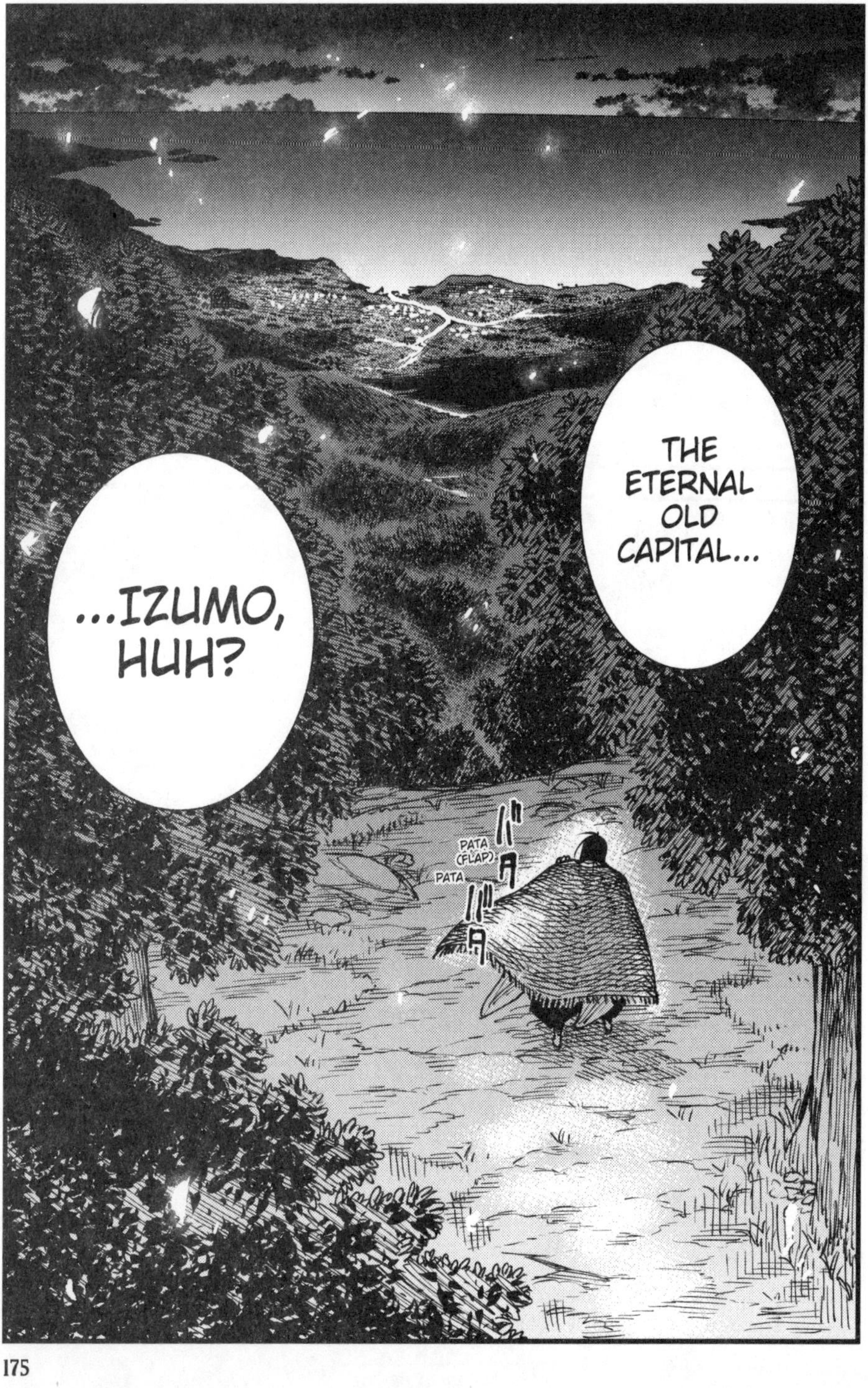
THE ETERNAL OLD CAPITAL...
...IZUMO, HUH?
PATA (FLAP) PATA
バタバタ

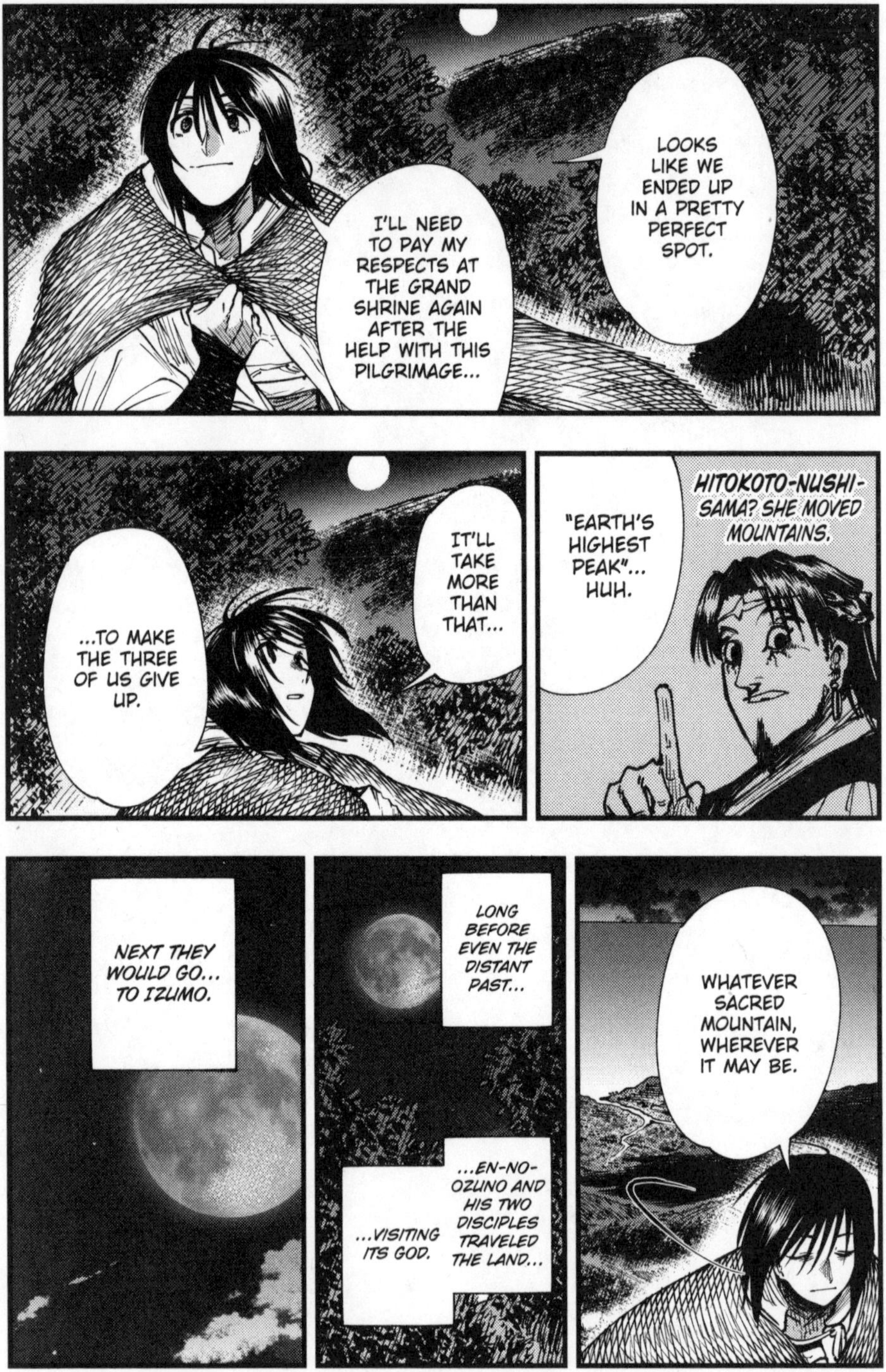
LOOKS LIKE WE ENDED UP IN A PRETTY PERFECT SPOT.
I'LL NEED TO PAY MY RESPECTS AT THE GRAND SHRINE AGAIN AFTER THE HELP WITH THIS PILGRIMAGE...
HITOKOTO-NUSHI-SAMA? SHE MOVED MOUNTAINS.
"EARTH'S HIGHEST PEAK"... HUH.
IT'LL TAKE MORE THAN THAT...
...TO MAKE THE THREE OF US GIVE UP.
WHATEVER SACRED MOUNTAIN, WHEREVER IT MAY BE.
LONG BEFORE EVEN THE DISTANT PAST...
...EN-NO-OZUNO AND HIS TWO DISCIPLES TRAVELED THE LAND...
...VISITING ITS GOD.
NEXT THEY WOULD GO... TO IZUMO.

CHAPTER XV END

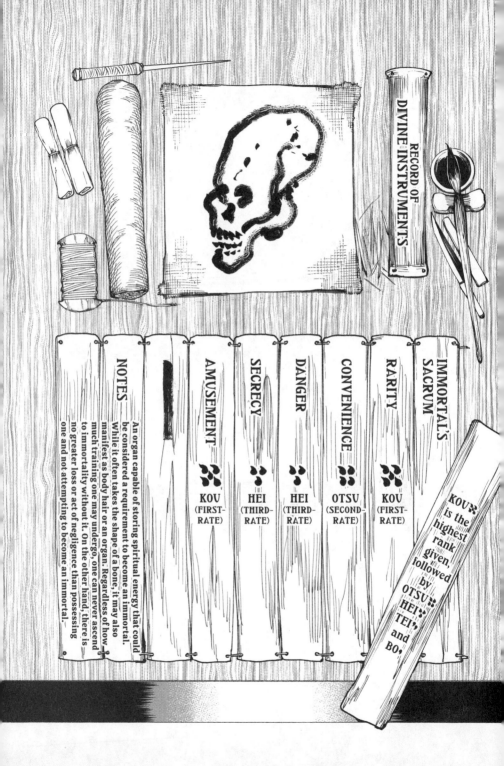

RECORD OF DIVINE INSTRUMENTS

IMMORTAL'S SACRUM

RARITY ✷✷ KOU (FIRST-RATE)

CONVENIENCE ✷✷ OTSU (SECOND-RATE)

DANGER ✷ HEI (THIRD-RATE)

SECRECY ✷ HEI (THIRD-RATE)

AMUSEMENT ✷✷✷ KOU (FIRST-RATE)

NOTES — An organ capable of storing spiritual energy that could be considered a requirement to become an immortal. While it often takes the shape of a bone, it may also manifest as body hair or an organ. Regardless of how much training one may undergo, one can never ascend to immortality without it. On the other hand, there is no greater loss or act of negligence than possessing one and not attempting to become an immortal.—

KOU ✷ is the highest rank given, followed by OTSU ✷ HEI ✷ TEI ✷ and BO ✷

TOUGE ONI

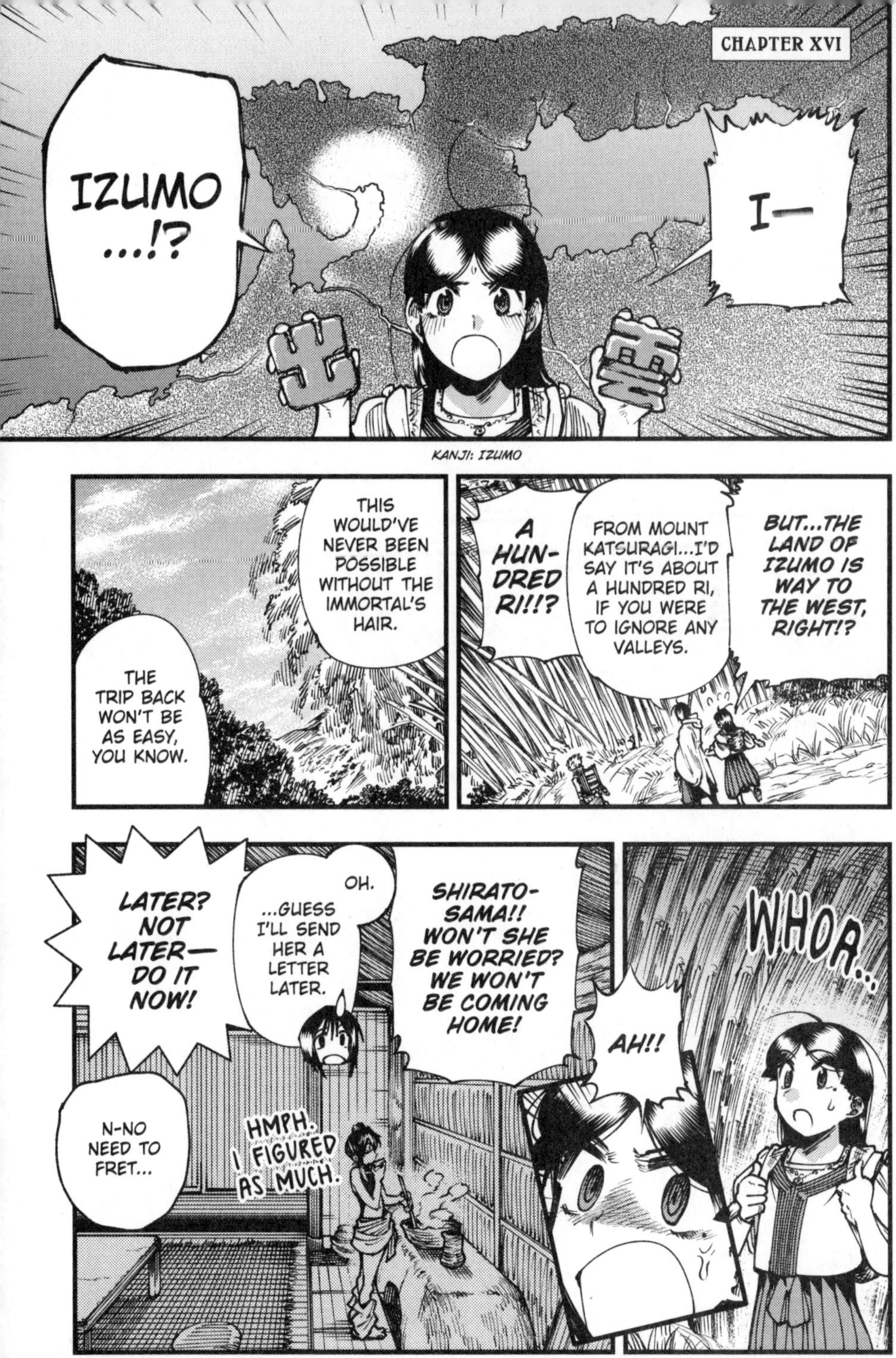
CHAPTER XVI
I—
IZUMO ...!?
KANJI: IZUMO
BUT...THE LAND OF IZUMO IS WAY TO THE WEST, RIGHT!?
FROM MOUNT KATSURAGI...I'D SAY IT'S ABOUT A HUNDRED RI, IF YOU WERE TO IGNORE ANY VALLEYS.
A HUNDRED RI!!?
THIS WOULD'VE NEVER BEEN POSSIBLE WITHOUT THE IMMORTAL'S HAIR.
THE TRIP BACK WON'T BE AS EASY, YOU KNOW.
WHOA...
AH!!
SHIRATO-SAMA!! WON'T SHE BE WORRIED? WE WON'T BE COMING HOME!
OH.
...GUESS I'LL SEND HER A LETTER LATER.
LATER? NOT LATER—DO IT NOW!
N-NO NEED TO FRET...
HMPH. I FIGURED AS MUCH.

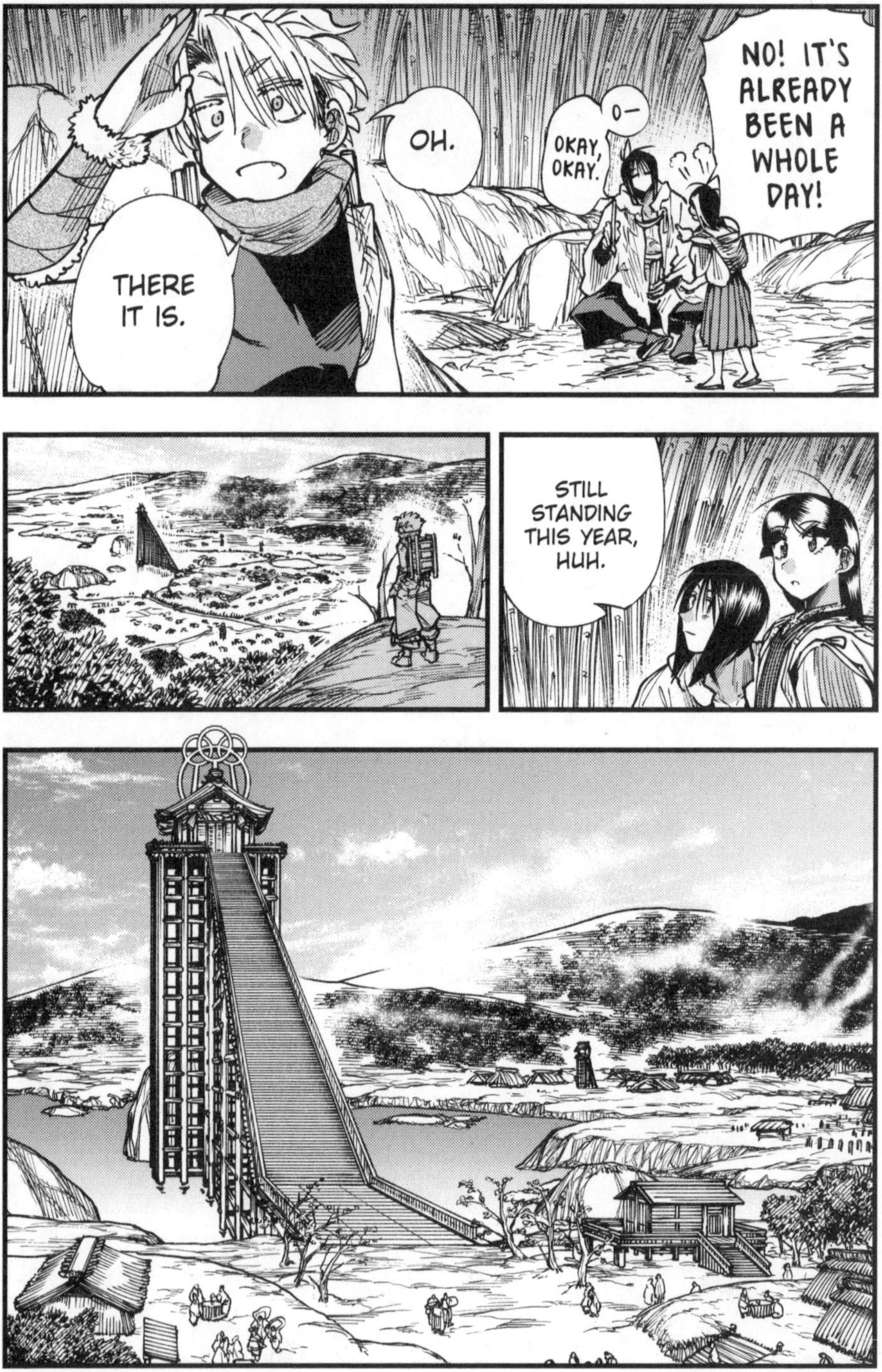
NO! IT'S ALREADY BEEN A WHOLE DAY!
O— OKAY, OKAY.
OH.
THERE IT IS.
STILL STANDING THIS YEAR, HUH.

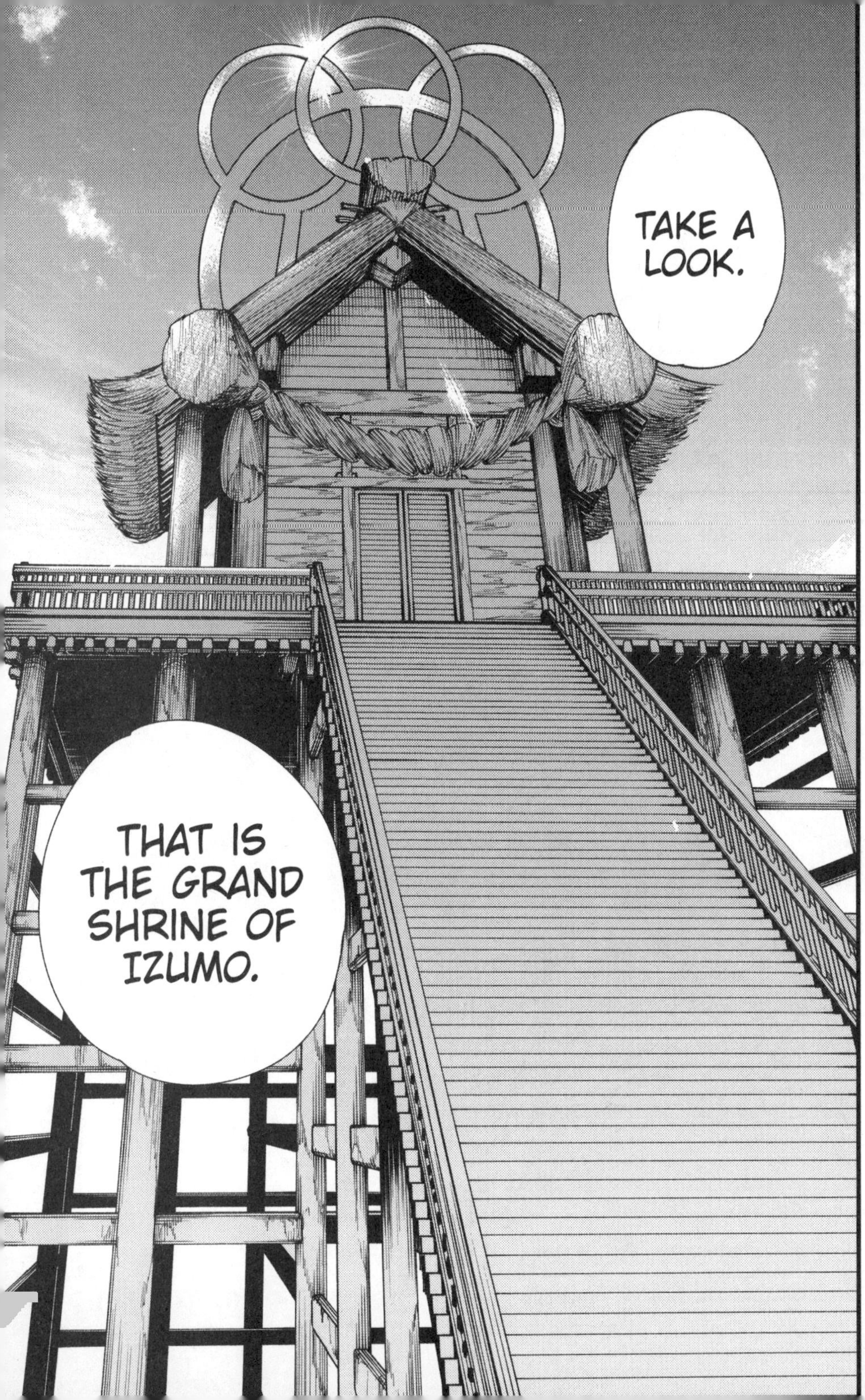
TAKE A LOOK.
THAT IS THE GRAND SHRINE OF IZUMO.

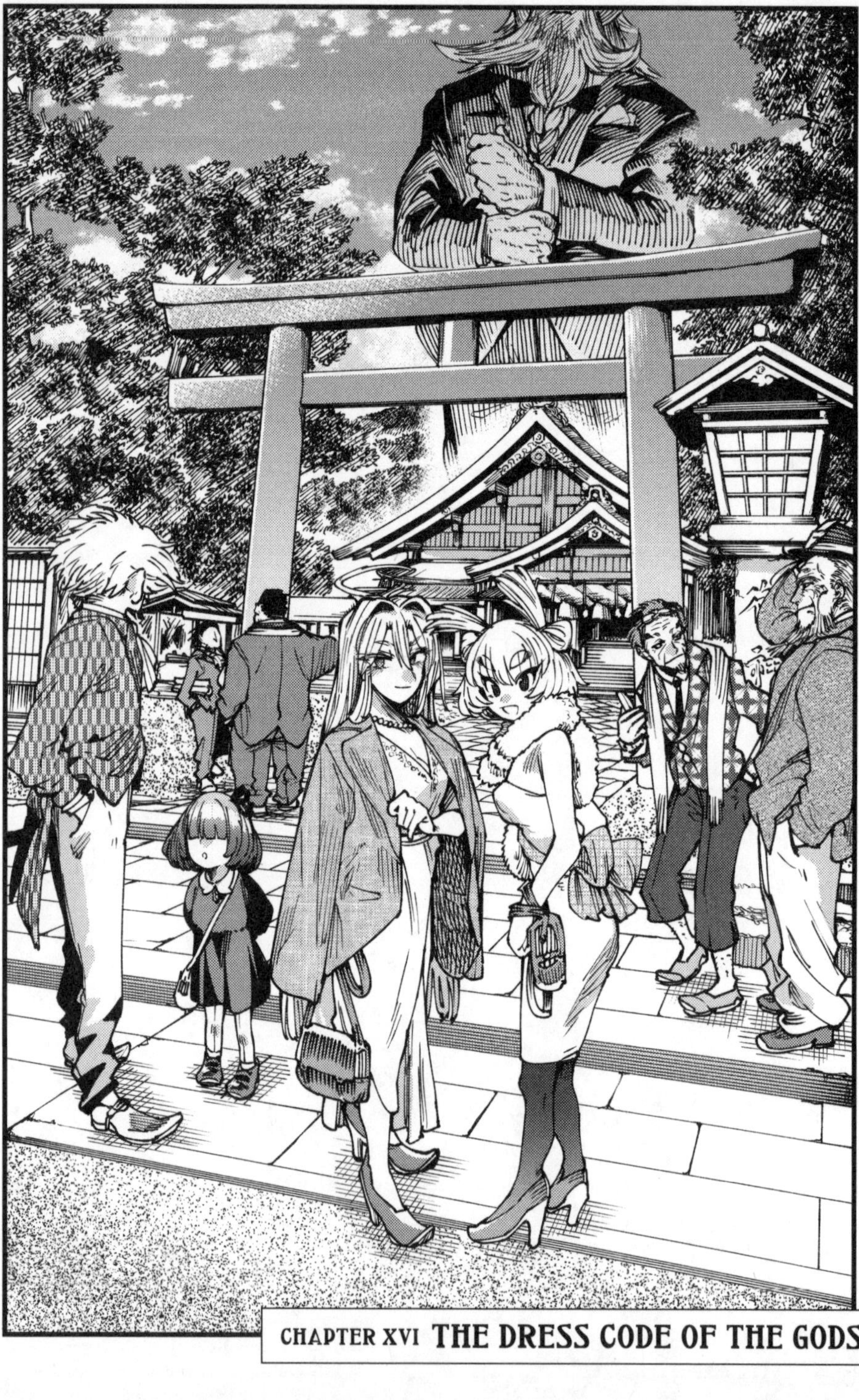

CHAPTER XVI THE DRESS CODE OF THE GODS

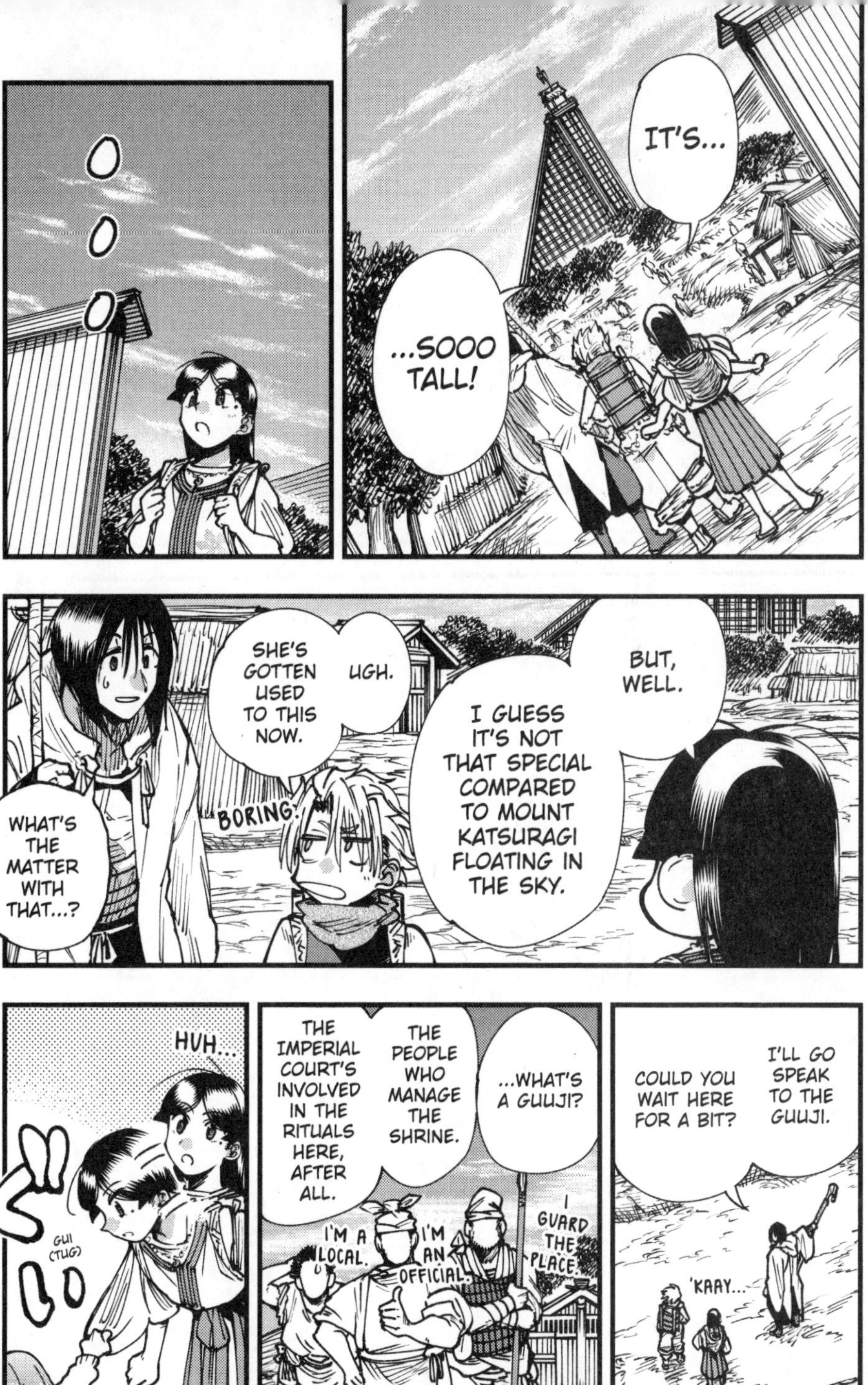
IT'S...
...SOOO TALL!
BUT, WELL.
I GUESS IT'S NOT THAT SPECIAL COMPARED TO MOUNT KATSURAGI FLOATING IN THE SKY.
UGH.
SHE'S GOTTEN USED TO THIS NOW.
BORING.
WHAT'S THE MATTER WITH THAT...?
I'LL GO SPEAK TO THE GUUJI.
COULD YOU WAIT HERE FOR A BIT?
'KAAY...
...WHAT'S A GUUJI?
THE PEOPLE WHO MANAGE THE SHRINE.
THE IMPERIAL COURT'S INVOLVED IN THE RITUALS HERE, AFTER ALL.
I GUARD THE PLACE.
I'M AN OFFICIAL.
I'M A LOCAL.
HUH...
GUI (TUG)

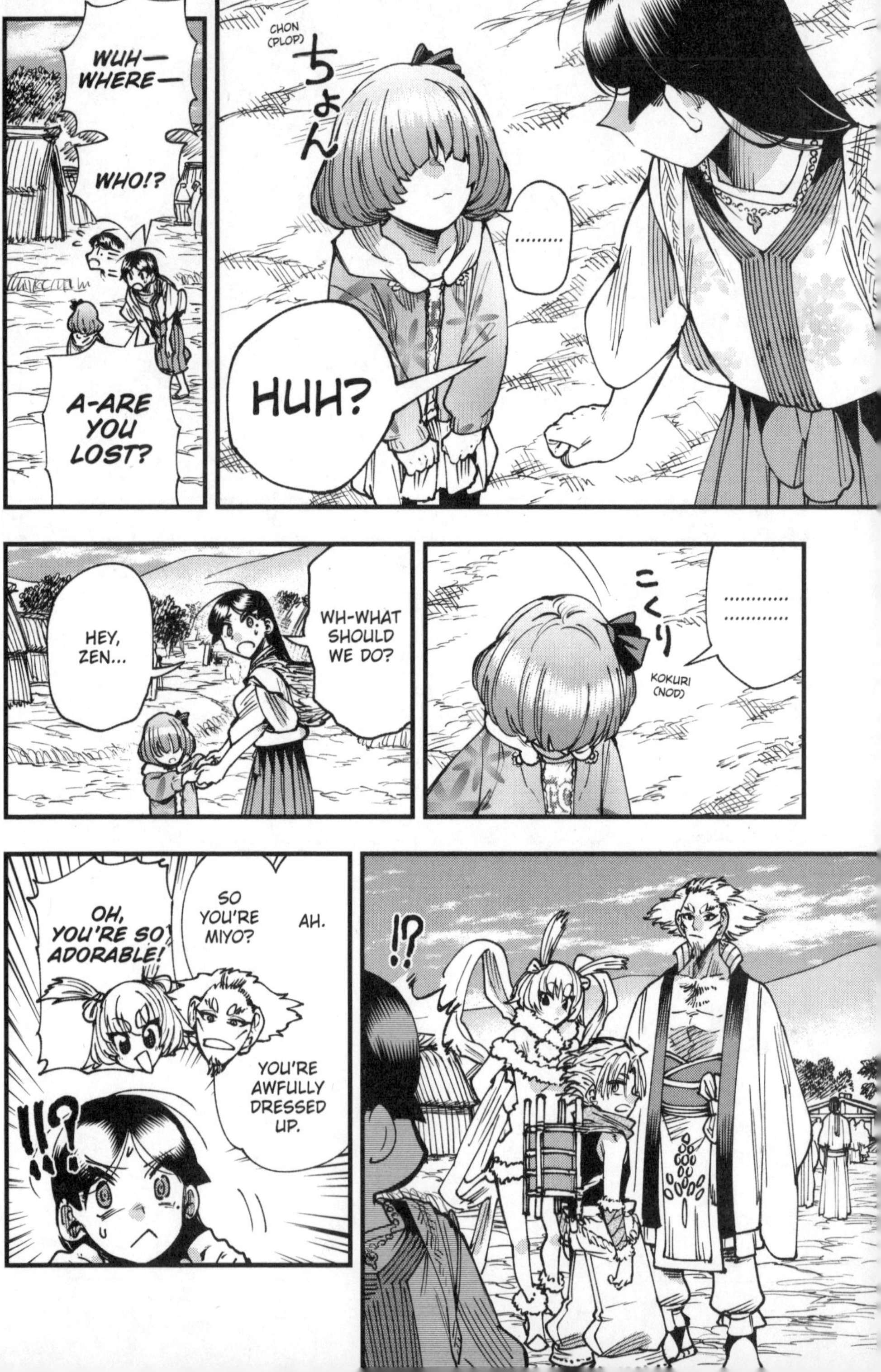
CHON (PLOP)
ちょん
....
HUH?
WUH— WHERE—
WHO!?
A-ARE YOU LOST?
....
こくり
KOKURI (NOD)
WH-WHAT SHOULD WE DO?
HEY, ZEN...
!?
AH.
SO YOU'RE MIYO?
OH, YOU'RE SO ADORABLE!
YOU'RE AWFULLY DRESSED UP.
!!?

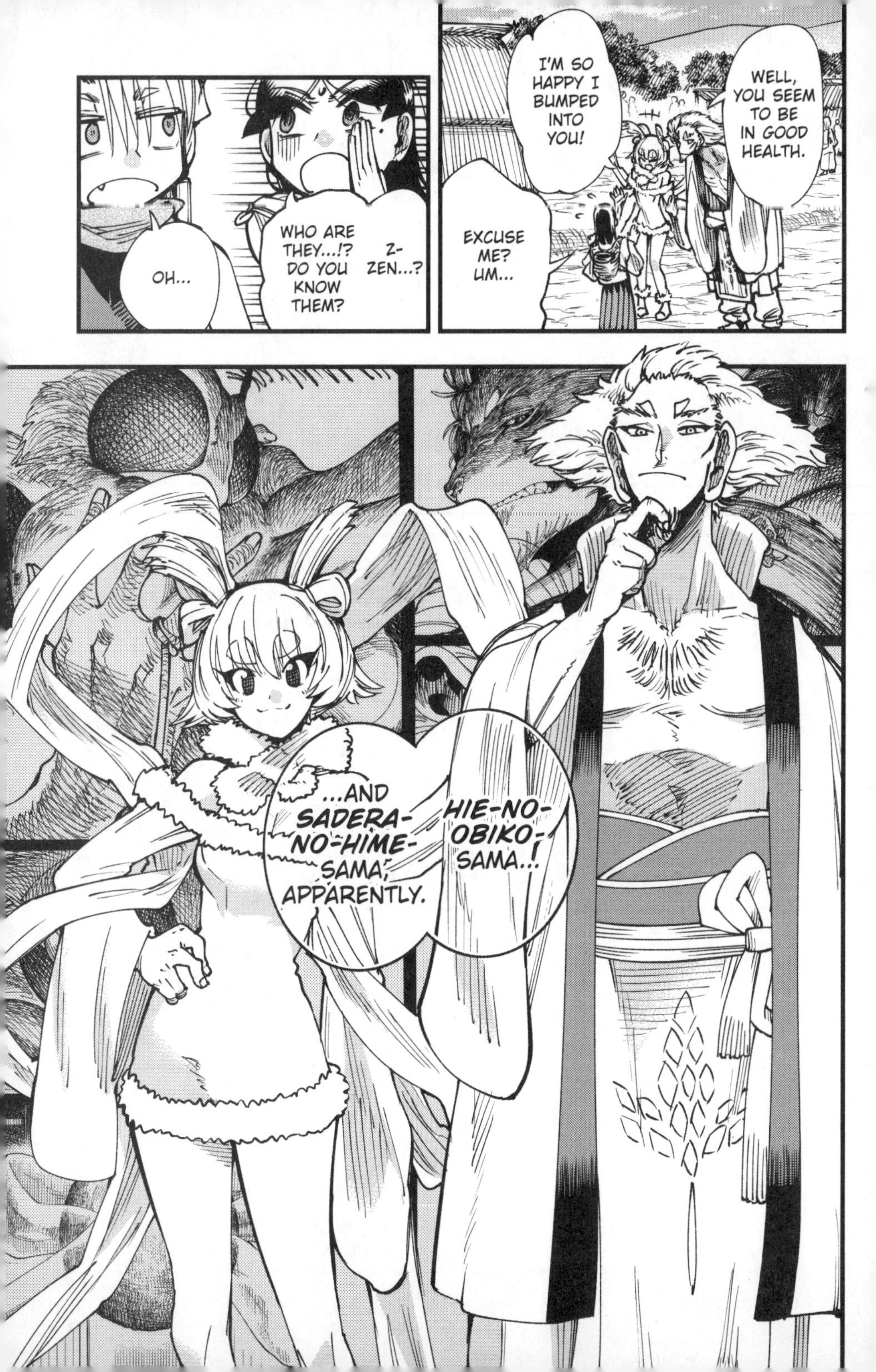
WELL, YOU SEEM TO BE IN GOOD HEALTH.
I'M SO HAPPY I BUMPED INTO YOU!
EXCUSE ME? UM...
Z-ZEN...?
WHO ARE THEY...!? DO YOU KNOW THEM?
OH...
HIE-NO-OBIKO-SAMA..!
...AND SADERA-NO-HIME-SAMA, APPARENTLY.

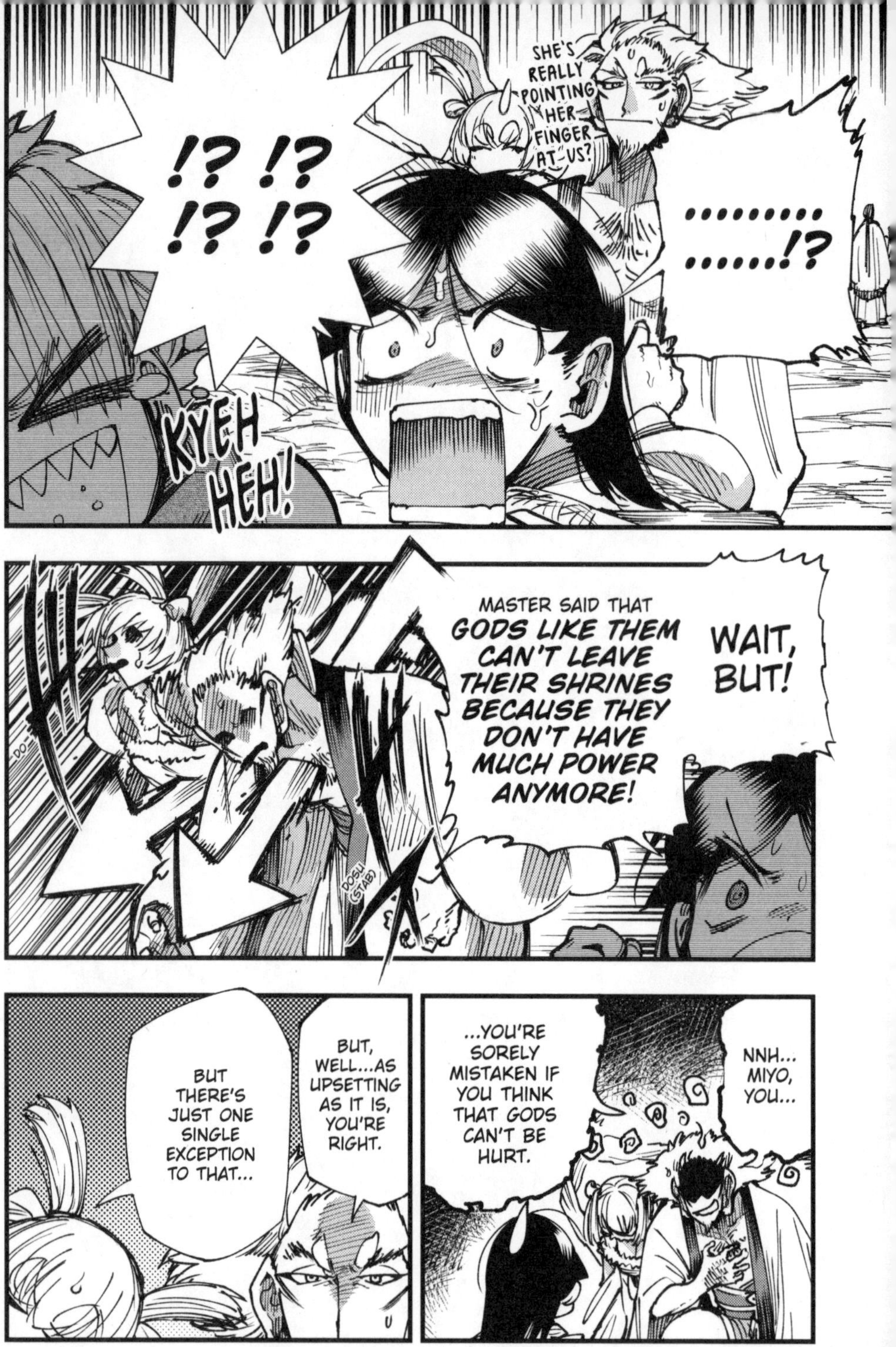
....
.......!?
SHE'S REALLY POINTING HER FINGER AT US?
!? !? !? !?
KYEH HEH!
WAIT, BUT!
MASTER SAID THAT GODS LIKE THEM CAN'T LEAVE THEIR SHRINES BECAUSE THEY DON'T HAVE MUCH POWER ANYMORE!
DOSU (STAB)
DO
NNH... MIYO, YOU...
...YOU'RE SORELY MISTAKEN IF YOU THINK THAT GODS CAN'T BE HURT.
BUT, WELL...AS UPSETTING AS IT IS, YOU'RE RIGHT.
BUT THERE'S JUST ONE SINGLE EXCEPTION TO THAT...

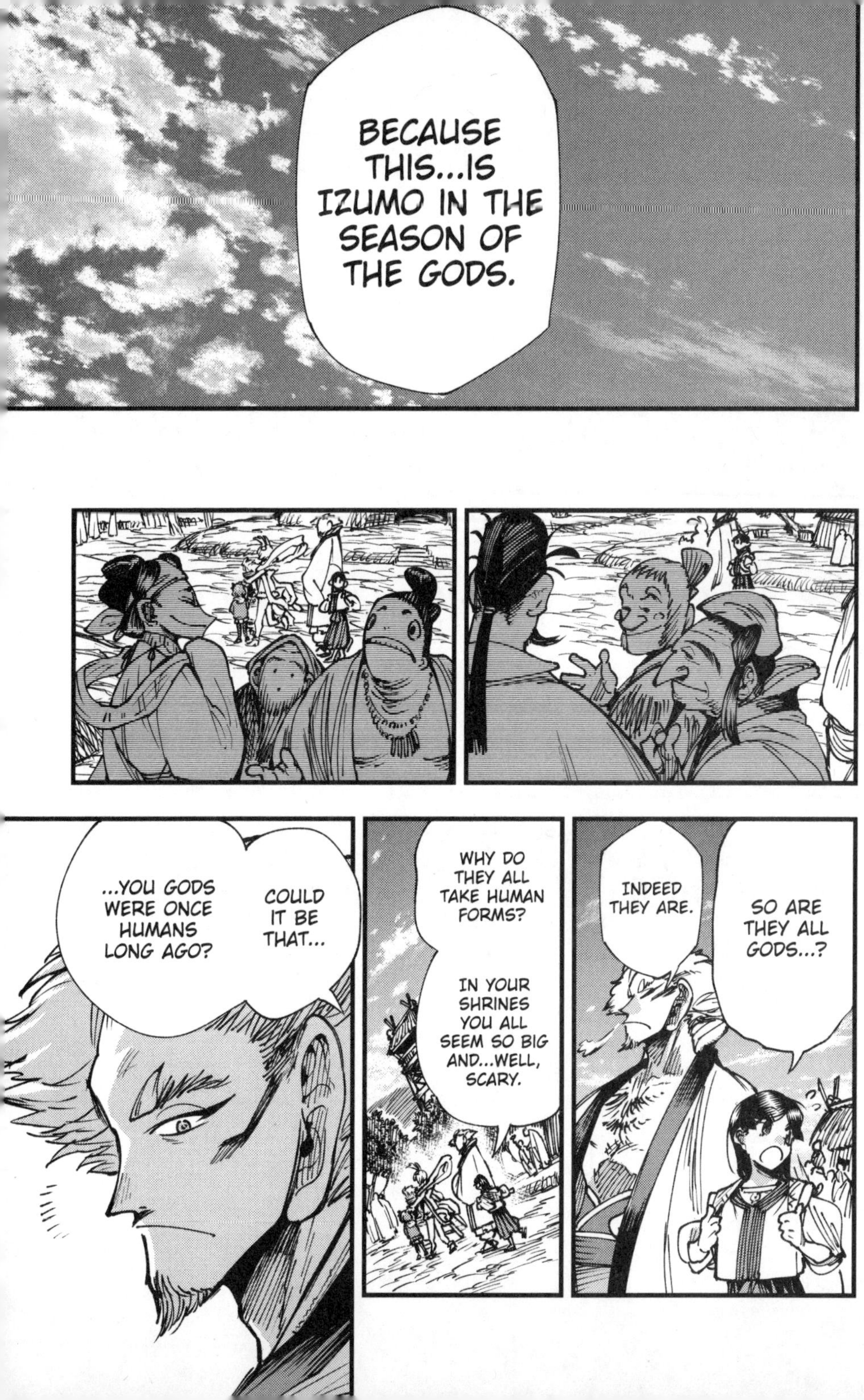
BECAUSE THIS...IS IZUMO IN THE SEASON OF THE GODS.
SO ARE THEY ALL GODS...?
INDEED THEY ARE.
WHY DO THEY ALL TAKE HUMAN FORMS?
IN YOUR SHRINES YOU ALL SEEM SO BIG AND...WELL, SCARY.
COULD IT BE THAT...
...YOU GODS WERE ONCE HUMANS LONG AGO?

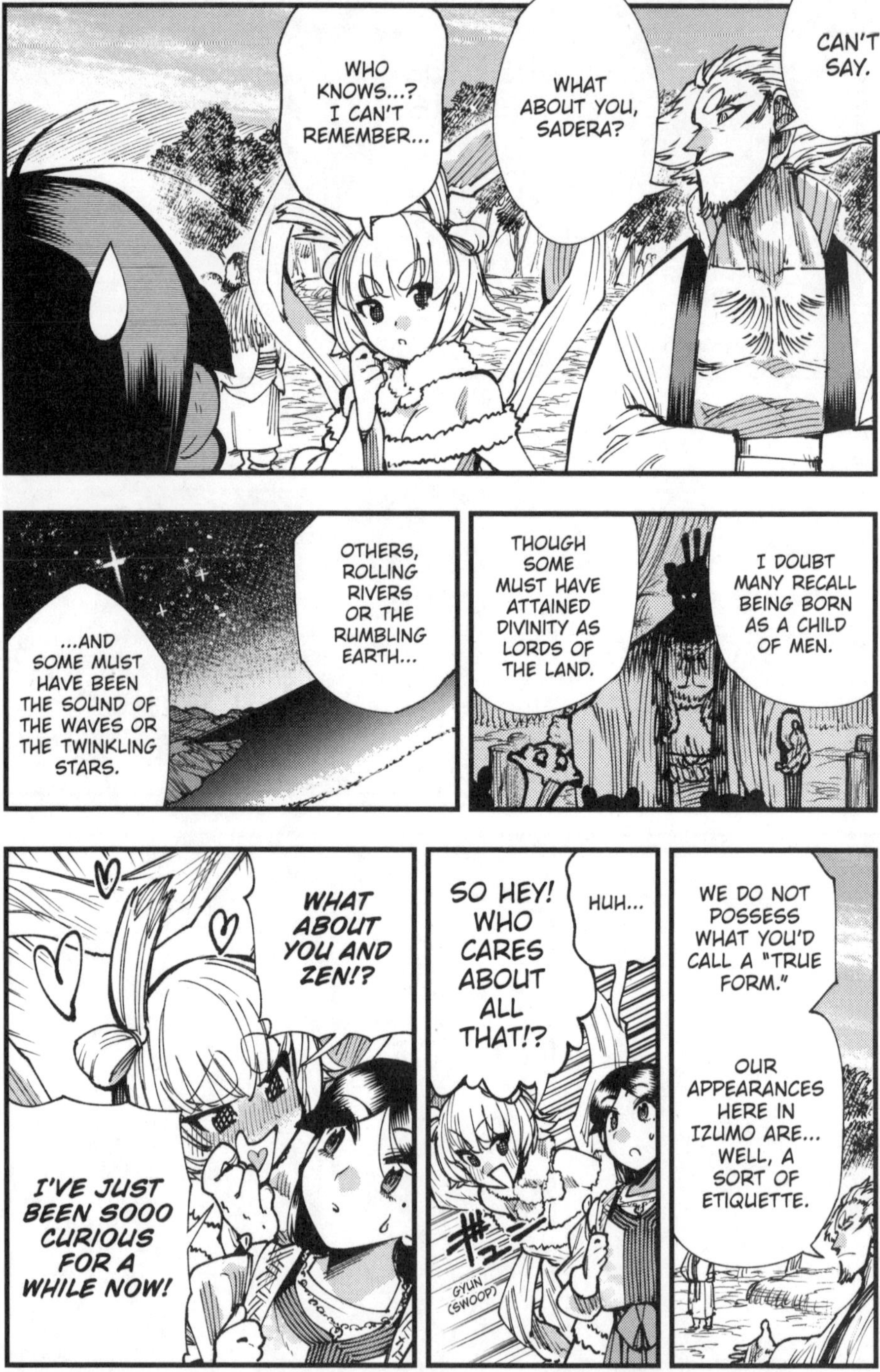
CAN'T SAY.
WHAT ABOUT YOU, SADERA?
WHO KNOWS...? I CAN'T REMEMBER...
I DOUBT MANY RECALL BEING BORN AS A CHILD OF MEN.
THOUGH SOME MUST HAVE ATTAINED DIVINITY AS LORDS OF THE LAND.
OTHERS, ROLLING RIVERS OR THE RUMBLING EARTH...
...AND SOME MUST HAVE BEEN THE SOUND OF THE WAVES OR THE TWINKLING STARS.
WE DO NOT POSSESS WHAT YOU'D CALL A "TRUE FORM."
OUR APPEARANCES HERE IN IZUMO ARE... WELL, A SORT OF ETIQUETTE.
HUH...
SO HEY! WHO CARES ABOUT ALL THAT!?
GYUN (SWOOP)
WHAT ABOUT YOU AND ZEN!?
I'VE JUST BEEN SOOO CURIOUS FOR A WHILE NOW!

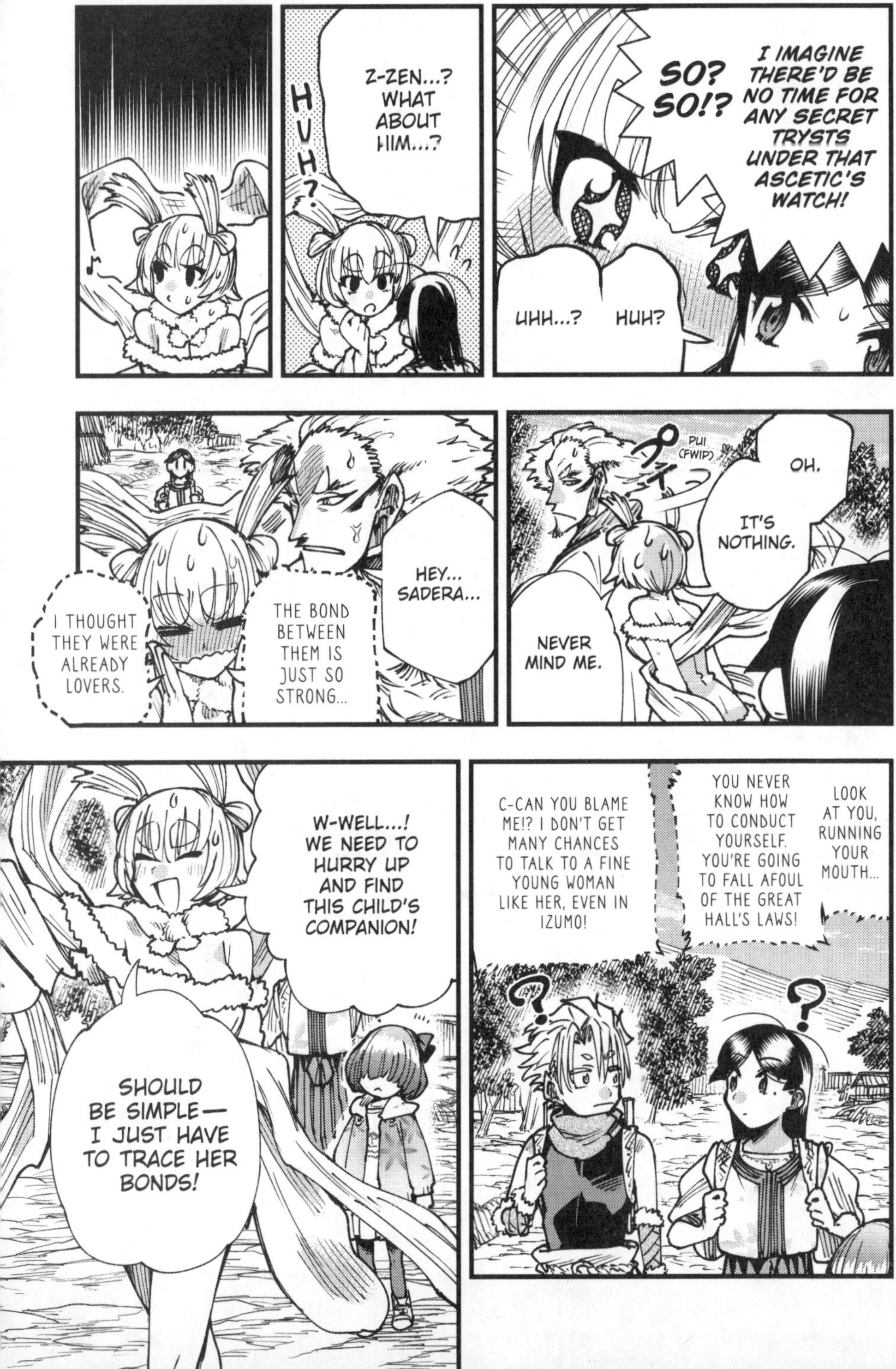
I IMAGINE THERE'D BE NO TIME FOR ANY SECRET TRYSTS UNDER THAT ASCETIC'S WATCH!
SO? SO!?
HUH?
UHH...?
Z-ZEN...? WHAT ABOUT HIM...?
HUH?
OH.
IT'S NOTHING.
PUI (FWIP)
NEVER MIND ME.
HEY... SADERA...
THE BOND BETWEEN THEM IS JUST SO STRONG...
I THOUGHT THEY WERE ALREADY LOVERS.
LOOK AT YOU, RUNNING YOUR MOUTH...
YOU NEVER KNOW HOW TO CONDUCT YOURSELF. YOU'RE GOING TO FALL AFOUL OF THE GREAT HALL'S LAWS!
C-CAN YOU BLAME ME!? I DON'T GET MANY CHANCES TO TALK TO A FINE YOUNG WOMAN LIKE HER, EVEN IN IZUMO!
W-WELL...! WE NEED TO HURRY UP AND FIND THIS CHILD'S COMPANION!
SHOULD BE SIMPLE— I JUST HAVE TO TRACE HER BONDS!

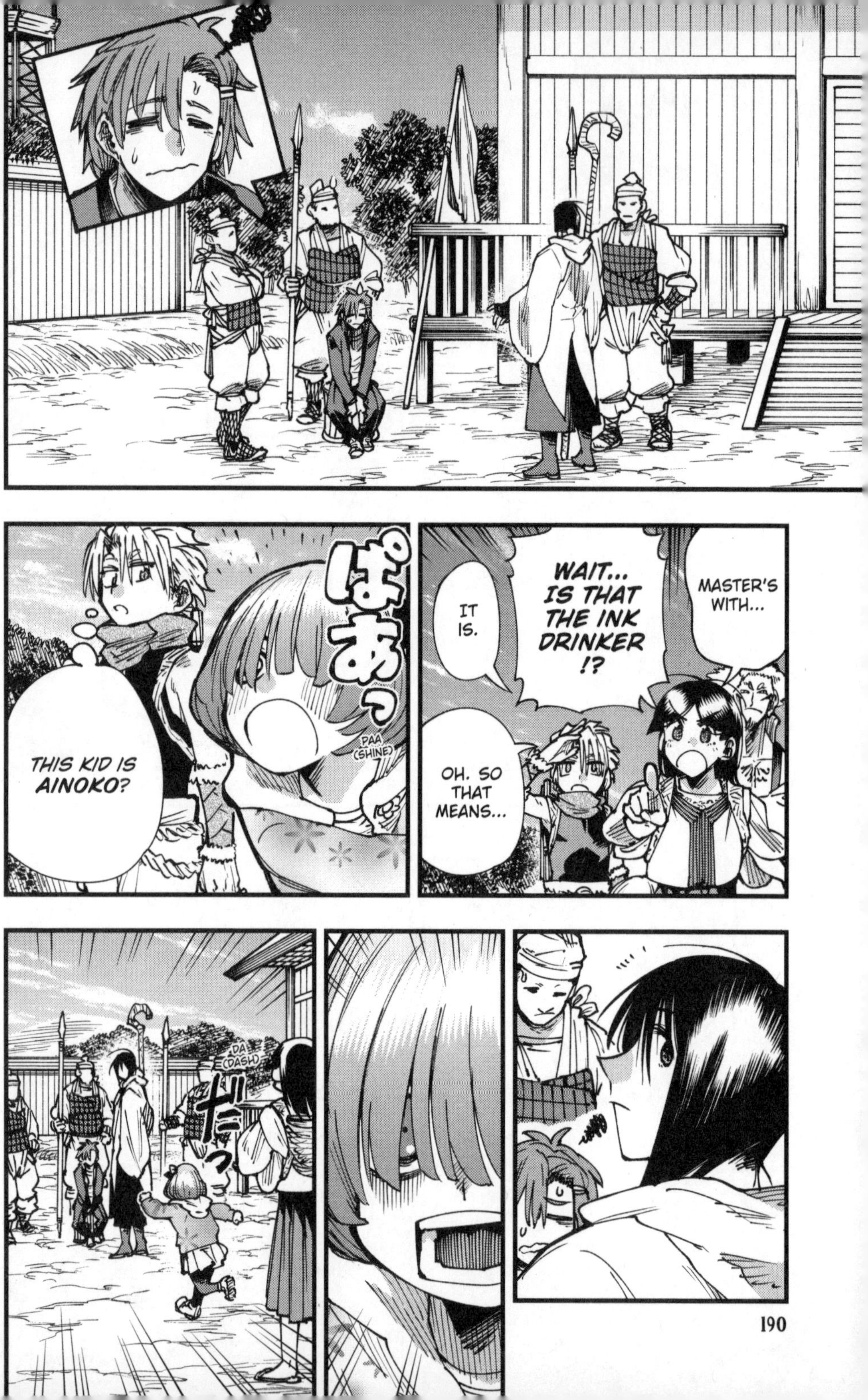
MASTER'S WITH...
WAIT... IS THAT THE INK DRINKER !?
IT IS.
OH. SO THAT MEANS...
ぱあっ
PAA (SHINE)
THIS KID IS AINOKO?
...
だっ
DA (DASH)

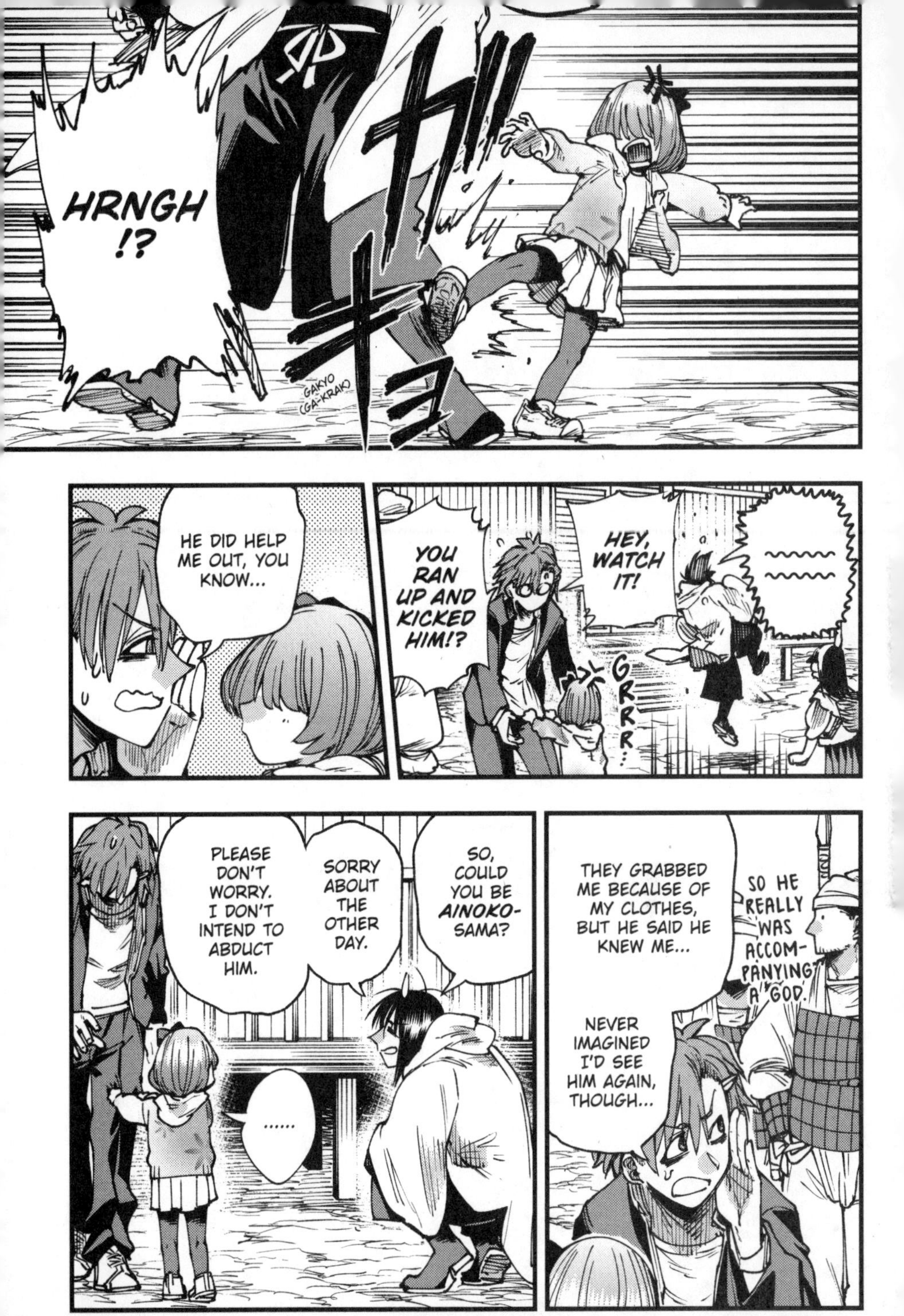
HRNGH !?
GAKYO (GA-KRAK)
~~~~~ ~~~~~
HEY, WATCH IT!
YOU RAN UP AND KICKED HIM!?
GRRR...
HE DID HELP ME OUT, YOU KNOW...
SO HE REALLY WAS ACCOMPANYING A GOD.
THEY GRABBED ME BECAUSE OF MY CLOTHES, BUT HE SAID HE KNEW ME...
NEVER IMAGINED I'D SEE HIM AGAIN, THOUGH...
SO, COULD YOU BE AINOKO-SAMA?
SORRY ABOUT THE OTHER DAY.
PLEASE DON'T WORRY. I DON'T INTEND TO ABDUCT HIM.
......
~~~~~

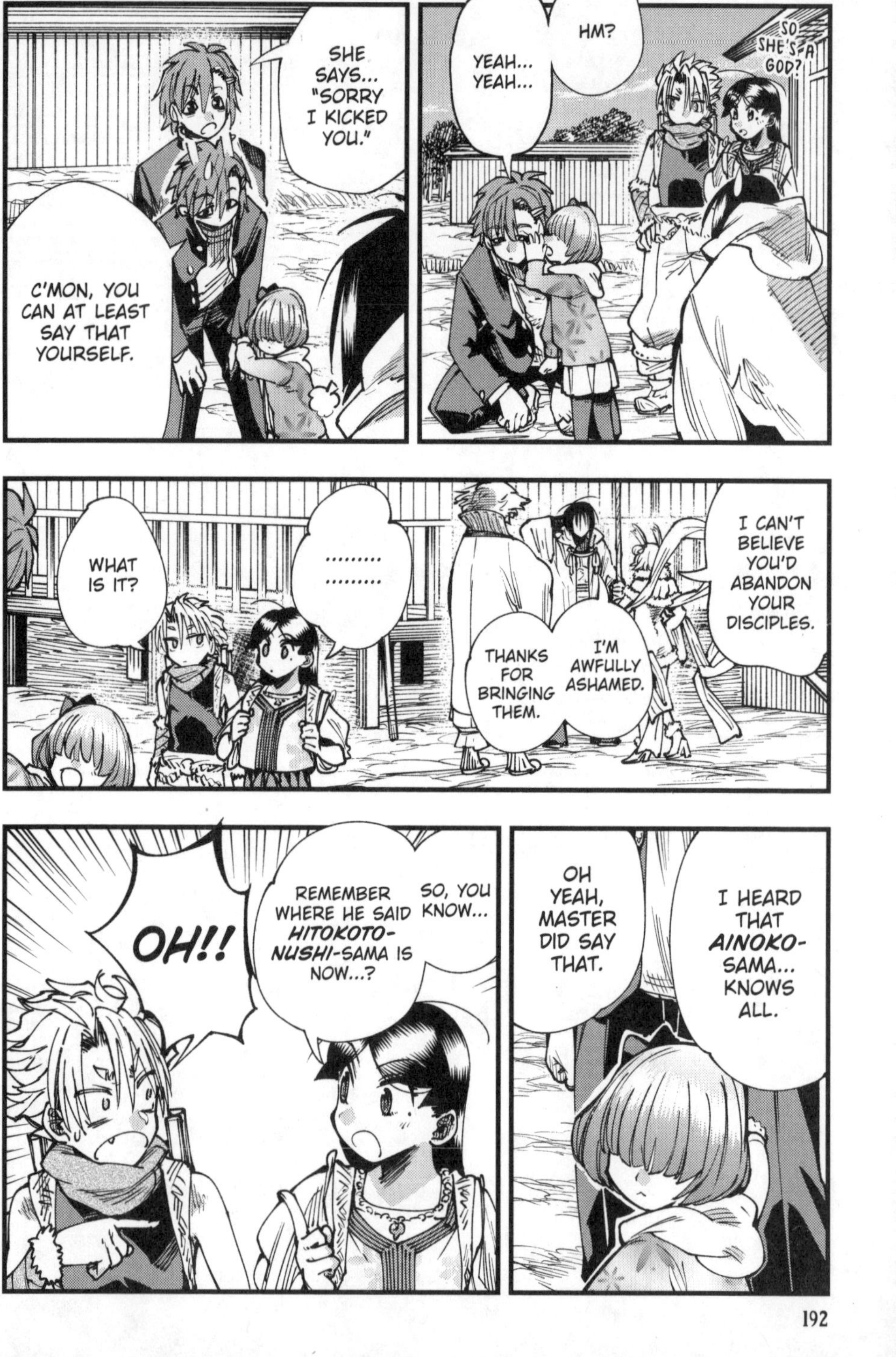
SO SHE'S A GOD?
HM?
YEAH... YEAH...
SHE SAYS... "SORRY I KICKED YOU."
C'MON, YOU CAN AT LEAST SAY THAT YOURSELF.
I CAN'T BELIEVE YOU'D ABANDON YOUR DISCIPLES.
I'M AWFULLY ASHAMED.
THANKS FOR BRINGING THEM.
....
....
WHAT IS IT?
I HEARD THAT *AINOKO*-SAMA... KNOWS ALL.
OH YEAH, MASTER DID SAY THAT.
SO, YOU KNOW...
REMEMBER WHERE HE SAID *HITOKOTO-NUSHI*-SAMA IS NOW...?
OH!!

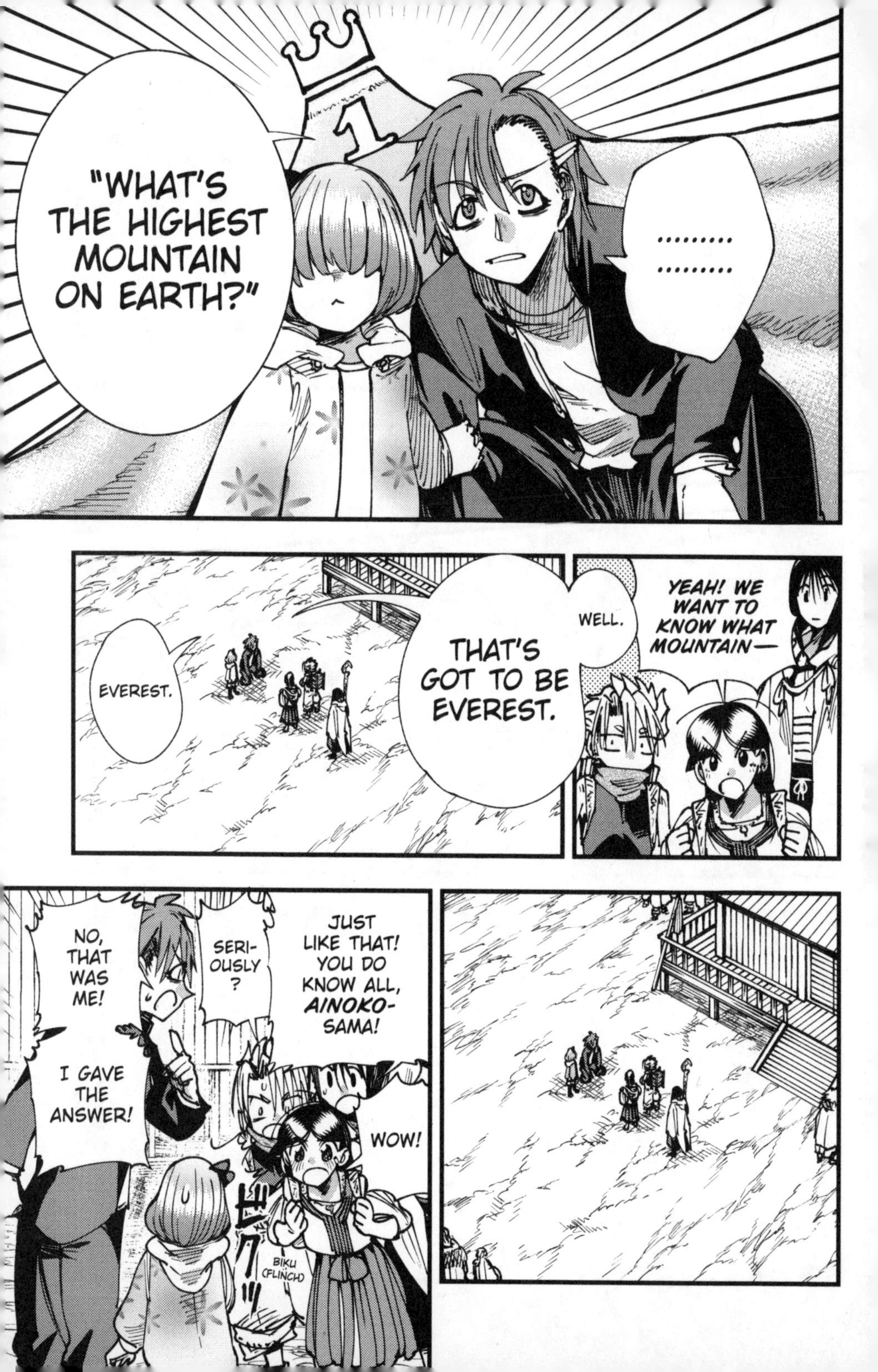
"WHAT'S THE HIGHEST MOUNTAIN ON EARTH?"
....
YEAH! WE WANT TO KNOW WHAT MOUNTAIN—
WELL.
THAT'S GOT TO BE EVEREST.
EVEREST.
JUST LIKE THAT! YOU DO KNOW ALL, AINOKO-SAMA!
SERI-OUSLY?
NO, THAT WAS ME!
I GAVE THE ANSWER!
WOW!
BIKU (FLINCH)

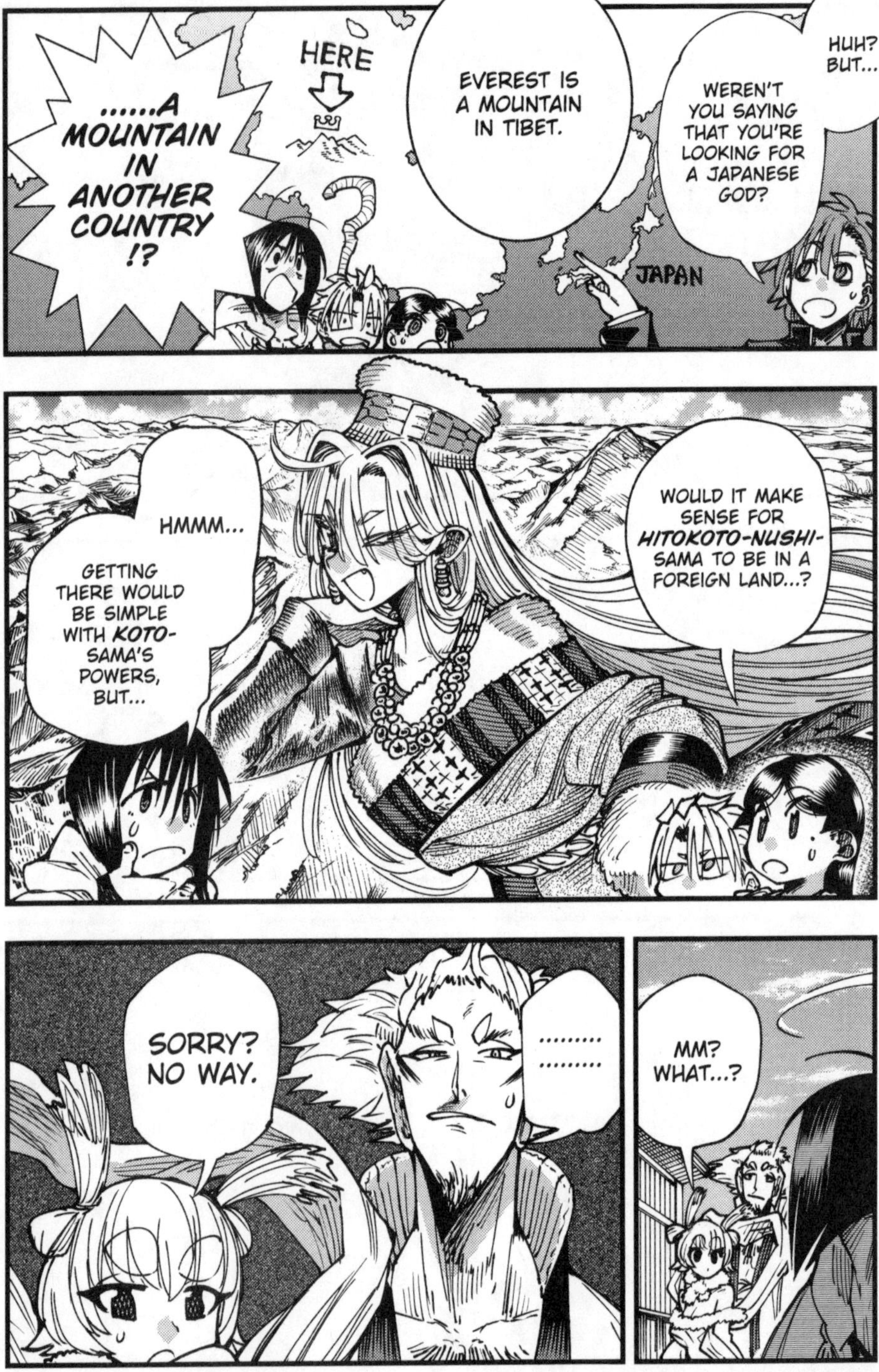
HUH? BUT...
WEREN'T YOU SAYING THAT YOU'RE LOOKING FOR A JAPANESE GOD?
JAPAN
EVEREST IS A MOUNTAIN IN TIBET.
HERE
......A MOUNTAIN IN ANOTHER COUNTRY !?
WOULD IT MAKE SENSE FOR *HITOKOTO-NUSHI*-SAMA TO BE IN A FOREIGN LAND...?
HMMM...
GETTING THERE WOULD BE SIMPLE WITH *KOTO*-SAMA'S POWERS, BUT...
MM? WHAT...?
....
....
SORRY? NO WAY.

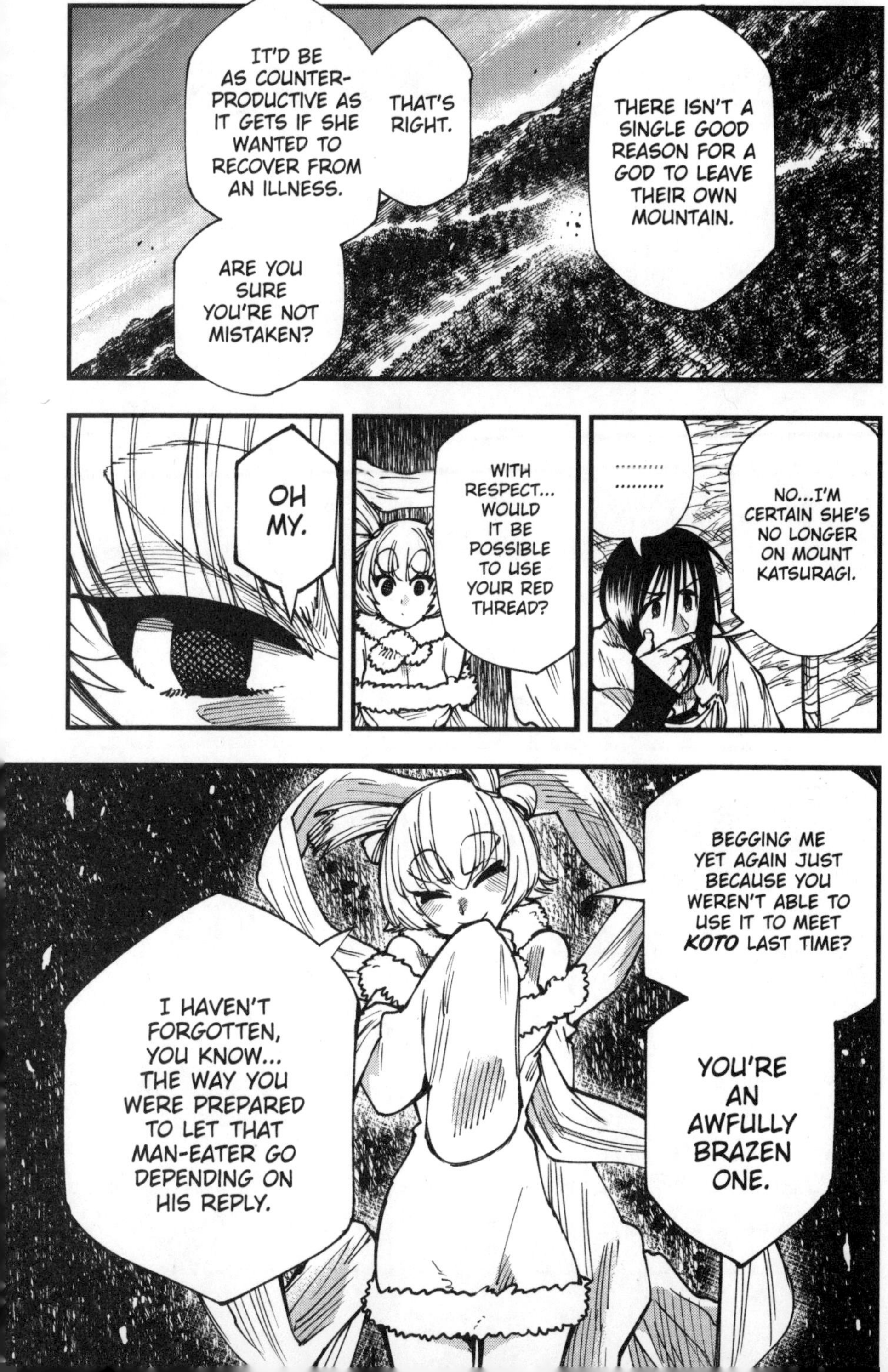
THERE ISN'T A SINGLE GOOD REASON FOR A GOD TO LEAVE THEIR OWN MOUNTAIN.
THAT'S RIGHT.
IT'D BE AS COUNTER-PRODUCTIVE AS IT GETS IF SHE WANTED TO RECOVER FROM AN ILLNESS.
ARE YOU SURE YOU'RE NOT MISTAKEN?
NO...I'M CERTAIN SHE'S NO LONGER ON MOUNT KATSURAGI.
....
WITH RESPECT... WOULD IT BE POSSIBLE TO USE YOUR RED THREAD?
OH MY.
BEGGING ME YET AGAIN JUST BECAUSE YOU WEREN'T ABLE TO USE IT TO MEET *KOTO* LAST TIME?
YOU'RE AN AWFULLY BRAZEN ONE.
I HAVEN'T FORGOTTEN, YOU KNOW... THE WAY YOU WERE PREPARED TO LET THAT MAN-EATER GO DEPENDING ON HIS REPLY.

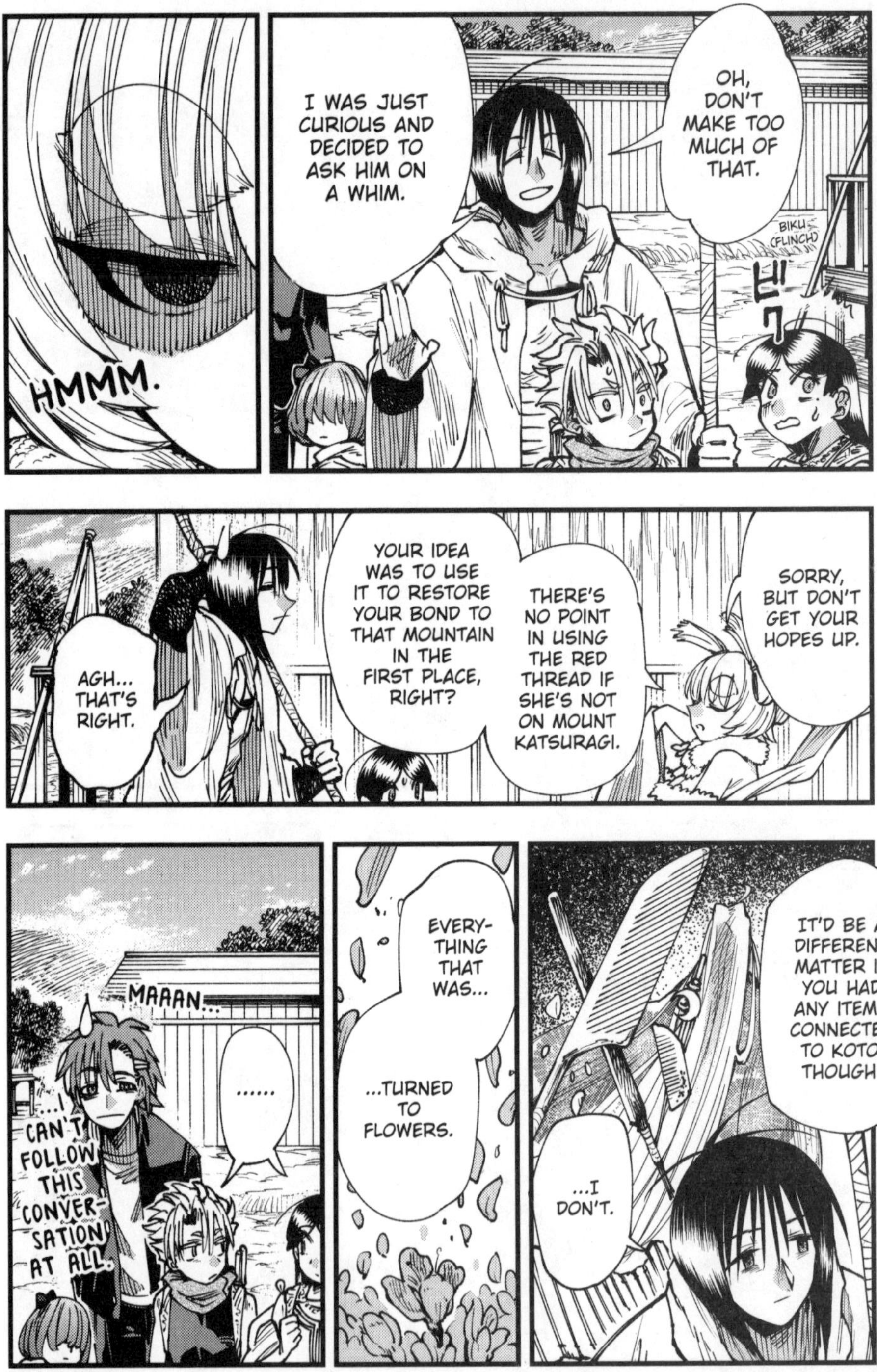
OH, DON'T MAKE TOO MUCH OF THAT.
I WAS JUST CURIOUS AND DECIDED TO ASK HIM ON A WHIM.
BIKU (FLINCH)
ビク
HMMM.
SORRY, BUT DON'T GET YOUR HOPES UP.
THERE'S NO POINT IN USING THE RED THREAD IF SHE'S NOT ON MOUNT KATSURAGI.
YOUR IDEA WAS TO USE IT TO RESTORE YOUR BOND TO THAT MOUNTAIN IN THE FIRST PLACE, RIGHT?
AGH... THAT'S RIGHT.
IT'D BE A DIFFERENT MATTER IF YOU HAD ANY ITEMS CONNECTED TO KOTO, THOUGH.
...I DON'T.
EVERY-THING THAT WAS...
...TURNED TO FLOWERS.
......
MAAAN...
...I CAN'T FOLLOW THIS CONVER-SATION AT ALL.

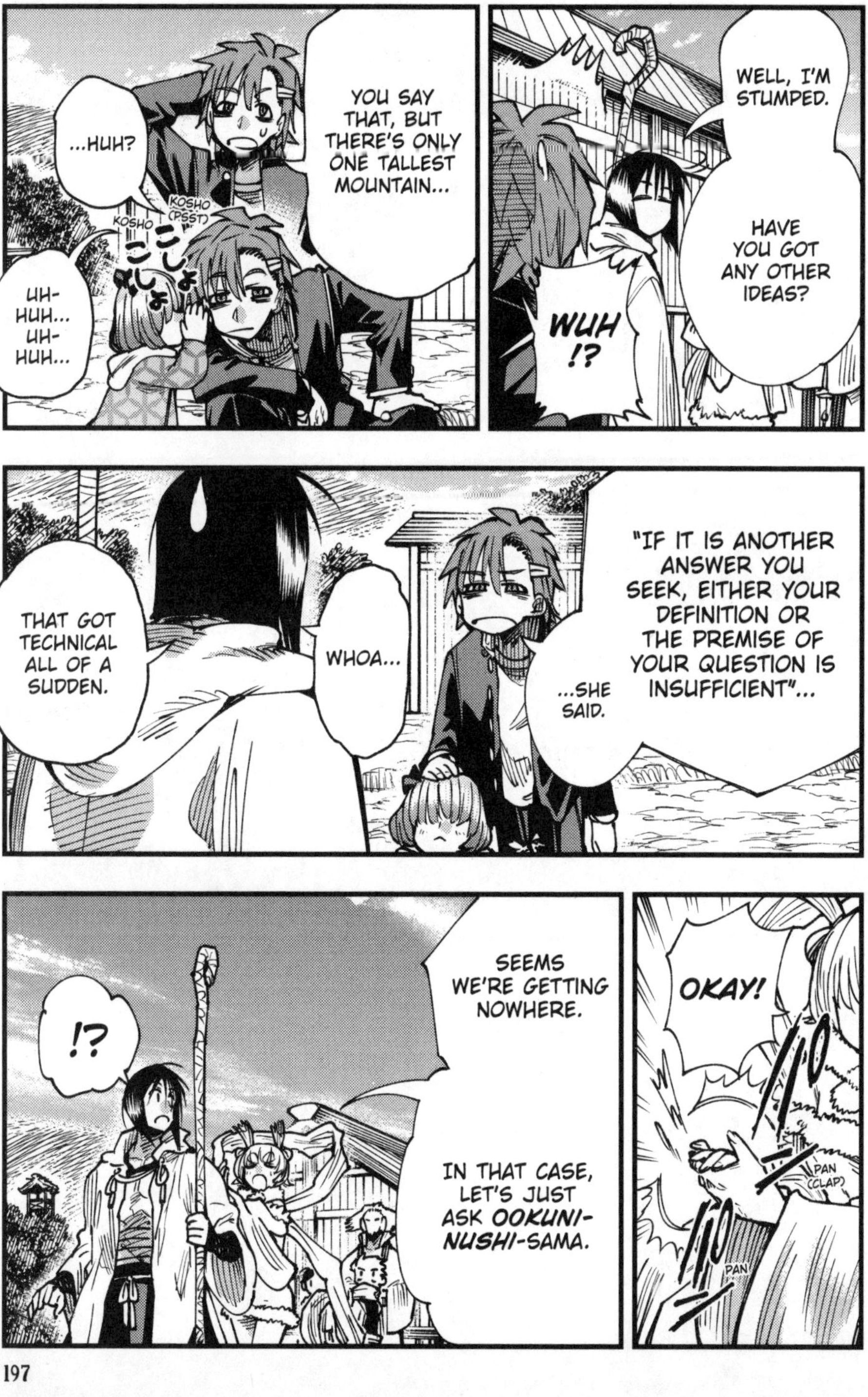
WELL, I'M STUMPED.
HAVE YOU GOT ANY OTHER IDEAS?
WUH!?
YOU SAY THAT, BUT THERE'S ONLY ONE TALLEST MOUNTAIN...
...HUH?
KOSHO (PSST)
こしょ
KOSHO
こしょ
UH-HUH... UH-HUH...
"IF IT IS ANOTHER ANSWER YOU SEEK, EITHER YOUR DEFINITION OR THE PREMISE OF YOUR QUESTION IS INSUFFICIENT"...
...SHE SAID.
WHOA...
THAT GOT TECHNICAL ALL OF A SUDDEN.
OKAY!
PAN (CLAP)
PAN
SEEMS WE'RE GETTING NOWHERE.
IN THAT CASE, LET'S JUST ASK *OOKUNI-NUSHI*-SAMA.
!?

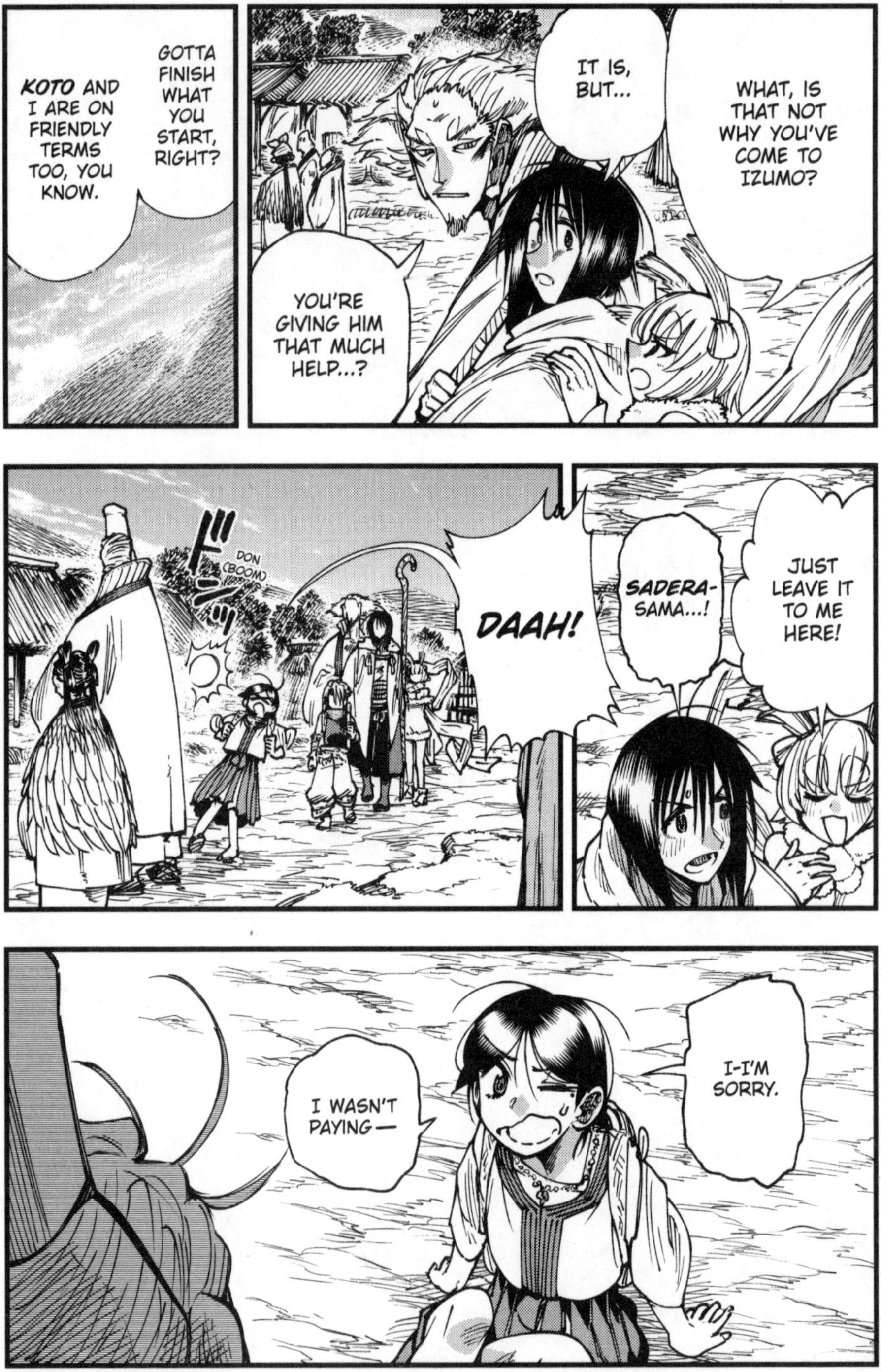
WHAT, IS THAT NOT WHY YOU'VE COME TO IZUMO?
IT IS, BUT...
YOU'RE GIVING HIM THAT MUCH HELP...?
GOTTA FINISH WHAT YOU START, RIGHT?
KOTO AND I ARE ON FRIENDLY TERMS TOO, YOU KNOW.
JUST LEAVE IT TO ME HERE!
SADERA-SAMA...!
DAAH!
DON (BOOM)
I-I'M SORRY.
I WASN'T PAYING—

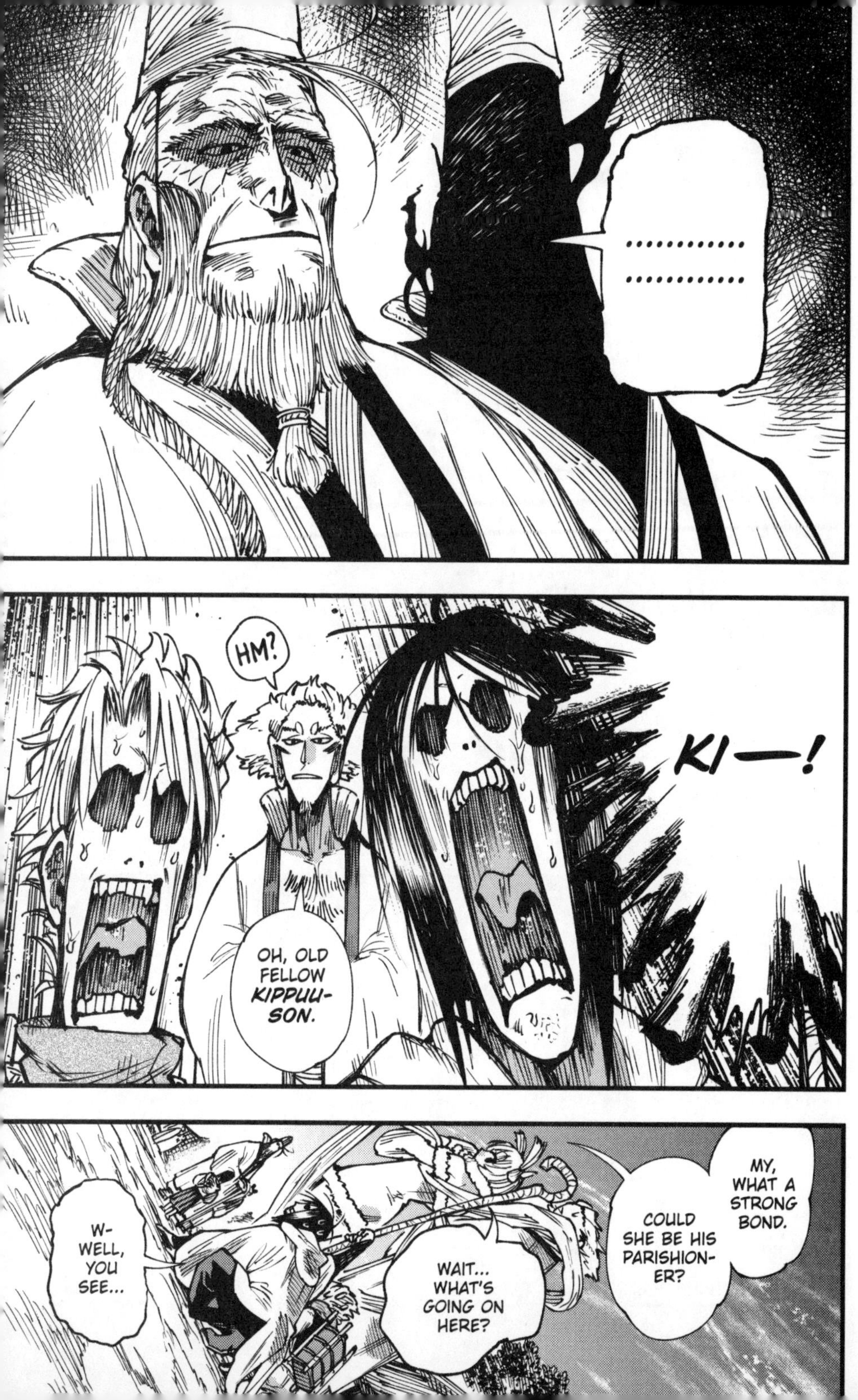
....
....
KI—!
HM?
OH, OLD FELLOW KIPPUU-SON.
MY, WHAT A STRONG BOND.
COULD SHE BE HIS PARISHIONER?
WAIT... WHAT'S GOING ON HERE?
W-WELL, YOU SEE...

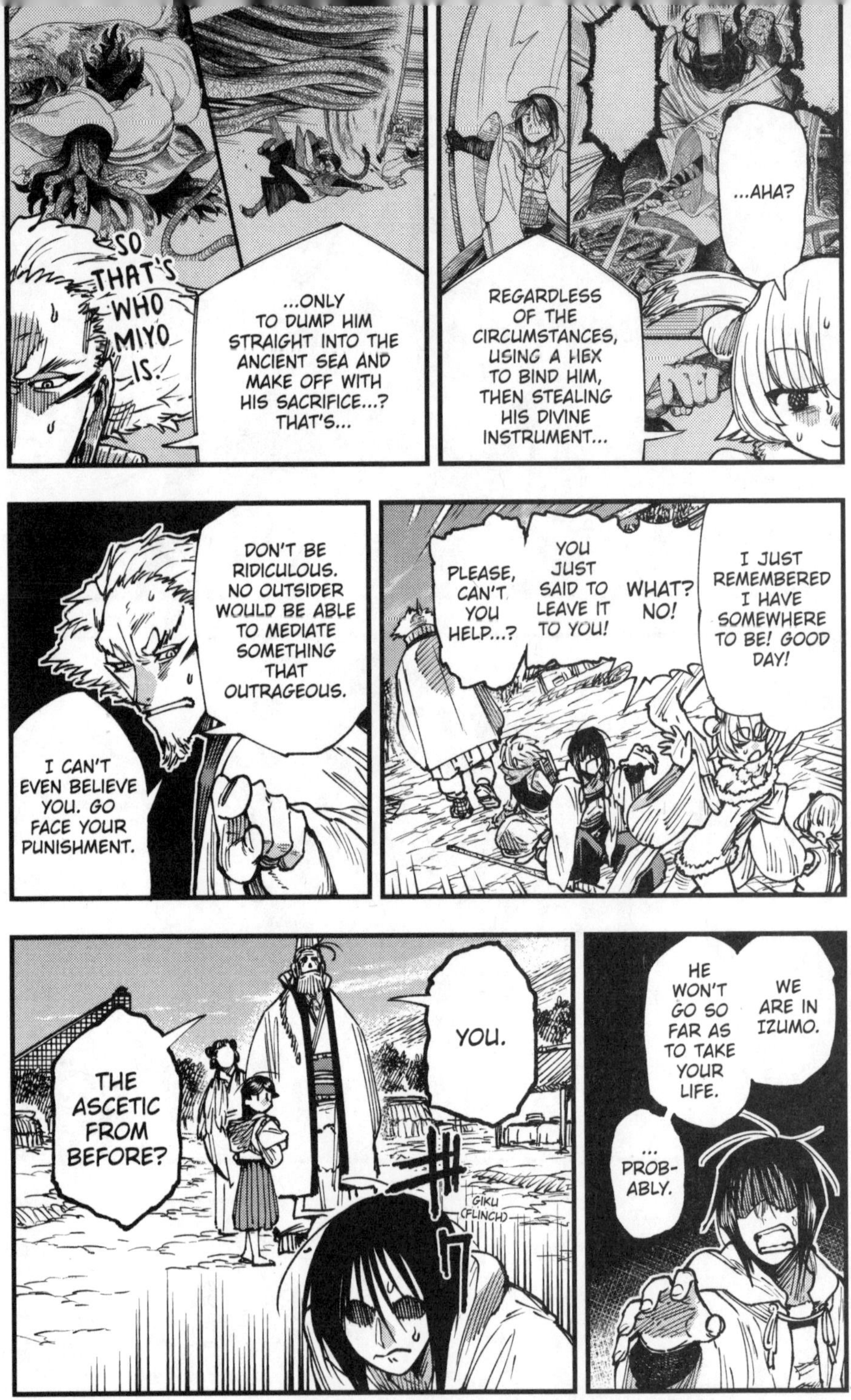

...AHA?
REGARDLESS OF THE CIRCUMSTANCES, USING A HEX TO BIND HIM, THEN STEALING HIS DIVINE INSTRUMENT...
...ONLY TO DUMP HIM STRAIGHT INTO THE ANCIENT SEA AND MAKE OFF WITH HIS SACRIFICE...? THAT'S...
SO THAT'S WHO MIYO IS.
I JUST REMEMBERED I HAVE SOMEWHERE TO BE! GOOD DAY!
WHAT? NO!
YOU JUST SAID TO LEAVE IT TO YOU!
PLEASE, CAN'T YOU HELP...?
DON'T BE RIDICULOUS. NO OUTSIDER WOULD BE ABLE TO MEDIATE SOMETHING THAT OUTRAGEOUS.
I CAN'T EVEN BELIEVE YOU. GO FACE YOUR PUNISHMENT.
WE ARE IN IZUMO.
HE WON'T GO SO FAR AS TO TAKE YOUR LIFE.
...PROBABLY.
YOU.
THE ASCETIC FROM BEFORE?
GIKU (FLINCH)

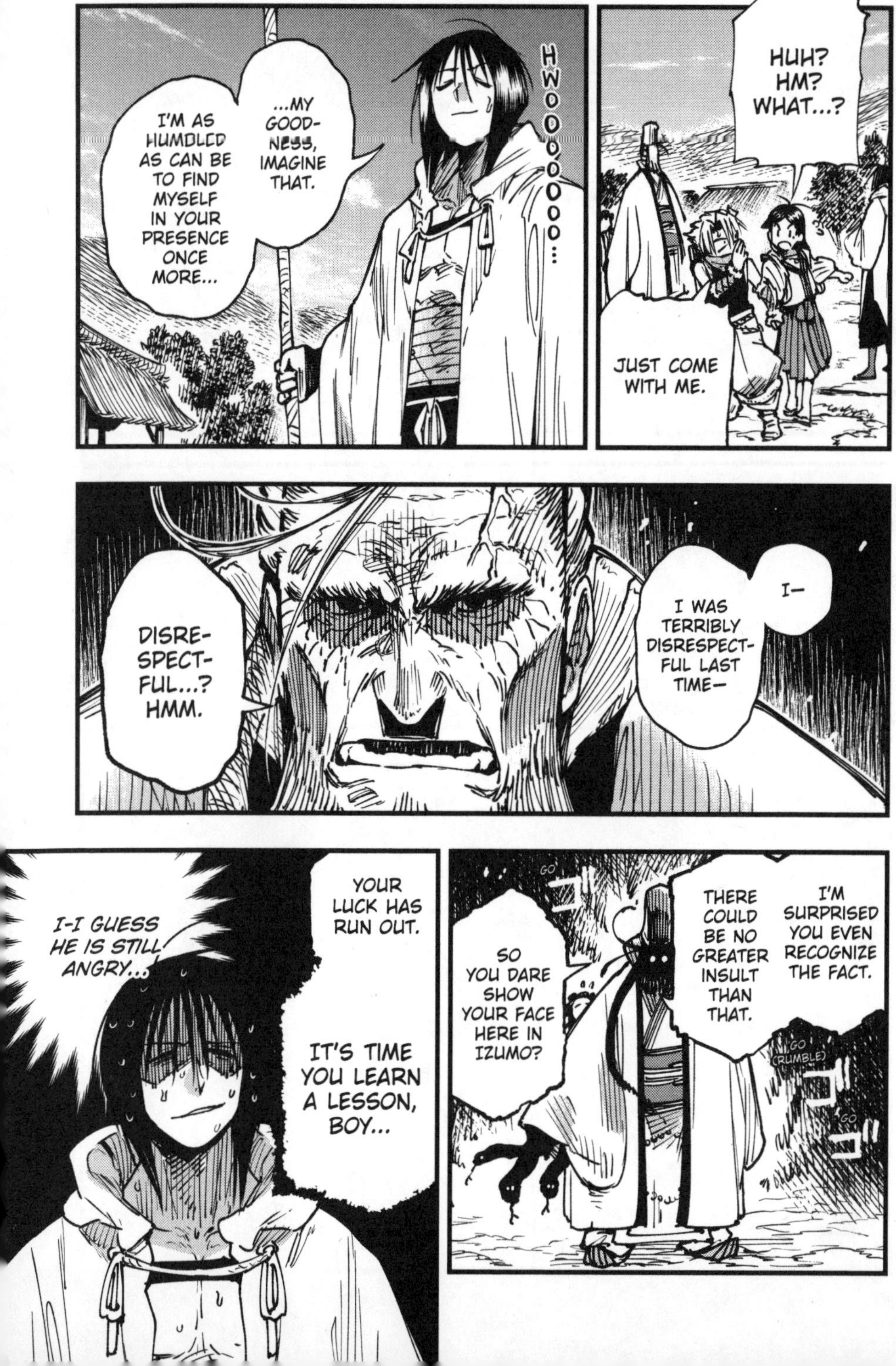
HUH? HM? WHAT...?
JUST COME WITH ME.
HWOOOOOOOO...
...MY GOODNESS, IMAGINE THAT.
I'M AS HUMBLED AS CAN BE TO FIND MYSELF IN YOUR PRESENCE ONCE MORE...
I—
I WAS TERRIBLY DISRESPECTFUL LAST TIME—
DISRESPECTFUL...? HMM.
I'M SURPRISED YOU EVEN RECOGNIZE THE FACT.
THERE COULD BE NO GREATER INSULT THAN THAT.
SO YOU DARE SHOW YOUR FACE HERE IN IZUMO?
GO
GO (RUMBLE)
GO
YOUR LUCK HAS RUN OUT.
IT'S TIME YOU LEARN A LESSON, BOY...
I-I GUESS HE IS STILL ANGRY...

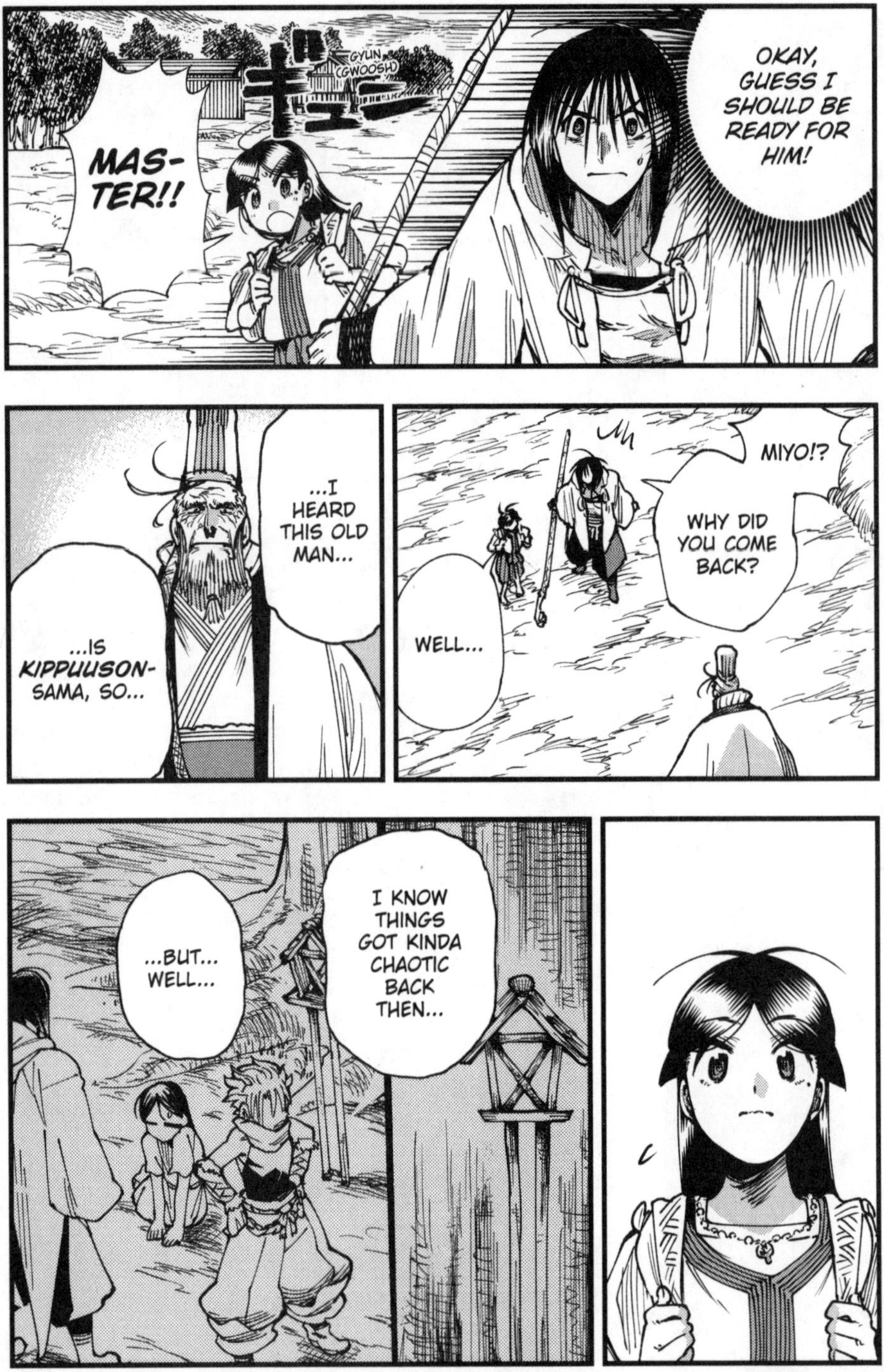
OKAY, GUESS I SHOULD BE READY FOR HIM!
GYUN (GWOOSH)
MAS-TER!!
MIYO!?
WHY DID YOU COME BACK?
WELL...
...I HEARD THIS OLD MAN...
...IS KIPPUUSON-SAMA, SO...
I KNOW THINGS GOT KINDA CHAOTIC BACK THEN...
...BUT... WELL...

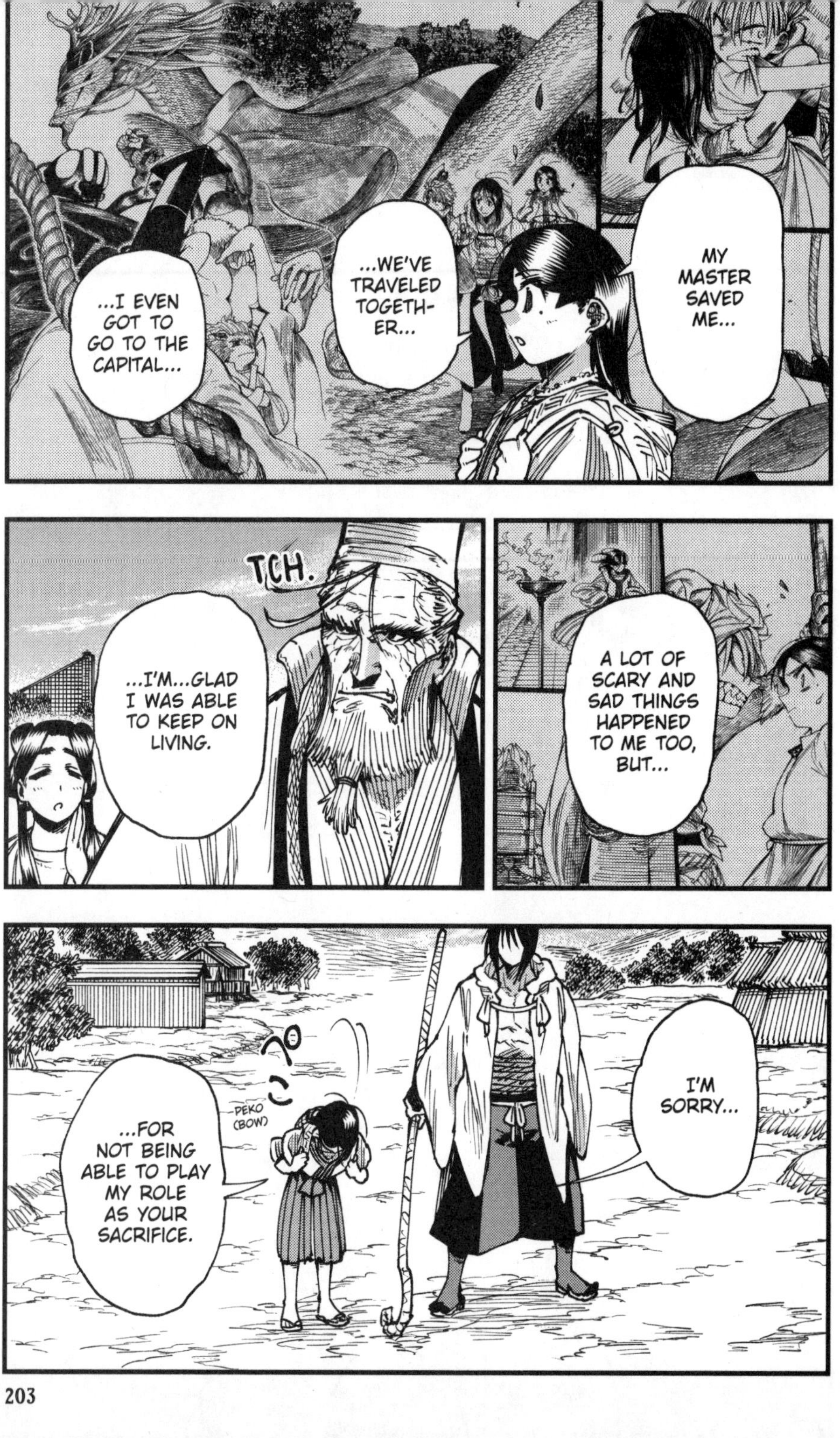
MY MASTER SAVED ME...
...WE'VE TRAVELED TOGETH-ER...
...I EVEN GOT TO GO TO THE CAPITAL...
A LOT OF SCARY AND SAD THINGS HAPPENED TO ME TOO, BUT...
TCH.
...I'M...GLAD I WAS ABLE TO KEEP ON LIVING.
I'M SORRY...
PEKO (BOW)
...FOR NOT BEING ABLE TO PLAY MY ROLE AS YOUR SACRIFICE.

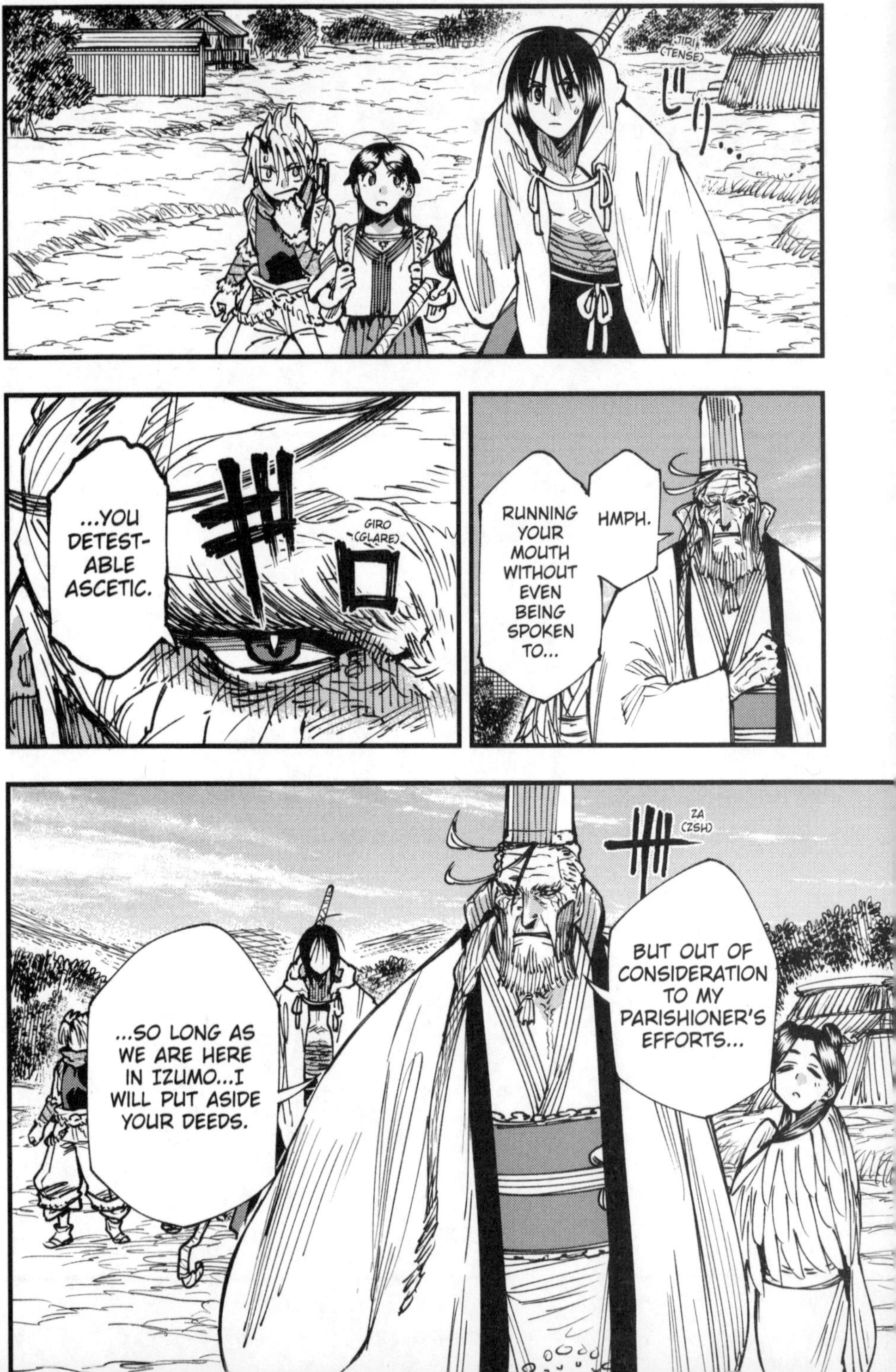
JIRI (TENSE)
じり…
HMPH.
RUNNING YOUR MOUTH WITHOUT EVEN BEING SPOKEN TO...
GIRO (GLARE)
ギロ
...YOU DETEST-ABLE ASCETIC.
ZA (ZSH)
BUT OUT OF CONSIDERATION TO MY PARISHIONER'S EFFORTS...
...SO LONG AS WE ARE HERE IN IZUMO...I WILL PUT ASIDE YOUR DEEDS.

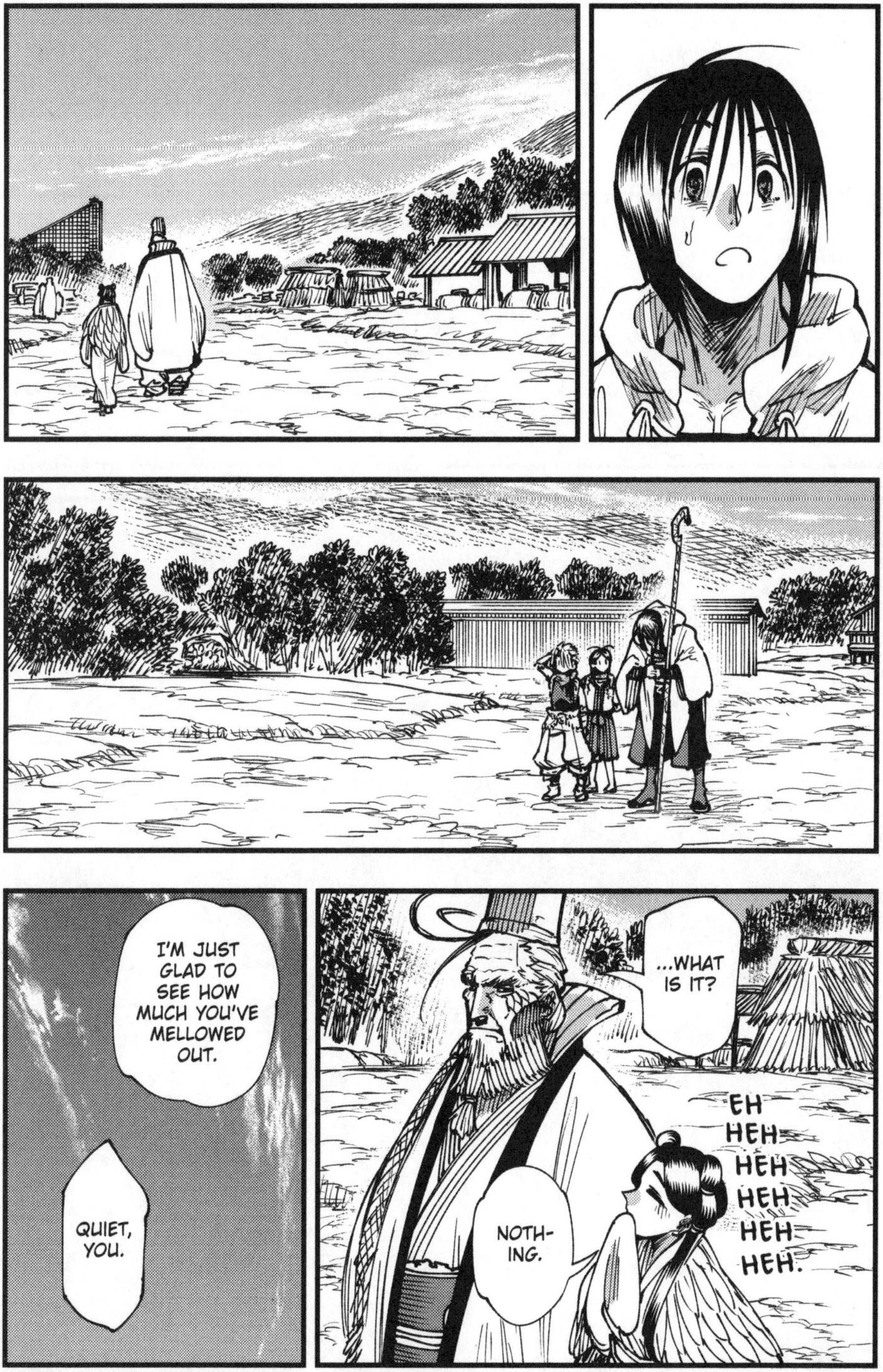
...WHAT IS IT?
EH HEH HEH HEH HEH HEH.
NOTH-ING.
I'M JUST GLAD TO SEE HOW MUCH YOU'VE MELLOWED OUT.
QUIET, YOU.

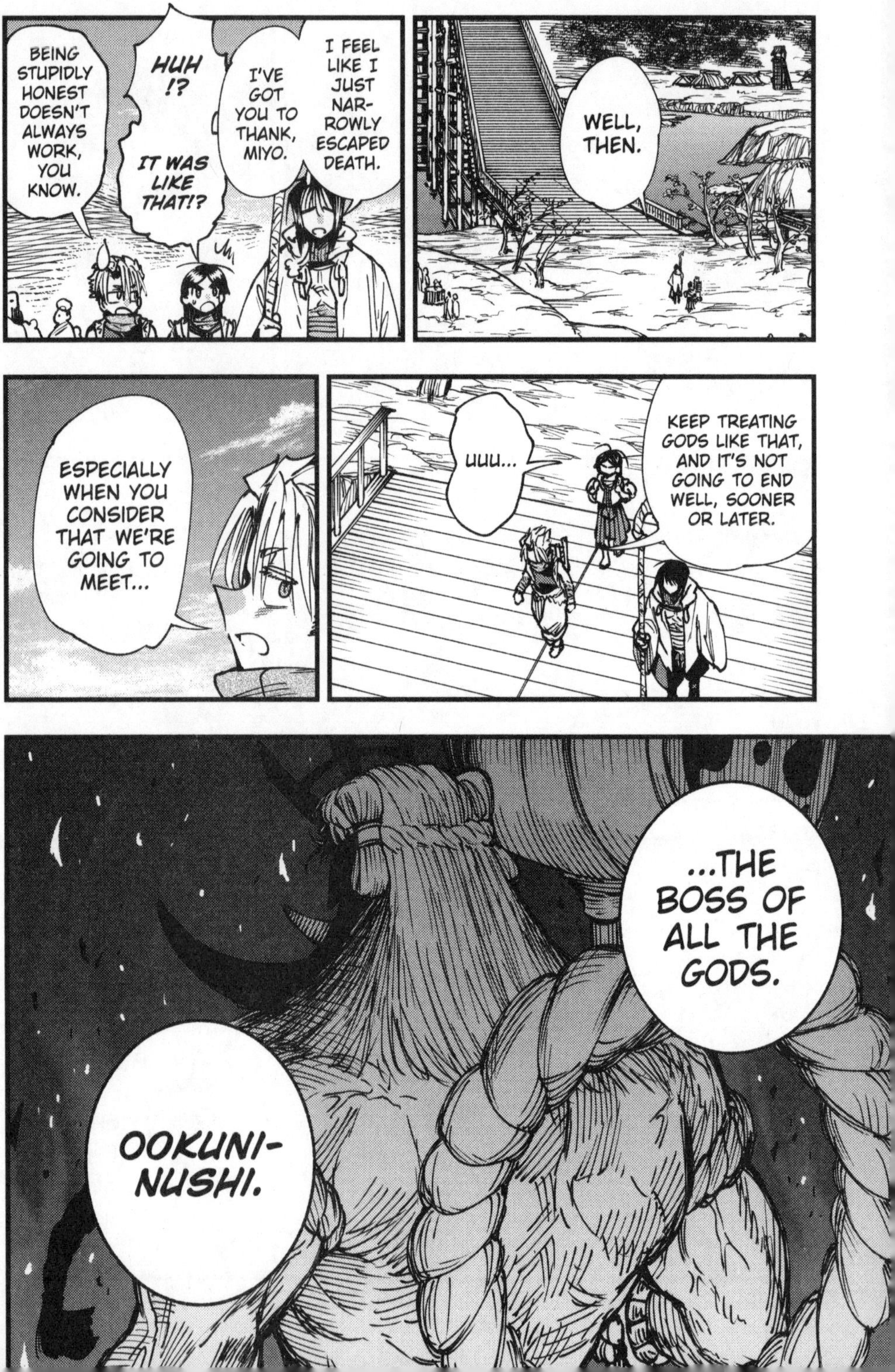
WELL, THEN.
I FEEL LIKE I JUST NAR-ROWLY ESCAPED DEATH.
I'VE GOT YOU TO THANK, MIYO.
HUH!? IT WAS LIKE THAT!?
BEING STUPIDLY HONEST DOESN'T ALWAYS WORK, YOU KNOW.
KEEP TREATING GODS LIKE THAT, AND IT'S NOT GOING TO END WELL, SOONER OR LATER.
uuu...
ESPECIALLY WHEN YOU CONSIDER THAT WE'RE GOING TO MEET...
...THE BOSS OF ALL THE GODS.
OOKUNI-NUSHI.

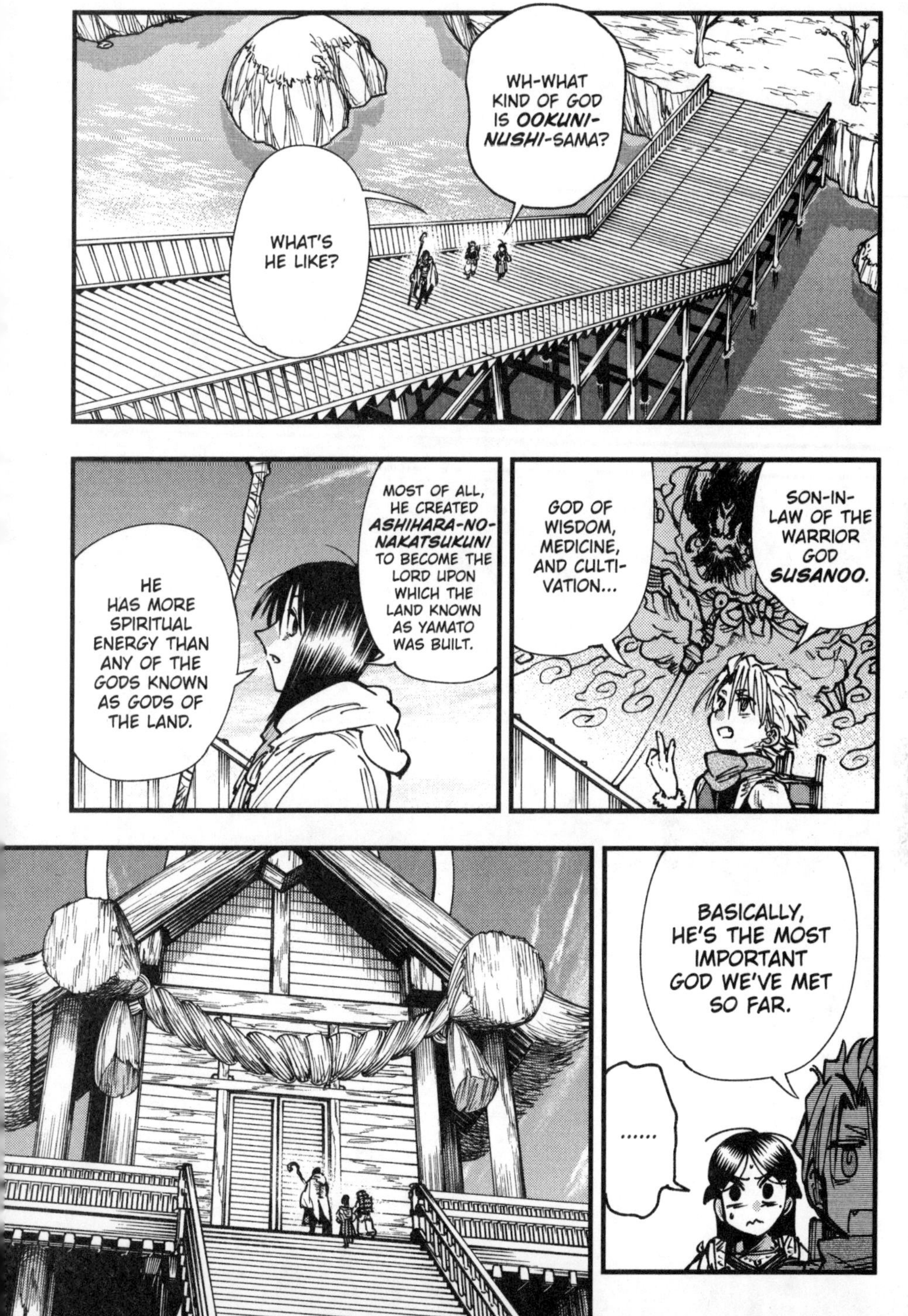
WH-WHAT KIND OF GOD IS OOKUNI-NUSHI-SAMA?
WHAT'S HE LIKE?
SON-IN-LAW OF THE WARRIOR GOD SUSANOO.
GOD OF WISDOM, MEDICINE, AND CULTI-VATION...
MOST OF ALL, HE CREATED ASHIHARA-NO-NAKATSUKUNI TO BECOME THE LORD UPON WHICH THE LAND KNOWN AS YAMATO WAS BUILT.
HE HAS MORE SPIRITUAL ENERGY THAN ANY OF THE GODS KNOWN AS GODS OF THE LAND.
BASICALLY, HE'S THE MOST IMPORTANT GOD WE'VE MET SO FAR.
......

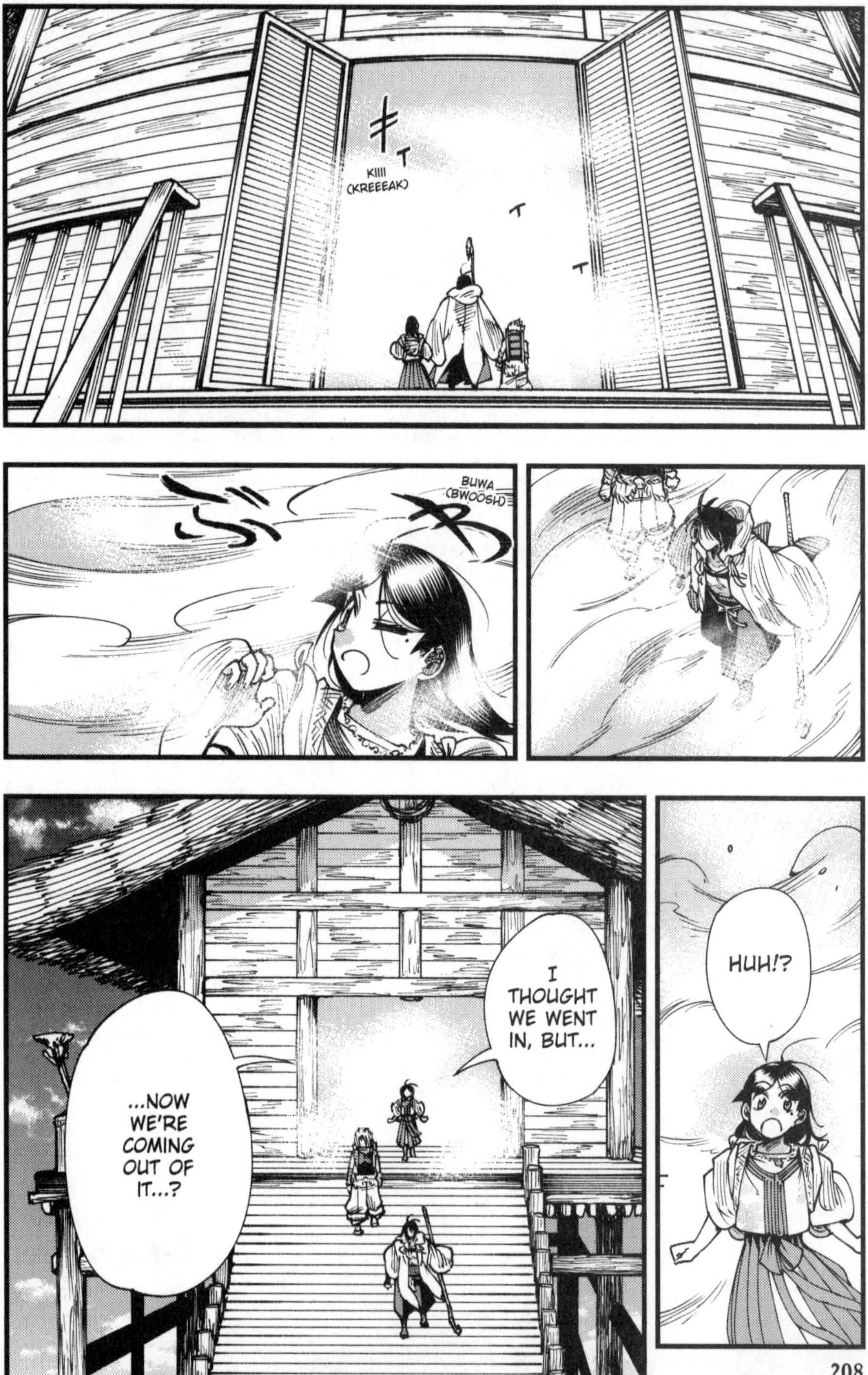
KIIII (KREEEAK)
BUWA (BWOOSH)
HUH!?
I THOUGHT WE WENT IN, BUT...
...NOW WE'RE COMING OUT OF IT...?

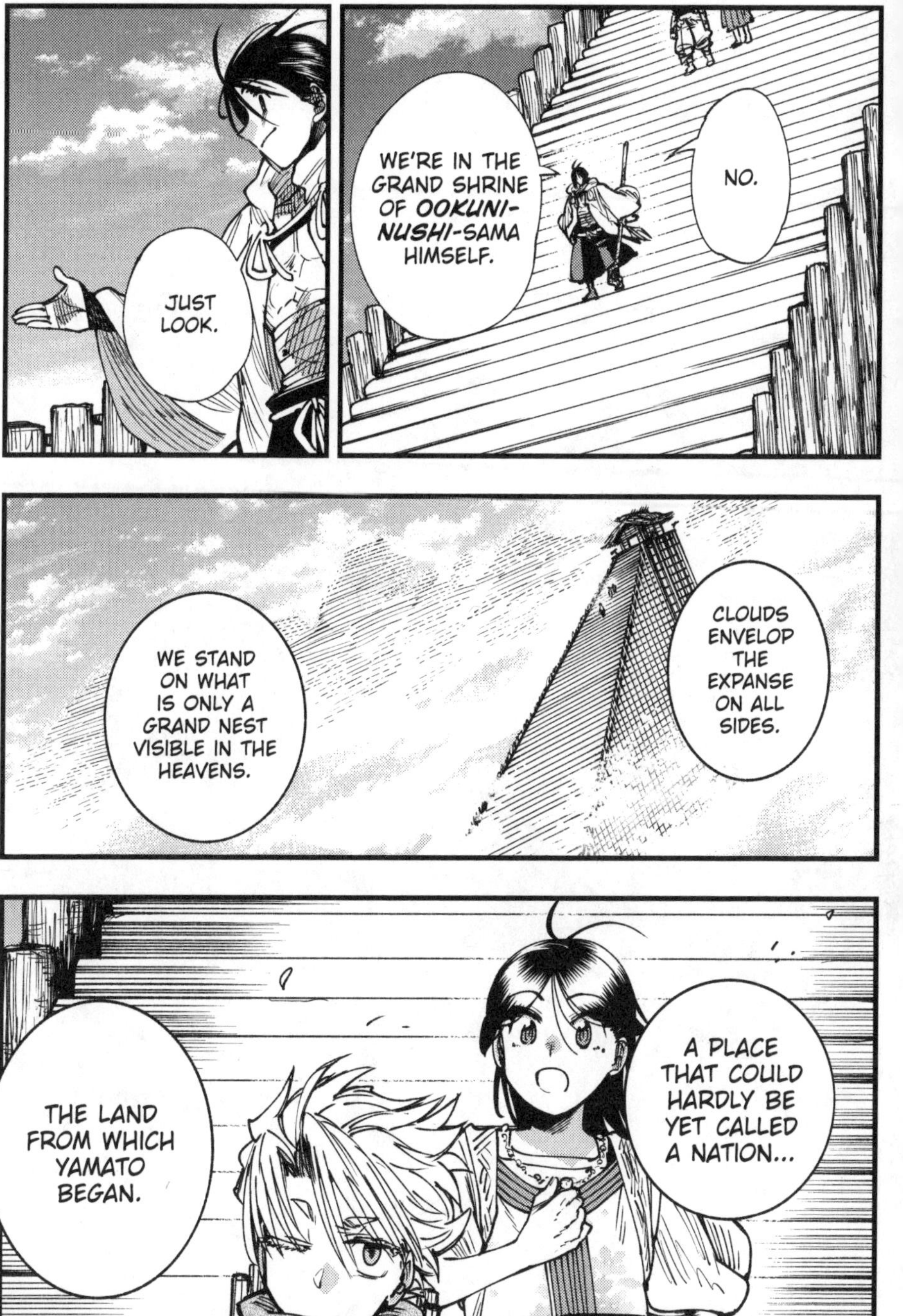
NO.
WE'RE IN THE GRAND SHRINE OF *OOKUNI-NUSHI*-SAMA HIMSELF.
JUST LOOK.
CLOUDS ENVELOP THE EXPANSE ON ALL SIDES.
WE STAND ON WHAT IS ONLY A GRAND NEST VISIBLE IN THE HEAVENS.
A PLACE THAT COULD HARDLY BE YET CALLED A NATION...
THE LAND FROM WHICH YAMATO BEGAN.

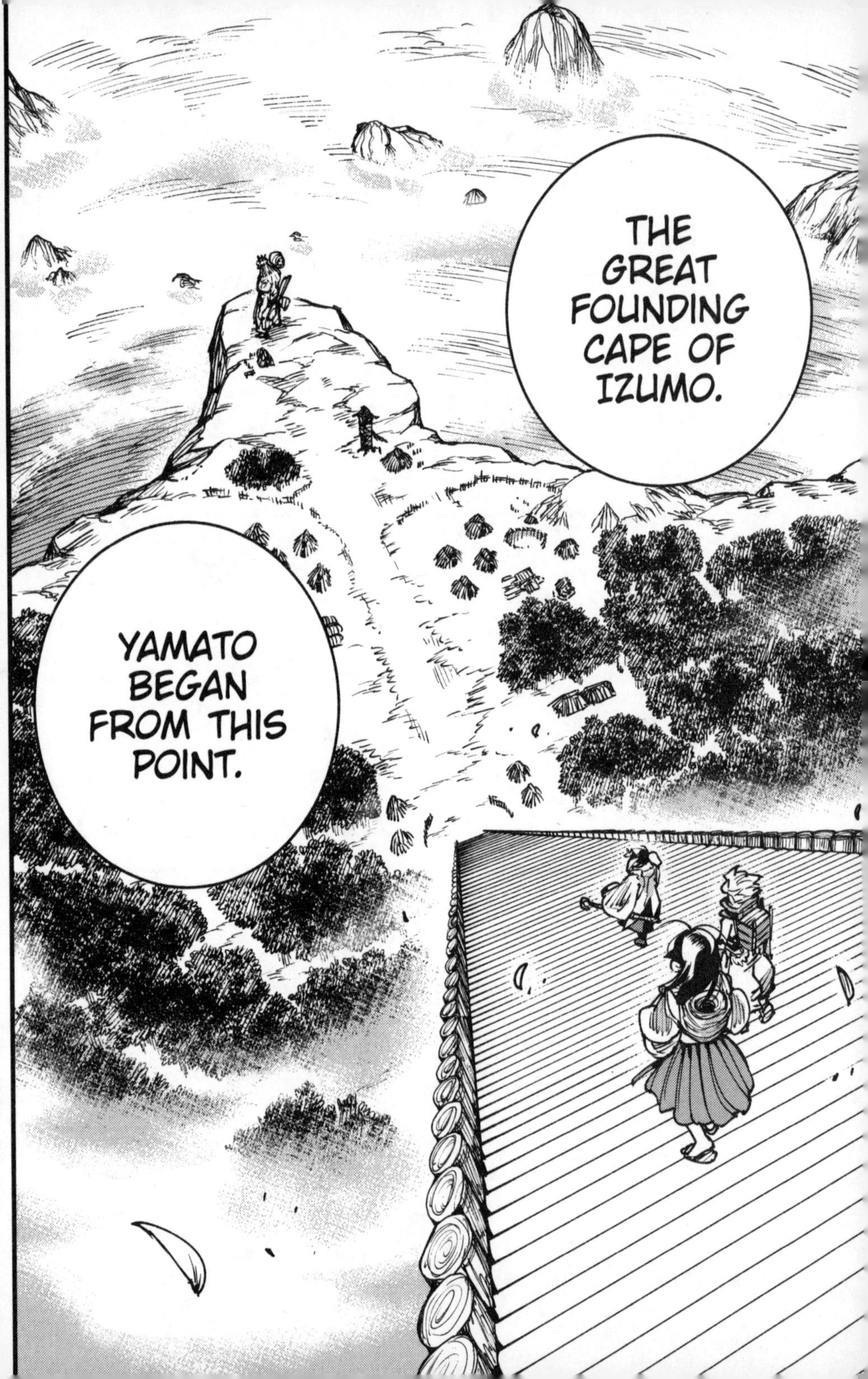
THE GREAT FOUNDING CAPE OF IZUMO.
YAMATO BEGAN FROM THIS POINT.

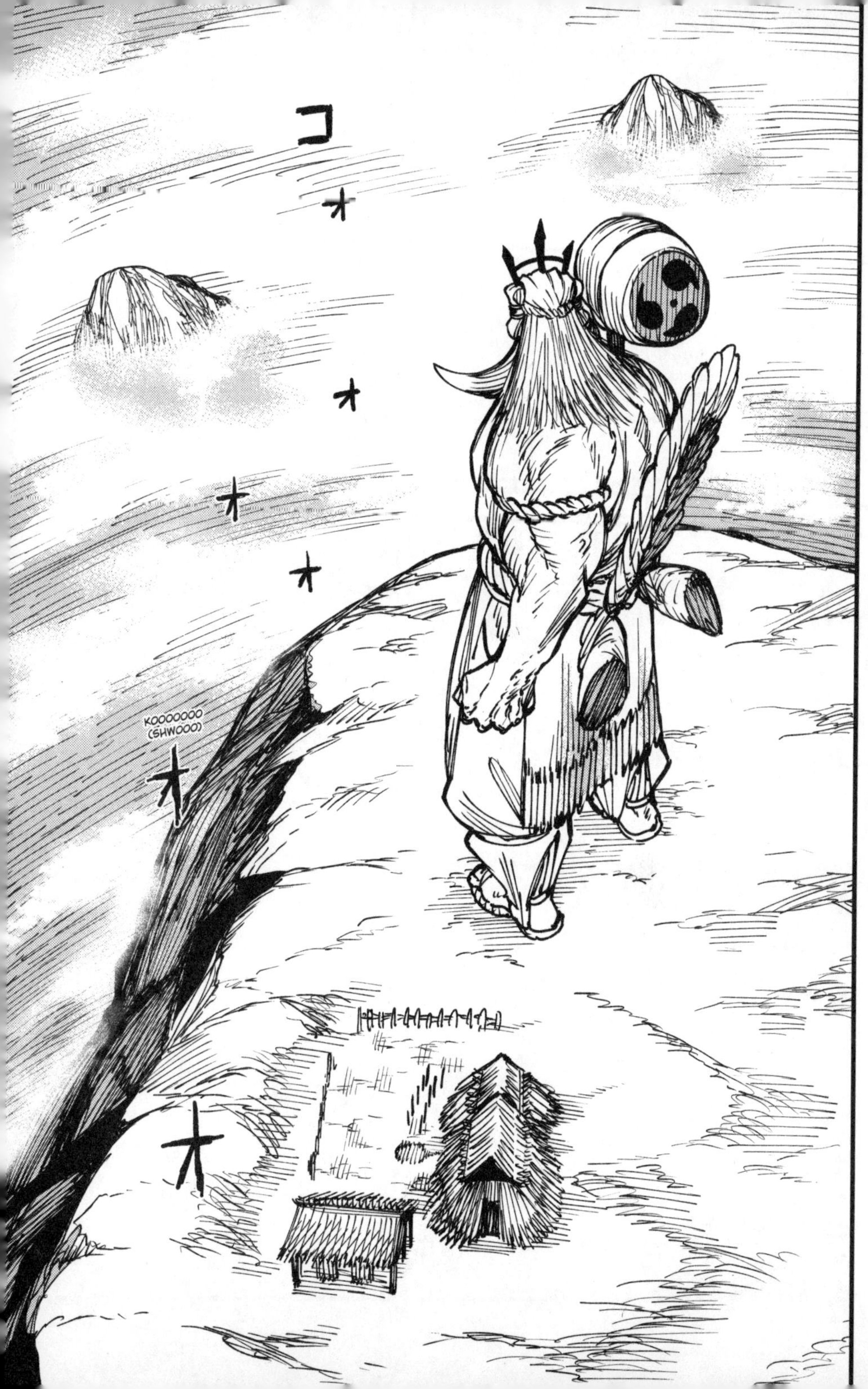
コオオオオオオ
KOOOOOOO
(SHWOOO)

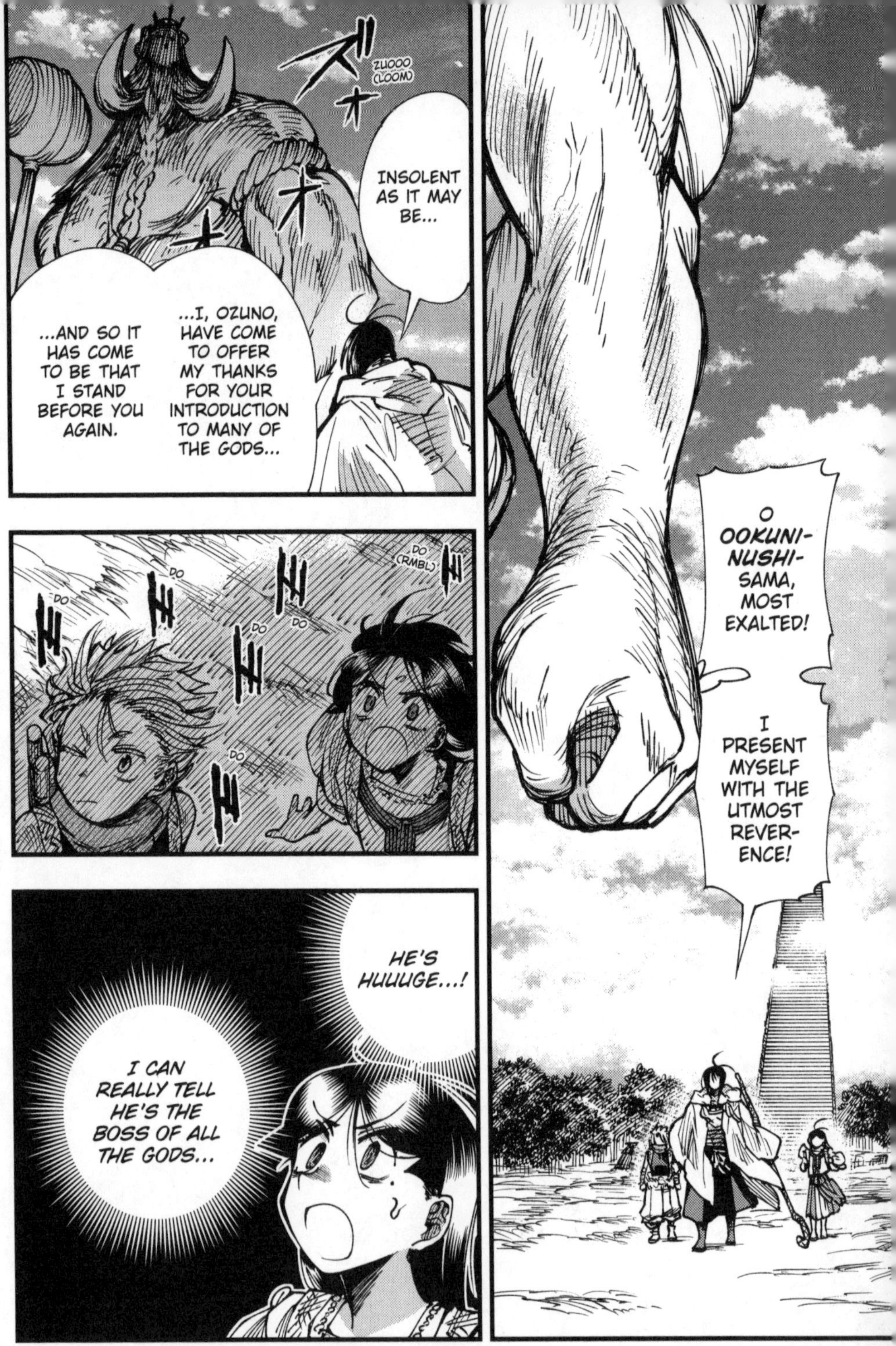
O OOKUNI-NUSHI-SAMA, MOST EXALTED!
I PRESENT MYSELF WITH THE UTMOST REVER-ENCE!
ZUOOO (LOOM)
INSOLENT AS IT MAY BE...
...I, OZUNO, HAVE COME TO OFFER MY THANKS FOR YOUR INTRODUCTION TO MANY OF THE GODS...
...AND SO IT HAS COME TO BE THAT I STAND BEFORE YOU AGAIN.
DO (RMBL)
DO
DO
DO
DO
DO
HE'S HUUUGE...!
I CAN REALLY TELL HE'S THE BOSS OF ALL THE GODS...

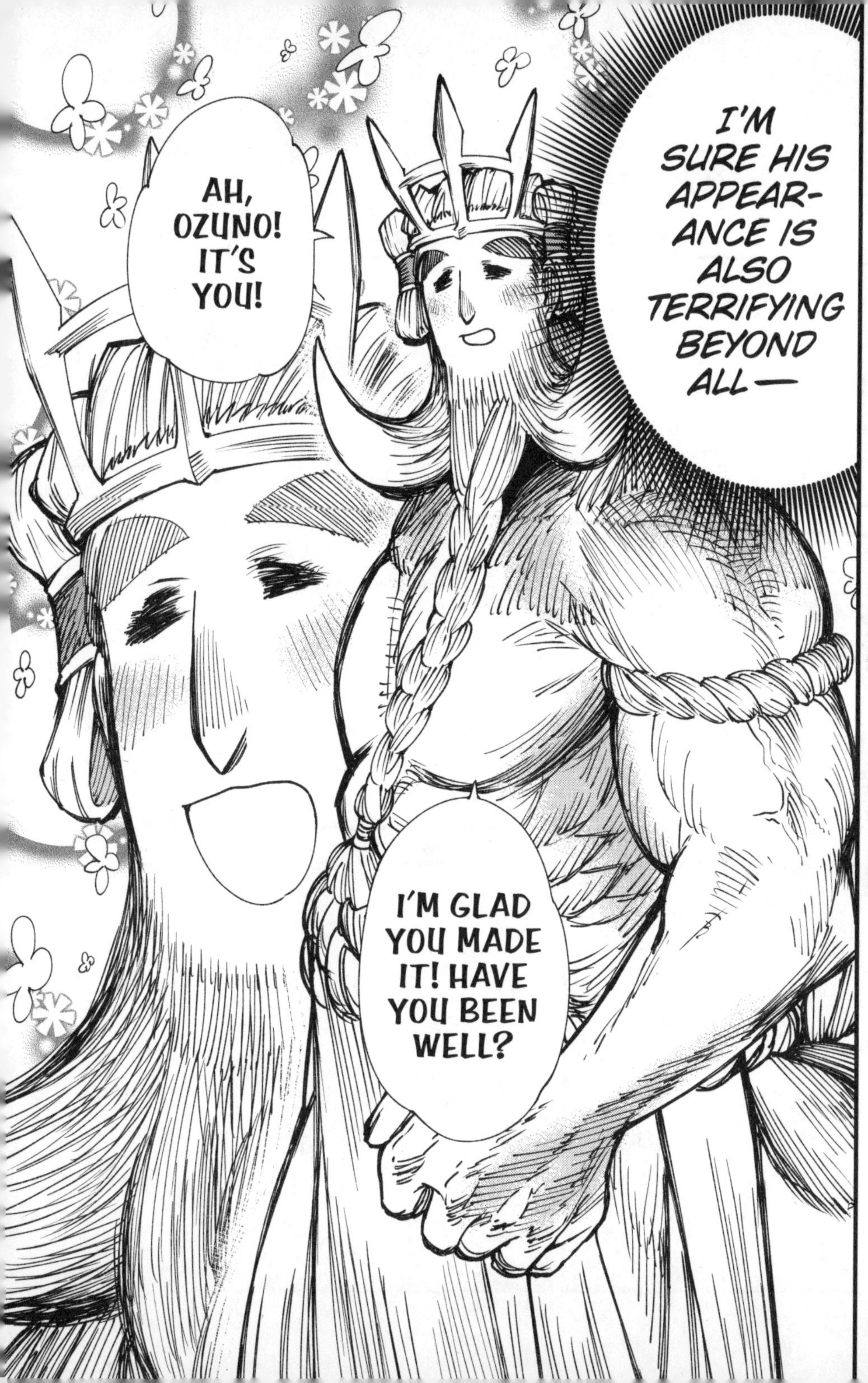
I'M SURE HIS APPEARANCE IS ALSO TERRIFYING BEYOND ALL—
AH, OZUNO! IT'S YOU!
I'M GLAD YOU MADE IT! HAVE YOU BEEN WELL?

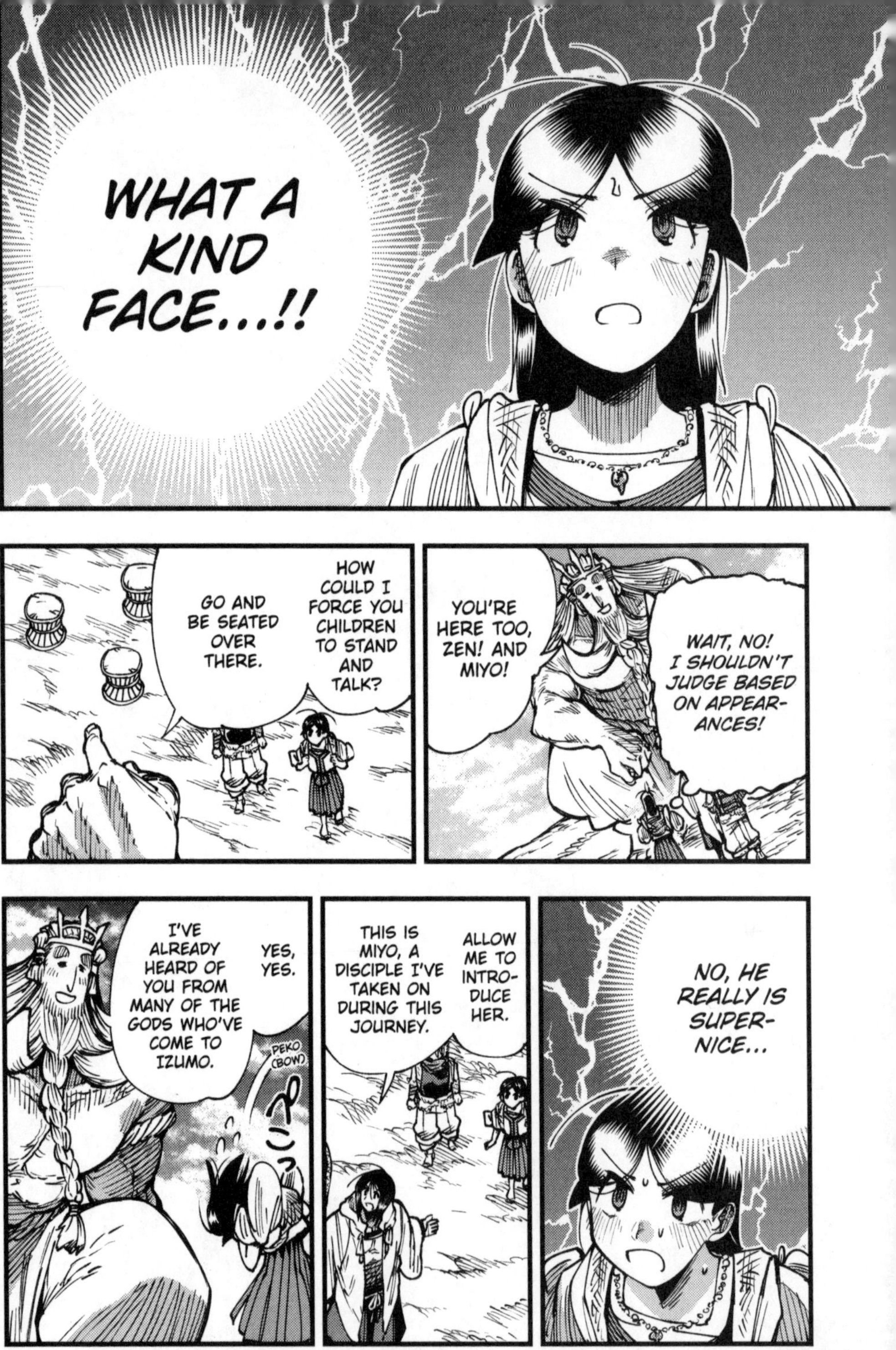
WHAT A KIND FACE...!!
WAIT, NO! I SHOULDN'T JUDGE BASED ON APPEAR-ANCES!
YOU'RE HERE TOO, ZEN! AND MIYO!
HOW COULD I FORCE YOU CHILDREN TO STAND AND TALK?
GO AND BE SEATED OVER THERE.
NO, HE REALLY IS SUPER-NICE...
ALLOW ME TO INTRO-DUCE HER.
THIS IS MIYO, A DISCIPLE I'VE TAKEN ON DURING THIS JOURNEY.
YES, YES.
I'VE ALREADY HEARD OF YOU FROM MANY OF THE GODS WHO'VE COME TO IZUMO.
PEKO (BOW)

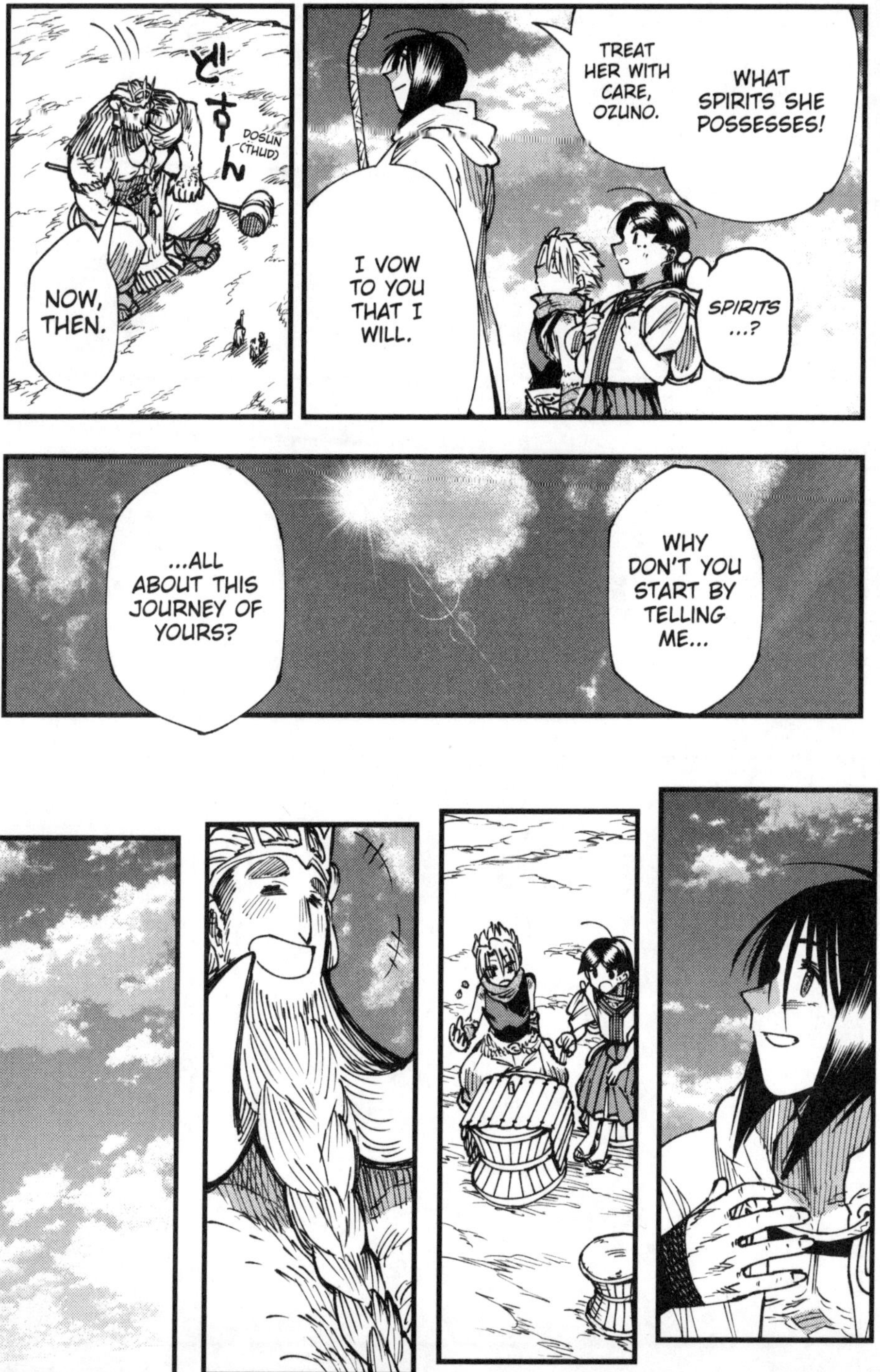
WHAT SPIRITS SHE POSSESSES!
TREAT HER WITH CARE, OZUNO.
SPIRITS ...?
I VOW TO YOU THAT I WILL.
どすん
DOSUN (THUD)
NOW, THEN.
WHY DON'T YOU START BY TELLING ME...
...ALL ABOUT THIS JOURNEY OF YOURS?

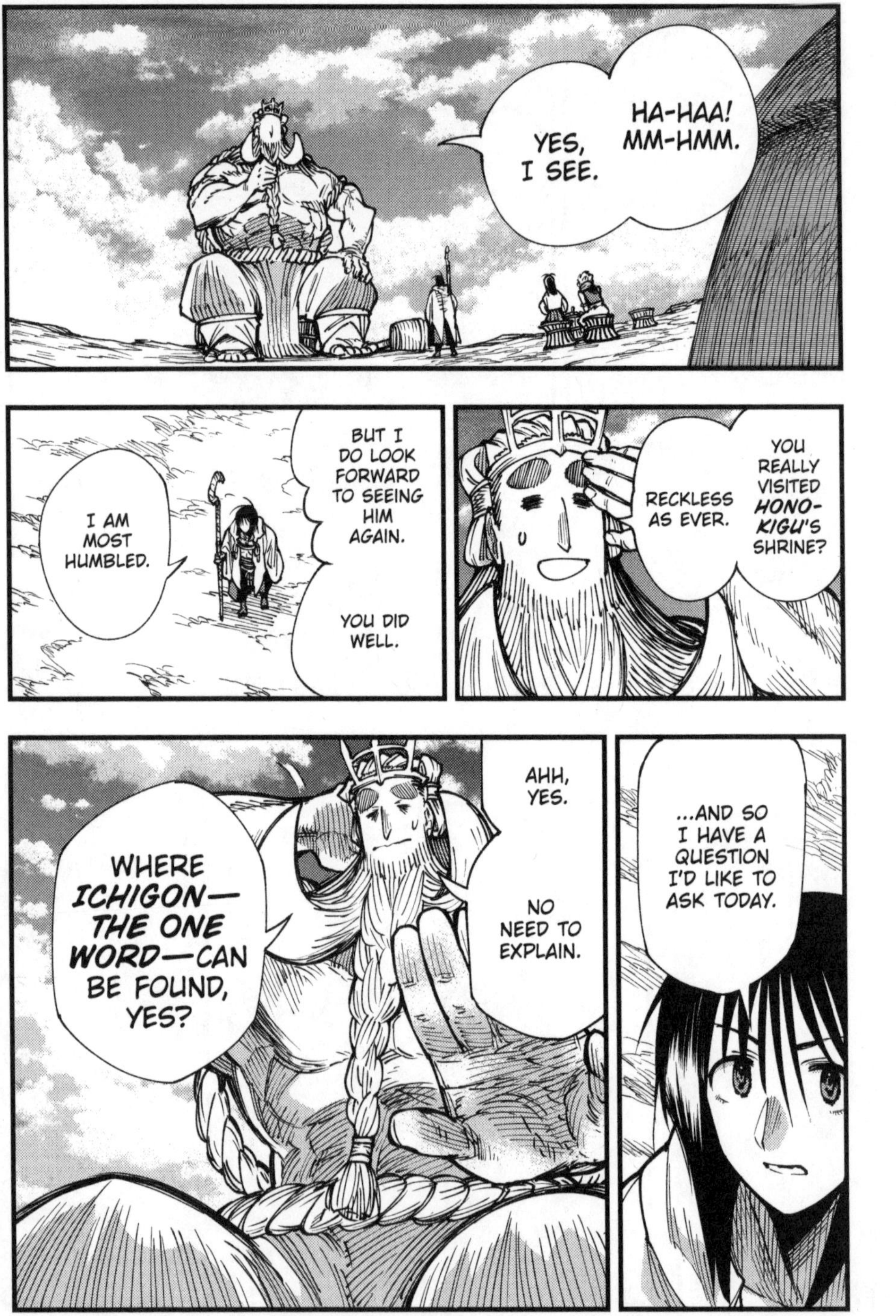
HA-HAA! MM-HMM.
YES, I SEE.
YOU REALLY VISITED HONO-KIGU'S SHRINE?
RECKLESS AS EVER.
BUT I DO LOOK FORWARD TO SEEING HIM AGAIN.
YOU DID WELL.
I AM MOST HUMBLED.
...AND SO I HAVE A QUESTION I'D LIKE TO ASK TODAY.
AHH, YES.
NO NEED TO EXPLAIN.
WHERE ICHIGON—THE ONE WORD—CAN BE FOUND, YES?

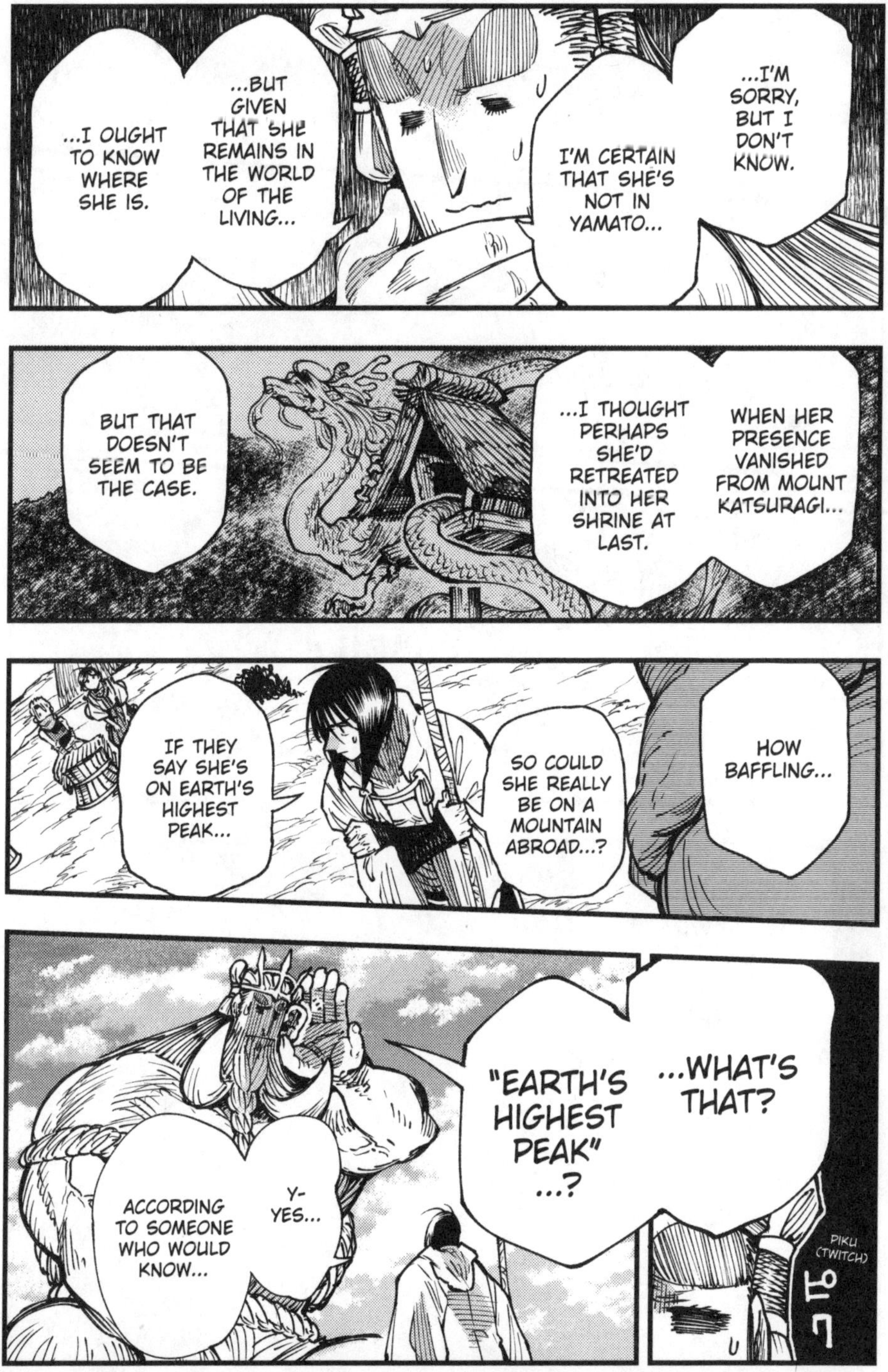
...I'M SORRY, BUT I DON'T KNOW.
I'M CERTAIN THAT SHE'S NOT IN YAMATO...
...BUT GIVEN THAT SHE REMAINS IN THE WORLD OF THE LIVING...
...I OUGHT TO KNOW WHERE SHE IS.
WHEN HER PRESENCE VANISHED FROM MOUNT KATSURAGI...
...I THOUGHT PERHAPS SHE'D RETREATED INTO HER SHRINE AT LAST.
BUT THAT DOESN'T SEEM TO BE THE CASE.
HOW BAFFLING...
SO COULD SHE REALLY BE ON A MOUNTAIN ABROAD...?
IF THEY SAY SHE'S ON EARTH'S HIGHEST PEAK...
PIKU (TWITCH)
...WHAT'S THAT?
"EARTH'S HIGHEST PEAK" ...?
Y-YES...
ACCORDING TO SOMEONE WHO WOULD KNOW...

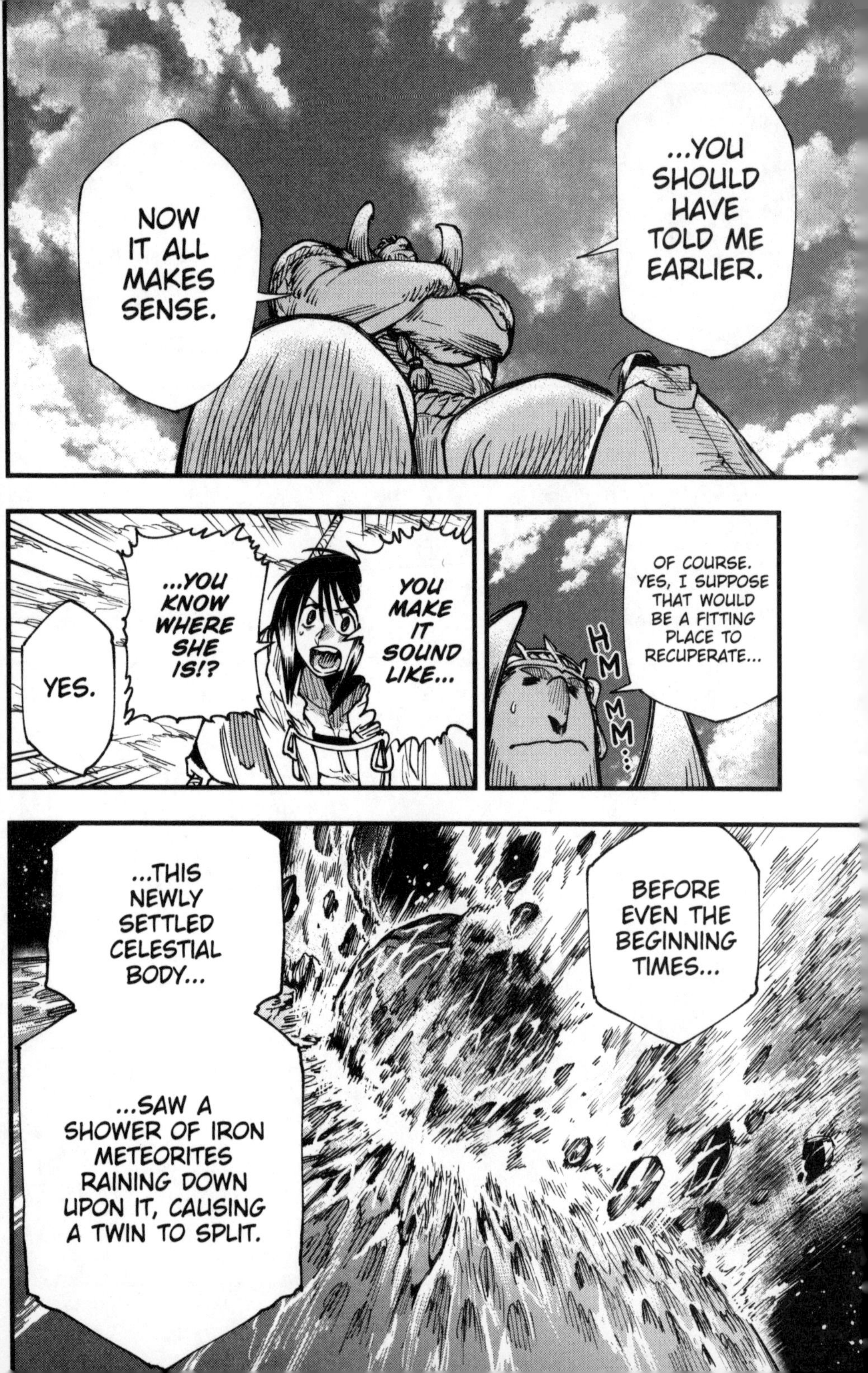
...YOU SHOULD HAVE TOLD ME EARLIER.
NOW IT ALL MAKES SENSE.
OF COURSE. YES, I SUPPOSE THAT WOULD BE A FITTING PLACE TO RECUPERATE...
HMMM...
YOU MAKE IT SOUND LIKE...
...YOU KNOW WHERE SHE IS!?
YES.
BEFORE EVEN THE BEGINNING TIMES...
...THIS NEWLY SETTLED CELESTIAL BODY...
...SAW A SHOWER OF IRON METEORITES RAINING DOWN UPON IT, CAUSING A TWIN TO SPLIT.

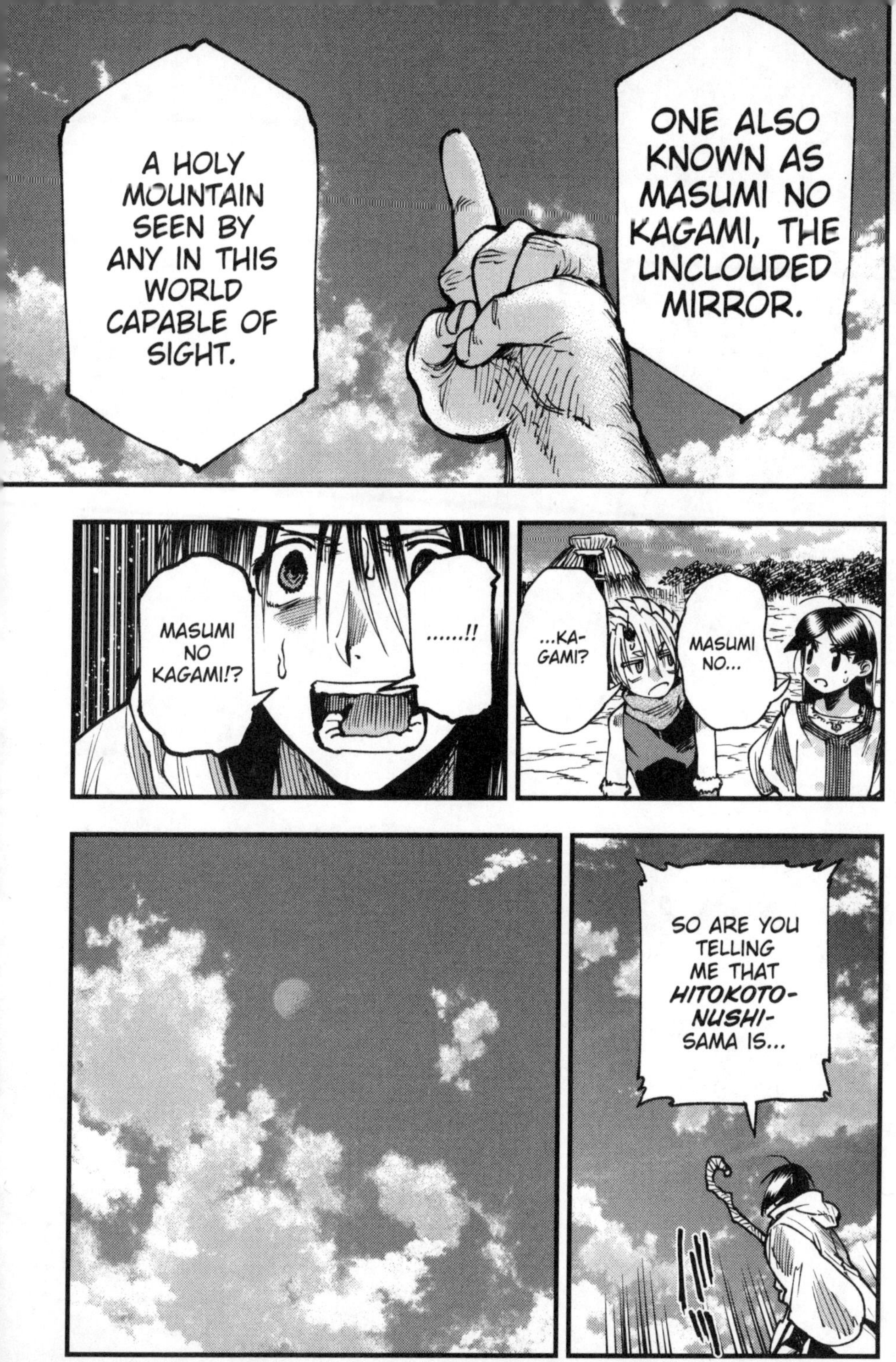
ONE ALSO KNOWN AS MASUMI NO KAGAMI, THE UNCLOUDED MIRROR.
A HOLY MOUNTAIN SEEN BY ANY IN THIS WORLD CAPABLE OF SIGHT.
MASUMI NO...
...KA-GAMI?
......!!
MASUMI NO KAGAMI!?
SO ARE YOU TELLING ME THAT *HITOKOTO-NUSHI*-SAMA IS...

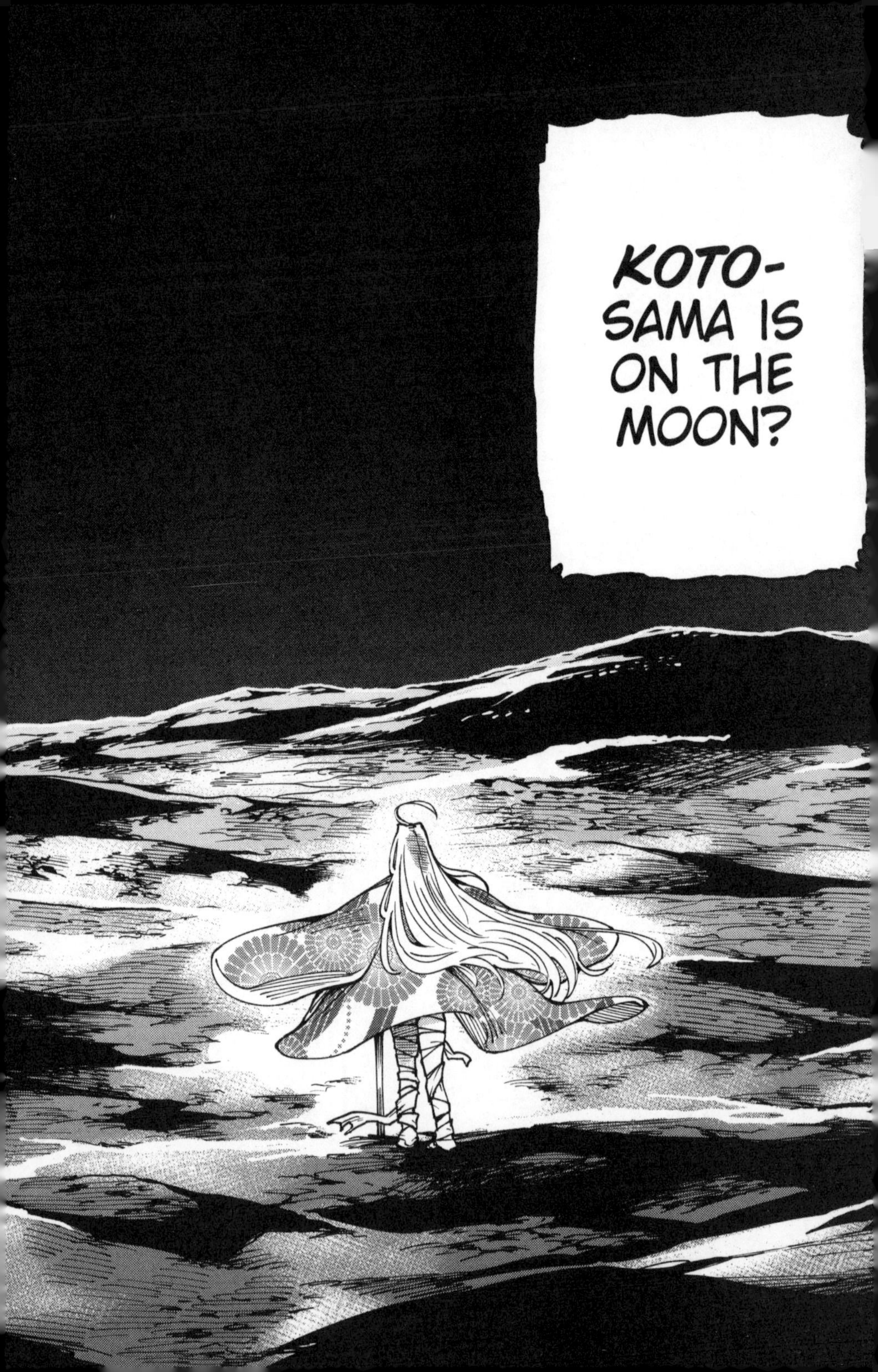
KOTO-SAMA IS ON THE MOON?

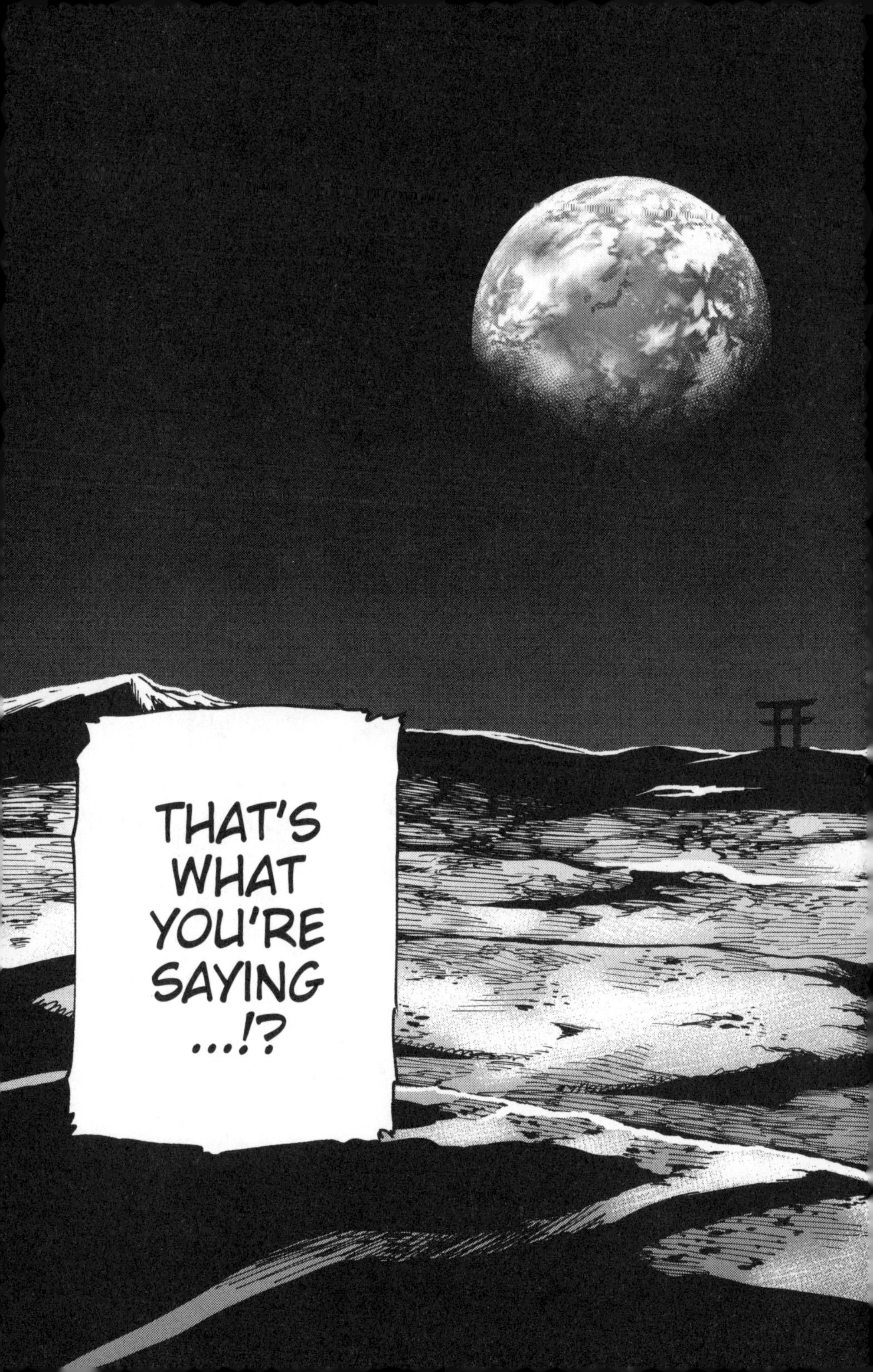
THAT'S WHAT YOU'RE SAYING ...!?

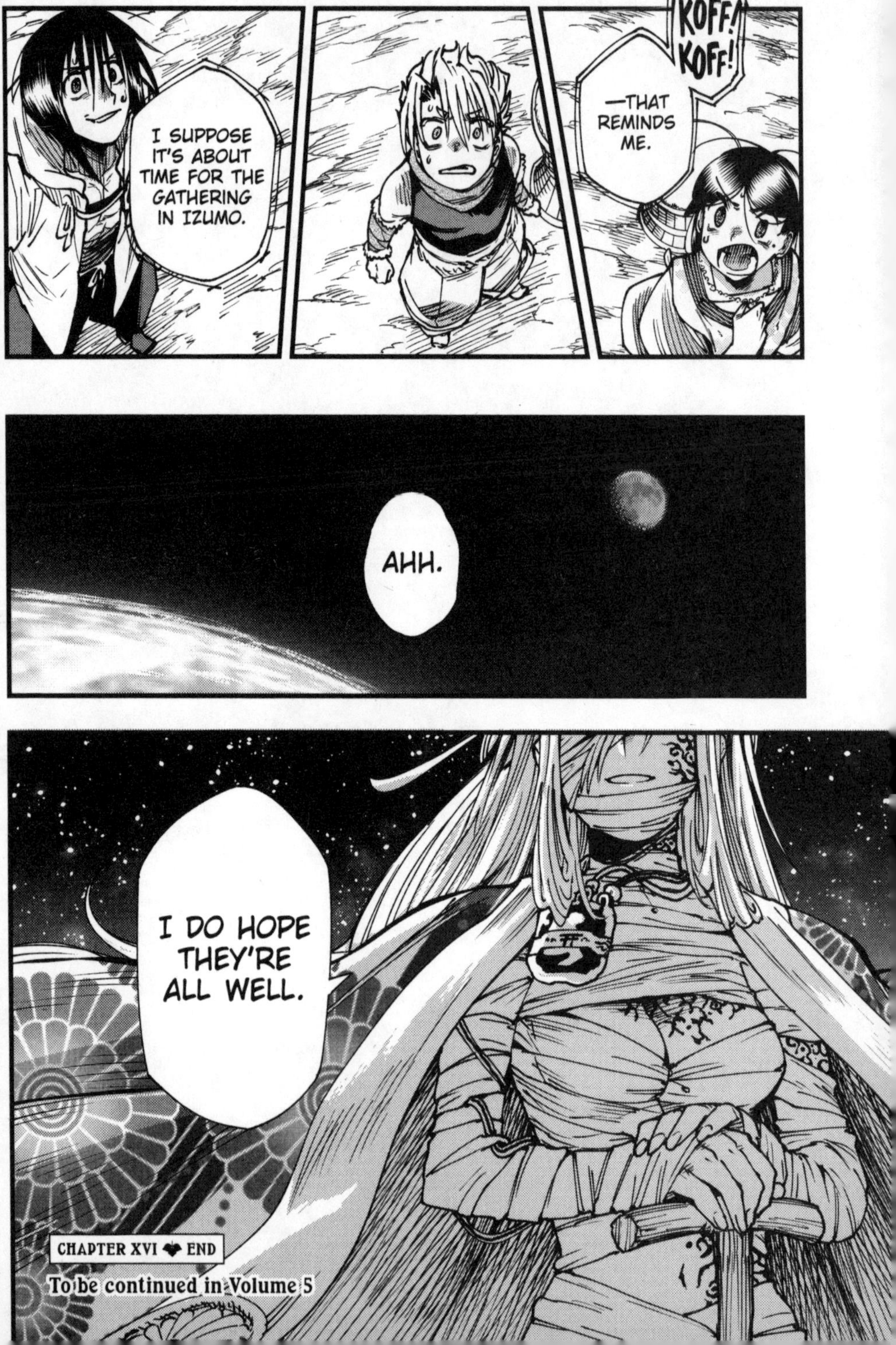
KOFF! KOFF!
—THAT REMINDS ME.
I SUPPOSE IT'S ABOUT TIME FOR THE GATHERING IN IZUMO.
AHH.
I DO HOPE THEY'RE ALL WELL.
CHAPTER XVI END
To be continued in Volume 5

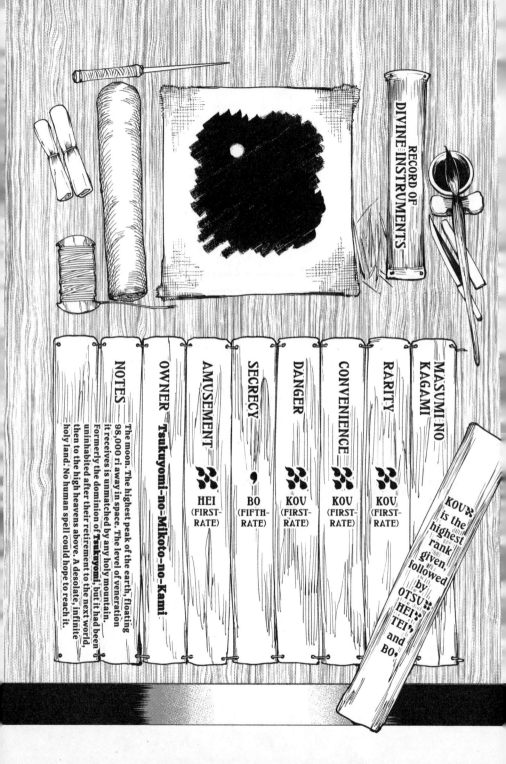

RECORD OF DIVINE INSTRUMENTS

MASUMI-NO KAGAMI

RARITY
KOU (FIRST-RATE)

CONVENIENCE
KOU (FIRST-RATE)

DANGER
KOU (FIRST-RATE)

SECRECY
BO (FIFTH-RATE)

AMUSEMENT
HEI (FIRST-RATE)

OWNER Tsukuyomi-no-Mikoto-no-Kami

NOTES The moon. The highest peak of the earth, floating 98,000 ri away in space. The level of veneration it receives is unmatched by any holy mountain. Formerly the dominion of Tsukuyomi, but it had been uninhabited after their retirement to the next world, then to the high heavens above. A desolate, infinite holy land: No human spell could hope to reach it.

KOU is the highest rank given, followed by OTSU, HEI, TEI, and BO,

Touge Oni 4

PRIMAL GODS IN ANCIENT TIMES

KENJI TSURUBUCHI

Translation: **KO RANSOM** Lettering: **ABIGAIL BLACKMAN**

TOGEONI Vol. 4
©Kenji Tsurubuchi 2021
First published in Japan in 2021 by KADOKAWA CORPORATION, Tokyo.
English translation rights arranged with KADOKAWA CORPORATION, Tokyo through TUTTLE-MORI AGENCY, INC., Tokyo.

English translation © 2024 by Yen Press, LLC

Yen Press
150 West 30th Street, 19th Floor
New York, NY 10001

Visit us at yenpress.com
facebook.com/yenpress • twitter.com/yenpress
yenpress.tumblr.com • instagram.com/yenpress

First Yen Press Edition: July 2024
Edited by Abigail Blackman and Yen Press Editorial: Carl Li
Designed by Yen Press Design: Lilliana Checo, Wendy Chan

Yen Press is an imprint of Yen Press, LLC.
The Yen Press name and logo are trademarks of Yen Press, LLC.

Library of Congress Control Number: 2023938326

ISBNs: 978-1-9753-6263-8 (paperback)
      978-1-9753-6264-5 (ebook)

10 9 8 7 6 5 4 3 2 1

WOR

Printed in the United States of America